The Developing Place of Portugal European Union

José M. Magone

The Developing Place of Portugal in the European Union

LONDON AND NEW YORK

First published 2004 by Transaction Publishers

2 Park Square, Milton Park, Abingdon, Oxfordshire OX14 4RN
711 Third Avenue, New York, NY 10017

Routledge is an imprint of the Taylor & Francis Group, an informa business

First issued in paperback 2017

Library of Congress Catalog Number: 2003054139

Library of Congress Cataloging-in-Publication Data

Magone, José M. (José María), 1962-
The developing place of Portugal in the European Union / José M. Magone.
p. cm.
Includes bibliographical references and index.
ISBN 0-7658-0206-6 (cloth: alk. paper)
1. European Union—Portugal. 2. Portugal—Politics and government—1974- I. Title.

HC240.25.P8M33 2003
341.242'2'09469—dc21

2003054139

ISBN 13: 978-0-7658-0206-4 (hbk)
ISBN 13: 978-1-138-51569-7 (pbk)

To my dear brother Rui and his wife Shana
in their pursuit of new linguistic frontiers

Mudam-se os tempos,mudam-se as vontades,
muda-se o ser,muda-se a confiança;
todo o mundo é composto de mudança,
tomando sempre novas qualidades.

Continuamente vemos novidades,
diferentes em tudo da esperança;
do mal ficam as mágoas na lembrança,
e do bem – se algum houve – as saudades.

(Luis de Camões, 1517-1580)

Contents

Acronyms ix

List of Figures and Tables xi

Acknowledgments xv

Introduction 1

1 The European Union and National Political Systems: Towards Systemic Integration 5

2 The Europeanization of the Core Political System 25

3 The Continuing Nationalization of the Portuguese Party System 55

4 Social Change and Political Culture: The Impact of the European Union 85

5 The Difficult Reform of Public Administration: The Importance and Challenge of Internationalization and Europeanization 101

6 National European Union Policy Coordination in Portugal: The Establishment of a Simple System 131

7 The Portuguese Euro-Elite and the Presidency of the European Union 2000. A Study of the Network of Interactions within the European Union Multilevel Governance System 165

8 Catching Up with the European Union: The Strategic Role of the Structural Funds 215

9 The Return of Portuguese Foreign Policy: Bridging the European Union and the Lusophone World 241

10 Conclusions: Challenges to Portuguese Democracy within the European Union 265

Selected Bibliography 271

Index 293

Acronyms

BE	Bloco de Esquerda/Block of the Left
CAP	Common Agriculture Policy
CDS/PP	Centro Democratico Social-Partido Popular/Democratic Social Centre-People´s Party
CDU	Coligação Democrática Unitária/Democratic Unitary Coalition
CFP	Common Fisheries Policy
CGTP-In	Confederação Geral dos Trabalhadores Portugueses-Intersindical/General Confederation of Portuguese Workers-Intersindical
CIP	Confederação da Industria Portuguesa/Confederation of Portuguese Industry
CPLP	Comunidade de Paises de Lingua Portuguesa/Community of Portuguese Speaking Countries
CSF	Common Support Framework
DGAC	Direccão Geral de Assuntos Comunitários/General-Directorate for Community Affairs
EC	European Community
EIA	Environmental Impact Assessment
EMU	Economic and Monetary Union
EP	European Parliament
EU	European Union
IMF	International Monetary Fund
MNE	Ministério dos Negócios Estrangeiros/Ministry of Foreign Affairs
NATO	North Atlantic Treaty Organization
OECD	Organization for Economic Cooperation and Development
PRD	Partido Renovador Democratic/Democratic Renewal Party
PS	Partido Socialista/Socialist Party
PSD	Partido Social Democrata/Social-Democratic Party
REPER.	Representação Permanente/Permanent Representation
SEA	Single European Act
SEM	Single European Market

UN	United Nations
UGT	União Geral dos Trabalhadores/General Union of Workers(P)
TEU	Treaty of the European Union/Maastricht Treaty

Figures and Tables

Figures

1.1	The European Union Political System	7
1.2	The European Union Multilevel Governance System and Different Forms of Europeanization	8
1.3	Sketch of a Europeanized Political System	15
2.1	Treatment of EU Issues in Plenary Sessions of Portuguese Parliament	42
3.1	Abstention in Portugal (1975-2002)	60
3.2	Evolution of Membership of Portuguese Parties (estimates)	62
3.3	Location of Portuguese Main Parties within the European Integration Cleavage	78
4.1	Completion of Upper Secondary School as Percentage of Population in Portugal and in the EU (1999)	87
4.2	Power Distance Perception (1997)	93
4.3	Satisfaction with National Democracy	94
4.4	Political Participation in 1997	95
5.1	Public Administration in Portugal (1968-1989)	111
5.2	Portuguese Civil Service in the 1990s	115
5.3	Distribution of Civil Service according to Ministries (1999)	116
5.4	Distribution of Civil Service according to NUTS II Regions	117
5.5	Education Background of Portuguese Civil Service (1999)	118
5.6	Seniority in Portuguese Civil Service according to Tiers of Government (1999)	119
6.1	National EU Policy Coordination in Portugal (domestic and supranational levels)	134
6.2	Renewal Rate of Staff in Permanent Representation, Brussels (1987-2003)	152
7.1	Gender of the Portuguese Euro-Elite	179
7.2	Age in Committee of European Affairs (Assembly of the Republic)	180

7.3	Age of Portuguese Members of European Parliament	181
7.4	Age of Government Ministers during the EU Presidency in 1992 and 2000	182
7.5	Local Origins of Members of Committee of European Affairs in Assembly of the Republic	182
7.6	Local Origins of Portuguese Members of the European Parliament	183
7.7	Local Origins of Government Members during the Presidency in 1992 and 2000	184
7.8	Educational Background of Members of Committee of European Affairs (Assembly of the Republic)	185
7.9	Educational Background of Portuguese Members of the European Parliament	186
7.10	Educational Background of Government Members during the EU Presidency in 1992 and 2000	187
7.11	Professional Background of Members of the Committee of European Affairs (Assembly of the Republic)	188
7.12	Professional Background of Portuguese Members of the European Parliament	189
7.13	Professional Background of Government Members during the EU Presidency in 1992 and 2000	190
7.14	Public Office Experience of the Members of the Committee of European Affairs (Assembly of the Republic)	191
7.15	Public Office Experience of the Portuguese Members of the European Parliament	192
7.16	Public Office Experience of Government Members during the EU Presidency of 1992 and 2000	193
7.17	Number of Meetings, Hours, and Days in Council, COREPER, and Working Groups during the Portuguese Presidency 2000	199
7.18	Appearances of Government before European Parliament	200
8.1	The Five Administrative Deconcentrated Regions and the Two Autonomous Governments of the Islands Azores and Madeira	224
8.2	Research and Development Financing (1997)	226
8.3	Internet Users in the European Union (per 100 inhabitants)	227
8.4	GDP per capita (EU15)	228
8.5	Regional Disparities in Portugal	229
9.1	Portuguese Contribution to Balkan Troops	248
9.2	Active Portuguese Armed Forces (December 2001)	250
9.3	The CPLP in Terms of Geographical Position	253
9.4	Quantitative Dimensions of CPLP Activities	255

Tables

1.1	The European Union Multilevel Governance System	10
1.2	The Layers of Top-Down Europeanization	13
2.1	Permanent Committees of 9th Legislature (2002)	43
2.2	The Meetings of the Conference of European Affairs Committees (COSAC/CEAC)	46
3.1.	Election Results in Portugal (1987-2002)	72
3.2.	Concentration of the Vote (1975-2002)	74
5.1	Guiding Principles for Engaging Citizens in Policymaking	107
5.2	Employment Longevity	120
5.3	The Ethical Chart of Portuguese Public Administration	123
6.1	The Departments of the General-Directorate for Community Affairs (DGAC)	145
7.1	Typology of National, Transnational, and Supranational Euro-Elites	171
7.2	Training for the Portuguese Presidency of the European Union (1998-1999)	195
7.3	Table of Events of Presidency (January-June 2000)	197
7.4	Number of Meetings, Hours, and Days Spent in Different Councils	201
7.5	Number of Meetings, Hours, and Days Spent in the Busiest Working Groups	202
7.6	The Agenda of the Portuguese Presidency (January-June 2000)	207
8.1	The Portuguese CSFIII (2000-06) According to Axis and Source of Financing in € Million	225
8.2	Distribution of Structural Funds among the EU Members	230
9.1	Some Data on the Member-States of CPLP	253
9.2	The Meetings of the Chiefs of State and Government of CPLP (1996-2002)	256

Acknowledgments

This book could not have been written without the help of many people. I want to thank the Faculty of Arts and Social Sciences at the University of Hull for a small grant from the Strategic Research Fund, which enabled me to conduct the last research trips to Portugal and Brussels in July and September 2002, respectively. Moreover, I am very grateful for the study leave in the fall of 2002, which led to the completion of the book. I want to thank the interviewees referred to in this book for taking time and giving me insight into the administrative structures of the Portuguese political system. I thank librarian José Nogueira of the CCR-N in Oporto for providing me with so much information on the Coordinating Regional Commission Norte, and I am extremely thankful to the librarians at the General Directorate for Community Affairs in the Ministry of Foreign Affairs for being so kind and providing me with a wealth of information. I want to thank Oxford University Press for giving permission to reprint some of the material included in two chapters on Portugal that I published in *The National Coordination of EU Policy. The Domestic Level* (2000), edited by Hussein Kassim, B. Guy Peters, and Vincent Wright (pp.141-160), and *The National Coordination of EU Policy: The European Level* (2001), edited by Hussein Kassim, Anand Menon, B. Guy Peters, and Vincent Wright (pp.118-190). Such material can be found in updated form in chapter six of this book. Earlier versions of chapters of the book were presented at different conferences. I wish to thank in particular the late Vincent Wright for inviting me to take part in one of his last projects related to the study of European Union policy coordination as well as Antonio Costa Pinto and Nuno Severiano Teixeira for inviting me to several conferences on Portugal and the European Union between 1997 and 2002. Last but not least, I want to thank Irving Louis Horowitz, Anne Schneider, and the Transaction team for all the support given throughout the production of the volume.

Introduction

After thirty years of Portuguese democracy, it is crucial to make an assessment of the long road that this small country has taken since the Revolution of Carnations of 25 April 1974. The fact that we are waiting for an objective history of the events of the Portuguese Revolution shows that even today these events are extremely alive in Portuguese politics. The mobilization of the population during 1974-75 does not compare with the present situation in Portugal, where the discourse of the political elites is quite distant from the average citizen. Indeed, the assessment of national democracy among Portuguese citizens has deteriorated considerably in the past two or three years, and this is certainly related to the sometimes autistic discourse of the Portuguese political elites. Although there is a discussion about reform of the electoral system to bring it closer to the citizens, in the end the Palace of São Bento, where the Portuguese Parliament is located, is not responding to the needs of the population in regard to better education, healthcare, and improvement of living conditions, despite the fact that actually much has been done in the past three decades to overcome this deficit. The Portuguese Parliament is among the institutions with the lowest of support rates in several polls since the mid-nineties, surpassed only by the low rating of the justice system.

Still today, Portugal is characterized by a high income disparity which is related to an educational division. Although many efforts were made over the last thirty years to overcome Portugal's educational gap in relation to other member-states of the European Union, this continues to be the main problem for further development of the Portuguese economy and labor market by the national employment plans of the European Union. Despite this negative outlook, there is hope that this monitoring by the European Union will help the country to overcome this gap in the next decades. At least, one can say that Portuguese elites are aware of the problems that the country has to face up to in this continuation on the long road to qualitative democracy.

Integration into the European Union is one of the most important events in the history of Portugal. After decades of isolation and a turbulent transition to democracy, it gave political, economic, social, and cultural stability to a country that had to overcome the trauma of losing an empire. Today, in spite of all the negative aspects related to the education system, Portugal has become a self-confident nation in global politics. The constitution clearly defines the parameters of its new foreign policy, which clearly aims at strengthening the international community and global governance. After the senseless colonial wars, Portuguese political elites and the population are keen to push for peaceful solutions to global crises. This became quite evident in the process towards the independence of East Timor, which became a major issue for Portuguese foreign policy. The successful outcome was to a great extent achieved by decades of diplomatic pressure exerted by Portugal in the United Nations and in the European Union. Quite a challenging role for the country is the foundation of the Community of Portuguese Speaking Countries, which restored the dialogue with the former colonies as well as with Brazil. In this sense, the past thirty years have been, in spite of all the setbacks, quite successful decades of Portuguese influence in the world for such a small country. The two presidencies of the European Union in 1992 and 2000 further helped to project the new found identity of the country within a pan-European community of democracies.

The organization of Expo ´98 led not only to an improvement of the quality of life in the capital, but in the country as well. New projects emerged that clearly helped to strengthen the self-confidence of this oldest of nation-states. The Handball World Championships in 2003 and the Soccer European Championships in 2004 are examples of the will of Portugal to contribute to the glory of its democracy. The greatest Portuguese footballer of all times, Eusebio, clearly contributed to bringing the European championship to Portugal. This is quite important, because it helps to strengthen the ability of the country to fulfill an international role and project the country within and outside the European Union.

This volume attempts to add to the study of how Portugal became part of the European Union as a political system, and illustrate how integration actually enhanced the national identity. It shows also that any discussion of Europeanization of the Portuguese political system is only one side of the coin. The other is that Portugal is also part of a so-called Domestication of European Union politics, of which the Austrian case during the Portuguese presidency was the best example. It clearly shows that more and more national policies are discussed by the member-states. The so-called Open Method of Coordination in Employment Policy, established during the Extraordinary European Council in Lisbon in March 2000, allows for joint monitoring of the employment policies of the member-states. This naturally is of extreme importance for the Portuguese economy. It opens up the political, economic, and social system to outward scrutiny, which in the end is actually domestized European Politics.

Chapter 1 presents a theoretical framework for the study of Europeanization while chapters 2, 3, and 4 discuss the political system, political parties, and Portuguese society in terms of Europeanization. Chapter 5 reviews the evolution of public administration in Portugal and how the European Union and the

OECD impacted on the modernization agenda. Chapter 6 examines national EU policy coordination. Chapter 7 is dedicated to the Portuguese Euro-elite and how they interacted in the Portuguese presidency and attempts to show the importance of actors in the European integration process. Chapter 8 discusses the impact of EU structural funds on Portugal, while chapter 9 scrutinizes Portuguese foreign and defense policies. Last but not least, the volume presents some conclusions relevant to the challenges that Portugal must face in the future.

1

The European Union and National Political Systems: Towards Systemic Integration

Understanding the European Union as a Political System

One of the major characteristics of the European integration process is that it remained almost unnoticed for the past fifty years. Indeed, the first real awareness of the populations of the member-states was before and after the Treaty of Maastricht, which set up the criteria and the schedule for the establishment of a Economic and Monetary Union by the beginning of the millennium. This smooth evolutionary process towards a new European Union multilevel governance system was constructed mostly by political and administrative elites. The populations of the European Union were only asked to give legitimacy after the introduction of the direct elections to the European Parliament, so that the "Eurosclerosis" of stagnating institution-building could be overcome. Indeed, since the mid-1980s, the European Union has been affected by a new wave of institution-building, but this time linked to the transition towards a new wave of globalization. In the past thirty years, the European Union has become the main actor of this transition, particularly since the fall of the Berlin wall in 1989. This coincidence of so many events in such a short period of time seems to suggest that this was a breaking point between the modern industrial society and the emergent knowledge society.

The introduction of the Euro in January 2002 in twelve democracies can be regarded as an important achievement, in spite of the doomsday prognosis of euroskepticism and more cautious academics. It represents the development towards a new era in the relations between the European Union and other major economies in the world. One should not lose sight of the real aim of the European Union, which is to strengthen the European economy in relation to the United States and Japan. One should be aware that there is still much to be done to achieve this aim. In addition, the Euro constitutes the first major symbol of a systemic integration between the supranational level and the national political systems. The so-called European System of Central Banks, headed by the European Central Bank, created a functioning integration of monetary systems. The importance of this fact cannot be underestimated. It constitutes the establishment of a supranational policy community, which will have cultural effects towards a shift of paradigm from national sovereignty to shared pooled sovereignty.[1]

It is important to contextualize the topic of this book—the impact of the European Union on the Portuguese political system—before we turn to the more concrete empirical study of the processes that affect small member-states in general, and Portugal in particular. It is central to study the inflated concept of *Europeanization* within the European Union Multilevel Governance System. It is important to give it more scientific rigor, so that the *Europeanizing* processes can be quantified and qualified. One thought that one must consider is that all member-states are now affected by different processes that are identified under the same label of *Europeanization*. We will make an effort to differentiate analytically between various forms of *Europeanization*, which will give us the ideal conditions to study empirically the effects on the Portuguese case. There is a tendency to look at national political systems as independent from the overall European Union system. I do not follow this route; I define the Portuguese political system as being engaged in a systemic interactive integrative process with the supranational level of the European Union. Each one has a distinct process of interactive integration, but they all constitute a political system that is still in the making. The dynamics of interaction is slowly reifying an inbetween level of cultural transnational integration, what Weiler calls infranationalism.[2] One major unnoticed aspect creating these transnational policy communities is naturally European law, which has a fifty-year history, has its translation into all languages of the European Union, and is now taken for granted as internalized "national" legislation.[3]

In sum, to understand the Portuguese political system, one needs to contextualize it in the new European Union multilevel governance system. This will lead us then to the conceptualization of *Europeanization*.

The European Union Multilevel Governance System

Any attempt to depict the European Union is always characterized by difficulty, because it is so complex. Most attempts are simplifications, maps of the actual reality of the European integration process. Maps help us to find places at home or abroad, but they never comprise all the information. This is the case of the multilevel governance (MLG) paradigm, which can be regarded as a major one to understand processes between different levels. Meanwhile it is finding its usefulness in discussing global governance. In this volume, we are keen to stick to the heuristic device created by Gary Marks

Figure 1.1
European Union Political System

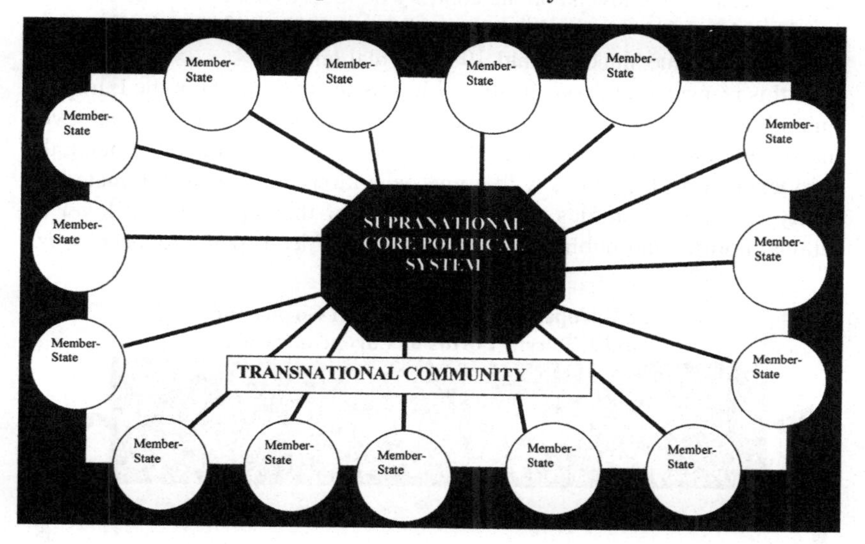

and Liesbet Hooghe throughout the 1990s. The literature on MLG has meanwhile become quite voluminous. Most of the research has been directed towards the relationship between subnational actors, such as the regions and the local authorities, and the national and supranational level. Another field in which the MLG approach has been used is in the means interest groups use to try to influence policy. Although the MLG approach is quite holistic in its nature, it is excellent for mapping the position of a country within a process of European integration. Combined with the concept of *Europeanization* we come to an approach that is able to take into account micro-, meso-, macro-, and meta-levels of analysis without having to leave the overall map.

Governance comprises the political institutions, civil society actors and the sum of all processes between these entities. It can be studied in different fields from the political/public field to the economic/cultural field. Moreover, it also can be applied to the policy process. All of these constitute different categories of the map, such as with geography where one can have political, physical, natural resources or other kinds of topic-specific maps. What makes Marks' and Hooghe's approach more appealing is that the map consists of different levels, meaning that one can study governance within and between the supranational, transnational, national, and regional level. This naturally shows that Marks and Hooghe are writing implicitly about an integrated political system already in the making.[4] Clearly, they follow many of the thoughts of another theorist of MLG, Philippe Schmitter.[5] He identifies the European Union as an imperfect polity. What makes the big difference between Marks/Hooghe and Schmitter is that the latter never makes the connection between the levels; on the contrary he focuses mainly on the supranational level and this is certainly an incomplete perception of what the European Union has become since the mid-1980s in real terms.

In this respect, on the one hand, one has to be cautious about the European Union literature, which tended to focus until now on the supranational level, and venture only sometimes to the transnational level. On the other hand, the Europeanization literature, with some exceptions, has been dominated by highly speculative studies about the impact of the supranational level on national politics and public policy. This naturally leads one to conceptualize

Figure 1.2
The European Union Muiltilevel Governance and Different Forms of Europeanization

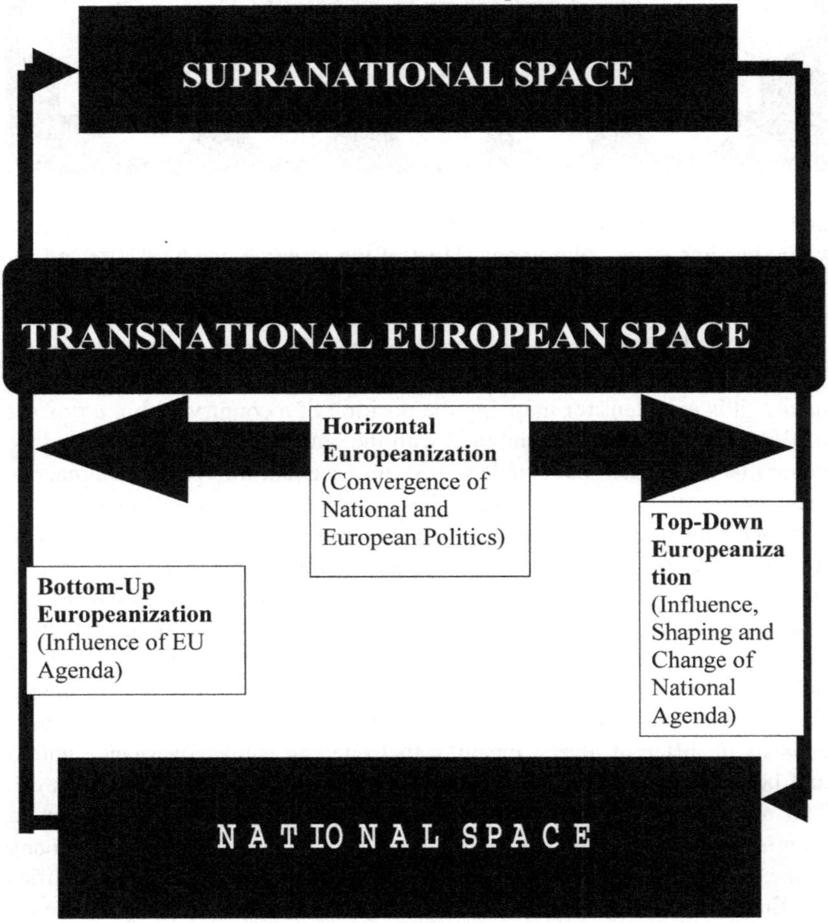

a separation of the levels of analysis from each other and a conceptualization of them being independent from each other. In reality, however, as we argue in this volume by studying the Portuguese case they are interconnected and interdependent with each other in an interactive integrated political system. This, however, is still a heuristic assumption in many ways, because the European Union MLG map developed by Marks and Hooghe is still in the making. Sometimes, the only thing we need to do is to gather the scattered research of the different levels and reconstruct it within the MLG paradigm; sometimes there is a strong need to start from scratch and do new research related to that. When studying a country such as Portugal from a MLG perspective we are bound to use comparative data to show the specific similarities and differences in the adjustment of the Portuguese political system within the wider multilevel governance system.

As mentioned before, each country is integrated within the MLG system in a different way. Some, particularly large countries, are major players and designers of the future of the European Union, while others, mostly smaller countries, tend to accept the positions taken by the larger countries. In each category, there are countries that may be so-called leaders in certain aspects and others laggards. This indicates the complexity, asymmetry, and diversity of the European Union multilevel governance system.

In this volume, we attempt to analyze the Portuguese case using the MLG system. This means that we will be looking at the Portuguese case from various perspectives and on different levels in order to show a more complex picture of the *Europeanization* of the Portuguese political system.

The systemic levels of the multilevel governance system are defined in Table 1.1.

Our main task will be to look at processes from the Portuguese national level of governance and relate it to the other governance levels (supranational, transnational, and local levels). Before that, however, we must go one step further and elucidate the various definitions of Europeanization.

The Concept of Europeanization

The concept of Europeanization became widespread in the 1990s. It characterizes the impact of the supranational level on the politics and policy of the member-states. This original meaning was extended later to other processes. One of the first to present a viable definition of Europeanization was Robert Ladrech in a much quoted article:

> Europeanization is an incremental process reorienting the direction and shape of politics to the degree that EC political and economic dynamics become part of the organizational logic of national politics and policy-making.[6]

Table 1.1
The European Union Multilevel Governance System

LEVELS OF GOVERNANCE IN THE EUROPEAN UNION	DESCRIPTION
Supranational Level	Comprises the core institutions of the European Union (Council, Commission, European Parliament) the so-called European civil Society (Eurogroups) and the interaction between them.
Transnational Level	Is the main field of interactions among supranational, national, and subnational levels. It creates transnational communities in different fields. It includes most of the comitology of the Commission; working groups and Coreper I and II of the Council, the Economic and Social Committee and the regular meetings with other similar committees, the committee of regions, policy communities such as the Eurogroup, European administrative space, Euroregions.
National Level	Comprises the political institutions, civil society, and citizens. It is more than the sum of all the processes among these actors.
Subnational Level	Comprises the regional/local institutions and regional/local civil societies as well as the regional populations. It is more than the sum of all the processes among these actors.

Ladrech concentrated his research on two main areas affecting French politics after the adoption of the Maastricht Treaty. The first area was constitutional revision and parliamentary development and the second area was related to the territorial organization of policymaking. He found that constitutional revision to accommodate the Maastricht Treaty actually led to a revival of the dormant Parliament of the Fifth Republic. In particularly, Parliament gained new powers to scrutinize EU legislation.[7] In terms of territorial organization Ladrech made the point that the regions are becoming more involved at the Brussels level and cooperating with other regions across Europe.[8]

Ladrech's definition of Europeanization led to the inflationary use of the concept, which in the end complicated the possibility of developing a rigorous definition of this concept.[9] One example that may be quoted here is Attila Agh´s definition of Europeanization for what is happening to the central and eastern European candidates for enlargement, which are already experiencing an *anticipatory Europeanization* by adjusting their structures to the European Union multilevel governance system. This, of course, was a broad definition of the concept, which should be used only for countries within the system, not those outside it.[10] This fact can be underlined by using the case of Sweden after its accession to the European Union. Indeed when Sweden entered the European Union it was confronted with immediate major pressures to adjust to the new European Union multilevel governance system, but it took some years after accession to absorb the rationale of the new political system. One of the major problems confronting Sweden was the need for a sufficient number of qualified personnel to have an efficient handling of the Europeanization process.[11] We are not dismissing as less relevant the process that candidate countries are subject to when preparing for accession than what happens to actual members, but there is a significant difference between insiders and outsiders. Insiders cannot afford to ignore the pressures coming from the European Union, while outsiders, at least theoretically, can still refrain from joining the European Union. Europeanization therefore is something that precludes membership, while the adaptation process of candidate countries can be subsumed under the broader, less specific concept of European integration.

Europeanization is also characterized by uneven effects. Indeed, it is an asymmetrical process that affects different layers with different temporal rhythm and different countries in a different way. One aspect that has been studied in depth is the implementation of EU directives in the fifteen member-states. More or less, the literature seems to argue that there is a north-south divide of leaders and laggards of implementation. However, this now has been refuted by the excellent studies of Tanja Börzel who clearly found that such a north-south divide is a simplification of the reality. In reality, some southern European countries do better in certain fields than others, sometimes even better than their northern counterparts. Börzel naturally focuses mainly on environmental policy.[12] In another study, she shows that quantitatively Portugal and Spain have a good middle of the road record, while Belgium, France, Greece, and Italy are the laggards of implementation.[13]

Before Jacques Delors took over the presidency of the Commission, Europeanization was almost nonexistent in the vocabulary of comparative European politics. It is only the voluntaristic drive of Delorsism towards a relaunching of the Single European Market and Economic and Monetary Union that led to the perception of such a process.[14] This led to a considerable incrementalism of European Union directives, policymaking processes, and monitoring pressures going from the supranational towards the national level. Such incrementalism began to decline only after 1995.[15]

In another way, one can study Europeanization through a different lens similar to that used by Laura Cram in her study on *Policy-Making in the EU*.[16]

We are here confronted with different perspectives and viewpoints which may bring to the fore different research results in the study of Europeanized political systems. One can take always a micro-, meso-, macro, or meta-approach to Europeanization which naturally lead to complementary research results.

In sum, Europeanization cannot be analyzed unidimensionally. On the contrary, one has to take various viewpoints to analyze the different aspects of Europeanization. A way of mapping the complex nature of Europeanization is to study Europeanization from three main viewpoints: (a) top-down Europeanization; (b) bottom-up Europeanization, and (c) horizontal, transnational Europeanization.

Top-Down Europeanization

This is probably the more frequently used concept, which means the impact of supranational policymaking, politics, and polity on a particular member-state. The literature clearly shows that Europeanization affects different parts of the domestic polity, politics, and policy in a different way. In a recent article, Alastair Cole shows how difficult it is to separate these forms of Europeanization. Political parties today are embedded in transnational networks and adopt common policy positions that may have a top-down impact on national parties. Political party networks can also be used to push the position of a specific political party, such as the French socialist party in employment policy at the European Union level.[17] Only in an artificial, analytical way are we able to recognize layers of top-down Europeanization.

The Europeanization of the core political system would lead to an adaptation to pressures coming from the supranational level. The creation of compatible filter institutions to adjust optimally to the pressures of policy implementation differ from country to country, but all of them have the same purpose of creating the most efficient structures of adjustment. Larger countries such as the UK, France, Germany, and Italy tend to locate their administrative structures close to the prime minister's office, while smaller member-states have located them in the foreign ministries.[18]

The core executive and Parliament may become more Europeanized, due to the growing involvement in transnational networks. It depends how much possibility of influence to control these pressures exists in each political system.

National parties are converging more and more in their electoral manifestos, this may be related to their development towards cartelization of politics.[19]

The most evident features of Europeanization can be found in public administration and in national public policy. These layers of top-down Europeanization are under considerable pressure to keep up with the growing number of European Union directives and the complexity of proper implementation. Sometimes assumptions of correct implementation, may be proved to be wrong. The Danish case is regarded as the best example for proper implementation of EU environmental legislation. One Danish expert, however, believes this to be a myth created by the Danes, who tend to be fast in legal implementation, but very discretionary in real implementation. Lack of monitoring by the Commission, the language, and others factors reinforce this positive superficial impression, which may be different if more closely scrutinized.[20]

The less studied area of Europeanization is the impact of the European integration process on the political life of national citizens. One question that arises is related to the rise of new cleavages and/or social movements. In some way, the emergence of euroskeptic parties in Denmark, UK, France, Austria, Italy, and Sweden has been related to the growing Europeanization of social and economic life. This, naturally, is still an open research area.[21] If we look at the electoral vote of the euroskeptic parties in European elections we can dismiss it as a negligible minority. Only in Denmark do the European elections create a party system distinct from that of national elections.[22]

In sum, top-down Europeanization affects mainly the public administration and the policy space and less so the political field. The national demoi

Table 1.2
The Layers of Top-Down Europeanization

LAYERS	DESCRIPTION
The Core Political System	The impact of European integration on political elites, core executive, Parliament, and political parties. Pressures to adjust to European integration. It also would include constitutional change.
Public Administration	Adjustment of public administration to the rationale of European programs such as the structural funds; legal implementation of EU legislation; creation and sustainability of EU policy coordination mechanisms.
The National Public Policy Space	The real implementation of European policies. Inclusion of private actors and interest groups. Creation of policy networks. Evaluation and monitoring mechanisms.
The National Public/ Political Space	Political expression of, for, and against European integration. Establishment of social movements related to the European integration process. Linkage political parties and voters. National political culture and European integration (Knowledge of European Union matters and institutions; support for European Union; benefit of European Union).

and political parties are still very much absorbed by national politics, inspite of certain Europeanizing tendencies.

Bottom-Up Europeanization

Bottom-up Europeanization is the ability of national actors to influence main paradigms of European integration. This may be related to actions of immediate response in regard to fellow member-states as happened during the Portuguese presidency in relation to the inclusion of the far right populist Freedom party of Jörg Haider in the Austrian government, which led to the temporary ostracism of Austria within the European Union [23]or it may be related to policy paradigms such as the discussion on employment between Tony Blair and Lionel Jospin leading up to the open method of coordination adopted at the extradionary Council of Lisbon in March 2000.[24]

Bottom-up Europeanization is clearly a strategy used by larger member-states that have more resources and abilities to bring in new paradigms about European integration. This bottom-up Europeanization does not lead to an improved policy by a country, but to general discussion with alternative solutions, which produces a compromise among the member-states over a lengthier period of time. Intergovernmental conferences and the European Councils can be regarded as the best fora for such bottom-up Europeanization.

In sum, bottom-up Europeanization allows national political actors to enjoy the possibility of liberal intergovernmentalism. Nevertheless, in the end this liberal intergovernmentalism where national prestige and national models are put forward as the main paradigm of EU polity, politics, or policy issues are watered down to a constructivist common position.[25]

Horizontal, Transnational Europeanization

Top-down and bottom-up Europeanization are bringing these member-states together towards what one could call horizontal, transnational Europeanization. As a result, the Economic Monetary Union, the Open Method of Coordination in Employment, Common Fisheries Policy, Common Agricultural Policy, Structural Funds, Common Foreign and Security Policy, and the policies of Justice and Home Affairs are creating transnational policy communities, which are leading to the socialization of policymakers across the European Union. This can be observed in relation to transnational party networks, the informal meetings of the Economic and Social Committees,[26] the European System of Central Banks,[27] Europol,[28] the Secretariat of Directorate-Generals of Public Administration Reform, [29]and the biannual conferences of the parliamentary committees of European affairs.[30] Other such transnational policy networks can be found in other policy areas. This, of course, makes the Europeanization debate more complex than one would think. It creates pressures on member-states without really being a top-down Europeanization, but a horizontal, transnational one. This horizontal process creates a culture of cooperative behavior, which includes the creation of regimes of benchmarking, stability, convergence, and harmonization. It may also create horizontal linkages to other transnational policy communities, which means that we are experiencing the development towards a thick, dense, complex transnational system of cooperation that is crucial for the sustainability and strengthening of the EU multilevel governance system. This naturally can include transnational social movements at European scale. This issue has been argued now for some time by Doug Imig and Sidney Tarrow. In a recent article, they made it aware of the transnational solidarity of workers in relation to lay-offs.[31] At the same time, the works council has become a major aspect of the transnationalization of European politics.

In sum, it is necessary to have all three forms of Europeanization in mind before engaging in a full-scale study of Europeanization. In this volume, we are focusing on the impact of European integration on Portugal. Most of the research will deal with the top-down dimension of Europeanization, but in certain instances we can see that Portuguese elites are engaged in bottom-up and horizontal Europeanization processes. Before we begin the full-scale investigation, let us contextualize Portugal in the European Union multi-level governance system.

Figure 1.3
Sketch of a Europeanized Political System

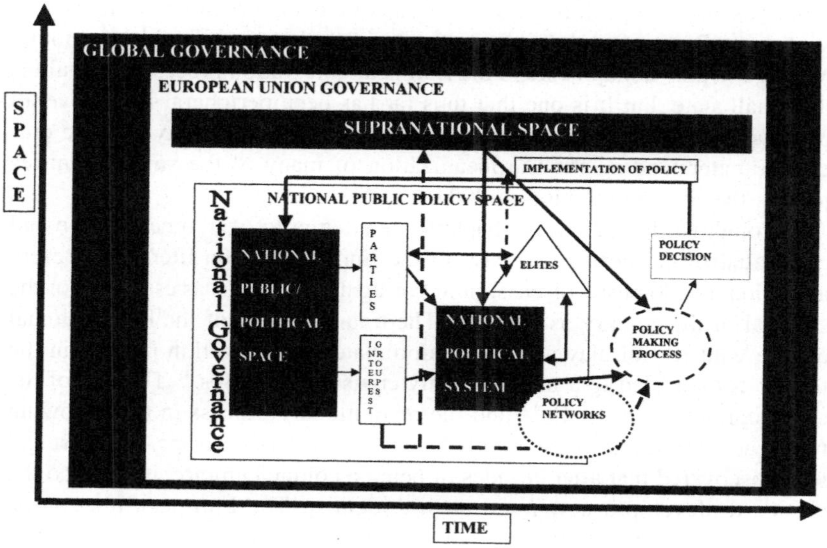

Europeanization of Small States: The Portuguese Case in Comparative Perspective

Portugal is probably one of the least researched countries in the literature on Europeanization. This latecomer to the club of democracies and European integration received considerable attention during the process towards enlargement, but afterwards very few studies were produced dealing with the Europeanization processes to which the Portuguese political system was exposed. Interestingly enough, the lack of interest in the impact of Europeanization on the Portuguese political system was not counterweighted by a domestic boom of academic studies in this area. On the contrary, studies on the Portuguese political system in general, and the impact of European integration in particular, continue to be a scarce commodity. Most of the studies that exist ignore completely the European dimension and seem to be absorbed by a national political system. Exceptions to the rule are the excellent studies of Francisco Torres who wrote several publications on the impact of Economic and Monetary Union on Portugal.[32] Other scholars that have published contributions in this area are José Medeiros Ferreira,[33] Federiga Bindi,[34]Carlos Gaspar,[35] and David Corkill.[36] The latter used the concept of Europeanization to discuss the impact of the European Union on the Portuguese economy. Although his study discusses the troubles of the Portuguese economy, which today have become a major problem for the incoming government, he fails to give a rigorous definition of Europeanization. In the 1990s, several edited volumes[37] in English and Portuguese helped to overcome the lack of studies as well as some journals specializing in International Relations and European Integration.[38] One of the main reasons for the lack of studies on Portugal is that it is a semiperipheral country[39] without enough leverage to play a major role in the European integration process. Not only is it a small state, but it is one that thus far has been peripheral in the overall process of European integration.[40] Nevertheless, Portugal may become crucial to understanding the Europeanization of many of the small countries joining the European Union in 2004.

Throughout the following chapters, we attempt to overcome this gap and contextualize the Portuguese case in the Europeanization literature. Before accession, the domestic discussion in Portugal viewed this as essential for the survival of the country as a nation. The traumatic loss of the huge colonial empire with feet of clay and the misfortunate decolonization process in the former colonies led to a major identity crisis in the 1980s.[41] The end of the authoritarian regime in 1974 and the revolutionary process in the following two years almost led to the establishment of a Cuba in Europe. But Portugal soon discovered that after decades of being a colonial empire, it now had the chance to develop a new more pacific identity. The European integration process became an important escapist route for the democratic political elites of the emerging new democratic Portugal. Integration into the European Union became a way out of the crisis for the Portuguese political elites. Even today, the process of European integration, although overwhelmingly supported by the population, is a elite-led project. Although a referendum on Economic and Monetary Union was scheduled before 1999, in the end the three main parties, the Socialist Party, the Socialdemocratic Party, and the anti-Maastricht People´s Party, backed by the constitutional Court, decided in the national interests to avoid such a referendum.[42] None of the treaties were subject to a referendum. In this sense, the European integration process is regarded as a project in the national interest, meaning that staying outside of any of the European projects is losing out in terms of influence.

Compared to other small member-states the Portuguese Euro-elite is extremely well prepared, having placed their best people at the forefront of the European integration process. This again confirms the paradigm of national interest in the Portuguese case. Although the public has become more critical and differentiated in assessing the benefits of EU membership, there is no major social movement against the European integration process. Three small parties—Communists, bourgeois People´s Party, and the trotzkyite Block of the Left-from time to time voice euroskeptic views, but their force is so small in terms of electoral support that they are not able to challenge the two pro-European main parties. This situation contrasts heavily with Denmark where the party system and society at large are extremely polarized between Euroskeptics and pro-Europeans. One problem that Portuguese political elites face is the dramatic high level of abstentionism at elections. This becomes even more salient in European elections, in which 60 percent of the electorate stayed at home in the 1999 elections. According to a study commissioned by the previous Socialist government a large part of the population does not identify themselves with any of the existing parties and there is a growing dissatisfaction with the political institutions, particularly Parliament.[43] This, however, is not a problem restricted to Portugal. According to the Eurobarometer studies across the European Union there is a growing discontentment with political parties and the main institutions.[44] Nevertheless, Portugal is among the countries, along with the United Kingdom, France, and Germany, to have the highest levels of abstentionism. If we look at European elections, European issues are almost irrelevant. The most recent European elections were regarded by the political elites as an indicator for the legislative elections in October 1999. Indeed, the result of the legislative elections was identical to that of the preceding European elections. This shows that the national public/political space is not Europeanized at all; national politics and the national interpretation of European politics prevails over alternative interpretations. The route for showing discontent, apathy, or withdrawal is abstention.[45]

The gap between political elites and the population led to a monopolization of the European debate by the former, which still use the argument of national interest, and which naturally jeopardizes the ability to increase the information of the population on the European Union. According to Eurobarometer studies, Portugal is at the bottom along with the United Kingdom in perceived knowledge of the European Union. Denmark, Sweden, and Austria are on the other side of the scale.[46] This monopolization of the European debate reinforces this elitist approach and the strong role given to national European Union policy coordination. The weak civil society, the lack of strong interest groups, and the problems of public administration to engage in a dialogue with the citizens is making it difficult to gain more input legitimacy from the population.

Portugal, which thus far has been in the process of catching up with the European Union, made substantial progress in the 1990s. Yet, despite that, Portugal continues to be one of the poorest countries with the highest levels of poverty.[47] In recent times, Portugal has been compared with successful Ireland which invested a good amount of structural funds in human resources and research and development. This naturally has led to negative assessments of the results of the structural funds in Portugal.[48] This is one of the reasons that make it difficult to draw comparisons. Indeed, after forty-eight years of authoritarian dictatorship until 1974, Portugal had to change the gear of development and this was only achieved with difficulties. Before Ireland joined the European Community in 1973, it was already a democracy with a pre-established policy style. It is a policy style that is close to the British one, which is used to consultation and networking. All this led to an optimal use of the structural funds.[49] The Portuguese case was still engaged in restructuring and democratizing the patrimonial public administration, when Portugal joined the EC/EU. Indeed, it was during this time that the European Union changed its gear and policy style towards an even more complex and rationalized process. Portuguese public administration had to achieve a double adjustment. First, it had to continue to democratize and decentralize a discredited public administration, and second, it had to adjust to the changing complex policy style of the European Union. This gave it a comparative disadvantage in relation to the Irish case.

The reason Portugal was quite uncritical in relation to the impact of processes of European integration on public administration and the national political system was because it could not afford to lose time. It was so engaged in a modernizing agenda, that it wanted only to catch up as soon as possible to become a truthful equal partner. It had to learn to appreciate the differences of the country over time. Indeed, during 1993 the Portuguese government under Prime Minister Cavaco Silva was the first to submit a Regional Development Plan for the period 1994 and 1999 to the European Commission in order to negotiate the Common Support Framework (1994-

99).[50] This is a concrete example of the general behavior of government and public administration, which, clearly, in the national interest did not want to lose time in such matters that were so important for the modernization of the country. Such an attitude began to change only before, during, and after the second presidency of the Council of the European Union. Portuguese diplomacy began to reflect on its abilities and importance within the European Union integration process. Particularly, in view of the forthcoming Eastern enlargement, diplomats regarded themselves as holders of important polity, politics, and policy knowledge in relation to the European Union and the process of accession. Indeed, in being useful to policymakers in central and eastern Europe, diplomats helped themselves to find the new identity of Portugal[51]—a Portugal that is actively engaged in the European integration process. Indeed, the European integration process helped this small country, which had engaged in seeking new continents and new maritime challenges in the fifteenth and sixteenth centuries, to finally discover herself.

Although the European Union was regarded as a *vincolo esterno,*[52] which would strengthen the new feeble democracy and modernize the structures of the country, after seventeen years of European integration, the Portuguese political and administrative elites were sufficiently socialized in the EU multilevel governance system that it became part of the national identity. The European Union became an internalized *vincolo interno* related to the democratic and economic well-being of the country. In this sense, the Portuguese case differs substantially from the Greek and Italian cases where the perception of *vincolo esterno* continued to be a main factor in adjusting to the pressures of coming to the European Union. Both Greece and Italy encountered greater difficulties in qualifying for EMU than Portugal. Italy had to raise new taxes to finance integration into EMU and Greece had to wait until 1 January 2001. Although Portugal is presently facing a difficult economic situation, it appears that it has reflexive mechanisms to react to the new challenges in an appropriate manner. This was one of the reasons that the present social-democratic government, immediately after taking over power, took drastic measures to cut the budget deficit and public debt, so that Portugal would not diverge from the rest of the countries of the European Union.

In sum, the Portuguese case is exceptionally interesting, because, after years of uncertainty and economic instability, the Portuguese political elite and public administration regard European integration as part of the new identity of the country.. In my view, Portugal has achieved a remarkable success in the past seventeen years. Despite the fact, that much has yet to be done, the Europeanization process will one day trickle down to the national public/political space after having been monopolized for so long by the political elites. This is necessary because the quality of the education and health sectors and the quality of life of a large part of the population are still below the EU average. Critical constructive voices from civil society are important in order to democratize and broaden the European debate that until now was so jealously monopolized and protected by the political elites.

Conclusions

Europeanization is a useful concept, but much in need of a more sophisticated conceptualization. In this first chapter we developed a framework to analyze various kinds of Europeanization. Portugal is regarded as a semiperipheral country in terms of its standing in the world economy and therefore peripheral to the whole European Union decision-making process. Therefore, most processes of Europeanization are top-down ones. The ability to influence European policy is restricted not only by the semiperipheral nature of the Portuguese economy, but because Portugal is also a small state. This naturally allows for very restricted bottom-up Europeanization processes, meaning influence in policymaking. Portugal's influence on policy areas happened mainly during its presidency of the European Union or in such matters of vital national interest.

Notes

1. Kenneth Dyson, "EMU as 'Europeanization': Convergence, Diversity and Contingency," *Journal of Common Market Studies* 38, 4, 2000: 645-66; particularly 657: "What emerges is a picture of an EMU policy community bound together by a sound money paradigm and of the privileged role of EU central bankers within that community as the bearers and beneficiaries of that paradigm. Just as the construction of the single European market centralized the regulatory function at the EU level, so EMU has centralized the economic stabilization function at the EU level. Seen in technocratic terms, the EU is no longer just a regulatory state. It is an emergent stabilization state, dedicated to improving the economic efficiency of Europe by establishing and safeguarding economic stability.This small, exclusive EMU policy community continues to define the meaning and boundaries of the EU as a stabilization state."
2. J.H.H. Weiler, "Epilogue: 'Comitology' as Revolution-Infranationalism, Constitutionalism and Democracy," in Christian Joerges, Ellen Vos (eds.), *EU Committees: Social Regulation, Law and Politics* (Oxford: Hart Publishing 1999), 339-350; particularly 342-343: "Infra-nationalism would...be a third paradigm which addresses a meso-level reality which operates below the public macro and the above the individual micro; is not a reflection of the State-Community paradigm and the contours and dynamics of which are ill-served by the perennial supranational-intergovernmental discourse; is, ...more administrative and managerial than constitutional and diplomatic; is polycentric, or even non-centric but certainly dualist; has dynamics which are neither national or *Communautaire*, but functional and sectoral; has a modus operandi which is less by negotiation and more by deliberation.

   Infranationalism does not obliterate the intergovernmental or the supranational but operates alongside them; if you think of the Community as governance, infranationalism helps define an important layer in the European multi-layered system. If you think of the Community as a polity, it is infranationalism which often conceptualises better a polity in which national controls were not only removed on the highways and at airports. Infranationalism is to Supranationalism and Intergovernmentalism what postmodernity is to modernity: it challenges the epistemic comfort of boundaries—and in this infranationalism becomes, arguably, the most dramatic expression of integration itself."

3. M. Rainer Lepsius, "Nationalstaat oder Nationalitätenstaat als Modell für die Weiterentwicklung der Europäischen Gemeinschaft," in Rudolf Wildenmann (ed.), *Staatswerdung Europas? Optionen für eine Europäische Union* (Baden-Baden: Nomos Verlagsgesellschaft 1991), 19-40; M. Rainer Lepsius, "Die Europäische Union. Ökonomische-Politiche Integration und kulturelle Identität," in Reinhold Viehoff, Rien T. Segers (eds.), *Kultur, Identität, Europa. Über Schwierigkeiten und Möglichkeiten einer Konstruktion* (Frankfurt A.M.: Suhrkamp, 1999), 201-222; particularly 203-206.
4. Meanwhile, the MLG literature has become very extensive. The best summary is by the leaders of this approach Liesbet Hooghe, Gary Marks, *Multilevel Governance and European Integration* (Lanham, MA: Rowman and Littlefield, 2001), and Gary Marks, Fritz Scharpf, Philippe Schmitter, and Wolfgang Streck, *Governance in the European Union* (London: SAGE, 1996).
5. Philippe Schmitter, *How to Democratize the European Union and Why Bother?*(Lanham, MA: Rowman and Littlefield, 2000).
6. Robert Ladrech, "Europeanization of Domestic Politics and Institutions: The Case of France, *Journal of Common Market Studies* 32, 1, March 1994: 69-88; particularly 69-70.
7. Ladrech, "Europeanization," 76-79.
8. Ibid., 83-84.
9. A good review of the literature on Europeanization can be found in Klaus H. Goetz, Simon Hix, "Introduction: European Integration and National Political Systems," in Klaus H. Goetz, Simon Hix (eds.), "Europeanised Politics? European Integration and National Political Systems," *West European Politics* 23, 4, October 2000: 1-26. Although the authors give a good account of the state of discipline, they avoid creating a rigorous framework for the study of Europeanization.
10. Attila Agh, "The Europeanization of ECE Polities and the Emergence of the New ECE Democratic Parliaments," in Attila Agh (ed.), *The Emergence of East Central Parliaments: The First Steps* (Budapest: Hungarian Centre of Democracy Studies, 1994), 9-21; Attila Agh, *The Politics of Central Europe* (London: SAGE, 1998), 24-45. One has to acknowledge that Attila Agh´s hard work on anticipatory Europeanization is quite valid, but for our purposes a bit confusing. We prefer to use the term in referring to the member-states, otherwise it is difficult to define when processes of Europeanization start for countries of the European Union.
11. Magnus Ekengreen, Bengt Sundelius, "Sweden: The State Joins the European Union," in Ben Soetendorp, Kenneth Hanf (eds.), *Adapting to European Integration. Small States and the European Union* (London: Longman, 1998), 131-148; particularly 138-140.
12. Tanja Börzel, "Why There is No Southern Problem: On Environmental Leaders and Laggards in the EU," *Journal of European Public Policy* 7, 1: 141-162.
13. _____, "Non-compliance in the European Union. Pathology or Statistical Artefact?" *Journal of European Public Policy* 8, 5, 2001: 803-824; particularly 819.
14. George Ross, *Jacques Delors and European Integration* (Cambridge: Polity, 1995).
15. Mark Pollack, "Creeping Competence: The Expanding Agenda of the European Community," *Journal of Public Policy* 14, 2, 1994: 95-140; Mark Pollack, "The

End of Creeping Competence? EU Policy-making Since Maastricht," *Journal of Common Market Studies* 38 3, September 2000: 519-538.

16. Laura Cram, *Policy Making in the European Union. Conceptual Lenses and the Integration Process* (London: Routledge, 1997).
17. Alastair Cole, "National and Partisan Contexts of Europeanization: The Case of French Socialists," *Journal of Common Market Studies* 39, 1, March 2001: 15-36; particularly 25-31.
18. An excellent comparative study is B. Guy Peters and Vincent Wright, "The National Co-ordination of European Policy-Making. Negotiating the Quagmire," in Jeremy Richardson (ed.), *European Union. Power and Policy-Making* (London: Routledge, 2001), 155-178.
19. According to Peter Mair, Europeanization of national political parties is actually still not very salient. See Peter Mair, "The Limited Impact of Europe on National Party Systems,"in Klaus H. Goetz, Simon Hix (eds.), "Europeanised Politics? European Integration and National Political Systems," Special Issue of *West European Politics* 23, 4, October 2000: 27-50.
20. Peter Pagh, "Denmark´s Compliance with European Community Environmental Law," *Journal of Environmental Law*11, 2, 1999: 301-319.
21. Paul Taggart, "New Populist Parties in Western Europe," *West European Politics* 18,1, January 1995: 34-51; Pia Knigge, "The Ecological Correlates of Right-wing Extremism in Western Europe," in *European Journal of Political Research* 34, 2, October 1998: 249-279;
22. Hans Joergen Nielsen, "Denmark," in Juliet Lodge (ed.), *The 1994 Election to the European Parliament* (London: Pinter 1996), 54-65; Hans Joergen Nielsen, "Denmark," in Juliet Lodge (ed.), *The 1999 Elections to the EuropeanParliament* (Basingstroke: Macmillan, 2001), 60-71.
23. Peter Pernthaler, Peter Hilpold, "Sanktionen als Instrument der Politikkontrolle-der Fall Österreich," in *Integration*, 23Jg, 2/2000: 105-110; Pierre Giacometti, "Les Européens face au cas Haider. La question Haider divise les opinions européennes," in Bruno Cautrés, Dominique Reyniè (eds.*), L´Opinion Européenne 2000* (Paris: Presses Sciences Po, 2000), 193-195; Michael Merlingen, Cas Mudde, and Ulrich Sedelmeier, "The Right and the Righteous? European Norms, Domestic Politics and the Sanctions Against Austria," in *Journal of Common Market Studies* 38, 1, March 2001: 59-77; particularly 71-72.
24. Maria Joao Rodrigues, "A Estratégia de Lisboa: Das Politicas Europeias às Politicas Nacionais," in *Europa. Novas Fronteiras*, 7, Junho 2000: 42-45.
25. This excellent point has been made by Michael Merlingen, "Identity, Politics and Germany´s Post-TEU Policy on EMU," *Journal of Common Market Studies* 39, 3, September 2001: 463-483; particularly 469-477.
26. José Magone, "La construzione di una societá civile europea:legami a più livelli tra comitati economici e sociali," in Antonio Varsori (ed.) *Il Comitato Economico e Sociale nella construzione europea* (Venice: Marsilio, 2000), 222-242.
27. This concept was taken from Kenneth Dyson, "EMU as 'Europeanization'," 646: "This 'top-down,' Europeanization is, however, complemented by a 'bottom-up' process in which domestic elites construct EMU by reference to distinctive domestic institutional arrangements and project these constructions at the EU level. Hence, the direction of change is complex." See also Alastair Cole, "National and Partisan Contexts of Europeanization: The Case of French Socialists," in *Journal of Common Market Studies* 39, 1, March 2001: 15-36; particularly 33-34.
28. Monica den Boer, William Wallace, "Justice and Home Affairs:Integration through Incrementalism," in Helen and William Wallace (eds.), *Policy-Making in the Euro-*

pean Union (Oxford:Oxford University Press, 2000), 494-525, particularly 512-519.

29. Republique Francaise, Ministére de la fonction publique de la reforme d'Etat et de la decentralisation, *Rapport annuel de relations internationales et de la cooperation administrative.1998-99* (Paris: MFPRED, 1999), 9-11.
30. Martin Westlake, "The View from Brussels," in Philip Norton (eds.), *National Parliaments and the European Union* (London: Frank Cass, 1995), 166-176, particularly 171-173.
31. Doug Imig and Sidney Tarrow, "Political Contention in a Europeanising Polity," in Klaus H. Goetz, Simon Hix (eds.), "Europeanised Politics? European Integration and National Political Systems," *West European Politics* 23, 4, October 2000: 73-93; particularly 73-77; Andrew Martin, George Ross, "European Integration and the Europeanization of Labour," in Emilio Gabaglio and Reiner Hoffmann (eds.), *The ETUC in the Mirror of Industrial Relations Research* (Brussels: European Trade Union Institute 1998), 247-293; particularly 272-273.
32. See, for example, Francisco Torres, "Lessons from Portugal's Long Transition to Economic and Monetary Union," in Alvaro de Vasconcelos, Maria Joao Seabra (eds.), *Portugal. A European Story* (Lisbon: Instituto de Estudos Estratégicos e Internacionais-Principia 2000), 99-130; Francisco Torres, "Portugal Towards Economic and Monetary Union: A Political Economy Perspective," in Jeffry Frieden, Francisco Torres (eds.), *Joining Europe's Monetary Club: The Challenges for Smaller Member States* (New York: St. Martin's Press, 1998), 171-202.
33. José Medeiros Ferreira, *A Nova Era Europeia. De Genebra a Amsterdao* (Lisbon: Noticias Editorial, 1999).
34. Federiga Bindi Calussi, "2000: O processo de tomada de decisoes em politica comunitária," *Analise Social* 154-155: 383-404.
35. Carlos Gaspar, "Portugal e o alargamento da Uniao Europeia," *Analise Social*154-155: 327-372.
36. David Corkill, *The Portuguese Economy. A Case of Europeanization* (London: Routledge 1999).
37. Special issue of *Analise Social* XXVII, 118-119,1992 José Silva Lopes (ed.), *Portugal and EC Membership Evaluated* (London: Pinter, 1994). Both include political studies of the relationship between the EU and the Portuguese political system, but they are superficially done, based very much on speculation. The strongest parts are the economic studies.
38. This is, for example, *Politica Internacional* of excellent quality and *Europa Novas Fronteiras* issued regularly by the new Jacques Delors Centre of Information based in Belém nearby Lisbon.
39. Here "semiperipheral" is used in terms of Immanuel Wallerstein. It is a position between the core capitalist countries and the peripheral ones (in Africa, Asia, and Latin America). The semiperipheral countries have characteristics of both peripheral and core countries. A thorough discussion of Portugal and Spain as semiperipheral countries was undertaken in my book José Magone, *The Changing Architecture of Iberian Politics (1974-1992). An Investigation on the Structuring of Democratic Political Systemic Culture in Semiperipheral Southern European Countries* (Lewiston, NY: Edwin Mellen Press, 1996), 85-137; see also Boaventura Sousa Santos, "Social Crisis and the State," in Kenneth Maxwell (ed.), *Portugal in the 1980s. Dilemmas of Democratic Consolidation* (New York: Greenwood, 1986), 168-195; Boaventura Sousa Santos, *O Estado e a Sociedade em Portugal (1974-1988,* (Porto: Afrontamento, 1990), and Joaquim Aguiar, "Partidos, estruturas patrimonialistas e poder funcional: A crise de legitimidade." *Análise Social* 21,

1985: 759-783; Boventura Sousa Santos (org.), *Portugal: Um Retrato Singular* (Porto: Edições Afrontamento, 1993).

40. Jan Beyers, Guido Dierickx, "The Working Groups of the Council of the European Union: Supranational or Intergovernmental Negotiations?" *Journal of Common Market Studies* 36, 3. 1998: 289-317; 305-306.
41. Rui Aragão, *Portugal: O Desafio Nacionalista. Psicologia e Identidade Nacionais* (Lisbon: Editorial Teorema, 1985), 259-278.
42. José Magone, "Portugal," in Ruud Koole, Richard S. Katz (eds.), Political Data Yearbook 2000, Special Issue of *European Journal of Political Research* 38, 3-4, December 2000: 499-510; particularly 504.
43. *Expresso*, 5 October 2001.
44. *Eurobarometer* 51, Spring 1999: B3-B4.
45. For a more detailed comparative study, see André Freire, "Participação e abstenção nas eleicoes legislativas portuguesas, 1975-1995," *Analise Social* 154-155; 115-145.
46. *Eurobarometer* 51, 1999: B.13.
47. European Commission, *The Social Situation in the European Union 2002* (Luxembourg: Office of the Official Publications of the European Communities, 2002).
48. *Die Zeit*, 20 September 2001, p. 33.
49. It is not argued here that Ireland had no difficulties at all with adapting to the European Union. On the contrary, the argument is that Ireland had a much longer period of democracy and membership in which to adjust more gradually to the pressures of the European Union in contrast to newcomer Portugal, which was still engaged in democratizing its structures from a lengthy authoritarian dictatorship, which for a long time prevented economic and social development in Portugal. For the Irish case, see Brigid Laffan and Etain Tannam, "Ireland: The Rewards of Pragmatism," in Kenneth Hanf, Ben Soetendorp (eds.), *Adapting to European Integration. Small States and the European Union* (London: Longman, 1998), 69-83. See also Neill Collins and Mary O´Shea, "The Republic of Ireland," in J. A. Chandler (ed.), *Comparative Public Administration* (London: Routledge 2000), 98-125.
50. José Magone, *European Portugal. The Difficult Road to Sustainable Democracy* (Basingstroke: Macmillan, 1997, 2001), 142-143.
51. See a collection of lessons brought to paper by Portuguese civil servants dealing with the European integration in Alvaro Vasconcelos, Maria João Seabra (eds.), *Portugal. A European Story* (Lisbon: Instituto de Estudos Estratégicos e Internacionais-Principia, 2000).
52. Kenneth Dyson, Kevin Featherstone, "Italy and EMU as a 'Vincolo Esterno': Empowering the Technocrats, Transforming the State,"in *South European Society and Politics*1, 2, Autumn 1996: 272-299.

2

The Europeanization of the Core Political System

The Process toward EU Membership

From the very start, the process of European integration was dominated as in other European countries by the political elites without too much input coming from civil society. During the authoritarian regime, the press and civil society were repressed by censorship, while during democracy, the EC membership was regarded as a matter of national survival which, after the traumatic loss of the colonial empire, could not be subject to popular scrutiny.

In this chapter, I will first review the developments toward and after membership, before discussing more thoroughly how the different institutions were recreated shortly before and after EU membership. All of them were tailored to fit into the European constitutional order, even if such an order is still in the making. The actors of the Portuguese political system had to transform their highly socialist pluralist constitution into a compatible liberal constitution. This also had effects on the different core institutions. The civilianization of the presidency became an important achievement in the hand-over of power by the military to the civilian politicians.

Europeanization effects after membership can be found in the government and the Parliament. They became involved in a multilevel nested game that had implications for policymaking.

In sum, Europeanization is asymmetrical and affects different institutions of the core political system at different times and in different ways.

The Road toward EC/EU Membership (1960-1985)

In the 1960s, the Portuguese authoritarian regime searched for better integration into the European markets. This was a major project of the Europeanist faction within the Salazarist elite, which was counteracted by the advocates of continuing an isolationist policy and strengthening the relationship to the colonial empire. This so-called "Africanist faction" wanted to avoid an opening up of the Portuguese economy toward the more competitive European processes. Negotiations to join the European Community in the 1960s and 1970s were blocked by the fact that Portugal was not a democracy, an essential precondition for membership. Portugal became a member of the alternative European Free Trade Area (EFTA) on 18 August 1961,along with the UK, Sweden, Norway, and Denmark. This association wanted to have enough leverage to negotiate with the EC, in terms of future membership of the individual members. In spite of this strategy spearheaded by the UK, which led to rejection of the accession twice through the French veto in 1965 and 1967,[1] the Portuguese case was further hampered by the fact that Portugal was not a democracy. The famous Birkelbach report of the European Parliament set the benchmark for any potential candidate:

> Only states which guarantee on their territories truly democratic practices and respect for the fundamental rights and freedoms can become members of our Community.[2]

The replacement of dictator Antonio Salazar by his protegé Marcelo Caetano in 1968, despite high expectations, did not lead to major reform or political change towards democracy. Although the rise of Caetano to the top job was regarded at first as a potentially new beginning, all hopes were soon dashed when, in 1973, the new dictator was pressured by the ultras within the regime to take a more repressive attitude towards the opposition. This move inevitably led to the Portuguese Revolution of Carnations on 25 April 1974. However, despite these domestic developments, the authoritarian regime continued negotiations with the European Community throughout the 1970s, achieving on 22 July 1972 a free trade agreement with the EC along with the other EFTA members.[3]

The Portuguese Revolution of 25 April 1974 attracted the attention of many international actors because of the uncertainty of its outcome. This first country embarking on democratic regime transition was not certain about its final outcome in the revolutionary process. The multiplicity of power centers led to a situation of double impotence, in which neither the government nor the new grassroots social movements were able to take over.[4] The radicalization of the Revolution in 1975 was a major concern to the international actors, particularly the United States, which was afraid that a kind of domino-scenario of regimes becoming communist one after another could become reality in Southern Europe as it had happened before in Indochina. The domino-scenario was related to the growing influence of Communist parties in Italy, Greece, Spain, and Portugal. If Communist parties gained influence in Southern Europe, this would severely affect the stability between West and East.[5]

From the start, the military political elites, highly influenced by the ideologies of the African liberation movements, were of the opinion that they had to liberate the country from the existing authoritarian structures. Therefore, their political design was very much influenced by Socialist models. There was no clarity about the final model. Indeed, different models were put forward during the summer 1975.

The model of a *People's Democracy,* as in the Eastern European countries, was put forward by Prime Minister Vasco Gonçalves and the Gonçalvists. Such a model had to be implemented against the will of a substantial part of the population. It was also not in the interest of the Soviet Union to establish a second "Cuba" on the southwestern fringe of Europe, because Brezhnev was more interested in the process of *detente* related to the scheduled conference on security and cooperation in Europe in Helsinki at the end of 1975. Therefore, the Gonçalvist project became isolated in August 1975 when all the parties, even the Communist Party, decided not to take part in the fifth provisional government. Subsequently, Prime Minister Vasco Gonçalves had to resign.

The model of a *"People's Power" Democracy* was supported by the smaller left-wing parties such as the terceiro-mundistas, trotzkyists, maoists, etc. It was a model based on the structures of the grassroots movements. Otelo Saraiva de Carvalho, the main organizer of the coup and commander of the special police COPCON, was the leader of this radical faction within the Movement of Armed Forces (*Movimento das Forças Armadas*-MFA) The decrease in mobilization after November 1975 as well as the multitude of designs coming from the different left-wing groups made this model unfeasible.

The model of "*Social-Democracy*" was presented by the Socialist Party. It had reached democratic legitimacy in the founding elections of 25 April 1975. This political design was also supported by the People's Democratic Party (*Partido Popular Democratico*-PPD). The idea of a "democratic socialism" appealed to large segments of the population. Social justice and the access of all citizens to education and cultural goods were postulated aims in a catalogue with the main intention of creating in Portugal a more just and solidaristic society.[6]

Already on 3 May 1974, the foreign minister of the first provisional government, Mário Soares, had gone to Brussels and made first contacts with EC high officials. Behind these first contacts was the hope of mobilizing EC aid for the Portuguese economy and deepening economic ties between Portugal and the EC by substituting the Special Relations Agreement of 1972 for an association agreement with a provision for full membership. Such an agreement would also make possible EC aid within a well-tried framework. During question time at the European Parliament on 14 May 1974, Sir Christopher Soames, vice president of the Commission, clearly stated that foreign minister Mário Soares wanted to see a close relationship established between Portugal and the Community. Moreover, the members of the Commission were pleased to hear that the new Portuguese administration wanted to install a democratic government as swiftly as possible.[7]

The attention of the European Community towards the situation in Portugal became more intense during the months previous to the scheduled founding elections. On 12-13 February, Sir Christopher Soames paid a visit to Lisbon. There he stressed

> the high hopes in the Community as a result of Portugal's efforts to establish a stable democratic government and the parallel moves to grant independence to its overseas territories.[8]

Although most of the talks were related to economic issues, Soames' reply to an oral question put to him in the European Parliament on 19 February, concerning the situation in Portugal and Portugal's relation with the Community, produced an expression of concern by the MEPs that the conservative christian-democratic Democratic Social Centre (*Centro Democratico e Social*-CDS) was prevented from holding its founding congress and that foreign minister Mário Soares was of the opinion that such interference in political life could bring about another dictatorship or even a civil war. According to Soames, all political figures in Lisbon were determined to hold elections. At that time, the relationship between Portugal and the European Community was restricted to the negotiation of a Free Trade Agreement. Although political leaders in Lisbon urged application for full membership in the Community, the Portuguese government hesitated with a formal submission.[9]

After the elections, the negotiations between the EEC and Portugal in view of a Free Trade Agreement continued on the agenda of the Joint EEC-Portugal Committee, however, nevertheless, the political question of the establishment of a pluralist democracy was the pre-condition for any financial support to the Portuguese government.

After 25 November 1975, the date that marks the end of the revolutionary process, the relationship between Portugal and the European Community became more conciliatory. The question about the establishment of a pluralist democracy was steadily replaced by the question regarding the form of the relationship that Portugal wanted with the EEC.[10]

Even if the Portuguese Constitution adopted on 2 April 1976 was dominated by Marxist vocabulary, Portugal could be considered a liberal democratic country with inherited elements coming from the revolutionary process. Subsequently, the constitution remained the ideological battlefield to adjust the political structures to the European model of democracy.

After 25 November 1975, military dominance within the new Portuguese democracy was gradually reduced. However, civilian governments had to deal with the supervisory institution created by the MFA called the "Council of the Revolution," which made it possible for the military to watch over the Portuguese democracy for a five-year period after approval of the constitution. Only after the revision of the constitution in 1982 was the Council of the Revolution abolished and a civilian Constitutional Court created. After the adoption of the National Defense Law in 1982 and the election of the civilian Mário Soares as president of the Republic in early 1986, the process of civilianization of the new political system was finally completed.[11]

Nevertheless, at the same time, the parties represented in the Assembly of the Republic, the unicameral Portuguese Parliament, apart from the Communist Party, were interested in speeding up the process towards membership of the European Community, partly to stabilize the democratic structures and partly to strengthen the desire for civilianization of the political system in view of adjustment to it.[12]

In this sense, the first decade of the new Portuguese democracy was characterized by a strong commitment to European integration as the only viable option to strengthen its democratic regime. The dire economic situation after the revolutionary period leading to the implementation of two International Monetary Fund austerity programs in 1978/79 and 1983/84, the political instability due to ideological differences between right and left, the lack of an overall national design in foreign policy and national defense, and the growing impatience with the EC negotiations further undermined the search for a new identity in Portugal. After the collapse of the authoritarian regime, the overall priorities of Portuguese foreign policy shifted from a mere Portuguese imperial foreign policy to a collective European one. A new democratic Ministry of Foreign Affairs had to take into account the shift in priorities. Since the establishment of the first constitutional government, European Community membership became the number one priority of the new democratic political system. Very early in the day, already on 28 February 1977, Portuguese Prime Minister Mário Soares submitted the Portuguese application for EU membership. Both the Council of Ministers as well as the Commission reacted quickly and positively to the intentions of this young democracy. With the positive opinion of the Commission on 19 May 1978, the first negotiations were started in autumn 1978, although the real negotiations began only in 1980.[13]

Due to governmental and economic instability between 1978 and 1985, no government was able actually to reform the public administration, in general, and the Ministry of Foreign Affairs, in particular. Instead, the Ministry of Foreign Affairs was characterized by continuity from the former authoritarian regime. Even if some adjustments were made to deal with the new European option of Portuguese foreign policy, most of the staff had shown a high degree of continuity to the previous regime despite a revolutionary period, during which a very anti-American foreign policy was pursued.

During the revolutionary process, the European Community put pressure on the Portuguese government to move towards liberal democracy.[14] Since 1976, the Ministry of Foreign Affairs began a major restructuring towards European integration, which required the socialization of civil servants as well as diplomats into the policymaking structures of the European Community. This process of socialization and the training of diplomats and civil servants was constrained by three main aspects.

The first was of an economic nature. The economic austerity to which the Portuguese administration was subject between 1978 and 1985 did not allow for too much investment in this area.

The second reason was related to the fact that the longer the negotiations took, the more insecure became the Portuguese government and Portuguese diplomacy in relation to the accession data and the chosen priority.

The third reason is related to the fact that governmental instability prevented any profound changes to the Portuguese Ministry of Foreign Affairs. A major restructuring took place only in 1985 by Jaime Gama, shortly before the accession of the European Community and then finally in 1994 by José Durão Barroso. In both cases, we see a reinforcement of the policymakers dealing with European Union affairs. While between 1980 and 1985 the Portuguese government sent some civil servants to community institutions such as the Commission for training, it was only in the last year before the accession that the Portuguese government made major efforts to strengthen the number of civil servants and diplomats dealing with European affairs. It is probably important to bear in mind that while in domestic policy matters, the overall institutional and personnel resources began to be massively upgraded only when there was stronger demand coming from Brussels, the staff dedicated exclusively to the European foreign policy contingent did not change as dramatically. The latter concentrated merely on sending a permanent delegation to the headquarters of NATO. The plenipotentiary ambassador and his advisers continued to do so after 1986, due to the fact that the situation remained unchanged. Moreover, once Portugal became a member of the WEU in 1988, the powers of the plenipotentiary ambassador were extended to the WEU, complying with the Portuguese interpretation that the WEU was merely the European pillar of NATO. In contrast, after signing the Treaty of Accession in Belém on 12 June 1986, in domestic aspects the government was bombarded by the institutions of the European Community to send representatives to several internal and external committees. According to the figures provided by the Portuguese Ministry of Foreign Affairs the Portuguese government was requested to nominate overnight representatives to the different structures of the European Community, as well as 250 committees and 500 expert groups, which work within the comitology structures of the Commission. In the first year of membership, Portuguese representatives had participated in over 2,500 meetings.[15]

Belonging to the European Union (1986-)

The overall situation changed after accession to the European Community. After the uncertainty and long-waiting Portuguese political elites achieved the main objective after transition to democracy. One has to recognize that it is difficult for any new member to adjust to the complexity of the EC/EU decision-making process. In the second half of the 1980s and 1990s, Portugal had to learn to deal with the pressures, particularly those related to the implementation of the Single European Market, coming from the supranational European Community. It is only after 1992 that Portuguese diplomacy became more confident in the European setting. The presidency of the Council of the European Union can be regarded as the decisive point of maturation of the Portuguese position.One can divide this period into two main phases: The Learning Phase (1986-1995) and The Assertive Phase (since 1996).

The Learning Phase (1986-1995)

In the *first phase,* Portuguese diplomacy was keen to learn to deal with the complexity of the EU political system. It invested much in defending a Portuguese position around the national interest without alienating the other member-states. It was a position of full support of the European integration process, while preserving the national interests related to social and economic cohesion in general and the structural funds in particular. Portugal was strongly engaged in the negotiations leading up to the reform of the structural funds and the Delors Package I, with the Portuguese government regarding the European integration process as the way to modernize the Portuguese economy and society. Modernization is the keyword to understand the position of Portugal during this phase. Indeed, the Portuguese position in relation to the Treaty of the European Union is quite skeptical until 1989. The government of Cavaco Silva was close to the position of Margaret Thatcher in relation to the design of the European Community as a Single European Market to be completed by 1993, without an Economic and Monetary Union. As Francisco Torres asserts, this changed slowly towards a positive supportive position of the Treaty of the European Union in 1991. It became an important strategic decision by Anibal Cavaco Silva, which led to the establishment of a convergence plan called Quantum (*National Framework of Adjustment to the Transition towards Economic and Monetary Union*) in June 1990, followed by QuantumII for the period 1992-95, designed to make possible Portuguese entry to the Exchange Rate Mechanism leading up to the Economic Monetary Union. It joined the ERM on 6 April 1992 during the Portuguese presidency. In spite of difficulties in the Portuguese economy during 1992 and 1993, Cavaco Silva kept the Portuguese economy on course to become a full member of the EMU. Cavaco Silva´s well-managing of the economy, despite a European recession in 1992-93 and the unexpected fall of the tax revenue due to increased unemployment, led to extremely good foundations for the incoming Socialists to continue the pursuit of membership in the Economic and Monetary Union. The budget deficit remained at 1 percent of the GDP. Cavaco Silva was able to gain cross-party consensus from the Socialists for his policies.[16] He was opposed by the two small anti-Maastricht parties, the Communists and the renamed People´s Party of Manuel Monteiro.

A climax to the Cavaco Silva administration was the organization of the Portuguese presidency in the first half of 1992. Portuguese administration decided to skip its turn in organizing the presidency of the European Union in 1987 due to the lack of experience within European Community institutions. Preparation for the presidency started quite early in 1988. A massive program of training of staff was set in motion, which led to an improvement of the knowledge of the European institutions. The presidency itself was an important historical moment for the Portuguese administration, because it had to manage the difficult question of ratification of Maastricht. The negative referendum in Denmark and the split vote in the French referendum had repercussions in Portugal. The former christian-democratic CDS-PP highly supportive position of European integration changed completely under the new leader Manuel Monteiro. Manuel Monteiro´s party moved towards a Euroskeptic line. It led to his exclusion from the European People´s Party. Euroskepticism was a sign that Portugal was becoming less consensual in relation to the European integration process. Although the anti-Maastricht potential was at that time not more than 20 percent (if we add the percentage of Communists and the Centrists together), it represented a different position in relation to the two main parties, PSD and PS, which were full supporters of the post-Maastricht integration efforts. During the Portuguese presidency, foreign minister João Deus Pinheiro made clear that the government did not intend to hold a referendum, due to the fact that the treaty was so complex that it could not be answered with a yes or no. Inspite of attempts of the smaller parties and civil associations to campaign for a referendum, this was not regarded as an option by the two main parties. In the end, the Maastricht Treaty led to the third revision of the constitution in 1992 and it was approved by the two main parties. Communists and Centrists voted against.[17]

The presidency allowed Portuguese diplomacy to play a role in the United Nations Environmental Summit in Rio de Janeiro in 1992 which laid the foundations for Kyoto. Moreover, it had to deal with the difficult crisis in Bosnia-Herzegovina. On top of all these issues, it also completed the McSharry Reform of the Common Agricultural Policy (CAP), which, in all possible terms, did not lead to any benefits to Portuguese farmers. In sum, the Portuguese presidency was engaged in crisis management for most of the time; however, it can be considered a success.[18]

After the presidency, Portuguese diplomacy was much more active in defending its national interest. This became quite evident during the Edinburgh European summit when Portuguese allied with the southern Europeans to defend the doubling of the structural funds, known as Delors II package. This southern European alliance should become a common feature in this policy field.[19] The economic situation worsened during 1994 and 1995. An alternance in power was becoming quite evident.

The Assertive Phase (since 1996)

The new Guterres government after October 1995 emphasized the continuity of policy in relation to the previous government. It set priorities in relation to the modernization of the education sector and decentralization. It advocated in the electoral manifesto the introduction of administrative regions in Portugal which would be subject to a referendum in due time. The major issues of the Guterres government were the referendum on regionalization on 8 November 1998, the membership of the third phase of the Euro in 1999, the process towards introduction of the Euro in 2002, and, last but not least, the presidency of the European Union in the first half of 2000.

The outcome of the referendum on regionalization of 8 November 1998 was quite embarassing for the Guterres government. For days Guterres could not comment on the results which led to its rejection by two-thirds of the voters. Although less than 50 percent of the electorate voted in the referendum and therefore the result is not binding, it was a major blow to the government program of Guterres. Regionalization is enshrined in the constitution of 1976, but it was never introduced. The general debate in Portugal led to a split between the left and the right. While the main left-wing parties, Socialists and Communists, were enthusiastic of regionalization, the right-center parties, Socialdemocrats and Centrists, were against regionalization. The argument of the opponents of regionalization included the fact that Portugal was too small to be partitioned into eight administrative regions, that the country´s culture was unitary and not regionalized, and that this would create a new layer of bureaucracy. For Socialists and Communists this was an opportunity to decentralize decision-making processes, to increase efficiency in terms of policy implementation, and to strengthen democratization at the grassroots.[20]

The regionalization question was quite important in the context of a "Europe of the Regions." The overall result was a major blow to the decentralization policies of the Socialist government. Indeed, this result led to a complete disarray of the policies of the Socialist government which seemed to be extremely linked to a positive result of this referendum. Indeed, this was the second referendum of the year. The first referendum on the relaxation of the abortion law was also rejected by the population and the turnout was quite low as well.[21] This naturally was a major blow for a government that wanted to introduce major reforms in the country.

This also led to the conclusion that it was too risky to put the membership question in stage three of the Economic and Monetary Union (EMU) to the population. Indeed, both the discussion on the ratification of the Amsterdam Treaty and membership of stage three of the EMU were controlled by the political class as a question of national interest.

Guterres was successful in preserving the continuity of the macroeconomic policies of Cavaco Silva. Both in 1997 and 1998 the government was able to meet the Maastricht criteria, much better than Italy or Belgium. The acceptance of the European Commission of Portugal as member of the first group of the Eurozone by 1 January 1999 was regarded as an important strategic victory for Antonio Guterres and the country in particular.[22]

One of the big challenges for the Guterres government was the second presidency of the European Union, due in the first half of 2000. The preparations began already in 1998 by the General-Directorate for Community Affairs (*Direcção-Geral para Assuntos Comunitários*-DGAC). One of the big successes of the presidency was the achievement of a compromise in terms of European employment policy and strategy achieved by Maria João Rodrigues during the extradionary European Council in Lisbon. Although a quite difficult and almost impossible task, the Guterres government was able to bring the two positions of Lionel Jospin and Tony Blair towards a compromise. The so-called "open method of coordination" became an important extension to the methodologies of European integration.[23]

After the presidency, the Guterres government showed signs of weariness and decline. Indeed, between September 2000 and the resignation of Prime Minister Guterres in December 2001 several reshuffles were undertaken due to resignations of ministers or due to attempts to revitalize the fortunes of the government. These were accompanied by the feeling that in spite of all the successes related to membership in the EMU and the Presidency, the Guterres government had neglected to undertake the necessary public reforms to make the Portuguese state more competitive. Already before 9/11 signs of a slowing down of the Portuguese economy created a gap between expected and real tax revenue. One of the major problems of Antonio Guterres was an inability to tackle the long overdue reform of the public administration, particularly in relation to the growing civil service, which was above 700,000 by 1999. Moreover, several public sector enterprises such as the national railway and national television were heavily in debt. This was causing problems for the government in terms of its ability to keep the budget deficit to below the prescribed mark of 3 percent of GDP. If the government would pass this threshold which was regarded as a cushion in times of difficulties, it would have to pay a fine and would not be able to receive must needed structural funds until the situation would be resolved.[24]

The lack of reform and a tendency towards inertia led to a major offensive of the opposition under the leadership of Manuel Durão Barroso, chairman of the social-democratic party.[25] Discontentment of the socialist grassroots with the leadership style of Guterres in the Socialist party conference of 3-5 May 2001 further discredited the ailing government.[26] The collapse of a bridge across the river Douro in the northern village of Castelo de Paiva on 5 March 2001 was a major setback for the government, which was geared towards modernization of the country. At the end of the year, on 16 December 2001, Prime Minister Guterres was confronted with a major defeat in the local elections and he decided to resign. The call for new elections of 17 March 2002 by President Jorge Sampaio was welcomed by the opposition which was criticizing the government due to Portugal's difficult financial situation. [27]

In the elections of 17 March 2002, Guterres goverment was replaced by a center-right coalition between the liberal social-democratic party under the leadership of Manuel Durão Barroso and the euroskeptic People´s Party of Paulo Portas. Their main priority was the sorting out of the Portuguese finances in view of the dramatic increase of the budget deficit to 4.1 percent of GDP, well above the 3 percent ceiling enshrined in the stability pact. Although Portugal introduced the Euro on 1 January 2002, one can say that asymmetrical shocks were already being felt, limiting sharply the maneuvering of the Portuguese government in terms of policymaking.

Constitutional Change and European Integration

The Portuguese Constitution adopted on 2 April 1976 was not an inclusive one. The right-center parties had doubts about the viability of a highly romantic eclectic constitution that was full of marxist language. The very radical constitution was dominated by the main elements of a liberal democracy, but constrained by what the left in general, and the Communist Party, in particular, would call the achievements of the Revolution of the Carnations, which ended on 25 November 1975. The first articles of the constitution clearly emphasized the fact that Portugal was engaged in transforming the country into a classless society (article 1) and to ensuring that through pluralism it would achieve the transition to socialism (article 2). The whole constitution made references to the institutions of the social movements that were spontaneously formed during the revolutionary process. It also made it imperative for the political class to defend the nationalization of most of the large industrial enterprises, banks, and other small and medium-sized enterprises. This would also include the occupation of the land estates in the southern region of Alentejo. Internationally, the constitution positions Portugal as a supporter of the decolonization process and peace across the world. One aspect that clearly restricted the powers of the political class was the fact that for five more years the entire consolidation process would be supervised by the military. The so-called Council of the Revolution (*Conselho da Revolução*-CR) created during the revolutionary transition period and consisting of members of the movement of armed forces, clearly had the task of making certain that any major changes of the socialist contents would not be touched by the political elite. The constitution limited considerably the civilian politicians in their quest to reform the economic and political systems and make them more compatible with the European Community. One of the pre-conditions for membership in the European Community was to strengthen the liberal constitutional elements and discard the socialist aspects.

Several revisions of the constitution had to be undertaken to achieve more compatibility of the Portuguese constitution with other European constitutions. Under the leadership of the right-center social democratic party two major constitutional revisions were undertaken in the 1980s. The first constitutional revision aimed at reducing the power of the military by abolishing the Council of the Revolution (article 277-285) and replacing it with a Constitutional Court (articles 277-291). The revision was carried out by the PSD, PS, and CDS. This was a major breakthrough in terms of achieving an adaptation to the other European democracies. It meant that the Portuguese constitution was being demilitarized and finally dominated by civilian politicians. The final civilianization of the political system was achieved when President General Antonio Ramalho Eanes was replaced by Mário Soares, the leader of the PS. In spite of the revision, many elements of the original constitution remained intact, particularly those related to the so-called "achievements of 25 April" which meant the preservation of the huge public sector created during the revolutionary process. The above-mentioned highly Marxist first articles of the constitution were kept as originally formulated in this first revision.

A more thorough second revision was undertaken during the absolute majorities of the Cavaco Silva governments in 1989. One of the main achievements of the Cavaco Silva administration was the introduction of major reforms to liberalize the Portuguese economy. A revision of the economic section of the constitution rebalanced the relationship between the public and private sector (articles 71-92). It also opened the road for the successful privatization of many public enterprises. The membership of the European Community was a major incentive to make these adjustments, which were also crucial for Portugal to be competitive in the Single European Market. In this revision, there was a major change in the first two articles by eliminating the references to classless society and socialism, respectively.

In 1992, Cavaco Silva introduced a third revision of the constitution. The main purpose was to adjust the constitution to the Treaty of the European Union. This became particularly evident in article 166f (changed to article to 161n in 1997) which are related to political and legislative competencies of the Assembly of the Republic, the Portuguese Parliament. There it is inscribed that the Assembly of the Republic is entitled to give its opinion on decisions related to European Union matters. Again, this revision was approved with the votes of the PSD, PS, and CDS against the PCP. While the other constitutional revisions can be regarded as adjustments of the original revolutionary constitution to the *acquis constitutionel* of the European Union member-states, the third revision of 1992 meant a major decision for systemic fusion between the European Union and the national political system. It responded to protocol 13 related to the role of national parliaments in the European Union. This Europeanization of the constitutional provision links the supranational and national levels and makes it now a multilevel nested game for the Portuguese political class and the population. This is probably one of the reasons why the smaller parties asked for a referendum on this matter. Maastricht is really a qualitative leap from national sovereignty to transnational shared sovereignty.

Five years after the last constitutional revision a new attempt was undertaken. In a negative climate of extreme bipolarization between the two main parties, the incumbent Socialist government initiated the fourth revision of the constitution, which aimed at making elected politicians more accountable to the constituencies. The idea was to introduce uninominal constituencies that would link the representative closer to the constituency. Moreover, individuals and lists of independents could take part in elections, which until then were monopolized by the parties. In spite of all the efforts, the overall final revision was a major disappointment, due to the fact that it achieved only minimalist changes to the overall system of representation. Indeed, political parties are still central to the political system and MPs do not represent the constituency, but the overall country. Although independents can take part in elections, so far this has been reduced to candidacies in local elections. In the last local elections of 16 December 2001, three independent citizens' lists were successful in three municipalities.

The fourth revision also addressed the aspects of transparency and accountability of the financing of political parties, which has been partly achieved. Although since 1995 annual reports on the finances of the individual parties have to be submitted to the Constitutional Court, the overall assessment is that this exercise has not led to more transparency because there is no system of penalties attached to it. According to Manuel Braga da Cruz the conflict between the two main parties led to a missed opportunity to strengthen democracy in Portugal. The high level of abstentionism simply confirms that the political class is quite distant from the electorate.[28]

The fifth constitutional revision took place after 9/11, the tragic events related to the Twin Towers of the World Trade Center and the Pentagon in September 2001. Although the five years necessary for undertaking a new constitutional revision had not passed, this event led to a major thrust towards Europeanization. Indeed, this constitutional revision has to be contextualized in the overall effort of the EU member-states to strengthen the capabilities of the police and the intelligence services to look for terrorists or major criminals. The constitutional revision mainly attacked the private rights of citizens. Unannouced night searches of suspected persons, extradition to other EU member-states, and adherence to the International Criminal Court were the major changes undertaken in the constitution. The attempt to extend the constitutional revision to other issues was rejected by the two main parties, because these could be addressed in the proper ordinary process of revision in 2002 or 2003. The Communist Party tried to introduce in the constitution compulsory referenda for European treaties, but these were rejected by the PS, PSD, and PP. The constitutional revision was approved on 4 October 2001. Most likely, this is a further element of this fusion of the political systems of the European Union. Indeed, this can be regarded as transnational, horizontal Europeanization, which is slowly creating a Europeanized level playing field for criminal investigations and prosecution. In this sense, the Portuguese political system is already fusing with other national political systems on the supranational level.

The Changing Role of the Presidency: The Process of Civilianization

The most stable of Portuguese institutions is the presidency of the Republic. The introduction of a directly elected presidency in the constitution of 1976 was an important device to strengthen Portuguese democracy. Indeed, over twenty-six years after the first presidential elections this institution is still working extremely well. Meanwhile, the country experienced three presidencies which were quite different in style. The first and second presidential elections were won by General Antonio Ramalho Eanes, who prevented on 25 November 1975 a coup attempt allegedly organized by the small extreme left-wing parties around Otelo with some support of the Communist Party. This naturally gave an heroic status to Ramalho Eanes in the period directly after the end of the revolutionary process. In spite of his support for liberal democracy, he was committed to the Movement of Armed Forces and the continuation of its importance in the political system through the Council of the Revolution. Therefore, civilian politicians regarded the presidency as still in control of the military, and one of the main aims of the political class was to demilitarize the political system and subordinate the military to civilian authority. In the first term of the presidency, Eanes clearly antagonized the parties, because he exerted immense power in a fragmented parliamentary situation, in which no party was able to create a stable coalition. In particular, the bad relations between the Socialists and Socialdemocrats allowed Eanes to play a pivotal role in government building. The climax of the crisis came in 1978 and 1979 when the president nominated against the parties three technocratic governments which had no support in the Parliament. Nonetheless, Eanes was able to gain support from the Socialist party, against the will of Mário Soares, for his reelection campaign at the end of December 1980. His main opponent was the socialdemocrat candidate Soares Carneiro who in the end was unable to prevent Eanes´ reelection. In contrast to the first term, Eanes engaged in a more constructive dialogue with the parties and allowed the constitutional revision of 1982 to go through without problems, which, among other things, limited the powers of the president. At the end of his presidency he decided to found a new party on the left, which intended to challenge the Socialist party and restore ethical politics among the political class. The so-called Party of Democratic Renewal (*Partido Renovador Democratico*-PRD) was able to win 17 percent of the votes overnight in the legislative elections of 1985 and reduce considerably the vote for the Socialist party.

The retreat of General Eanes from the presidency allowed for a complete civilianization of the political system. Mario Soares' victory in the second round of the presidential elections of January 1986 above all had a symbolic significance. The new civilian president finally completed the long process of democratic consolidation which reduced the continuing presence of the military in the main institutions of the core political system. At the same time, Mário Soares started his presidency directly after Portugal became a member of the European Community, a process to which he had contributed considerably. Mário Soares was reelected in 1991 without problems. In his first term, he clearly used his power to further stabilize the political system. Prime Minister Cavaco Silva was supported by President Soares, both during the first minority and second absolute majority governments. Indeed, the trade-off for his low profile toward the Cavaco Silva government, was support for his reelection in 1991. The cohabitation between Soares and Cavaco Silva acted as a detriment to the Socialist party, which was now under the control of most party opponents of Mário Soares. However, during his presidency he was able to gain a high level of popularity among the population. His so-called open presidencies (*presidencia aberta*) led to periodic visits to the different parts of the country.

After his reelection, Mário Soares changed his style and began to be more critical towards the Cavaco Silva government. One spoke of an institutional conflict between Soares and Cavaco Silva. Cavaco Silva was able to win a second absolute majority in 1991. This naturally gave him the opportunity to dominate Parliament without difficulties. Soares regarded himself as one of the few checks and balances in relation to the government. Several legislative bills were either vetoed by the government or sent to the Constitutional Court to be scrutinized in relation to their constitutionality. Soares had nothing to lose in this second term and he was able to play this role of monitoring the government because he was not allowed to run for a third term.[29]

In the elections of 1996, Jorge Sampaio emerged as the winner over Cavaco Silva. All other candidates on the left decided to renounce in favor of Sampaio and against Cavaco Silva, a move that had major significance. It meant that the presidency remained in the hands of the left. The right-center candidates have had difficulties in conquering the presidency. Sampaio was a low profile president. He was reelected in January 2001 without difficulties. Similar to Mario Soares he enjoys high levels of popularity. In his first term and at the beginning of the second term he could count on a Socialist government under the leadership of Antonio Guterres. This, naturally, was quite important for a stable government, after the institutional conflict between Soares and Cavaco Silva. After his reelection he voiced concern about the handling of the economy by the Guterres government, particularly in relation to the budget deficit which was coming close to the 3 percent of GDP defined as part of the stability pact by the European Central Bank. After catastrophic local elections, the Guterres government resigned and new legislative elections were called for 17 March 2002. This was the first major test for Sampaio, who made this decision after properly consulting the Council of State.

In sum, Portuguese semipresidentialism is quite soft. It has become civilianized since entry into the EC/EU, which was naturally enhanced the role of the presidency as the main factor of stability of the political system. It is a precious element in the institutional architecture of Portuguese politics.

Government and Bottom-Up Europeanization

Portugal has to be regarded as a small country with a limited possibility of influence on the main trends of European integration. Nevertheless, Portuguese diplomacy made a substantial effort to play a constructive role in the major Intergovernmental Conferences (IGCs) of the 1990s and in the present millennium. Since membership to the EC/EU Portuguese governments have gained in stability, but at the same time are under considerable pressure to respond to supranational policies and decision-making processes. Between 1974 and 1985, Portugal experienced nine governments, while between 1985 and 2002 there were only five governments. This fact allowed for a more coherent response to the different Intergovernmental Conferences that took place during the 1990s.

Initially, the Portuguese position was quite defensive and was in alliance with the Mediterranean countries France, Italy, Spain, and Greece. Until the mid-1990s, the Portuguese position was unclear and based on shifting alliances in view of preserving her interests. A major more protagonistic position began to be taken with the Socialist government. Although foreign minister Manuel Durão Barroso was able to improve the influence capabilities of Portugal until the mid-1990s, it was only when the Socialist party came to power, that Portuguese diplomacy attempted to develop a coherent long-term strategy of the Portuguese position in relation to the IGC in 1996 and 2000.[30]

The new State Secretary for European Affairs Francisco Seixas da Costa changed the overall strategy of Portugal. From then on, Portugal took an intermediate position between the integrationists (Belgium and Luxembourg) and the intergovernmentalists (United Kingdom). It clearly also had a strong affinity with the concerns of small countries such as Finland, Belgium, the Netherlands, and Greece. It is a highly flexible position that allows for negotiation throughout the process. Several important issues for the Portuguese government have included the weighting of the vote in the Council, which led to major protests during the final negotiations of the Nice treaty in December 2000, and the preservation of a commissioner in the Commission (see chapter 6). It clearly supports a strong role for the European Parliament even with the possibility of the election of the president of the Commission by the Parliament. Portugal emphasizes aspects of intra-community solidarity related to the structural funds and, since the IGC 1996, the social dimension of the European Union, in particular related to employment policies. Portugal is disappointed with the progress of the Common Foreign and Security Policy (CFSP) and the Justice and Home Affairs (JHA). It particularly criticizes the lack of development in the area of Justice and Home Affairs. Portugal was also very supportive of the Charter of Fundamental Citizen's Rights. Moreover, Portugal wanted the role of national parliaments strengthened.[31] It was a realistic position, but pro-active in terms of ensuring maximum influence for a small country like Portugal.

Both during the IGC 1996 towards the Treaty of Amsterdam and during the IGC 2000 leading up to the Nice Treaty, Portuguese diplomacy was well prepared, having started early in setting the parameters of the Portuguese position. Indeed, Portugal chaired the first half of the IGC 2000, which led to major compromises at an early stage. This last IGC was not very successful for small countries in general. The weighting of the vote in the Council has strengthened the larger countries to the detriment of the smaller countries. This was due mainly to an alliance between the French and British to push through the new configuration which will be valid after the completed enlargement towards 27 members. For Portugal the position was and remains that the main cleavage is not between larger and smaller countries, but between countries with different levels of development or different interests.[32]

Indeed, already on 7 June 2000, Minister of Foreign Affairs Jaime Gama declared that the IGC model was completely exhausted and it was necessary to overcome the main divide between integrationists and intergovernmentalists. This meant that a long-term balance between national identities and European coherence had to be found in the perspective of properly integrating the candidate countries.[33]

Portugal became a major supporter of the enlargement to Central and Eastern Europe. The main argument was one of solidarity with the newcomers of European integration. The enlargement was regarded as positive, because it would alter substantially the nature of the European integration process in terms of social and economic development. It would in some way constrain the power of the larger, richer countries and strengthen the position of smaller countries with a lower level of economic and social development. During the presidency, Portuguese diplomacy was clearly supportive of the process towards enlargement.[34]

In sum, the position of Portugal within the negotiation process has improved considerably. Although Portugal is not one of the main players of the European integration process, it was able to upgrade its ability to make an impact on the whole process. This can be said particularly for the introduction of a social dimension and employment policy onto the agenda of the IGC 1996 and 2000 in conjunction with other countries as well as the Charter of Fundamental Rights of European Citizens. The main trend was a gradual overcoming of the isolationist position of preserving national sovereignty towards one of shared sovereignty. One can speak therefore of a limited bottom-up Europeanization which is highly flexible and open for negotiations.

Portuguese Parliamentarianism and the Impact of the European Union

Portuguese parliamentarianism has gained in self-confidence in the past decade. Naturally, the dominance of government over Parliament still prevails, but the structures and routines inside Parliament have become more established and institutionalized. The committee work improved consider-

Figure 2.1
Treatment of EU Issues in Plenary Sessions of Portuguese Parliament

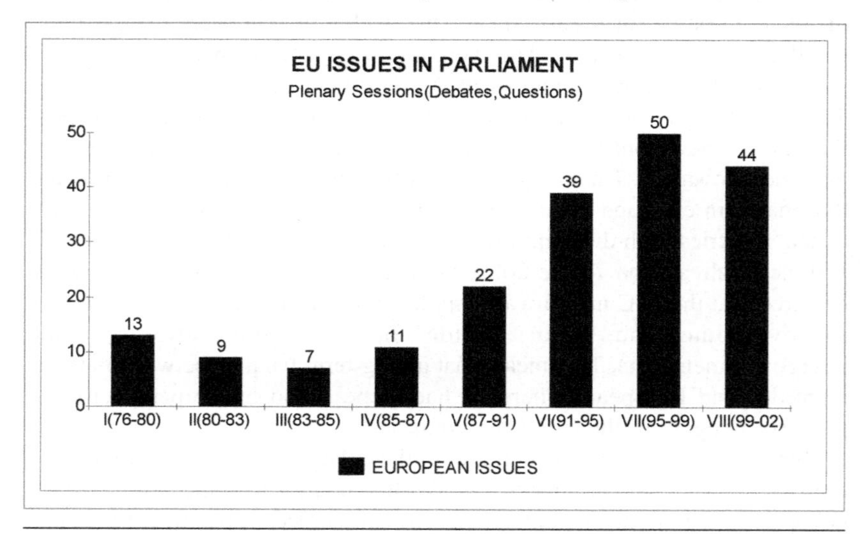

Source: Author's calculations based on *Diários da Assembleia da República*, 1976-2002

ably in the 1990s, particularly because it was able to connect Parliament with civil society. Indeed, many debates were held within the Parliament related to the regionalization referendum in 1998, the Maastricht Treaty, and the Economic and Monetary Union. Despite all the investment in the structures of Parliament, one basic problem remained the lack of professionalization of a parliamentary political class. The levels of renewal were between 40 and 50 percent between 1976 and 1999,[35] which posed major implications for the establishment of a stronger pool of experts in the Portuguese Parliament.

In the present ninth legislation, eleven committees were set up. The Committee of the European Affairs (*Comissão de Assuntos Europeus*-CAE), which was standing on its own, was now merged with the Committee of External Affairs. The new committee is called Committee of External and European Affairs(*Comissão de Assuntos Europeus e Externos*). Former foreign minister Jaime Gama is the new chair of this new committee. This may mean a further decline in the importance of the committee within the parliamentary structure and executive-legislative relations. Members of this merged committee will now be overburdened and unable to carry out a thorough scrutiny of EU legislation work.

In sum, parliamentarianism has gained in stability in Portugal, but it still has a low level of routinization and professionalization in comparison with similar counterparts in Germany, Denmark, the Netherlands, or even Spain. In terms of image among the public, the Portuguese Parliament has problems of projecting itself and achieving high levels of trust.[36]

Scrutiny of European Union legislation by the Assembly of the Republic

Although scrutiny of EU legislation through a Committee of European Affairs has been regulated since 1987, a proper scrutiny of European Union

Table 2.1
Permanent Committees of 9th Legislature (2002-)

1.	Constitutional Issues Committee
2.	Committee of European and External Affairs
3.	National Defense Committee
4.	Committee on Local Government, Territorial Organization, and Environment
5.	Economy and Finances Committee
6.	Budget Implementation Committee
7.	Committee on Education,Science, and Culture
8.	Committee on Employment and Social Affairs
9.	Committee on Public Works,Transport, and Communications
10.	Committee on Agriculture, Rural Development, and Fisheries
11.	Ethics Committee

legislation by the Assembly of the Republic started only after the introduction of the new law 20/94 of 15 June 1994, in the context of the ratification of the Treaty of the European Union, which includes a protocol on the role that national parliaments ought to play in the European integration process. Before 1994, scrutiny of EU legislation was sporadic and inconsistent, always dependent on the protagonism of the chair of the Committee of European Affairs. A qualitative improvement took place when former finance minister Jorge Braga Macedo took over the Committee of European Affairs and introduced the necessary reforms, so that it was able to scrutinize the translation of EU legislation by the government. The main bulk of the legislation is enacted by the government through decree-laws. Afterwards, the government issues an annual report called *Portugal in the European Union (Portugal na União Europeia),*which is submitted to the Committee of European Affairs. After collecting reports from all relevant permanent committees, the Committee of European Affairs issues a report that discusses the problems of the report of the government.[37]

Meanwhile, the Committee of European Affairs was able to scrutinize all the reports of the government since 1994. One of the main criticisms of the committee was that the report of the government lacked analytical depth. The report was mainly a reproduction of the transposition of the directives without giving any qualitative judgment. Moreover, former chairs of the committee such as José Medeiros Ferreira and Manuel dos Santos criticized the fact that a discussion of the report was scheduled always on Fridays or at end of the week and remained almost unnoticed by the government. Although the government is required to send a representative to take part in the discussion, this has not always been the case.[38]

Inspite of these criticisms the practice of EU legislation scrutiny is much more routinized, particularly since the last years of the Cavaco Silva and the two Guterres governments. A stronger and more open relationship between government and Parliament can be witnessed. The flow of information has improved considerably in the past eight years. Monthly visits of the junior minister for European affairs to the Committee of European Affairs has enhanced its role. Indeed, between 1995 and 2001 we can observe a dynamic Committee of European Affairs liaisoning strongly with civil society. In some sense, Parliament took over the role of educating the public about the ongoing process of European integration. This became quite evident during the process to approve the Treaty of Amsterdam, the Treaty of Nice, and to join the third stage of the Economic and Monetary Union.[39] Several universities were asked for assessment reports of the impact on Portugal.[40] The Portuguese Parliament, in 2001 began a major debate on the future of the European Union which strengthened the links to civil society.[41] In this sense, one can say that the Assembly of the Republic has increased its activity to educate the public and play a role in shaping the European integration process.

Comparatively speaking, the Committee of European Affairs is among the weakest with Spain and Greece in terms of EU scrutiny of the European Union. This naturally extends discretion and decision-making power to the government. The Portuguese Parliament in EU matters is neither a policy influencing, nor a policy making legislature; it is simply a weak legislature. According to a study by Andreas Maurer, the Portuguese Committee of European Affairs is clearly not well informed about all activities happening at European Union level. The information is selective and prepared in advance. The Portuguese legislature is not able to offer any input in relation to the specific legislation, only general comments for the next report.[42]

The Performance of the Portuguese Delegation in COSAC

Since 1989, the Committees of European Affairs of the European Union have met at least twice a year to discuss European issues in the so-called COSAC/CEAC (*Conference des organes specialisés dans les affaires communautaires/Conference of European Affairs Committees*). The meetings are a device to better integrate national parliaments into the process of European integration and so contribute to overcoming the democratic deficit. Although the committees of European affairs are quite different in outlook, this horizontal informal cooperation contributes to a process of transnational Europeanization. The meetings, which have become more sophisticated and interesting over the years, take place in the country in which the presidency currently resides.[43] We could say that since the COSAC meeting in Vienna in the second half of 1998, the work of this conference has been far more interesting. A positive occurrence in the past four years is the effort of the conference to become more institutionalized and better informed about the participating member-states. Several questionnaires were distributed among the different parliamentary delegations, which led to a general overview of the way scrutiny is undertaken in the different member-states. Some of the results were made available during the Swedish presidency in 2001, which clearly emphasized aspects of openness and transparency.[44] In recent times, we have also seen a stronger presence of the European Parliament and the parliaments of the candidate countries. Some national parliaments have created liaison bureaus with the European Parliament and the other supranational institutions in Brussels.

The Portuguese delegations so far have shown a keen interest in active participation. For the past COSAC meetings Portuguese contributions on the Treaties of Amsterdam and Nice were sent well in advance of the meetings. Integration into COSAC clearly is an opportunity for Portuguese MPs to exchange information and learn parliamentary strategies of other countries vis-à-vis their governments. Such short contributions on actual developments of European integration were sent to the COSAC in Sweden and Belgium in

2001.[45] COSAC is an important socialization structure for the Portuguese MPs from which they gain more expertise in relation to scrutiny of EU legislation. Their participation in COSAC has always been regarded as integral to the work done by the committee. However, one must recognize that the Portuguese contribution to a parliamentarization of European Union affairs can only be a modest one. The main reason for this is a lack of resources and also the importance of Parliament within the Portuguese political system in terms of adoption of EU legislation. As such, the conference is merely a forum to obtain more direct knowledge of ongoing European Union processes. As such it enables the Portuguese delegations to gain more self-confidence in asserting themselves in the scrutiny of EU legislation in relation to the government.

Table 2.2
The Meetings of the Conference of European Affairs Committees (COSAC/CEAC)

Meeting	Place	Date
27th	Copenhagen (Denmark)	14-15 October 2002
26th	Madrid (Spain)	12-14 May 2002
25th COSAC	Brussels (Belgium)	4-5 October 2001
24th COSAC	Stockholm (Sweden)	20-22 May 2001
23rd COSAC	Versailles (France)	16-17 October 2000
22nd COSAC	Lisbon (Portugal)	29-30 May 2000
21st COSAC	Helsinki (Finland)	11-12 October 1999
20th COSAC	Berlin (Germany)	30 May-1 June 1999
19th COSAC	Vienna (Austria)	23-24 November 1998
18th COSAC	London (United Kingdom)	18-19 May 1998
17th COSAC	Luxembourg (Luxembourg)	13-14 November 1997
16th COSAC	The Hague (The Netherlands)	9-10 June 1997
15th COSAC	Dublin (Ireland)	15-16 October 1996
14th COSAC	Rome (Italy)	24-25 June 1996
13th COSAC	Madrid (Spain)	8 November 1995
12th COSAC	Paris (France)	27-28 February 1995
11th COSAC	Bonn (Germany)	24-25 October 1994
10th COSAC	Athens (Greece)	9-10 May 1994
9th COSAC	Brussels (Belgium)	22-23 November 1993
8th COSAC	Copenhagen (Denmark)	3-4 May 1993
7th COSAC	London (United Kingdom)	10-11 November 1992
6th COSAC	Lisbon (Portugal)	4-5 May 1992
5th COSAC	The Hague (The Netherlands)	4-5 November 1991
4th COSAC	Luxembourg (Luxembourg)	6-7 May 1991
3rd COSAC	Rome (Italy)	1-2 November 1990
2nd COSAC	Cork (Ireland)	10-11 May 1990
1st COSAC	Paris (France)	16-17 November 1989

Source: http://www.cosac.org

The Constitutional Court: Moderating Party Politics

The role of the Constitutional Court in the Portuguese political system has grown in importance over the years. Indeed, it has become an important institution to refer to in cases where one suspects that laws are not constitutional. Although one cannot speak directly of a Europeanization of the Constitutional Court, there is some indirect influence particularly of rulings of counterparts in other countries. Quite a monumental reference point is the German Federal Constitutional Court, which in the 1990s became very active in ruling on the relationship between the German constitution and the European Union. The Portuguese Constitutional Court replaced the Constitutional Commission of the Council of Revolution after the first revision of the constitution in 1982. Since then, it has played an important role in moderating party political ambitions to politicize certain issues. Although ten judges are appointed by the Assembly of the Republic by two-thirds majority and further three are coopted by the ten judges, in reality the two main parties are in charge of preparing the list of potential candidates in consultation with the other smaller parties. Interestingly enough, the Court refrained from party politics and remained a consensual anti-majoritarian institution, which may represent a force to be reckoned with during absolute majorities such as the one under Anibal Cavaco Silva. The Court can be used both by the government or the opposition to review the constitutionality of proposed legislation.. The Communist Party used the Court through the 1980s to review legislation proposed by the Cavaco Silva government, while the Cavaco Silva minority government of 1985-87 engaged the Court to get its enormous amount of governmental legislation approved.[46]

Quite interesting was the ruling of the Constitutional Court in relation to the organization of a referendum on the Euro. It clearly ruled against it because it was not an issue that could be responded to with a clear "yes"or "no." This, of course, ended the discussion on the referendum. I suppose that the ruling was meant more or less to strengthen the position of the two main parties against the smaller euroskeptic People's Party and the critical Communists (decision no. S31/98).

In some way, the Constitutional Court was able to gain a strong reputation and prevent a politicization of the judiciary. It also remained moderate in trying to judicialize politics. In sum, it represents a moderating influence upon the heated legislative debates in the Assembly of the Republic.

Judiciary: The Lack of Reform

As in many other West European countries, the Portuguese judiciary is in a deep crisis, a condition which definitely affects the morale within the sector. And the Portuguese crisis of the judiciary is of a cumulative nature.

First of all, despite almost thirty years of democratic rule, many elements of the judicial codes of the former authoritarian regime are still valid. As a result, this has created a close-minded system that is not able to integrate innovative and reform elements from the judicial sciences done around the world. This lack of openness prevents a modernization of the procedures and ways of dealing with different kinds of crime.[47]

Secondly, the judiciary is faced with a lack of personnel such as judges and support staff. Indeed, in 1998, Portugal had only 1324 judges who were faced with a growing number of cases. Each judge on average had to deal annually with 552 new cases. He/she closed 468 cases, but he/she still had 802 pending cases that had been accumulated over the years. The result was an increase of the backlog of open and pending cases. It became clear, particularly in the second half of the 1990s, that the judiciary was becoming overwhelmed by the growing number of cases.[48] Obviously, the main way to solve this problem was to integrate more judges and support staff, so that the backlog could be reduced. Moreover, a better differentiation needed to be made between severe criminal cases and small cases so that smaller cases could be solved faster and with less cost at a lower level. Thirdly, the prison system has reached its limits. In 1998, 14,368 persons were in prison, most of whom had poor education records.

This overcrowding of prisons and lack of education implies that the justice system is the weakest link of the Portuguese political system.[49] In some manner, it needs to open up and learn, particularly from the European Union.

According to a major study undertaken by a team under the leadership of Boaventura Sousa Santos suspects and indicted persons do not trust the public institutions to represent them and prefer to hire their own lawyers, despite the fact that they cannot afford it financially.[50] This indicates that the Portuguese judicial system still has Kafkaesque elements in it.

Conclusions

Despite Portugal's almost thirty years of democracy, its political system is still being reconstructed and democratized. The European integration process has led to an opening up of all major institutions, although it has had an asymmetrical impact on each one of them. Europeanization processes can be found particularly in the core institutions of government and Parliament, but less so in relation to the presidency of the Republic and the judiciary. These institutions as well had to adjust to the European integration process, however at a much slower rate than the others. Although there are still many problems to be solved, the Portuguese political system is more and more integrated into top-down, bottom-up and transnational Europeanization processes. These processes have to be measured against the same processes in relation to other members of the European Union. In this respect, one has to assert that the semiperipheral nature of the Portuguese economy, society, and politics has led to a stronger top-down and horizontal receiving than a bottom-up influencing Europeanization.

Notes

1. Manuel Tavares Castilho, *A Ideia de Europa no Marcelismo (1968-1974)* (Lisbon: Colecção Parlamento, 2000), 87-97.
2. Geoffrey Pridham, "The Politics of the European Community, Transnational Networks and Democratic Transition in Southern Europe," in Geoffrey Pridham (ed.), *Encouraging Democracy:The International Context of Regime Transition in Southern Europe* (London: Leicester University Press, 1991), 211-245; quotation on 215. The exact name of the report is "Assemblée Parlementaire Européenne, Aspects politiques et institutionels de l´adhesion ou de l´association à la Communauté-Discussion d´un rapport de M.Birkelbach, fait au nom de la Commission politique," Séance du Mardi 23 Janvier 1962.
3. Manuel Tavares Castilho, *A Ideia de Europa no Marcelismo (1968-1974)* (Lisbon: Colecção Parlamento, 2000), 157-164.
4. Boaventura de Sousa Santos, "Crise e Reconstituição do Estado em Portugal (1974-1984)," *Revista Critica de Ciencias Sociais* 14, Novembro 1984: 7-29; quoted on 16.
5. José Freire Antunes, *Os Americanos e Portugal. Vol I: Os Anos de Richard Nixon 1969-1974* (Lisbon: Publicações Dom Quixote, 1986), 348-354.
6. José Magone, *The Changing Architecture of Iberian Politics (1974-1992). An Investigation on the Structuring of Democratic Political Systemic Culture in Semiperipheral Southern European Societies* (Lewiston, NY: Mellen University Press, 1996), 321-323.
7. *Bulletin of the EC*, 5, 1974: 65.
8. Ibid., 2, 1975: 55.
9. Ibid., 2, 1975: 61.
10. A more thorough study of the relationship EEC-Portugal can be found in my "A integração e a construção da democracia portuguesa," *Penelope* 18, 1998: 123-63; particularly 134-139. Here I had little space to highlight the importance of the German political foundations, the social-democratic Friedrich Ebert Foundation, and the christian-democratic Konrad Adenauer Foundation, in providing the party-building logistics in the Portuguese case. See the excellent book by Rainer Eisfeld, *Sozialistischer Pluralismus in Europa. Ansätze und Scheitern am Beispiel Portugal* (Köln: Verlag Wissenschaft und Politik, 1984). Eisfeld brings to the fore also the efforts made by the sister communist party of the official GDR main party SED in supporting financially and logistically the Portuguese Communist Party. The German influence in the Portuguese transition and consolidation to democracy cannot be emphasized strongly enough.
11. On civilianization and democratization, see the study by Felipe Agüero, "Democratic Consolidation and the Military in Southern Europe and South America," in Richard Gunther, P. Nikiforos Diamandouros, Hans-Jürgen Puhle (eds.), *The Politics of Democratic Consolidation. Southern Europe in Comparative Perspective* (Baltimore, MD: John Hopkins University Press, 1995), 124-165; particularly 131;144.
12. Berta Alvarez-Miranda, "On the Edge of Europe: Southern European Political Debates on Membership," *South European Society and Politics* 1, 2, 206-118; this

is a summary of her book *El Sur de Europa y la adhesion a la Comunidad. Los debates politicos* (Madrid: CIS, 1996).

13. José Magone, "A integração Europeia e a construção da democracia portuguesa," *Penelope* 18, 1998: 123-163; 139-141.
14. During the revolutionary process, there were six provisional governments and four different foreign ministers. For a study on the Minister of Foreign Affairs, see Jorge Campinos, *O Ministro dos Negócios Estrangeiros. Estudo de Direito Internacional Publico e de Direito Constitucional Comparado* (Lisbon: Moraes Editores, 1977).
15. Ministério dos Negócios Estrangeiros, *Portugal nas Comunidades Europeias. Primeiro Ano 1986* (Lisbon: MNE, 1987), 181-182.
16. Francisco Torres, "The Case for Economic and Monetary Union: Europe and Portugal,"*Nação e Defesa*, n°85, Primavera 1998, 2 Série: 29-69; particularly 42-44; Anibal Cavaco Silva, *As Reformas da Decada (1986-1995)* (Lisbon: Bertrand Editora, 1995), 105-112
17. José Magone, *European Portugal. The Difficult Road to Sustainable Democracy* (Basingstroke: Macmillan, 1997), 103-106.
18. A summary of the Portuguese presidency can be found in José M. Magone, *European Portugal*, 164-170.
19. Liesbet Hooghe,Gary Marks, *Multi-level Governance and European Integration* (Rowman and Little, 2001), 98.
20. António Guterres, *Regionalização Faz a Força. Discurso de António Guterres na Comissão Nacional do PS* (Lisbon: PS, 1998); Tom Gallagher, "Unconvinced by Europe of the Regions: The 1998 Regionalization Referendum in Portugal,"*South European Society and Politics* 4, 1, 1999: 132-148; Alvaro Xosé López Mira, "Portugal: The Resistance to Change in the State Model," *Regional and Federal Studies*, 9, 2, 1999: 98-115; Michael A. Baum and André Freire, "Political Parties, Cleavage Structures and Referendum Voting: Electoral Behaviour in the Portuguese Regionalization Referendum 1998," in *South European Society and Politics*, 6, 1, Summer 2001: 1-26; António Barreto (ed.), *Regionalização Sim ou Não* (Lisbon: Dom Quixote, 1998); "Ministério do Equipamento e da Administracao do Território" *(MEPAT), Descentralização, Regionalização e Reforma do Estado* (Lisbon: MEPAT, 1998).
21. David Corkill, "Portugal's 1998 Referendums,"*West European Politics* 22, 2, 1999: 186-92.
22. Francisco Torres, "The Case for Economic and Monetary Union," 44-45.
23. For a more thorough discussion on the Portuguese presidency 2000, see chapter 7.
24. José M. Magone, "Portugal," Special Issue Political Data Yearbook 2001, *European Journal of Political Research* 40, 3-4, December 2001: 396-401; particularly 399-400; *The Economist*, "A Survey of Portugal. Half-Way There," 2 December 2000, p.11.
25. José M. Magone, "Portugal," Special Issue European Political Data Yearbook 2001, *European Journal of Political Research* 42; 3-4; December 2002: 1068-1074.
26. *Expresso*, 12 May 2001.
27. José M. Magone, "Portugal," Special Issue European Political Data Yearbook 2001, *European Journal of Political Research* 41, 3-4, December 2002: 1068-1074.
28. Manuel Braga da Cruz, "A revisão falhada do sistema eleitoral," *Analise Social* 35, 154-155, Summer 2000: 45-53, particularly 52-53.
29. Maritheresa Frain, "Relações entre o Presidente e o primeiro-ministro em Portugal:1985-1995," *Análise Social*, 30133, 1995: 653-578.

30. Carlos Gaspar, "Portugal e o alargamento da União Europeia," *Análise Social* XXV(154-155),2000: 327-372; particularly 361-368; Francisco Torres, "A dinamica das novas adesões à UE e as opções europeias," *Europa. Novas Fronteiras*, December 1999: 85-87; Alvaro Vasconcelos, Maria João Seabra (eds.), *Portugal. A European Story* (Lisbon: Principia, 2000).
31. Ministério dos Negócios Estrangeiros, *Portugal e a Conferencia Intergovernmental para a Revisão do Tratado da União Europeia* (Lisbon: MNE Marco, 1996); Francisco Seixas da Costa, "Uma Reforma Indispensável," *Europa, Novas Fronteiras*, June 1999: 4-10; Francisco Seixas da Costa, "Tratado de Amsterdão: História de uma negociação," *Politica Internacional*1, 15-16, Winter 1997: 23-47.
32. Cécile Barbier, "La répartition des pouvoirs dans l'Union européenne aprés Nice," *Notabene* 119, Février 2001: 11-17; Interview with Francisco Seixas da Costa in *Publico1 January* 5 2000.
33. *Publico*, 8 June 2000.
34. Carlos Gaspar, "Portugal e o alargamento da União Europeia," *Análise Social* XXV(154-155), 2000: 327-372; particularly 370-372.
35. José M. Magone, "Political Recruitment and Elite Transformation in Modern Portugal 1870-1999: The Late Arrival of Mass Representation." in Heinrich Best, Maurizio Cotta (eds.), *Parliamentary Representatives in Europe 1848-2000. Legislative Recruitment and Careers in Eleven European Countries* (Oxford: Oxford University Press, 2000), 341-370; particularly 365.
36. Here is not the place to discuss the performance of the Assembleia da Republica. See, in this respect, Cristina Leston-Bandeira, *Da Legislação à Legitimação: O Papel do Parlamento Portugues* (Lisbon: ICS, 2002), and António Filipe, *As Oposicões Parlamentares em Portugal. Práticas e Intervenções (1976-2000)* (Lisbon: Vega, 2002).
37. José M. Magone, "The Portuguese Assembleia da República: Discovering Europe," in Philip Norton (ed.), *National Parliaments and the European Union* (London: Frank Cass, 1996), 151-165; particularly 161-162. See also Ana Fraga, "The Parliament in Portugal: Loyal Scrutiny and Informal Influence," in Andreas Maurer, Wolfgang Wessels (eds.), *National Parliaments on Their Ways to Europe:Losers or Latecomers?* (Baden-Baden: Nomos Verlagsgesellschaft, 2001), 359-376.
38. Diário da Assembleia da República, VI Legislatura, 2 Sessão Legislativa, No. 53, 25 March 1993; Diário da Assembleia da Republica, VI Legislatura, 2 Sessão Legislativa, No. 55, 31 March 1993; Diário da Assembleia da Republica, VI Legislatura, 3 Sessão Legislativa, 21 April 1994; Diário da Assembleia da Republica, VI Legislatura, 4 Sessão Legislativa, No. 46, 24 February 1995; Diário da Assembleia da República, VI Legislatura, 4 Sessão Legislativa, No. 86, 8 June 1995; Diário da Assembleia da Republica,VII Legislatura, 3 Sessão Legislativa, No. 8, 25 October 1997, 270; Diário da Assembleia da Republica, VII Legislatura, 1 Sessão Legislativa, No. 20, 23 December 1995; Diário da Assembleia da Republica, VII Legislatura, 4 Sessão Legislativa, No. 61, 18 March 1999; Diário da Assembleia da Republica, VII Legislatura, 4 Sessão Legislativa, No. 79, 29 April 1999; Diario da Assembleia da Republica,VII, 4 Sessão Legislativa, No. 102,14 July 1999 Diario da Assembleia da Republica, 2 Sessão Legislativa No. 37, 17 January 2001.
39. Comissão de Assuntos Europeus, *Acompanhamento parlamentar da Revisão do Tratado da Uniao Europeia na Conferencia Intergovernmental de 1996. 2 volumes* (Lisbon: Assembleia da Republica, 1995); Comissão de Assuntos Europeus, *Relatório sobre a Proposta n°59/VIII que aprova para ratificação, o tratado de*

Nice que altera o Tratado da União Europeia, Os Tratados que instituem as Comunidades Europeias e alguns actos relativos a esses Tratados, assinado em Nice, em 26 de Fevereiro de 2001 (Lisbon: Assembleia da Republica 2001); Comissão de Assuntos Europeus, *Opcões Europeias de Portugal. União Económica e Monetária* (Lisbon: Assembleia da Republica, 1998).

40. Maria Eduarda Goncalves, Pedro Quartin Graça, João Salis Gomes, *O Tratado de Nice e o Futuro da Europa* (Lisbon: ISCTE, 2001); Miguel Gorjão Henriques, *Novas Reflexões sobre o Sistema Institucional Comunitário Antes e Depois de Nice* (Coimbra: Faculdade de Direito, Universidade de Coimbra, 2001);Miguel Poiares Maduro, *O Tratado de Nice e o Futuro da Europa* (Lisbon: Faculdade de Direito da Universidade Nova de Lisboa, 2001); Carlos Botelho Moniz, Andreia Soares, Maria João Ferreira, Eduardo Henriques, Miguel Fontoura, *O Tratado de Nice e o Futuro da União Europeia* (Lisbon: Universidade Técnica de Lisboa, 2001).
41. Comissão de Assuntos Europeus, *Mesa Redonda sobre o Tratado de Nice e o Futuro da Europa* (Lisbon: Assembleia da Republica, 2001).
42. Andreas Maurer, "National Parliament after Amsterdam: Adaptation, Recalibration and Europeanization by Process." Paper for working group meeting, XXIVth COSAC, 8-9 April 2001, 19; see also Torbjörn Bergman, "National Parliaments and EU Affairs Committees: Notes on Empirical Variation and Competing Explanations," *Journal of European Public Policy*, 3, 1997: 373-87; Ana Fraga, *O Papel dos Parlamentos Nacionais e a Legitimidade da Construcao Europeia* (Lisbon: Cosmos, 2002).
43. Martin Westlake, "The View from 'Brussels'," in Philip Norton (ed.), *National Parliaments and the European Union* (London: Frank Cass, 1996), 166-176.
44. http://www.cosac.org.
45. Ibid.; on the Portuguese contribution to the XVI in Hague, and XVII in Luxembourg during 1997, see Comissao de Assuntos Europeus, *Portugal Na União Europeia em 1996 e 1997. Apreciação Parlamentar* (Lisbon: Assembleia da Republica, 1998) 221-246; on the Portuguese contribution to the XIV COSAC in Rome and XV COSAC in Dublin during 1996, see Comissão de Assuntos Europeus, *Portugal na União Europeia em 1995 e 1996. Apreciação Parlamentar* (Lisbon: Assembleia da Republica, 1997), 171-232.
46. António de Araújo, *O Tribunal Constitucional (1989-1996).Um estudo de comportamento judicial* (Coimbra: Coimbra Editora, 1997); António de Araújo, Pedro Coutinho Magalhães, "A justiça constitucional: Uma instituição contra as maiorias," *Análise Social* XXXV (154-155), 2000: 207-246.
47. This is naturally related to the patrimonial nature of the Portuguese political system, which still has a legal culture influenced by the historical legacy of cumulative discontinuous regimes. Legal production is not very transparent. The fragmentation of the judicial profession further adds to the difficulty of reform. José Magone, "Democratic Consolidation and Political Corruption in the Southern European Semiperiphery: Some Research Notes on the Portuguese Case, 1974-1993,"in Patrick Dunleavy and Jeffrey Stanyer (eds.), *Contemporary Political Studies 1994. Volume Two* (Belfast: Political Studies Association, 1994), 751-764; particularly 753-755; Pierre Guibentif, "Rechtskultur und Rechtsproduktion: Das Beispiel Portugal," *Zeitschrift für Rechtssoziologie* heft 2, 1989: 148-169; Diogo Freitas do Amaral, "A crise da justiça," *Analise Social* XXXV (154-155), 2000: 247-257; particularly 252-255.
48. António Barreto, Clara Valadas Preto, "Indicadores sociais: Portugal,1960-2000, "in António Barreto (ed.), *A Situação Social em Portugal 1960-1999. Vol. II.*

Indicadores sociais em Portugal e na União Europeia (Lisbon: Instituto de Ciencias Sociais, 2001), 197-199.

49. Ibid., 210-211.
50. Boaventura Sousa Santos, Maria Manuel Leitão Marques, João Pedroso, Pedro Lopes Ferreira, *Os Tribunais nas Sociedades Contemporaneas.O Caso Portugues* (Porto: Edições Afrontamento, 1996), 497.

3

The Continuing Nationalization of the Portuguese Party System

The Party System Change in Portugal

In a recent article, Peter Mair made the point that the national party systems of the member-states of the European Union are barely being touched by the European integration processes. They remained mainly conditioned by domestic factors such as the party financing system and the conflict patterns of each national society. Although some parties in some countries campaigned on a single anti-European ticket, they were not able to achieve much success. Instead, right-wing parties that were able to include the euroskeptic message in their repertoire were able to profit from any feelings of discontentment among the population. According to Mair, one of the main reasons for a lack of Europeanization is the still undefined nonexistent European party system, which is still awaiting a connection to some form of party government or executive presidential election in relation to the European Commission. In this sense, the so-called Euro-parties are still loose confederations of many national parties, which refuse to lose their autonomy to the establishment of a genuine European party system. Both in terms of format and the mechanics of the national party system the European dimension is still insignificant because it lacks structuration.[1]

Although Mair is cautious enough not to speak about the "more recently democratized polities of Greece, Portugal, and Spain,"[2] the same generalization can be made about them. The Portuguese party system, in particular, is extremely conditioned by national factors. The lack of interest in European elections over the past fifteen years shows that the European Union did not create a relevant cleavage within Portuguese society. Although some parties such as the People's Party and the Communist Party, have some euroskepticism in their repertoire, in the end it has not been rigid and dogmatic. The People's Party is anxious to be accepted by the two main parties and tends to support policies of European integration, inspite of the fact that it fights elections with a nationalist opportunistic tone. The main reason is that it hopes to win discontented segments of the population in electoral terms.

Compared to other party systems, the Portuguese system has remained quite stable in terms of its format. Since the founding elections of 1975, it consists of four main parties. Other parties may emerge from time to time but they tend to disappear after a while. The overwhelming majority of the electorate is moderate making preferences in the center. A tiny part of not more than 3 percent tends to vote to extreme left-wing parties, which are highly fragmented into many smaller parties. Since the elections of 1999, a new, extreme left-wing party, carried mostly by intellectuals from Lisbon and Oporto as well as by younger voters, was able to achieve representation in the Assembly of the Republic. The Block of the Left (*Bloco da Esquerda-BE*) was able to get two MPs elected in 1999 and three MPs in 2002. While the centrist electorate is under the control by the two main parties, the Social-Democrats and Socialists, the two smaller parties, Communists and People's Party, are losing votes and importance from election to election. This concentration of the share of the vote between the two main parties and the reduction of the share of the vote of the smaller parties clearly shows that in comparison to other West European countries, the Portuguese party system is becoming more concentrated.This concentration becomes quite evident, if we make cross-electoral arena comparisons. While the two main parties are gaining more control over the offices available in the political system, both the Communists and the People´s Party are losing it, particularly from local election to local election.

This naturally leads to the identification of a further property of the political system, which is that in spite of the fact that the parties are elected by a simple D´Hondt electoral system without any electoral threshold and more or less large multinominal constituencies and the admission to elections requiring only 5,000 signatures, very few new parties were able to change the format of the political system. The only case in which the party system format came near to changing to a five-party system was when President General Antonio Ramalho Eanes decided to found his own party, the Party of Democratic Renewal (*Partido Renovador Democratico*-PRD). It was able to gain over 17 percent of the vote in the elections of 1985, but it collapsed two years later in the elections of 1987. Most of Eanes' votes were transferred to the Social-Democratic Party under the charismatic figure of Anibal Cavaco Silva. This move contributed to the first absolute majority of Cavaco Silva, which would last for two legislature periods until 1995.

This was probably the turning point of the Portuguese party system, because from then on it evolved towards a bipolar party system. This bipolarization can be attributed to the fact that the two other smaller parties were not really alternatives in a society that had moved towards marketization of electoral politics. The two smaller parties represented archaic fringes of the Portuguese society. On the one hand, the Communists under Alvaro Cunhal, and later Carlos Carvalhas, kept their orthodox-leninist ideological position and identity. They were unable to renew themselves, becoming more and more a party of old people which refused to connect to the realities of a changing electoral arena. On the other hand, the People's Party appealed only to the very conservative segments of the population related to the former authoritarian regime or the small landowners in northern Portugal. It tried to use the anti-Maastricht nationalist ticket to boost its electoral chances. While these two parties became more rigid in ideological terms, communism and nationalism, the two centrist parties, Social-Democrats and Socialists, became more heterogeneous in their appeal for voters. They simply responded to the emergence of electoral market behavior in Portugal. The adjustment to the electoral market meant that policies became more personalized around leaders.

Anibal Cavaco Silva was the first to use what later has been called the "presidentialization of the prime minister" meaning that two main political parties fought elections around charismatic personalities, as if they were contesting presidential elections.[3] This is quite bizarre because the Portuguese political system is a semipresidential one and this development towards presidentialization is responding to a phenomenon that can be found across the European countries. This cannot be referred to as Europeanization. It is better to characterize it as Americanization. In the United Kingdom, commentators tend to refer to Prime Minister Tony Blair as "President Blair" due to the way he fights elections, his rebranding of his party as New Labour, and his keen interest in keeping a strong relationship with the United States. This phenomenon can also be found in Italy where in the last two legislative elections of 1996 and 2001, the two main candidates for prime minister advertised themselves as candidates to the presidency. Naturally, they did not mean the presidency of the Republic, which is clearly occupied by Giancarlo Ciampi, but the presidency of the Council of Ministers. Once again, Prime Minister Silvio Berlusconi´s leadership style shows strong similarities to the style of the American presidency. This can also be seen in Spain where similar to the Italian case, José Maria Aznar,and before him, Felipe Gonzalez presented themselves at elections as candidates to the presidency, in spite of Spain's being a constitutional monarchy. Indeed, in Spain the equivalent of the word prime minister is *El Presidente*, meaning naturally the presidency of the Council of Ministers. The Spanish system naturally allows for the strong role of the prime minister in relation to the Spanish Cortes, because it is extremely difficult to topple the prime minister. In sum, the Portuguese presidentialism of legislative elections is more related to a general trend across the European Union countries to personalize politics and converge to a simílar electoral arena as in the

United States. It means that ideology becomes more flexible and heterogeneous. The major parties have become shopping centers in which all products can be found, while the smaller parties are more than ever specialized "boutique parties" with small constituencies.[4]

Such an emergence of the electoral market means that the former frozen cleavages of West European politics, which endured until the late 1960s, were exposed to considerable change in the 1970s and 1980s. This means that collective ideological identities were replaced by more individualized consumers of electoral products.[5] Such marketization of electoral politics was quite gradual in most established West European democracies, but it became the level playing field for the Portuguese party system from the very beginning.

As Klaus von Beyme asserts, the southern, central and eastern European party systems did not have to undergo the whole process of party formation and transformation, which existed in most West European democracies. They became from the onset Americanized cartel parties, whose main task was to achieve the highest numbers of voters.[6] Portuguese parties never became mass parties, although they tried hard to follow this route. Instead they were always cartel parties, although they failed to recognize it until the mid-1980s, up to the rise of Anibal Cavaco Silva. Portuguese parties clearly are highly dependent on the public subsidy system that was created after 1975. Failing to get good results in elections means that parties may become highly indebted. In some cases, personalities within the parties pay themselves for their electoral campaigns or those of their party. This was the case of Marcelo Rebelo Sousa who became one of the interim leaders after the resignation of Anibal Cavaco Silva. Due to the fact that in the 1995 elections the party lost over 16 percent of the vote, there was a considerable reduction in the public subsidy. Marcelo Rebelo Sousa had to streamline the administration inside the party and was faced with several debts of the local and regional branches of the party.[7] Similar stories can be found in regard to the Socialist party, which, between 1986 and 1992, was faced with many debts left by former party leader Mário Soares.[8] This desperate state of affairs was also related to the fact that electoral campaigns were becoming more and more expensive. The parties were fortunate that before 1994 there was no real control of party financing by the Constitutional Court. The first submission of party financing reports by the parties receiving public subsidies occurred in 1995. Since then, the Constitutional Court has issued scrutiny reports of the declarations made by the parties. Nevertheless, these reports have been so far very negative, with the Constitutional Court finding many improprieties and gaps in the reports.[9] However, the actual process of some scrutiny can be regarded as a highly positive development in Portuguese politics. Other laws related to the transparency of the financial situation of incumbents of public offices were approved in the 1990s.[10]

The cartel nature of political parties in Portugal clearly makes it difficult to rely on any organizations close to the parties, for example, trade unions. The individualization of society and the lack of stable political cleavages means that voting behavior is more fluid. Joaquim Aguiar had discovered already in 1985 that this was an extremely important property of the Portuguese party system.[11] The Portuguese party system is ultra-stable in terms of format, but quite fluid in terms of voting behavior relative to the two main parties. The voters in the center are more or less highly mobile voters of the new middle classes, which tend to make the final outcome of elections quite unpredictible. Electoral behavior is conditioned more and more by experiences with the previous government, the charismatic leadership of the prime minister, the cohesion of the party, and, naturally, the state of the economy. This fluidity may even lead to the support of a new party, which may disappear in the following election. These new middle classes are quite choosy and are looking particularly for a government that will be able to offer political and economic stability over the long run. They are conservative in terms of experiments; they are interested in results. If one of the main parties fails to deliver, they may choose a change.

One of the major worries of the Portuguese party system is the growing alienation of the population. Abstention has been high since the 1980s. This has been blamed on the fact that the registration of voters is not updated and mistakes of the actual number of voters may occur. In reality, a major review of the registered voters in the 1998 shows that, inspite of such mistakes of a technical nature abstention is still quite high. It is assumed that about 10 percent of all registered voters are either dead, emigrated, or double counts. A change in this situation can be achieved only in medium-term perspective.[12] Real abstention is particularly high in the regions of inner Portugal and in the Azores, where many elderly people are living and gradually cut off from the political system. Abstention emerges also in the larger urban centers and becomes a national phenomenon. Indeed, abstention is probably the largest "party" in Portugal with four out of ten Portuguese not voting. This apathy and the discontentment of an ever growing part of the electorate with the Portuguese parties is causing a major crisis. The situation is definitely worrisome when contrasted with the high levels of participation in the first elections back in the 1970s.[13]

In sum, one can speak of an Americanization of the Portuguese party system which is more or less shaped by message polling, focus groups, and political marketing. Because Portuguese political parties were never able to rely on members, out of necessity they have to use the media and other means to reach the electorate. The party system is an electoral market as in most advanced West European countries, [14] although the political economy underlying it is still patrimonial and semiperipheral. In this sense, insufficient control of party financing and patrimonial patronage arrangements may lead

Figure 3.1
Abstention in Portugal (1975-2002)

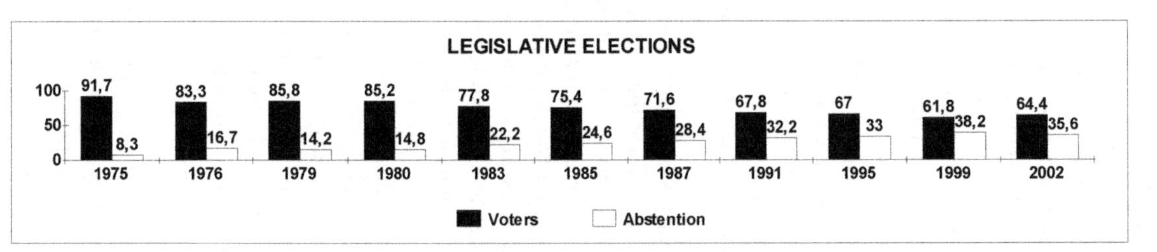

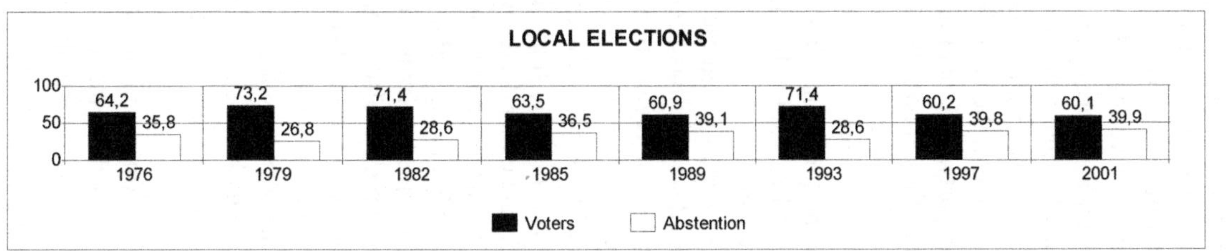

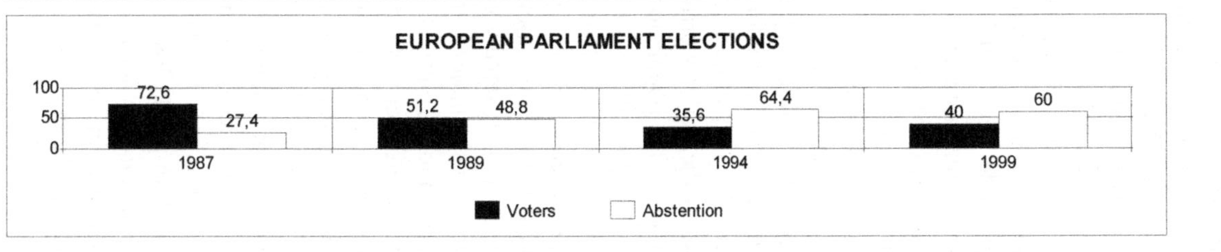

Source: Comissão National De Eleições (CNE) http://www.cne.pt.

to the autonomy of the political class from the voters. Indeed, Portuguese party politics and electoral market politics are still highly patrimonial and more about distributive politics to clienteles than electoral competition.[15] This factor has become quite dangerous within restricted budgetary conditions imposed by the European Union

The Transformation of Political Parties

The growing Americanization of the electoral process had major repercussions for the strategies and organization of Portuguese political parties. Following the characterization of Richard Katz and Peter Mair, Portuguese parties are cartel parties extremely interested in doing well in elections, which is their main source of income, due to the fact that membership fees are only raised irregularly by the parties. Loss of votes from election to election naturally means an automatic loss of income. The state funding of parties is related to the number of votes each party receives at elections. As Katz and Mair clearly state, the main aim of cartel parties is to achieve the maximum number of relevant positions in the state either in the legislative, executive, or even judicative.[16] Office-seeking by the parties clearly is a dominant strategy among the Socialists, Social-Democrats, the People's Party, and the Block of the Left. The Communist Party is the only one of the parliamentary parties with ambitions to be a mass party and follow a class strategy, in spite of the fact that the logics of the electoral market are showing a growing gap between this strategy and the reality of Portuguese politics. This became quite evident when the Communists lost one-third of the vote in the last legislative elections, declining from 10 to 7 percent.[17]

The figures on the membership of Portuguese political parties, however, are quite unreliable. They are more or less estimates. There was a stronger effort of the PSD after 1996 and now the PS to collect the exact membership figures by writing to all the members and trying to find out which members were still active, which shows that only at elections do militants of the two main parties and the People's Party become more actively engaged in the political process. In the period between elections, political party activism is quite low. The Communist Party attempts to preserve a high level of mobilization among party activists, but it has major difficulties in recruiting younger members and is subject to a geriatrization of its grassroots.

A reconstruction of the membership of the different parties can only be obtained from different sources. The Social-Democratic party has presently a membership of around 93,000, of which 76 percent are male, and 24 percent are female. Over 51 percent are between twenty and forty years of age and 15 percent are holders of administrative positions. The majority of members live in the constituency of Porto (21 percent) and the Beira Litoral. Members pay around € 6 yearly.

Figure 3.2
Evolution of Membership of Portuguese Parties (estimates)

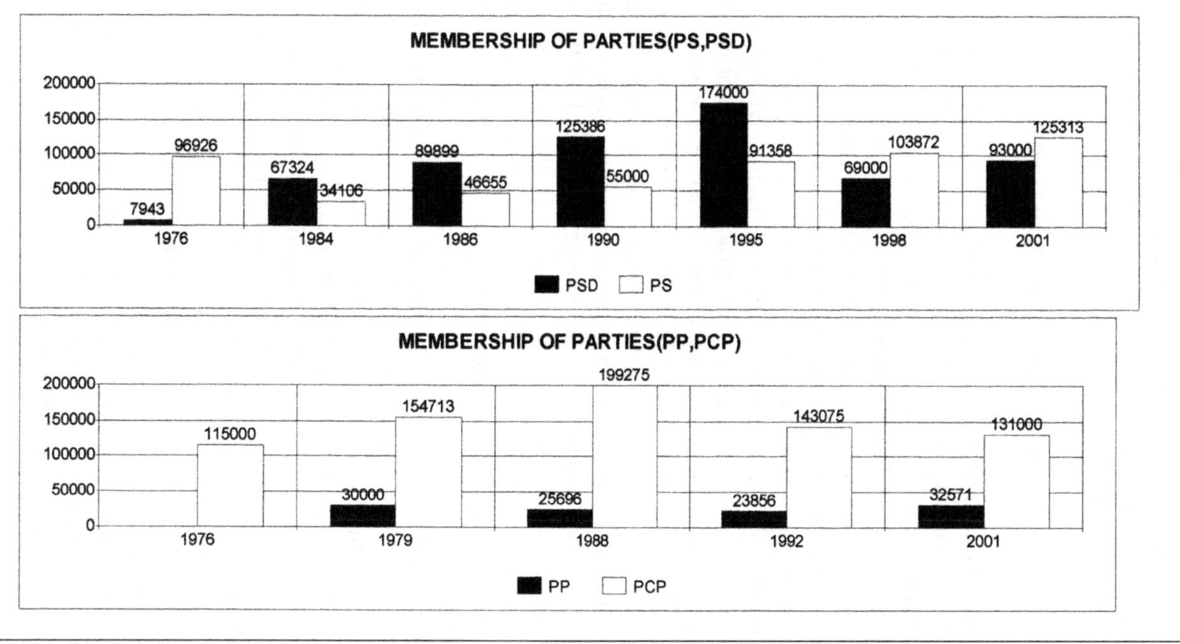

Sources: Own reconstruction based on data from *Expresso* 4.7.1992, pp.20-21R; *Expresso*,13.4.2001; Maritherese Frain, "The Right in Portugal: The PSD and the CDS/PP." In Thomas C. Bruneau (ed.), *Political Parties and Democracy in Portugal. Organizations, Elections, and Public Opinion* (Boulder, CO: Westview Press 1997), pp. 94 and 98; Fundação Mário Soares, Partido Socialista, 25 Anos de Documentos e Imagens-Fontes para a História do Partido Socialista. Fontes para a Historia do Partido Socialista. CD-Rom, 1998.

Although the Socialist Party reached 125,313 members in 2001, a major census conducted among members pointed to the probability of a halving of its membership by November 2002. The main reason was that, apart from the fact that some members may be not have been active for several years, the return to the opposition led certainly to an outflow of fellow travellers.[18] Most members are male (76 percent) and over forty years old (67 percent). Professionally, most members are technicians or employees (22 percent). They are concentrated in the constituencies of Porto (17 percent) and Lisbon (16 percent). Members pay a € 6 membership fee, which is managed by the local branch.

The People´s Party had 32,571 members in 2001. Similar to the two main parties most members are male (72 percent), but in contrast 34 percent are less than thirty years old and 21 percent are students. They are concentrated in Porto (21 percent) and Beira Litoral (18 percent). They pay membership fees, but without defined guidelines.

The Communist Party is probably the strongest in terms of membership, although there are no exact estimates. In 2001, the official figures were of 131,000 members, of which 75 percent were male, 55 percent are older than fifty years of age and 53 percent were workers. Although there are no reliable figures on the concentration of their membership, traditionally members come from the industrial belt around Lisbon and the Alentejo.[19]

There are no reliable studies available on the new party Block of the Left, and estimates on membership are difficult to make, but it is certainly below 10,000 members. It is a party that evolved from the merger between two extreme left-wing parties, the Revolutionary Socialist Party (*Partido Socialista Revolucionário*-PSR) and the People's Democratic Union (*União Democratica Popular*-UDP), which, if they competed individually, would not be able to go beyond 1 percent each. The strategy of joining forces led also to a watering down of the extremely rigid Trotzkyite and Maoist ideologies that they represent respectively. The Block of the Left has its stronghold among intellectuals of the libertarian Left in Lisbon and Porto and the smaller suburban towns of the main cities. Their leaders are normally recruited from the politicized middle classes. Francisco Louçã and several members of his family, including Antonio Louçã, originate from the middle classes; this can be said also of Miguel Portas, who is the brother of PP leader Paulo Portas.

Regardless of the fact that all parties are state funded, they all are, as previously mentioned, in extreme financial difficulties. The best example is the PSD, which, after the catastrophic elections of 1995, lost 15 percent of the vote and the corresponding state-funded share. After a decade of Cavaquismo, the new leaders Fernando Nogueira, Marcelo Rebelo de Sousa, and Manuel Durão Barroso had to foot the bill. Marcelo Rebelo de Sousa had to pay for electoral campaigns from his own pockets, while Durão Barroso was faced with empty coffers when he became leader before the June 1999 elections to the European Parliament.[20] The same can be noted for the Socialist Party, which, after Mário Soares became president of the Republic, had to deal with the loss of income after a long period of bad electoral results during Cavaquismo, while inheriting debts from previous campaigns. Such problems may also be common among the People's Party and the Communist Party, although there is less knowledge about them. The Communist Party was financially supported by Moscow up until the fall of the wall. Now the Communist Party must rely heavily on its own efforts to raise funds. These factors undoubtedly put strong pressures on a declining subculture of Portuguese politics.[21]

After thirty years, the main Portuguese parties are well established, although similar to most West European politics a low level of trust exists. According to *Eurobarometer* figures of 1999, Portugal was only slightly above the EU average of 19 percent of persons trusting political parties. Indeed, only 18 percent of the respondents tended to trust political parties in comparison to 40 percent in the Netherlands, 27 percent in Denmark and Luxembourg. The lowest scores could be found in France with only 11 percent, Italy and the UK with 16 percent, and Germany with 18 percent of respondents trusting parties.[22] On the one hand, one could interpret this as a normalization of Portuguese politics in relation to other countries with more established democracies. On the other hand, it may be interpreted as a rejection of the present performance of political parties, which is characterized by conflict, rather than cooperation and consensus.

One has to acknowledge that the image of political parties is quite negative, chiefly because of the impression of moving towards partyocracy and the establishment of a political class. This could be observed during the various party conferences of the 1990s, in which the ideology was replaced by leadership contests or factionalism in some cases. This is valid for all four main parties. It is necessary for the Block of the Left to maintain a high degree of unity to avoid a decline of its electoral strength.

The PSD is the most Portuguese of the parties founded and as such is charaterized by many Portuguese vices. The party is still influenced by a strong factionalism,[23] and personalities are extremely important in the conduct of inner party politics. Therefore, the characteristic of *personalismo*, meaning that personal likes and dislikes are stronger determinants of the politics of the individual politicians than the common ground, always creates divisions within the party.[24] From time to time a strong leader may appear and keep all the factions under control, but during phases when there is a lack of strong leaders, factionalism around personalities reappear and gives the electorate a negative image. The best periods for the PSD were under the leadership of Anibal Cavaco Silva, who won two consecutive absolute majorities and introduced major reforms in Portuguese politics between 1985 and 1995. Although factions existed, he was able to tame them. Cavaco Silva was a more clever leader than even the legendary first leader of the PSD Francisco Sá Carneiro, who died tragically in a aviation accident when travelling to support the presidential candidate Soares Carneiro in the presidential elections of 1980. Sá Carneiro was one of the founders of the party in 1974. In the authoritarian regime, he was known as a representative of the liberal wing of the National Assembly, the rubber stamp parliament. While Sá Carneiro was a charismatic leader who tried to assert himself against Mário Soares,his main drawback was his impatience as a leader. Cavaco Silva was more patient and had a strong ability to learn by doing. Cavaquismo could be characterized as the most stable phase of the new Portuguese democratic politics.[25]

After Cavaco Silva left politics, the PSD had three different leaders. Cavaco Silva tried to push forward Fernando Nogueira as his successor, but Nogueira was too weak to fight against the continuing factionalism within the party. He was replaced by Marcelo Rebelo de Sousa, a university professor, in 1996, who made major reforms within the party, particularly in downsizing the party organization. He tried to push the idea of a renewed Democratic Alliance with the People's Party, but it was opposed by some factions within the party. Although Rebelo de Sousa was supported by two-thirds of the party in the party conference of February 1999, two months later he resigned unexpectedly, leaving the party without a leader before the European elections and legislative elections of 1999. Marcelo Rebelo de Sousa was replaced by Manuel Durão Barroso, the former Minister of Foreign Affairs of Cavaquismo, in an extradionary party conference in May 1999, shortly before the European elections. Rebelo de Sousa´s withdrawal from the party leadership led to a major withdrawal of persons who did not want to work with Durão Barroso, among them Leonor Beleza, which again emphasizes the dominance of personalistic politics within the party.[26] Inside the party factionalism and personalism continued to affect Durão Barroso's leadership. After defeat both in the European elections and legislative elections, Durão Barroso was unsuccessfully challenged by the charismatic Santana Lopes in the party congress of February 2000 in Viseu.[27] However, Durão Barroso´s persistent opposition from 2000 to 2002 against the Guterres government clearly paid off. In the most recent congress on 12-14 July 2002, there was almost no challenge to his leadership. Indeed, Durão Barroso was able to reconcile with Lopes by integrating many of his followers in the main bodies of the party. The relationship between Durão Barroso and Lopes was always a strange one for outsiders. It was a combination of friendship and political rivalry. Santana Lopes is now the mayor of Lisbon and is able to play a major role within the party alongside Durão Barroso. More problematic is the relationship between Rebelo de Sousa and Durão Barroso. Rebelo de Sousa decided to stay away from the congress, because Durão Barroso withdrew the voting privileges of former leaders of the party in a quest for renewal of internal party democracy.

The number of party congresses since the resignation of Anibal Cavaco Silva is a sign that the question of leadership has so far undermined stability in the party. Between February 1995 and July 2002 there were eight congresses, more than one per year. It is expected that such struggles between main personalities of the party may begin anew, if Durão Barroso is not able to deliver in terms of national policies.

In comparison to the PSD, the Socialists were better able to control their internal factionalism. This does not mean that factionalism does not exist inside the Socialist party.[28] On the contrary, since 1974, the party has had to face several factions from the left.[29] The party became more stable in the 1980s and 1990s. After the election of Mário Soares as president of the Republic, the PS struggled with financial difficulties. Soares' successor, Vitor Constancio, was able to improve the financial situation of the party while at the same time dealing with the opposition of Soares' followers, the so-called *Soaristas*, who certainly created difficulties for his leadership. One of his main contestants was Jaime Gama who lost both in the fifth (1986) and sixth party (1988) conferences against him. Constancio was replaced in the seventh party conference in 1988 by Jorge Sampaio, who was on the left of the party. Although Sampaio introduced some renewal of the party, he was not able to win elections against Cavaco Silva. After the legislative elections of 1991, he was replaced by Antonio Guterres in the party conference of 1992. Guterres, in conjunction with Antonio Vitorino, the present Portuguese Commissioner, was able to renew the party and make it more attractive for the new middle classes. The ideological profile in particular moved more towards a Blairite Third Way position.[30] Guterres' strategy was to gain the next legislative elections in 1995, and he was able to mobilize the party and parts of civil society sympathetic to the Socialist program for this purpose.

The so-called *Estados Gerais* (General Estates) were meetings of civil society actors and members of the Socialist Party organized throughout the country, which culminated in a general meeting in Lisbon, and which mobilized over 30,000 persons. The consultation process that led to the so-called legislative contract (*contracto de legislatura*) with the electorate, included major reform projects such as decentralization of public administration via regionalization, investment in education, health, and public services, and continuing affirmative integration of Portugal in the European Union. Guterres'capacity to integrate the different factions within the party cannot be overestimated.[31] Nevertheless, throughout the seven years of government, one could observe a so-called emptying out of the innovative and creative forces within the party. The priority of staying in power consumed most of the talented forces in the successive governments, and led to a wearing out of the quality of government work from the first to the second legislature. At some stage, Guterres had to find independents to fill positions in government, such as the right-center Luis Braga da Cruz, the last minister of the economy, or to promote junior ministers to heads of ministry.

Already in 1998, it was felt that Guterrismo was undermining internal party democracy. The enlargement of the national bodies of the party, so that the quota of women would be fulfilled, strengthened Guterres' position. Although the electronic election of the party list was quite modern and trendy, it was far from democratic, because there was only the list of Guterres to choose from. Such a decline of internal democracy became even more evident in the party congress of 3-5 May 2001, which was a mere rubber stamp exercise. The grassroots sector was extremely unhappy with the last months of Guterrismo. It appeared that both inside the party as well as in government, Guterres was engaged in a mere survival exercise.[32] The difficulties of government were piling up and he was unable to turn it around. There was a strong feeling among the parliamentary group that the government was no longer communicating to the party structures. This growing discontentment of the Socialist parliamentary group and the government became evident before the local elections of 14 December 2001. Antonio Guterres' resignation after the local elections was symptomatic of his personal performance since the end of the presidency of the European Union.[33] Guterres' resignation took the Socialist leadership by surprise. Very soon, they had to find a replacement for him, because president Sampaio called for early elections for 17 March 2002. After approaching Commissioner Antonio Vitorino, who declined the offer, they decided on a prominent member of the Guterres government, Eduardo Luis Ferro Rodrigues, who is of the same generation as Guterres and quite popular among the population. He has a degree in economy, was a university teacher, and a public servant. He was able to defend well the position of the Socialist party in the last legislative elections of March 2002, keeping the losses to an absolute minimum. The PSD was only able to form a government with the PP, meaning that strategically the Socialists have a good chance to come back into government in the next legislature.

The main problem for Ferro Rodrigues is keeping the reappearing factions under control. After a decade of Guterrismo,there is strong opposition against Guterrismo from the left. Indeed, there is a danger that some parts of the left may leave the party if the ideology of the PS moves even more towards the third way Blairite ideology or even more catch-all, throwing out all aspects of a left-wing agenda.[34] A good example for this rethinking within the party is the so-called reflection group *Margem Esquerda* (Left Margin) which integrates one of the presidents of the Regional Coordinating Commission, one of the deconcentrated services of the Ministry of Planning. Left Margin clearly points to the emptying out of the party after Guterrismo. The party needed to make the necessary reform to adjust to the new realities.[35] Such major discussion took place before the 13th congress on 17-18 November 2002. In the congress, Ferro Rodrigues was confirmed as leader of the party. Most Guterristas are no longer part of the team, and there was a major shift to the left in the party. The party congress was used to prepare the campaign for the European, regional, local, presidential, and legislative elections all of which will take place between 2004 and 2006.[36]

The People's Party is also characterized by strong factionalism. After a generation of notables who were still active under the authoritarian regime, such as Adriano Moreira and Freitas do Amaral, in the 1990s a change of generations took place which contributed to a revival of the party, which at that time was under the threat of disappearing altogether. Such a threat is still far from over, but the party received a prolongation of life due to the strong commitment of two young charismatic leaders. In 1992, Manuel Monteiro became the new leader of the party and made efforts to modernize the message. Monteiro brought forward a strong nationalist message related to the threatened national sovereignty of the country due to European integration. He became one of the main voices against the Maastricht Treaty demanding along with the Communist Party a referendum. His position towards further integration was perceived negatively by the European People's Party, which expelled this traditionally christian-democratic party from their European Parliament group.

Nevertheless, Monteiro continued his hardline intransigent position and was able to win votes among the losers of European integration such as fishermen and farmers. Although Monteiro was not able to improve his stance considerably in local elections, he doubled the electoral share of the vote at the national level. This situation presented a dilemma for the People's Party. Although the party was disappearing as a local party from election to election, it still was able to resist against all odds in the national elections. After the poor results at local elections in December 1997, Monteiro was replaced by Paulo Portas in the March 1998 party conference, which contributed to the moderation of the party. Paulo Portas is a clever, charismatic politician in the Portuguese context. He always scores highest in popularity of all the leaders, a fact that naturally contributes to the overall image of the party. Since his emergence as party leader in the party congress of March 1998, the PP became one of the main parties of government, meaning that it supported most of the policies related to furthering European integration in the name of national interest, in spite of a grassroots movement that is dominated by euroskeptic militants. This became quite evident during discussion over the referendum on the euro. Portas took the position that although he and a large part of his party were against Economic Monetary Union, he would support participation because it was in the national interest. This was a strange declaration, but typical of the power politics and the compromising attitude of the PP leader.[37] Indeed, during the leadership of Marcelo Rebelo de Sousa, it was the intention of the PSD to pursue a coalition government under the name of Democratic Alternative (*Alternativa Democrática*) which was quite similar to the arrangement in which the two parties were engaged between 1979 and 1983 under the umbrella of Democratic Alliance (*Aliança Democrática*-AD). In the PSD February 1999 congress, Rebelo de Sousa gained the support of two-thirds of the participants for it, but in the end he resigned and the Democratic Alternative project was not followed up.

Nevertheless, after the elections of March 2002 with the PSD short of an absolute majority, it had to coalesce with the PP to achieve an hegemony over the left. Portas, a former journalist and university teacher, is presently the vice prime minister in a coalition with the Social-Democratic party and more popular than Durão Barroso. Although Manuel Monteiro continues to challenge Paulo Portas in the party congresses, the latter had no difficulty in being reelected as leader. One of the major decisions made in the congress held on 18-20 January 2002 in terms of organization is that the party will now have a secretary-general instead of a president.[38] In sum, Paulo Portas' leadership greatly benefited the stability of the party and strengthened the PP among the electorate.

The Communists remain the only parliamentary party that adheres to a traditional approach to politics. They characterize themselves as a mass party, which is defined by a Marxist-Leninist identity. The party has not changed much since its foundation. The secretary-general Carlos Carvalhas is quite orthodox in his views. He clearly follows closely the advice of the *eminence grise* Alvaro Cunhal, who is still a power in the background. Although in the 1999 European elections the party was able to achieve 10.32 percent of the vote, overall support for the party has been declining since the 1990s. Recent local and legislative elections in December 2001 and March 2002, respectively, led to a major outflow of Communist voters to other parties, particularly to the Socialists, which caused them to receive the lowest score of 6.92 percent in the 2002 legislative elections and the loss of over 100,000 voters.[39] Obviously, there is growing discontentment within the party, particularly in relation to the lack of internal democracy inside the party. Between 1987 and 1991, several members were expelled, and this is now threatening the most prominent older members of the party, who fought against the authoritarian regime. Such was the case in regard to veterans of the party, Carlos Brito, Edgar Correia, and Carlos Luis Figueira. It has led to solidarity events of other Communists with these veterans awaiting disciplinary processes, [40] all of which is creating a negative image of the main anti-fascist party, a party of resistance among the electorate. One of the main requests of this new group of dissidents was to organize a party congress before the legislative elections of 2002, so that changes to the overall electoral campaign could be made. In the end the leadership rejected the organization of a party conference.[41] The party conference in December 2000 led to the victory of the orthodox leadership over the list advocating a renewal of the party, which only confirmed the highly democratic centralist stand of the orthodox leadership under the chairmanship of Carlos Carvalhas.[42]

In the past decade, the Communist Party has expelled many talented people from the party, the most prominent of which include Zita Seabra, José Barros Moura, Pina Moura, José Luis Judas, José Magalhães, and Miguel Portas. Some of these became prominent Socialist members.[43] Pina Moura became the Minister of Economy during the first Guterres government. Miguel Portas is now one of the leaders of the Block of Left, which may attract younger voters in the left-wing spectrum. There is a growing feeling among a vast number of prominent leaders of the party, that a tendency towards radicalization and neo-Stalinist practices exists among the present leadership toward any internal criticism. Reform is vital if the party wants to survive as the fourth largest party. Indeed, the Block of the Left is a major threat to the Communist Party, because it is able to gain young votes in the urban centers. The slight decline in the abstention rate, which in the end penalized their stagnant or decreasing number of voters, had a major effect on the Communists in the last election.

The Block of the Left is still very much an electoral platform rather than a party. Founded in 1999 shortly before the European elections, it achieved 1.79 percent. In the legislative elections it was able to improve the result to 2.46 percent and two seats in the Assembly of the Republic. This newcomer was also successful in improving the results in the 2002 legislative elections to 2.8 percent and increasing the numbers of voters by over 20,000. The Block of the Left is a joint electoral platform of the Trotzkyite Revolutionary Socialist Party, dominated by Francisco Louçã, a well-known intellectual from Lisbon, and the Maoist Democratic People's Union. Individually, each of these two parties had difficulties in getting a representative elected, but together they are able to capitalize on joint forces. As a party they can afford to reflect on the new problems of society in general. Their agenda is quite postmodernist and related to the quality of life. Their electoral potential is concentrated in the larger cities of Lisbon, Porto, and Setubal. In recent elections, the party was able to take some voters from the Socialists and the Communists. The Block of the Left continues to be a loose alliance without the heavy bureaucratic structures of the other parties. It also represents the radical left, which was so prominent during the Revolution and in the post-revolutionary process.

In sum, political parties are under pressure to respond to the electoral market. All parties, apart from the Communist Party, have made their party structures more compatible with the electoral market. Some major changes have to be undertaken in the Communist Party if they are to survive as one of the four main parties. The electorate is stable, but more volatile than ever. In this respect, national politics is still the main arena, while European politics are read through national partisan lenses.[44]

The Dynamics of Multilevel Electoral Arenas

Since the emergence of Cavaquismo, Portuguese elections have become more electoral market oriented, a characteristic that becomes more relevant from election to election. Manuel Castells calls this process, which is common to most European democracies, the Americanization of politics. He emphasizes particularly the ascendancy of the media system as the chief means of bridging the gap between party and potential electorate. Indeed, political marketing "with constant opinion polling, feedback systems between polling and politicking, media spinning, computerized direct mailing and phone banks, and real time adjustments of candidates and issues to the format that can win" is pushing boundaries towards a constructed, controlled political market behavior.[45] Party congresses and party conventions are staged accordingly, so that they become media spectacles. Such careful choreography has transformed the relationship into a constructed one, which clearly is reinforced by the media as becoming more and more what has been referred as *infotainment* (combining the words information+entertainment). Although studies on this aspect of the marketization of Portuguese politics are rare, a recent analysis of several party congresses and party conventions clearly shows the patterns of established relationships between the media and the political marketing personnel of the individual parties. There is a tendency to simplify the complex political reality, so that news can be transmitted easily to the viewers. Indeed, the overall practice of spin-doctoring is a phenomenon of cartel parties, which need the media in general, but television in particular, to transmit their messages due to the growing loss in numbers that has plagued their membership in the 1990s.[46] This process of mediatization is also reinforced by constant opinion polling regarding the different chances of the political parties. The emergence of private channels on television in the early ninetíes has led to a stronger competition in this field. Indeed, four channels RTP1, RTP2, SIC, and TVI are eager to present political sensations. In recent times, Portuguese television news bulletins have closely copied the American CNN style, which means that there is a permanent flow of written information across the screen, making it difficult to concentrate on the real news.

Legislative elections are still at the center of Portuguese politics and both local as well as European elections tend to be used as barometers in relation to it. In the 1990s, legislative elections produced more or less stable electoral results, although the 1995 and 1999 elections failed to produce absolute majorities for the Socialist Party. This became the main factor in the difficulties of the Socialist Party to follow a program of major reforms. In the end, a poor result in the local elections of 14 December 2001 led to the resignation of prime minister Antonio Guterres—an unprecedented event in the history of the young Portuguese democracy. Indeed, Cavaco Silva had to face a nega-

Table 3.1
Election Results in Portugal (1987-2002)

Legislative Elections

	1987		1991		1995		1999		2002	
	%	Seats	%	Seats	%	Seats	%	Seats	%	Seats
PS	22.24	60	29.3	72	43.76	112	44	115	37.8	96
PPD/PSD	50.22	148	50.4	135	34.17	88	32.3	81	40.2	105
CDS-PP	4.44	4	4.4	5	9.08	15	8.4	15	8.8	14
CDU(PCP/ PEV)	12.14	31	8.8	17	8.65	15	9	17	6,9	12
PRD	4.91	7								
PSN			1.7	1	0.21					
BE							2.5	2	2.8	3
Other	6.07		5.4		4.13		3.8		3.5	-
		250		**230**		**230**		**230**		**230**

Source: Comissão Nacional de Eleições, http://www.cne.pt

Local Elections

	1989		1993		1997		2001	
	%	Seats	%	Seats	%	Seats	%	Seats
PS	32.3	11 201	36.1	12 312	38.1	13 697	26.57	12 142
PPD/PSD	31.4	13 261	33.7	13 679	32.9	12 947	33.86	13181
CDS-PP	9.1	3 434	8.4	2 719	5.64	1 843	3.62	968
CDU(PCP/ PEV)	12.8	2 929	12.8	2 747	11.99	2 730	11.20	2469
BE							1.10	46
PS-PCP-PEV					3.19	409	2.54	310
PSD-PP					3.88	561	8.17	2106
Citizens' Groups					2.81	1584	4.42	2392

Source: Comissão Nacional de Eleições, http://www.cne.pt

European Elections

	1987		1989		1994		1999	
PS	26.9	8	28.52	8	34.8	10	43.05	12
PSD	37.4	9	32.70	9	34.4	9	31.10	8
CDU	11.5	3	14.40	4	12.5	3	10.32	2
CDS/PP	15.4	4	14.13	3	11.2	3	8.17	2
B.E.			-	-	-	-	1.79	-

Source: MAI, 1987, 1989, 1994, htt://www.europeias.dgsi.pt

Table 3.1 (cont.)

Autonomous Regions Elections

	AZORES				MADEIRA			
Year	1996		2000		1996		2000	
	%	Seats	%	Seats	%	Seats	%	Seats
PSD	42.3	20	32.5	18	56.9	41	55.9	41
PS	44.3	19	49.2	30	24.8	13	21	13
CDS/PP	6.4	2	9.6	2	7.3	2	9.7	3
PCP/PEV	4.2	1	4.9	2	4	2	4.6	2
UDP	1.01				4	1	4.8	2
PSN					0.6	-	1.7	-
B.E.			1.37	-				

Source: Comissão Nacional de Eleições, http://www.cne.pt

tive electoral result in the local elections of 1989, but two years later he managed to win a second absolute majority in the legislative elections.

Although local elections normally follow events in local politics, they also have a national dimension that may reappear in times of crises, such as was the situation in 2001 due to government inertia. What the elections of 1995, 1999, and 2002 have shown is that there is in the center a highly volatile electorate, coming predominantly from the new middle classes, which tends to swing between the two parties according to the circumstances.[47] The first appearance of this electorate was in the elections of October 1985, when the new Democratic Renewal Party (*Partido Renovador Democratico*-PRD) was able to catch 17.9 percent of the vote, mostly from the Socialist Party. In the following legislative elections of July 1987, this electorate went straight to the PSD, while the PRD was reduced to about 4 percent. Cavaco Silva was able to transmit the message that he was the only representative of political and economic stability against a divided and discredited opposition.

Although national politics is the dominant arena, for the first time the electorate has also been asked to vote at European elections on the same date. This shows that the European dimension is attached to the decision-making of the electorate in legislative elections.[48] This electorate of the new middle classes constitutes about 20 to 30 percent of the electorate. It may vote for one of the main two parties or abstain. The same happened in the reverse direction from the PSD to the PS. The resignation of Cavaco Silva and a credible platform presented by Guterres led to a reverse process of this mobile electorate. While in 1999, the Socialist Party was able to keep most of these volatile voters on its side, by 2002, after the resignation of the highly popular Antonio Guterres and his replacement by Eduardo Ferro Rodrigues, it lost some of the voters to the PSD under the less popular Manuel Durão Barroso; however, it was not a seismic change to the Social-Democrats. Both parties share this electorate, but circumstances matter.[49] This means that Manuel Durão Barroso is not able to convince the electorate of his major reforms. Indeed, the first three months of Durão Barroso's government led to a negative perception of the government in the opinion polls.[50]

This is the reason why the PS moved much closer to the center during the Guterres period. Guterres clearly wanted to develop the Socialist Party towards a catch-all moderate position and thus challenge the potential moderate electorate of the PSD. The difficulty Manuel Durão Barroso had in crossing the 40 percent barrier during the Guterres government shows that it is not so much the message that is affecting the possibilities of the PSD, but the messenger.

European elections have so far reflected the dominance of the two main parties and the decline of the two smaller parties. In the 1990s, the PS was able to improve considerably, achieving similar results as at legislative elections. In fact, the June 1999 legislative elections produced exactly the same results as the October 1999 legislative elections. This illustrates the use of the European dimension in the function of national politics. Issues of national importance are discussed and used at European elections. The 1999 European elections were regarded as the first test for Guterres' government after losing the referenda of 1998. Guterres was able to win over Mário Soares to lead the

Table 3.2
Concentration of the Vote (1975-2002)

Legislative Elections

	1976	1983	1985	1987	1991	1995	1999	2002
PS+PSD	51.7	63.1	50.7	72.5	79.7	78	76	78
PCP+PP	30.4	31.3	25.5	16.5	13.2	18.5	17	15.7
Other	17.9	5.6	23.8	11	7.1	3.5	7	6.3

Local Elections

	1976	1985	1989	1993	1997	2001
PS+PSD	57.9	61.4	62.7	69.8	70.88	62.34
PCP+PP	34.5	29.1	21.9	21.2	17.67	19.6
Other	7.6	9.2	15.4	11.45	11.45	18.1

European Elections

	1987	1989	1994	1999
PS+PSD	64.3	61.2	69.2	74.2
PCP+PP	26.9	28.5	23.7	18.4
Other	8.8	10.3	7.1	7.36

Source: Comissão Nacional de Eleições, http://www.cne.pt

European list. This led to a good result for the Socialist Party against the other parties. In fact, the leader of the PSD list, José Pacheco Pereira, expressed his feelings by saying that Mário Soares as a candidate was like Amália Rodrigues competing in the song contest, meaning that this was a unequal fight. In the end, the 1999 elections were instrumentalized as a test for the more important legislative elections.[51] Mário Soares also played an important role in the European elections of June 1994 as president of the Republic. He tended to intervene in the European debate and make his views heard. He presented federalist views in relation to the future of the European Union.[52]

One has to acknowledge that the last two European elections took place in a period where the PSD was internally quite divided and in a crisis. In 1994, there was already a feeling that the political cycle of Cavaco Silva was coming to an end, while in 1999 Durão Barroso was elected as leader at the last minute, which naturally prevented the PSD from presenting a coherent European policy. Both the Communists and People's Party were euroskeptic in relation to further integration. They lost votes and Members of the European Parliament in both elections, which clearly shows a decline of the two parties in the second-order elections, be they local or European.

One European aspect that was highly divisive during the 1999 campaign in relation to the Kosovo question was the bombardment of Serbia . Although Guterres supported NATO and was seconded by Paulo Portas, inside the PS, PSD, and the PCP, there was strong opposition against such a drastic measure. João Soares, then mayor of Lisbon, went to Belgrade to show solidarity with the Serbian people. José Pacheco Pereira and Ilda Figueiredo, leaders of the list to the European Parliament, were also against this NATO action.[53]

The elections in the autonomous regions in the Azores and in Madeira seem to confirm the fact that personalism is an important feature of Portuguese politics. In the Azores, after the stepping down of Mota Amaral as president, the Socialist party was able to gain control of the archipelago. In contrast, Madeira continues to be dominated by the charismatic populist Alberto João Jardim of the PSD. In some way, the regional autonomous governments follow a completely different logic from that of the continent. Their enhanced status within Portuguese politics makes them literally *islands of political microclimates* that refer only partly to what happens in Lisbon.

Although euroskepticism is quite moderate in Portugal, one has to realize that there is some dissatisfaction with the policies of the main parties on the fringes of the party system. Both the Communists and the People's Party appear to capitalize on it. Although the main cleavages of the Portuguese political system are still territorial, there is a growing move towards a value-oriented electorate, which looks more at aspects related to performance of the economy, quality of life, and delivery of public goods. This naturally shows the growing Americanization of the Portuguese electoral market, a process similar to that happening in other European democracies. It implies a growing integration of the population into consumerist patterns of behavior and into the individualization of society. Indeed, recent studies show that the vote related to economic performance of governments or expected economic benefits plays a role in shaping the electoral choice. Thus, the general good-feel factor may confirm a successful party's continuing to stay in power.[54]

All of these factors led to major transformations of the electoral geography in Portugal. Until 1985, one could speak of an electoral geography that could be interpreted by a left-right cleavage. Since 1987, the intensity of consumer market construction has led to a decline of classistic identities and a move towards more mobile, new middle classes, which still have some elements of class identity, but clearly are being replaced by new value-oriented electorates. One can recognize at least two main cleavages. The first is naturally the north-south territorial cleavage, which is essentially informed by a left-right rationale. This is an old cleavage of Portuguese politics that goes back to the establishment of the first Republic. Indeed, the conservative north tended to support the monarchy against the republic. During the Portuguese Revolution, this north-south divide could have led to a civil war during the hot summer of 1975. Amazingly, the more recent presidential elections of January 1996 and January 2001 showed how resilient this cleavage is in terms of electoral geography. Presidential elections led to a bipolarization of the electorate. The north was normally dominated by the candidates of the right such as Anibal Cavaco Silva and Ferreira do Amaral, while the south tended to vote for the left-wing candidate, in this case Jorge Sampaio. This north-south cleavage explains also why the strongholds of the PSD and the PP are in the north and in the islands of Madeira and the Azores. The still-existing, strongly fragmented possession of small estates by small farmers leads to support of the right-center parties, which may be added to a secular-religious cleavage, which also became quite evident during the Revolution when farmers were mobilized by the Church to put Communist branches in northern Portugal on fire. The growing marketization and secularization of Portuguese society is eroding the still religiously motivated enclaves of northern Portugal, which are strongly supportive of the PP because of its christian-democratic origins. This enclave is fairly resilient between Viseu and Guarda in the Beira Interior. Slowly, particularly in local elections, the PSD or the PS are penetrating these enclaves of the PP.

The PSD is especially strong in the urban centers and medium-sized towns. It clearly represents a modernist discourse and is certainly less engaged in a religious discourse. The PSD is now the strongest party in the north. It is only in the east of Beira Baixa and the major cities of Oporto and Coimbra that the PS is stronger.

PSD penetration abilities in the south is somewhat limited. This area, so far, has been the stronghold of the left. In particular, the Communist Party was able to resist until the early 1990s as the main party in Alentejo. It was supported by the land laborers, but the situation became less so when the Socialists began to penetrate these enclaves of the Communist Party. Now the Socialists are the main party of Alentejo,but enclaves of party resistance against absolute control still exist in the districts of Beja and Portalegre. The Algarve is also predominantly Socialist, although the center and northeast are PSD strongholds.

This cleavage is clearly the most important one in terms of bipolarization between left and right. The two main parties share part of the moderate electorate, which may, according to circumstances, vote for one party or the other.

Portugal's second territorial cleavage between the coast and the inner section of the country can be characterized as a urban-rural cleavage. There is growing desertification of the inner regions of Portugal (Trás-Os-Montes, Beira Alta, Beira Baixa, Beira Interior, East Alentejo). Emigration from the rural parts of inner Portugal to the larger cities of the coast or abroad has been pronounced since the end of the second world war, which shows that there is a geriatrization process going on in these regions. Despite EU structural funds to reverse this situation, the bipolarization became even sharper. In this cleavage, one can see that the PSD and the PP are still the main parties dominating the regions of inner Portugal. Nevertheless, the PS was able in the elections of 1995 and 1999 to achieve a more balanced electorate between their strongholds in the urban centers of the coast and new electorates in inner Portugal. In the 2002 elections, the PSD was able to make substantial gains in the inner regions, while the enclaves of the PP are showing penetration by the PSD. In Alentejo, the Communists are quite strong in the regions that are most remote to the capital.

The Block of Left emerged as a new phenomenon in this cleavage. Although almost nonexistent in inner Portugal, it is strong in the suburban regions of the southern coast.

The traditional Lipset-Rokkan cleavages Church vs. State and Workers vs. Employers have lost importance over time. The cleavage Church vs. State is still resisting in the northern inner regions of Portugal, but eroding from election to election, while the Workers vs. Employers still matters in terms of the strength of the Communist Party in the suburban towns of Lisbon and Porto. It is expected that the growing tertiarization will lead to an erosion of this cleavage as well. In this sense, Portugal as a latecomer to the club of West European democracies, is experiencing a much earlier party system change.[55]

This party system change is not only a social realignment due to tertiarization, individualization, and adjustment to electoral market hehavior, but also, intrinsically, a response to the European integration and the modernization agenda of the main parties. Some parties, such as the Communist and the People's Party, represent constituencies that are being threatened by further integration, while the two main parties have gained constituencies that have profited from European integration. Although not visible as in the Danish case in which European elections form a distinct party system configuration to normal legislative elections, elements of new cleavages emerging related to further European integration can be found, which are integrated in the overall national discourse. This means that the European issues are presented in a national package by the different parties.

Using the heuristic grid developed by Stefano Bartolini, based on two dimensions *European Integration* vs. *National Independence* and *Exit Control* vs. *Exit Options*, we are able to allocate the five parties of the political system.[56] Indeed, the best integrated parties are the Socialists and the People's Party while PSD and PCP are between quadrants. Even the most nationalist of parliamentary parties, the PP, can act more moderately and pro-integrationist when it is asked to take into account the national interest and the wish of the vast majority that votes for the two main parties. The Communists have changed

Figure 3.3
Location of Portuguese Main Parties within the European Integration Cleavage

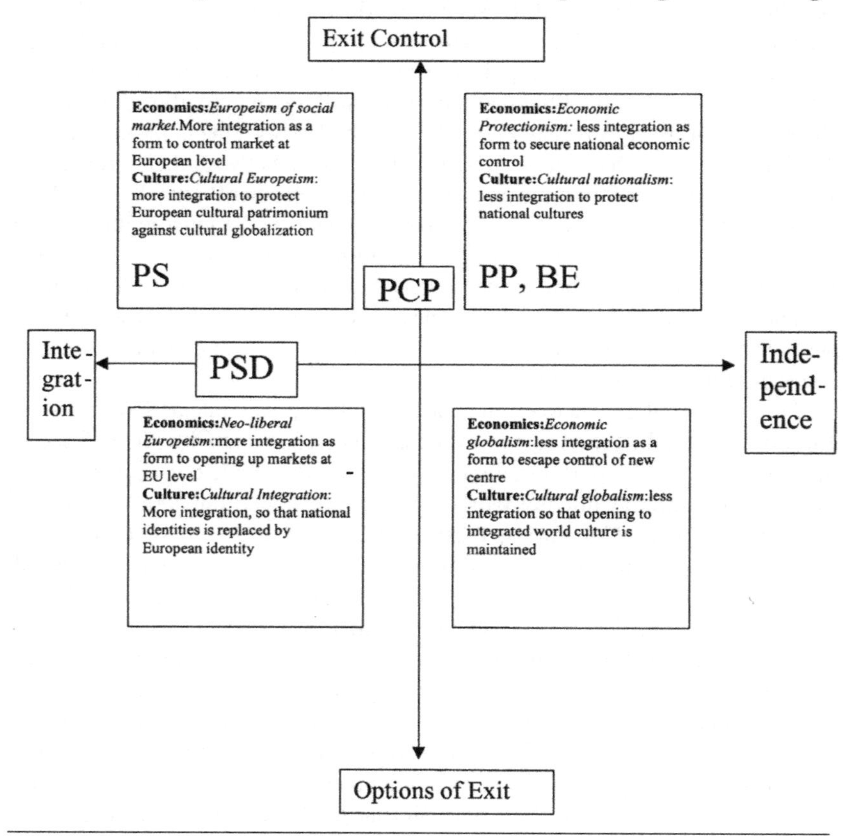

Source: Adapted by the author for the Portuguese case from Stefano Bartolini, "A integração europeia provocará uma reestruturação dos sistemas de clivagens nacionais?" *Sociologia. Problemas e Práticas*, 37, 2001: 104.

their position considerably to one towards social Europe, nevertheless still advocating a strong nationalist cultural stand. This means that there is an internalization of the European integration cleavage among parties going on, but invisibly as part of the national discourse of modernization and distribution of goods from election to election (see fig. 3.3).

In sum, the Portuguese political system is characterized by a double hegemony of the two main parties, which acts in terms of bipolarization. The smaller parties are in a situation of resistance and may in a particular election captivate some of the protest vote. The new phenomenon of the Block of the Left is naturally related to the aggregation of forces between the extreme left-wing Trotzkyite PSR and the Maoist UDP. Although it achieves more than the sum of the single electoral strengths of these two parties, and therefore is more than the sum of the forces, it may have difficulties in enlarging the electorate, if it does not overcome the highly antiquated discourse of Maoism and Trotzkyism.

Conclusions

The Portuguese party system has experienced considerable transformation since 1987. Indeed, the bipolarization of the party system has led to a decline of ideology and the former cleavages Workers vs. Employers and Church vs. State. The main cleavage is between north and south which corresponds to a cleavage between right and left. The individualization of society, the loosening of the former class system towards a consumer market society has also transformed voters into consumers of politics as a package. This factor led to an articulation of the predominantly cartel parties of the Portuguese party system towards the electoral market, which means that the difference between the two main parties disappeared almost completely. Portuguese politics is becoming Americanized, similar to what is happening in Spain, Italy, Greece, and the UK, while the European dimension is being fully integrated and filtered through the national partisan lenses.

Notes

1. Peter Mair, "The Limited Impact of Europe on National Party System," in Klaus H. Goetz, Simon Hix (eds.), "Europeanised Politics? European Integration and National Political Systems," Special Issue of *West European Politics* 23, 4, October 2000: 27-51.
2. Ibid., 30.
3. Adriano Moreira, "O Regime: O presidencialismo do primeiro ministro." in Mário Baptista Coelho (org.), *Portugal. O Sistema Politico e Constitucional 1974-1987* (Lisbon: ICS, 1989), 31-37.
4. Herbert Kitschelt, "European Party Systems: Continuity and Change," in Martin Rhodes, Paul Heywood, and Vincent Wright (eds.), *Developments in West Euro-*

pean Politics (Basingstroke: Macmillan, 1997), 136-147; Herbert Kitschelt, "A Silent Revolution in Europe?" in Jack Hayward, Ed Page (eds.), *Governing the New Europe* (Oxford: Oxford University Press, 1995), 123-165.

5. Paul Pennings and Jan Erik Lane, "Introduction" (1-19) and Svante Ersson and Jan Erik Lane, "Electoral Instability and Party System Change in Western Europe" (23-39), both in Paul Pennings and Jan-Erik Lane (eds.), *Comparing Party System Change* (London: Routledge, 1998).
6. Klaus von Beyme, "Party Leadership and Change in Party Systems:Towards a Postmodern Party State?" *Government and Opposition* 31, 2, 1996: 135-159, particularly 140.
7. Maritheresa Frain, *PPD/PSD e a consolidação do regime democrático* (Lisbon: editorial noticias, 1998), 233.
8. Vitor Constancio, *Relatório do Secretário Geral, VII Congresso do Partido Socialista,1988* (Lisbon: Partido Socialista, 1988).
9. The new law of party financing and electoral campaigns (Law 72/93) was issued on 30 November 1993. Presentation of reports by the individual parliamentary and some extraparliamentary parties started in 1994. Meanwhile the following decisions were taken by the Constitutional Court Acordão no. 979/96 for the year of 1994; Acordão no. 531/97 for the year 1995; Acordão no. 682/98 for the year 1996; Acordão no. 453/99 for the year 1997; Acordão no.578/00 for the year 1998; Acordão no. 371/01 for the year 1999; Acordão no. 357/02; *Expresso*, 17 August 2002. See also Ingrid van Biezen, "Party Financing in New Democracies: Spain and Portugal," in *Party Politics* 6, 3, 2001: 329-342.
10. For a more detailed study, see Luis de Sousa, "2001: Political Parties and Corruption in Portugal," *West European Politics* 24, 1, January 2001: 157-180, and Ingrid van Biezen, "Sobre o equilibrio interno do poder: As organizções partidárias nas novas democracias," *Análise Social* 33, 1998: 685-708.
11. Aguiar, Joaquim, "Portugal: The Hidden Fluidity in a Ultra-Stable Party System," in Walter C. Opello and Eduardo de Sousa Ferreira (eds.), *Conflict and Change in Modern Portugal 1974-1984* (Lisbon: Teorema, 1985), 101-126.
12. Francisco Soares, Teresa Evaristo, "Recenseamento eleitoral:disfuncionamentos e novas perspectives," *Análise Social*, XXXV, 154-155, 2000: 25-43; particularly 35-42.
13. After decades of neglect, several pioneering studies on abstentionism in Portugal were or are being undertaken in the framework of a national project financed by several ministries, the Assembly of the Republic, and the Tinker Foundation on the electoral behavior of the Portuguese since 1996. See Pedro Magalhães, "Desigualdade, desinteresse e desconfiança: A abstenção nas eleições legislativas de 1999," *Análise Social*, XXXV, 157, 2001: 1079-1093; André Freire, "Participação e abstenção nas eleicões legislativas portuguesas, 1975-1995," *Análise Social* XXXV, 154-155, 2000: 115-145; André Freire, Pedro Magalhães, *A abstenção eleitoral em Portugal* (Lisbon: ICS, 2002).
14. See Herbert Kitschelt, *The Transformation of European Social Democracy* (Cambridge: Cambridge University Press, 1994); Stefano Bartolini, Peter Mair, *Identity,Competition and Electoral Availability:The Stabilization of European Electorates 1885-1985* (Cambridge: Cambridge University Press, 1990), 295-98.
15. On neopatrimonialism in the Portuguese case, see Joaquim Aguiar, "Partidos, estruturas patrimonialistas e poder funcional: a crise de legitimidade," *Análise Social* XXI, 87-88-89,1985: 759-763; Boaventura de Sousa Santos, *O Estado e a Sociedade em Portugal (1974-1988)* (Porto: Edições Afrontamento, 1990); Luis de Sousa, "Political Parties and Corruption in Portugal," *West European Politics*

24, 1, January 2001: 157-140; José M. Magone, "Portugal: Das patrimoniale Erbe und die Entstehung einer demokratischen politischen Klasse," in Jens Borchert unter Mitarbeit von Jürgen Zeiß (eds.), *Politik als Beruf. Die politische Klasse in westlichen Demokratien* (Opladen: Leske+Budrich, 1999): 396-414.

16. Richard Katz, Peter Mair, "Changing Models of Party Organisation and Party Democracy: The Emergence of the Cartel Party," *Party Politics* 1995: 5-28.
17. On the structures of the Portuguese party organizations in comparative European perspective using Katz and Mair findings, see Ingrid van Biezen, "Sobre o equilibrio interno do poder:as organizacoes partidárias nas novas democracies," *Análise Social* XXXVIII, 148, 4, 1998: 685-708.
18. *Publico*, 13 July 2002, p.11; according to first figures of the ongoing census Lisbon and Oporto have the highest number of members (one-third).
19. *Expresso*, 13 April 2001.
20. *Expresso*, 22 May 1999.
21. Carlos Cunha, "The Portuguese Communist Party," in Thomas C. Bruneau (ed.), *Political Parties and Democracy in Portugal* (Boulder, CO: Westview Press, 1997), 23-54, particularly 27.
22. *Eurobarometer* 51, Spring 1999: B.3-B.4.
23. For the development until the end of the 1990s, see the unparalleled, unpublished study by Maria José Stock, "Elites, Facções e Conflito Interpartidário: O PPD/PSD e o processo político portugues de 1974 a 1985," Ph.D. diss., University of Évora, 1989. Recently Marcelo Rebelo de Sousa wrote his personal account of the genesis of the PSD; see Marcelo Rebelo de Sousa, *A Revolução e o Nascimento do PPD*, 2 volumes (Lisbon: Bertrand Editora, 2000). Although this account is quite a personal account, it includes a good deal of information, including photographs and documents on the PSD.
24. This concept is taken from Douglas Wheeler, *Republican Portugal. A Political History 1910-1926* (Madison: University of Wisconsin Press, 1978).
25. Maritheresa Frain, *PPD/PSD e a consolidação do regime democrático* (Lisbon: editorial noticias, 1998), 92-127.
26. José M. Magone, "Portugal," European Political Data Yearbook 2000, Special Issue of *European Journal for Political Research* 38, 3-4: 499-510; particularly 504.
27. *Expresso*, 12 July 2002 ,p.8.
28. The history of the Portuguese Socialist Party is now being systematically studied by the Fundação Mário Soares. It has already published a cd-rom with all major documents of the party since 1945; see "Partido Socialista, Fundação Mário Soares," *Fontes Para a História do PS, Fontes para a História do PS 1, 25 Anos em Documentos e Imagens-Fontes Para a História do Partido Socialista* (Lisbon, 1998); a good study of the international connections of the PS during and after the revolutionary process is Juliet Antunes Sablovsky, *PS e a transição para a democracia* (Lisbon: editorial noticias, 2000); the best critical insider well-documented study is Rui Mateus, *Contos Proibidos. Memórias para um PS Desconhecido* (Lisbon: Dom Quixote, 1996). This latter study clearly gives us a very personal account of what happens inside the patrimonial party dominated by leader Mário Soares. Mateus' account is not only well documented, it gives a dramatic turn at the end, when he becomes himself victim to the intrigues within the party. Moreover, the study is certainly useful because Mateus's autobiographical account is moderated by his Swedish background. Another critical study, which preceded Sablovsky´s work is Rainer Eisfeld, *Sozialistischer Pluralismus in Westeuropa.Ansätze und Scheitern am Beispiel Portugal* (Köln: Wissenschaft und Politik, 1984).

29. See José M. Magone, "The Portuguese Socialist Party," in Robert Ladrech, Philippe Marliér (eds.), *Social Democratic Parties in the European Union* (Basingstroke: Macmillan, 1999), 116-175; 166-169.
30. On the development towards Guterrismo, see Marina Costa Lobo, Pedro C. Magalhães, "From 'Third Wave' to 'Third Way': Europe and the Portuguese Socialists," *Journal of Southern Europe and the Balkans*, 3, 1, 2001: 25-35; see also José M. Magone, "The Portuguese Socialist Party," in Robert Ladrech, Philippe Marliére (eds.), *Socialdemocratic Parties in the European Union. History, Organization, Policies* (Basingstoke: Macmillan, 1999), 166-175.
31. Maria José Stock and José M. Magone, "Portugal," European Political Data Yearbook 1996 Special Issue of *European Journal for Political Research* 30, 3-4, December 1996: 445-452; particularly 450-52.
32. *Expresso*, 12 May 2001.
33. *Publico,* 17 December 2001; *Publico*, 18 December 2001. According to a minister of the last Guterres government, he did not even inform the cabinet beforehand; they also were taken by surprise.
34. *Publico*, 14 July 2002, p.14.
35. *Visão*, 11 July 2002, pp.15-17.
36. *Expresso*, 23 November 2002; *Expresso*, 30 November 2002.
37. Magone, "Portugal," EPDY 2000, op.cit. 503-504.
38. *Expresso*, 26 January 2002.
39. *Expresso*, 23 March 2002.
40. *Expresso*, 6 July 2002, pp. 6-7.
41. *Expresso*, 26 January 2002; *Expresso*, 19 January 2002; *Expresso*, 6 July 2002, p.7.
42. Michael Baum, André Freire, "Clivagens, economia e voto em Portugal 1999: Uma análise das eleições parlamentares com dados agregados," *Sociologia-Problemas e Práticas*, 37, November 2001: 15-140; particularly 122-123.
43. *Expresso*, 6 July 2002, p. 9.
44. Alistair Cole, "National and Partisan Contexts of Europeanisation: The Case of French Socialists," *Journal of Common Market Studies* 39, 1, March 2001: 15-36; particularly 26-31.
45. Manuel Castells, *The Power of Identity. Volume II of Information Age, Economy, Society and Culture* (London: Blackwell, 1997), 317-318.
46. Rogério Santos, Isabel Ventura e Vanda Calado, "Congressos e convenções partidárias-como se relacionam os políticos e os jornalistas de televisão," *Observatório*, 5, May 2002: 9-25; this study contrasts heavily with the preoccupation of party conferences in the early 1980s which was very much about membership. See the study by Maria José Stock,*Os Partidos do Poder. Dez Anos depois do 25 de Abril* (Évora: Universidade de Évora, 1986).
47. Isabel André and Jorge Gaspar, "Geografia eleitoral 1974 e 1987," Mário Baptista Coelho (ed.), *Portugal. O Sistema Politico e Constitucional.1974-1987* (Lisbon: ICS, 1989), 257-277, particularly 268-277.
48. Juan Carlos González Hernandez, *Desarollo Político y Consolidacion Democrática en Portugal(1974-1998)*.(Madrid: Centro de Investigaciones Sociologicas, 1999), 194-202.
49. Joaquim Aguiar, "Eleições, configurações e clivagens:os resultados eleitorais de 1995," *Análise Social* XXXV, 154-155, 2000: 55-84; 75; Joaquim Aguiar, "Partidos, eleições, dinamica politica (1975-1991)," *Análise Social* XXIX, 125-126, 1994: 171-236; particularly 230-235.
50. *Visão*, 11 July 2002, pp. 42-49.

51. José Magone, "Portugal," in Juliet Lodge (ed.), *The 1999 Elections to the European Parliament* (Basingstroke: Palgrave, 2001), 171-184; particularly 175-182.
52. José Magone, "Portugal," in Juliet Lodge (ed.), *The 1994 European Parliament Elections* (London: Pinter, 1996), 147-156; particularly 151-155.
53. José Magone, "Portugal," in Lodge, 2001, 176.
54. A most extensive study on this economic factor has been done by Marina Costa Lobo; see "A evolução do sistema partidário portugues á luz de mudanças económicas e politicas," *Analise Social* XXXI, 139, 1996: 1085-1116; see also André Freire, Michael Baum, "Clivagens, Economia e Voto em Portugal 1999: Uma análise das eleições parlamentares com dados agregados," *Sociologia. Problemas e Prácticas* 37, 2001: 115-140.
55. See José Magone, "Portugal: Party System Installation and Consolidation," in David Broughton, Mark Donovan (eds.), *Changing Party Systems in Western Europe* (London: Pinter, 1999), 232-253; 245-247, and 251-253.
56. Stefano Bartolini, "A integração europeia provocará uma reestruturação dos sistemas de clivagens nacionais?" *Sociologia. Problemas e Práticas* 37, 2001: 91-114; particularly 104-105.

4

Social Change and Political Culture: The Impact of the European Union

Introduction: The Problems of Fast Social Change

Major social and economic transformations have taken place in Portugal after integration into the European Union. When Portugal became a member of the European Union one of the main problems was to find reliable statistics on the social and economic conditions of the population. Until 1988 and 1989, it was difficult to prepare plans of regional development because of a lack of reliable data. The European integration process made sure that knowledge about Portuguese society became more reliable and accurate.[1] The number of socioeconomic studies boomed throughout the 1980s and 1990s. It started with an incredible boom in the education sciences and went on to more accurate studies in other areas such as social policy and, particularly, employment policy. In spite of these transformations, many of the problems of Portuguese society still remain. Indeed, despite more modern infrastructures, better roads, the coverage of sanitation and water supply, structural change, particularly in terms of social capital, Portuguese society did make only modest progress. This paradox became quite evident, when it was discovered that although the structural funds related to the fund for regional development (FEDER) were well-used, the European Social Fund was either abused, or did not achieve a major quality change of the fabric of qualifications of Portuguese workers.[2] The single major problem that Portuguese society has yet to overcome is the continuing persistence of an education divide, which leads to a high level of economic and social inequality. Although after the Revolution there was ambition to make social security and social protection universal rights for all Portuguese, in the 1980s successive governments watered down this ambition by making it dependent on existing resources. This means that in times of crises the present stand of social protection may well be reduced to accommodate budgetary problems.

Regardless of an overwhelming culture of the market, many Portuguese are still struggling to make a daily living, a situation that may become even worse if the economic condition is not able to afford the already fragile system of social protection and insurance. In this chapter, it is my intention to explore the social bases of the Portuguese democracy, which is completing its thirtieth year. Seymour Martin Lipset in his *Political Man* clearly emphasized that a successful democracy needs a strong middle class.[3] Indeed, Nancy Bermeo goes even further in her seminal article on the transition in Spain and Portugal, by noting that such a process towards the establishment of a middle class in Portugal began shortly before the revolutionary transition of 1974, but such a heterogeneous group was quite incipient. One characteristic that was lagging behind in the establishment of the middle classes, was the small number of people belonging to the new middle classes in relation to the traditional middle classes.[4] While the traditional middle classes could be found among shopkeepers, teachers, and other professions, the new middle classes are linked to new professions that work with new techologies and are highly mobile. They are professional technicians, executive employees, and independent workers. In the past three decades, the new middle classes have grown steadily, creating the conditions for a more political market of highly mobile and individualized behavior. One crucial factor determining this lack of new middle classes is the weakness of the education sector, which, to this day continues to reproduce a class society based on the level of education.

In sum, Portuguese society is still polarized by the educational divide. Although government has tried to correct this, the fast social change has led to disarticulation between policy areas, particularly between the education system and the labor market.

In this chapter, we will discuss the problems that Portuguese society still faces in its effort to reach the European average in terms of quality of life. In the following section, we will discuss the main features of the new Portuguese society after European Integration, including the problems of consumerism, social exclusion, and the new phenomenon of immigration to Portugal. This is followed by a study of attitudes towards the political system and afterwards European integration. Last but not least, conclusions are drawn from this chapter.

The Main Features of the New Portuguese Society after European Integration

The major progress of Portuguese society in the past three decades is due in many ways to Portugal's orientation towards European integration. This progress has to be measured against the background of a long period of authoritarianism that existed between 1926 and 1974. Although it may be unfair to attribute all the problems to the dictatorship of Antonio Salazar and

Marcelo Caetano, one has to acknowledge that this time period is still the root of many problems that the Portuguese are facing now. Until the mid-1970s, little was done to improve the socioeconomic conditions of the population. Most of the economic improvement was induced by colonial wars which contributed to the completion of the national market. Up until the 1960s, the Portuguese market was quite fragmented and lacked integration. One particular element, which is still felt in Portugal, was the authoritarian dictatorship's lack of commitment to education. Until the late 1950s, education was regarded as a danger to the regime. The high level of illiteracy, over 30 percent, when the Revolution of the Carnations took place on 25 April 1974 speaks for itself. The further a region was from the western coast where the main cities of Lisbon, Porto, Coimbra and Setubal were located, the more illiterate was the population. Although many efforts were made by several governments to eradicate illiteracy, pockets of it still persist and many Portuguese can barely write their name. This is not merely a generation problem, as many politicians have contended to simplify the facts, because illiteracy continues to persist even in younger generations.[5] In 1991, between 11 and

Figure 4.1
Completion of Upper Secondary School as Percentage of Population in Portugal and the EU (1999)

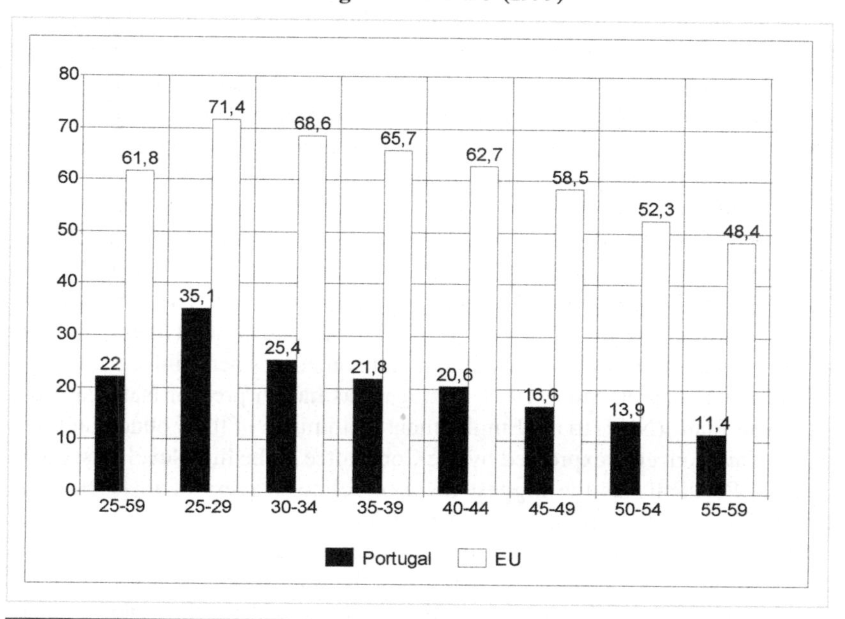

Source: Eurostat, *100 Basic Indicators from Yearbook 2001. The Statistical Guide to Europe. Data 1989-99* (Brussels: Eurostat 2001), p.10.

15.3 percent of the population was illiterate, and in 2000 it was over 7 percent. Another aspect that has been a major problem for policymakers in the area of education is the high level of school-leavers before or during the secondary school. This trend has been attributed to several factors, but mainly to the fact that the poor segments of the population cannot afford to send their children to school for a full period of nine years (basic schooling).

First of all, there is a tendency to see education as a burden on the poor's weak salaries, not as a personal enrichment that will lead to a better life in the labor market. Secondly, there is pressure to contribute to the family income by early entry into the labor market. Naturally, this leads to a reproduction of the level of qualifications of the previous family. Thirdly, with no incentive from parents and society to complete the basic schooling, many youngsters have the general feeling that education as such is not important. More significant is the short-term rationale of becoming part of the labor market. Meanwhile many studies on education have been undertaken which confirm that school-leavers can be found among the poorest segments of the population. The highest levels of school-leavers are among the rural populations (small farmers and workers), the less qualified industrial workers and the unemployed. Among these categories, school-leaving reaches values between 40 and 50 percent, which is highly problematic for the future of the Portuguese labor market. Regionally, the highest level of school drop-outs can be found in places away from the western coast, such as Trás-Os-Montes (Bragança, Vila Real), Alentejo (Portalegre), the islands of Azores, and Madeira.[6] The reason for this can be attributed to the legacy of the authoritarian regime, which neglected the inner parts of continental Portugal as well as the islands. The state's minimalist engagement in these regions led to a preservation of the culture of illiteracy, which was glorified by Salazar.[7]

Naturally, the present situation is related to the policies of democratic governments that clearly were not able to overturn this trend, thus leading to extreme social inequalities in Portugal. Policies were ill-designed, discontinuous, and not adjusted to the needs of the labor market. The consequence is the continuation of what one could call the patrimonial labor market, where jobs are precarious, low paying, and sometimes semi-informal. It is a fragile labor market. Since 1998, Portugal has had to present National Employment Plans (NEP) to the Employment Committee of the Council and one of the main concerns expressed by the Committee is the high level of school-leavers. Portugal has the highest level of school-leavers of the European Union Community, reaching 43.1 percent in 2001.

It was recommended that Portuguese governments adopt new strategies to overcome this main obstacle to improving the qualifications of the working population while at the same time taking action to address the gender imbalance across many sectors, in spite of the high rate of female employment in Portugal.[8] The recommendations to overcome the situations were as follows:

After due analysis, it appears that more efforts are required in response to the employment guidelines and recommendations concerning: lifelong learning and skills; the partnership approach; and gender imbalance:

Portugal should therefore:

1. Better articulate the lifelong learning strategy, by improving education and training systems in order to avoid skills shortages, increase the supply of skilled labour and thus promote the creation of medium and highly skilled jobs and raise labour productivity;
2. Pursue efforts to implement a partnership approach and promote concrete commitments from the social partners, in particular in the areas of modernisation of work organisation and adaptation of employment relations, including labour regulations, carefully monitoring the implementation of the agreements signed by the government and the social partners;
3. Pursue efforts to reconcile family and working life, in particular by extending childcare facilities, and examine new ways to promote better gender balance and sectoral level.[9]

The third recommendation, in particular, is quite relevant, because it addresses the problem of mismatch between family and working life. This naturally has to include an improvement of the income of poorer families so that they can afford education for their children.

Although absolute illiteracy has declined steadily to single figures, Portugal is faced with a high level of structural illiteracy, which is related to the short period of education that most people have had. In a major national study on education in Portugal in the mid-1990s, it was found out that 47.3 percent of the population had a very basic structural literacy which reached from complete incapacity to solve any tasks related to reading, writing, and calculus to a basic fulfilment of such tasks. This deficiency contributes to exclusion from a labor market that is asking for more and more skills.[10]

The past thirty years have led also to a growth of wealth in Portuguese society. The tertiarization of society contributed to an increase of the new middle classes, which today are clearly a major factor in shaping the politics of the center. Their shifting behavior in political terms may lead to a victory of one of the main parties, which is probably the most important development in Portuguese society because it contributes to the dissemination of political and economic market behavior. According to Fernando Luis Machado and Antonio Firmino da Costa, the new middle classes represented 47.3 percent of the population in 1991, and continued to expand throughout the 1990s, passing certainly the 50 percent mark.[11] These new middle classes are replacing the traditional middle classes. By contrast, the share of farmers and industrial workers is steadily decreasing in the population. These social changes have led to a polarized social structure, in some ways due to the levels of income between the richest and poorest segments of the population. According to the most recent figures of the European Commission, on average the richest segment of the population earns 7.2 times more than the poorest, while countries like Denmark with 2.7, Finland with 3, and Sweden with 3.4 are closer to a more equitative distribution of income. This means that 20 percent of the poorest part of the population received only 6 percent of income, while 20 percent of the richest part of the population had 45 percent of the income.[12] While salaries for the poorest are the lowest in the European Union, salaries for the richest in many cases exceed the highest paid in other European countries. The education divide is a critical factor in producing this inequality in income distribution.[13] It creates major problems for the country because 22 percent of the population is living in absolute poverty as compared to 15 percent in the EU average. Other figures suggest that the situation is even worse than these figures indicate.[14] In any case, Portuguese society can be regarded as a highly unequal society by any standards. The recent introduction of the so-called Minimum Guaranteed Income (*Rendimento Garantido Minimo*-RGM) in 1996 was a move in the right direction, but too little and too late for a vast majority of the population. Inequalities have increased in the 1990s and are reflected in all aspects of society such as in access to health, education, housing, and, of course, the consumer market. Structural poverty may likely affect more than 40 percent of the population.

A major trend in Portuguese society is towards individualization. As with other European Union countries, similar trends towards diversity of living forms in society are becoming more common. An example is the decline of Catholic marriages in Portuguese society in the past three decades. Although religion is still important in Portugal, particularly in the northern rural areas, secularization and the process of modernity have had a major effect on the changing attitudes towards the Church. Slowly, the meanings associated with Catholicism are being emptied out, leading to a decline of religious practices. The growing number of divorces has contributed further to the decline of marriage as an important social institution,[15] and has consequences for the structure of families. Portugal is moving slowly towards a diverse family structure that is common in the Scandinavian countries and the United Kingdom. One of most prominent features of this move is the rise in monoparental families that are headed by mothers and fathers with predominantly lower levels of education.[16] Nevertheless, this movement is relatively slow and fits into a general pattern that we describe as a southern European pattern, because of its similarity to what is happening in Spain, Italy, and Greece.[17]

This transformation of social life is certainly an adjustment to the growth of the market structure of the past thirty-five in Portugal, and in some ways is transforming economic and social relations in the country. The marketization of society has been rapid, leading in many cases to high levels of debt. Indeed, the introduction of credit cards and other flexible forms of payment led to 92 percent of the people being in debt. This Americanized way of life clearly changes perceptions about society. Integration into the market means, naturally, the consumption of prestigious goods, which may create major payment problems for a vast majority of the population. The marketization of society also means a standardization of living conditions through the main medium television. In some way, access to the market has become asymmetrical.[18] While the new middle classes are able to afford the most expensive luxurious goods, 30 to 40 percent of the population is struggling to make ends meet. As a result, this creates major problems for social and economic cohesion or for any ambition to achieve more equality of opportunities in Portuguese society.

Successive governments have made huge efforts to raise the social expenditure to European levels, however, the Portuguese social protection system is still exceedingly fragile. The fragility of the system can be detected in the way government just privatized the welfare provision to the excluded population. According to a study, the Portuguese state decided to create a secondary civil society, meaning that most recognized private charities are financed by the state by up to 70 percent. The rest of the funding must be paid by the clients, which means that the socially excluded and vulnerable people are only partially protected. This entire approach was reformed recently by decentralizing the whole process towards the local level, but the overall relationship between the state and the so-called charities is one of neopatrimonialism.[19] These charities carry 93 percent of all activities related to the social protection system, but they are insufficiently controlled. Indeed, control within the charities and by the state is sometimes nonexistent to avoid extra costs. Naturally, this seems strange, when one considers that these charities are being awarded subsidies from the state that are in the end taxpayers´money.[20] There is also a feeling among the poorest that they have to compete for any social benefits. This attitude undoubtedly creates major feelings of alienation towards the political institutions. Indeed, there is a general feeling that before elections the social benefits of the social protection system are used in exchange for votes for the ruling party. This naturally leads to even more withdrawal by the excluded population, which generally has a low level of education and is too proud to seek help from the state because it is not aware of its right to submit applications.[21] Although the previous Socialist government tried to change this situation between 1996 and 2000, soon it was confronted with the limits of the budget. By 2001, the government had to make substantial cuts to continue on track in relation to the EU's growth and stability pact.

A further major social change is the fact that after decades of being a country sending emigrants to all possible parts of the world, Portugal has itself become a target for economic immmigrants. Although the numbers are still quite low compared to other European countries, they have been growing over the past two decades, with the majority of immigrants coming from

Africa and Europe. Most African immigrants have poor education records and tend to work in the informal sector without protection or any kind of contract. The fact that they are also in an illegal situation often makes them vulnerable to exploitation. The demand for cheap labor in the construction sector is high, due to the dynamics initiated by the structural funds, the Expo98, and the European Championship in 2004. The majority of African immigrants come from Portuguese-speaking countries such as Cape Verde Islands, Guinea-Bissau, Angola, and Mozambique. In 1999, 89,516 legal immigrants entered Portugal, coming from Africa, particularly from Cape Verde. Europeans were the second largest group with 56,731 legal immigrants, of which slightly over 4,000 came from outside the European Union. There were also 35,989 immigrants from North America and 25,818 from South America. Among the latter, 20,887 came from Brazil. Europeans and North and South Americans tend to have higher qualified jobs, which, in some cases, cannot be filled by the Portuguese labor force due to its low level of qualifications. In sum, Portugal had 190,896 immigrants in 1999. It is estimated that between 80,000 and 120,000 immigrants are in the country illegally, most of them coming from Africa, Central and Eastern European countries, or the former republics of the Soviet Union. They will find jobs in the informal economy of the construction sector in the Algarve, Lisbon, and Oporto.[22] Such an increase over the past two decades has created new problems related to the welfare of these immigrants. Indeed, the different charities affiliated with the Catholic Church, which are dealing with immigrants, acknowledge that they are overburdened by this task, and have demanded a fast-track procedure for legalization. Indeed, the Portuguese government has established a High Commission for Ethnic Minorities and Immigration to deal with these matters.[23]

According to a major study on attitudes towards black people, it appears that Portuguese expressions of racism are becoming similar to those of other European countries. The authors of the study contrast overt racism with subtle racism, showing that there is a tendency towards subtle racism. While overt racism can be quite discriminatory on grounds of race and culture and may be related to security or economic threat, subtle racism does not attribute any negative values to the exogroup (black people), but tends to look at the endogroup (white people) in a more positive fashion than the exogroup. The authors also came to the conclusion that Portuguese political parties never problematize racism, which means that they clearly advocate a position of subtle racism, which becomes then the overall culture of the country.[24] According to another study that focuses on the relationship between media and discrimination, its authors found that the written press as well as television tends to offer negative images of the African and the Gypsy communities. Both are linked to anti-social behavior, violence, and crime. The social and economic background of these communities is not problematized in most reports, and, therefore naturally becomes part of the constructed social reality.[25] It contributes certainly to the prevalence of a subtle racism.

In sum, Portugal has made major progress in the past thirty years of democracy, however, Portuguese society is more unequal than it was some thirty years ago, or even one decade ago. This situation is no longer a legacy of the authoritarian regime, but has now become a question of long-term policy priorities. The European Union has become a major factor in exposing the existing sad social situation of this country, which, naturally, has negative repercussions within the Portuguese political system and affects also the often autistic political elites.

Attitudes towards the Political System: Growing Alienation of the Population

After thirty years of democracy, the political elites did not manage to make the political system more democratic. On the contrary, the majority of the population feels quite distant to the discourse and the actions of the political elite. Thus, the actions of political elites are very much autonomous from the

Figure 4.2
Power Distance Perception (1997)

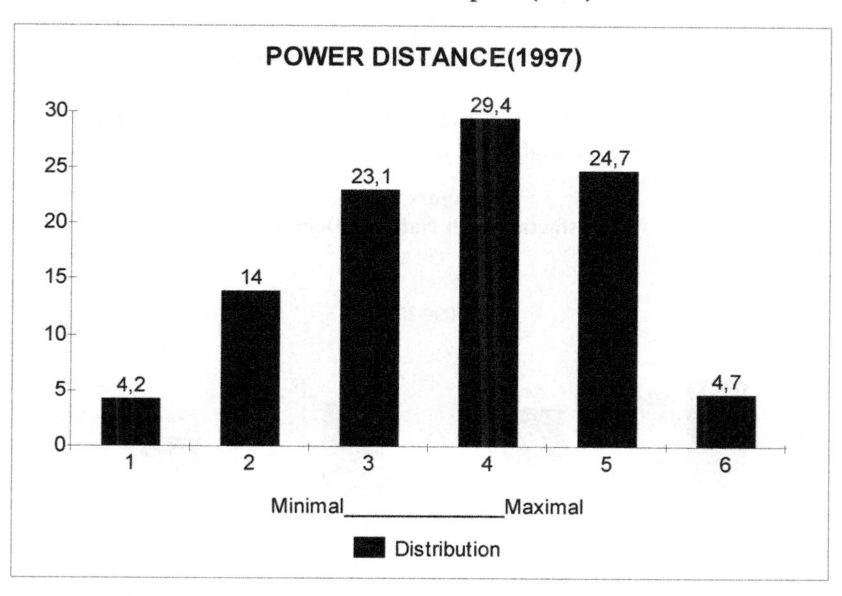

Source: Author's graph based on results of the study by Manuel Villaverde Cabral, "O exercicio da cidadania em Portugal." In Manuel Villaverde Cabral, Jorge Vala, Joao Freire (eds.), *Trabalho e Cidadania* (Lisbon: Imprensa de Ciencias Sociais 2000), p.155.

life of the population. According to a study by Manuel Villaverde Cabral, this distance has achieved alarming proportions. On a scale from 1 (minimal distance to the political elite) to 6 (maximal distance to the political elite) Portuguese respondents scored 3.7. When compared with survey results of 1968, it appears that feelings of distance toward the political elite have increased substantially.[26]

According to Villaverde Cabral's study, 58.8 percent of the respondents score showing distance in relation to the political class, a fact that is highly problematic after thirty years of democracy. A Eurobarometer study of 2001 confirmed the fact, indicating that Portuguese were beginning to be less satisfied with Portuguese democracy, in a pattern similar to that of the Italians.

Indeed, substantial change has been noted since 1990.[27] The decline in the 1990s dipped to below 60 percent, and in the extremely difficult year of 2001, an overwhelming majority of the population was dissatisfied with national democracy. Clearly, this is symptomatic of the gap that is widening between the political elite and the population. Other symptoms include the high level of abstentionism, the weak civil society, and the small number of people who are actively engaged. According to Cabral, political participation in Portugal is weak, having reached a score of 4.5 on a scale from 1 (strong) to 5 (none). This weakness reflects on the activities that Portuguese citizens are prepared to undertake to achieve political goals. Indeed, Portuguese citizens are quite conventional and more or less passive in terms of political action.[28] A low level of education and income inequality further reinforces this pattern of subject culture[29] in the Portuguese case.

This strong disarticulation between the political offer and the political demand clearly creates a high level of dissatisfaction and alienation from the

Figure 4.3
Satisfaction with National Democracy

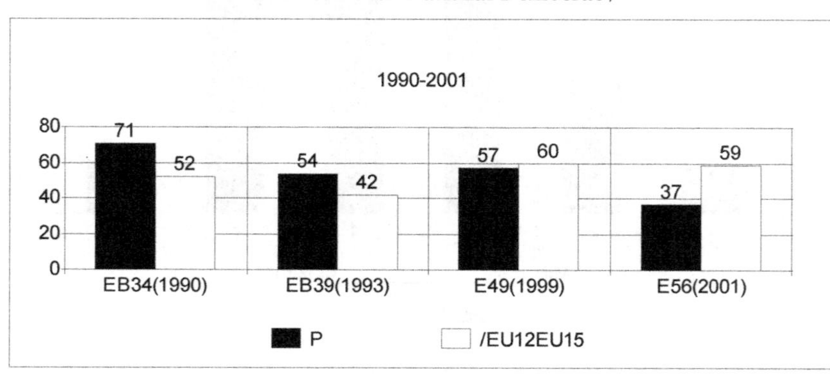

Source: Eurobarometer, 34, 1990; Eurobarometer 39, 1993; Eurobarometer, 49, 1999; and Eurobarometer, 56, 2001.

political system.[30] This autonomization of the political class from the political market needs was prevalent during 2001. A major study undertaken by the Socialist government concluded that most Portuguese are dissatisfied with the political choice offered. They also have a low opinion of political institutions, in particular the Parliament, which is a further indication of the split between *paese legale* and *paese reale*.[31] Indeed, a recent poll conducted for the newspaper *Expresso* shows that an overwhelming 62 percent of the population does not trust politicians, and 49 percent believe that the present political class is worse than it was twenty years ago. Only 26 percent think that it has improved.[32]

The consequence of this political climate is a closing of the political system, of which the main gatekeepers are the political parties, to the ordinary citizen. The selection processes do not allow for integration of new blood. Thus, they tend to reproduce the same political elite, without daring to include the vast majority of citizens with a lower level of education.[33] The overall image of Parliament is that it is controlled by the middle classes with reduced numbers coming from other social classes.[34] Naturally, one can argue that such a situation exists in other parliamentary systems and it is essential

Figure 4.4
Political Participation in 1997

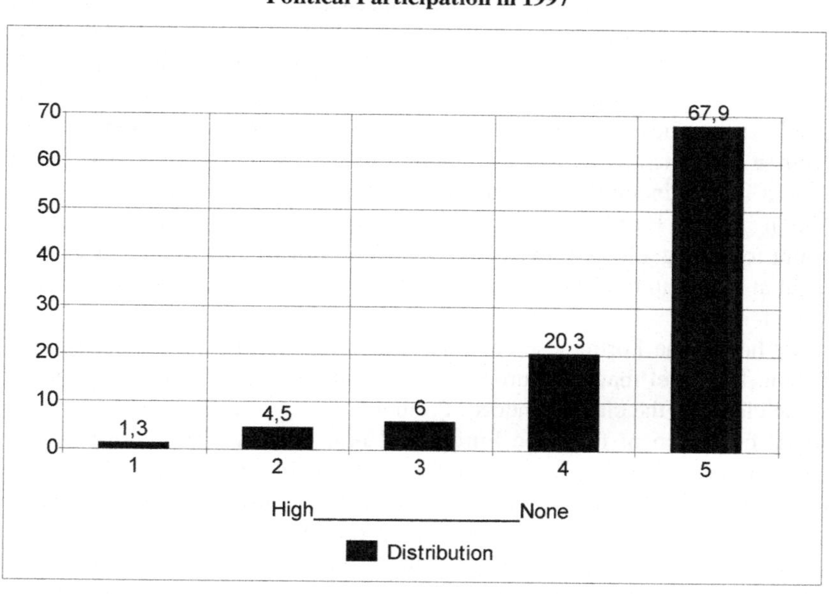

Source: Author's graph based on results of the study by Manuel Villaverde Cabral, "O exercicio da cidadania em Portugal." In Manuel Villaverde Cabral, Jorge Vala, Joao Freire (eds.), *Trabalho e Cidadania* (Lisbon: Imprensa de Ciencias Sociais 2000), p. 155.

that the highly qualified representatives are elected to Parliament.[35] However, in a highly unequal society, based on an education divide, there is a need for representation of the vast part of the population that still struggles to live in a complex society, hampered bya low level of educational qualifications and consequently a low income.

In sum, a growing divide is emerging between the political class and the citizens. Disarticulation of the political market between political offer and demand only adds to the alienation and apathy among the population.

Attitudes towards European Integration

After accession to the EC/EU, the Portuguese were among the most enthusiastic supporters of European integration. Scores related to membership support rose from 30 percent before accession to 49 to 80 percent afterwards and during the past two decades. The scores are even more convincing when the question of whether Portugal benefitted from membership is asked. Indeed, regularly 60 to70 percent of respondents gave a positive answer to this question. The Portuguese are also enthusiastic about further European unification, a fact that includes them in the southern European pattern, along with the Spaniards, Italians, and Greeks.[36]

However, these positive scores are actually accompanied by findings that the majority of Portuguese respondents do not know how the EU political system works. They represent 57 percent of respondents that have a low income, are of a working-class background, and have a low educational record; in addition, a lack of knowledge about the EU was more widespread among woman than men. And it is astonishing that 40 percent of the population with a higher income is also not aware of the workings of the European Union.[37] Most Eurobarometers of the 1990s revealed that the Portuguese admit to having a low knowledge of the European Union, which places Portugal at the bottom of the European Union, along with Spain and the United Kingdom.[38]

Although the Portuguese are satisfied with democracy in the European Union, they feel that the European Union should make a greater effort to come closer to the citizen. Indeed, Portuguese respondents expect a stronger social commitment from the European Union, which they believe should target peacekeeping and security and the fight against crime, the fight against unemployment, the fight against poverty, quality control of food, and protection of the environment. At the bottom of their priorities is enlargement and reform of the institutions.[39] Nevertheless, recent polls suggest that Portuguese in their vast majority do support a strengthening of the EU political system, particularly by adopting a European constitution (51 percent against 32 percent) and the election of a European president (69 percent against 13 percent). This can be interpreted as an escapist strategy, as in the Italian case, to overcome the dominance of the national political class in decision-making.[40]

The low level of education among the majority of Portuguese is a major problem in making them aware of the present developments of the European Union. It appears that Europeanization of the Portuguese population in terms of political culture is only superficial and related only to visible symbols such as the euro. A diffuse understanding of the process of enlargement persists. All this reinforces the position of the political class in the political system, and the illiteracy of the population in relation to EU aspects strengthens the autonomy of the political class. This was obvious in relation to the way the government overcame the problem of a referendum on the European Monetary Union. One cannot be certain that the decision by the Constitutional Court was the correct one in terms of legitimizing the position of the political class in this direction.

Conclusions: Superficial Europeanization of National Political Culture

The main intention of this chapter was to look at the problems of present Portuguese society in terms of education, employability, and social exclusion. It is a fragile society with a high level of structural illiteracy, and is characterized by an educational divide that is no longer tolerable after thirty years of democracy. This educational divide has led to a political break between the political class and the population. The political class's autonomy from the real problems of Portuguese society leads to the inevitable mismatch between political offer and demand. In terms of political culture, the vast majority of Portuguese citizens are still confined to a subject culture and some even to a parochial culture. A low level of education, low income, and latent poverty prevent Portuguese citizens from becoming more engaged in European affairs. They feel out of place in this respect and allow the political class to control the discussion, which, of course, means that there is a superficial Europeanization of Portuguese society. While the society is characterized by strong enthusiasm it is simultaneously accompanied by a lack of knowledge of the workings of the EU by the population.

Notes

1. Luis Madureira Pires, *A Politica Regional Europeia e Portugal* (Lisbon: Fundação Calouste Gulbenkian, 1998), 44.
2. Only 3 percent of the working population takes part in vocational training courses. The Portuguese figures are only better than the Greek ones, which have only 1 percent of the working population taking part in vocational training courses. *Expresso*, Emprego, 29 June 2002.
3. Martin Seymor Lipset, *Political Man. The Social Conditions of the Political Order* (London: Heinemann Group of Publishers, 1964): "From Aristotle down to the

present, men have argued that only in a wealthy society in which relatively few citizens lived at the level of real poverty could there be a situation in which the mass of the population intelligently participate in politics and develop the self-restraint necessary to avoid succumbing to the appeals of irresponsible demagogues. A society divided between a large impoverished mass and a small favored elite results either in oligarchy (dictatorial rule of the small upper stratum) or in tyranny (popular-based dictatorship)." (p. 50).

4. Nancy Bermeo, *A Teoria da Democracia e as Realidades da Europa do Sul* (Lisbon: Difel 2000), 154-167.
5. Luis Capucha, Ana Sofia Marques, José Luis Castro, Carlos Pereira e Paula Monteiro, "Vulnerabilidade e Exclusão Social," in DEPP/MTS (ed.), *Portugal 1995-2000. Perpectivas da Evolução Social* (Lisbon: Celta, 2002), 215-251; 221.
6. João Sebastião, "Os Dilemas da Escolaridade. Universalização, diversidade e inovação" in José Manuel Leite Viegas, António Firmino da Costa (eds.), *Portugal, que Modernidade?* (Lisbon: Celta, 1998), 311-327; particularly 319-321; see also Raul Iturra, *A Construção Social do Insucesso Escolar. Memória e Aprendizagem em Vila Ruiva* (Lisbon: Escher, 1990).
7. See Stephen Stoehr, *Educação e Mudança Social em Portugal 1970-1980. Uma decada de transição* (Porto: Edições Afrontamento, 1986).
8. Commission of the European Communities, *Council Recommendation on the Implementation of Member States' Employment Policies*, Brussels, 12 September 2001, COM (2001), 512 final, p. 17.
9. Ibid., 17-18.
10. Capucha, et al.,"Vulnerabilidade," p.223; this is quite problematic, because it may keep a large part of the population away from the political system, even for registration in the centers of employment. It leads to a subject culture which has difficulties in relating to the administrative culture of the state See the excellent lesser known study by Wolfgang Sieber, *Agrarentwicklung und ländlicher sozialer Wandel in Portugal* (Saarbrücken: Breitenbach, 1990).
11. Fernando Luis Machado, Antonio Firmino da Costa, "Processos de Uma Modernidade Inacabada. Mudanças Estruturais e Mobilidade Social," in José Manuel Leite Viegas, António Firmino da Costa (eds.), *Portugal, Que Modernidade?* (Lisbon: Celta, 1998), 17-58, particularly 33-38; on the process of tertiarization, see João Ferrão, "Terciarização e território: Emergencia de novas configurações espaciais? *Análise Social* XXVI, 5, 1991: 829-845.
12. European Commission, *The Social Situation in the European Union 2002* (Luxembourg: Office of the Official Publications of the European Union, 2002), 89 and 125.
13. José Luis Albuquerque, Teresa Bomba, Isabel Matias, Carlos Farinha Rodrigues e Gisela Santos, "Distribuição de Rendimentos e Condições de Vida," in DEPP/MTS (ed.), *Portugal 1995-2000. Perspectivas de Evolução Social* (Lisbon: Celta, 2002), 67-86; particularly 67-71.
14. Luis Manuel Antunes Capucha, "Pobreza, Exclusão Social e Marginalidades," in José Manuel Leite Viegas, Antonio Firmino da Costa (eds.), *Portugal, Que Modernidade?* (Lisbon: Celta, 1998), 209-242, 214-217; see also the classic studies of João Ferreira de Almeida, Luis Capucha, Antonio Firmino da Costa, Fernando Luis Machado, Isabel Nicolau, and Elisabeth Reis, *Exclusão Social. Factores e Tipos de Pobreza em Portugal* (Oeiras: Celta, 1992), and Alfredo Bruto da Costa, Manuela Silva, J. Pereirinha, and Madalena Matos, *A Pobreza em Portugal* (Lisbon: Fundação Calouste Gulbenkian, 1985).
15. Ana Nunes de Almeida, Maria das Dores Guerreiro, Cristina Lobo, Amália Torres, Karin Wall, "Relações Familiares: Mudanças e Diversidade," in José Manuel Leite

Viegas, António Firmino da Costa (eds.), *Portugal, Que Modernidade?* (Lisbon: Celta, 1998), 45-78; 67-74.

16. Karin Wall, Cristina Lobo, "Familias monoparentais em Portugal." *Analise Social* XXXIV, October 1999: 123-145; particularly 135-136.
17. Manuel Castells, *The Power of Identity. Volume II: The Information Age: Economy, Society and Culture* (London: Blackwell, 2000), 221-228; Eurostat, *Como somos los europeos?Todos los Datos* (Madrid: El Pais, 1999), 73.
18. Norberto Pinto dos Santos, *A Sociedade de Consumo E Os Espaços Vividos pelas Familias.A Dualidade dos espaços, a turbulencia dos percursos e a identidade social* (Lisbon: Edições Colibri, 2001).
19. Pedro Hespanha, Alcina Monteiro, A.Cardoso Ferreira, Fernanda Rodrigues, M. Helena Nunes, M. José Hespanha, Rosa Madeira, Rudy van den Hoven, Silvia Portugal, *Entre o Estado e o Mercado.As fragilidades das instituições da protecção social em Portugal* (Coimbra: Quarteto, 2000), 136-143.
20. Ibid., 228; 238-239; 247.
21. Ibid., 112-113, 271; 322-323.
22. Figures from Capucha, Vulnerabilidade, p.231-232; Maria Ioannis Baganha, João Ferrão, Jorge Macaista Malheiros, "Os imigrantes e o mercado de trabalho: O caso portugues," *Análise Social* XXXIV, 150, 1999: 147-173. On the employment situation and the informal sector, see particularly pp. 161-169. According to a study, the number of Romanians, Ukrainians, Russians, and Moldavians has increased considerably in the past years. Only in January 2001, 77,711 residence permits were given to Ukrainians. This shows that the immigration from the East is becoming more important than that from Africa (*Publico*, 3 July 2002, p. 54).
23. *Publico*, 3 July 2002, p.13.
24. Jorge Vala, Rodrigo Brito, Diniz Lopes, *Expressões dos racismos em Portugal. Estudos e Investigações 11* (Lisbon: Imprensa de Ciencias Sociais, 1997), 192-193.
25. Isabel Ferin Cunha, Verónica Policarpo, Teresa Líbano Monteiro e Rita Figueiras, "Media e discriminação: Um estudo exploratório do caso portugues," *Observatório* 5, May 2002: 27-38; particularly 36-37.
26. Manuel Villaverde Cabral, "O exercicio da cidadania em Portugal," in Manuel Villaverde Cabral, Jorge Vala, Joao Freire (eds.), *Trabalho e Cidadania* (Lisbon: Imprensa de Ciencias Sociais, 2000), 123-162.
27. The best study on this phenomenon in Italy is Leonardo Morlino, Mario Tarchi, "The Dissatisfied Society: The Roots of Political Change in Italy," *European Journal for Political Research* 30, July 1996: 41-63.
28. Ibid., 141-142.
29. Subject culture refers to the classic study by Gabriel A. Almond, Sidney Verba, *The Civic Culture. Political Attitudes and Democracy in Five Nations* (London: SAGE, 1989), 168-169: "Just as the citizen role may be performed more or less competently, so may the subject be more or less competent. But the competence of the subject is different from that of the citizen. The competent citizen has a role in the formation of general policy. Furthermore, he plays an influential role in this decision-making process: he participates by using explicit or implicit threats of some form of deprivation if the official does not comply with his demand. This subject does not comply with his demand. The subject does not participate in making rules, nor does his participation involve the use of political influence. His participation comes at the point at which general policy has been made and is being applied. The competence of the subject is more a matter of being aware of his rights under the rules than of participating in the making of rules. And though the subject

may attempt to make the government official responsive, he appeals rather than demands. His appeal may be to the set of administrative rules that are supposed to guide the action of the government official, or he may appeal to his considerateness. If the government official responds, it is because he is following these rules or because he is being considerate—not because influence has been applied to him."

30. Ibid., 156.
31. According to a study commissioned by the government, both political parties and the political institutions including the Parliament were in low esteem among the population. Up to 53 percent of the population did not feel represented by any of the main Portuguese parties (*Expresso*, 5 October 2001). A major legitimacy crisis emerged in November, when it was found out that President Sampaio ratified the new Law of Military Programming and a new law regulating the Elections to Local Offices, in spite of the fact that the necessary quorum of half of all MPs had approved the law, but their presence was wrongly notified in the official parliamentary records *Diario da Assembleia da Republica*. Both laws had to be sent to the Constitutional Court for scrutiny of their constitutionality (*Expresso*, 10 November 2001; *Expresso*, 17 November 2001). This led to another scandal related to the level of unjustified absences of MPs in the plenary sessions, in spite of a new statute approved recently which leads to automatic suspension of the office if an individual MP has three unjustified absences (*Expresso*, 17 November 2001; *Expresso*, 24 November 2001).
32. *Expresso*, 1 November 2002.
33. Juan Mozzicafreddo, *Estado Providencia e Cidadania em Portugal* (Oeiras: Celta, 1997), 206-207; Antonio Vitorino, "A Democracia Representativa," in *Portugal Hoje* (Oeiras: INA, 1995), 329-350.
34. José M. Magone, "Political Recruitment and Elite Transformation in Modern Portugal 1870-1999: The Late Arrival of Mass Representation," in Heinrich Best, Maurizio Cotta (eds.), *Parliamentary Representatives in Europe 1848-2000. Legislative Recruitment and Careers in Eleven European Countries* (Oxford: Oxford University Press, 2000), 341-370; particularly 359.
35. If we look at the Portuguese Members of the European Parliament, we have a good indicator about their working ethics. Indeed, a newspaper report during the summer 2002 showed that with exceptions, the majority of Portuguese representatives in Brussels are not at all hardworking and have a strong record of absenteeism. This naturally may be related to the kind of parliamentary culture they are used to domestically. This contradicts the thesis that better qualification means also more value for money (see *Expresso*, 9 July 2002).
36. *Eurobarometer* 44, April 1996: 30; *Eurobarometer* 48, March 1998: 34; *Eurobarometer* 49, September 1998: 33; *Eurobarometer* 54, Autumn 2000; *Eurobarometer* 56, Autumn 2001: 34; *Eurobarometer* 57, Spring 2002: 37.
37. *Eurobarometer, As fontes de informação sobre a União Europeia, O Alargamento e as Relações entre as Instituições, os Estados Membros e os Cidadãos.Estudo realizado para a Representação da Comissão Europeia em Portugal,* 2002, 40-41.
38. *Eurobarometer* 48, March 1998: 10; *Eurobarometer* 49, September 1998: 3.
39. *Eurobarometer, As fontes de informação*, p. 49.
40. *Expresso*, 1 November 2002.

5

The Difficult Reform of Public Administration: The Importance and Challenge of Internationalization and Europeanization

Introduction

The growing Europeanization of political systems within the European Union is leading to a growing necessity for cooperation among the national public administrations and the European Commission. In recent years, several initiatives have been initiated to bring the sixteen administrations (15 member-states+ the European Commission) together. The sharing of best practices or the implementation of new public management initiatives related to total quality management are among those aspects that are leading to a convergence of administrative traditions in Europe. Indeed, recently one does not speak only of the "Europe of Administrations," but more so of a "European Administrative Space." Cooperation reached a climax during the Portuguese presidency when the First Quality Conference of Sharing Best Practices was organized by the Portuguese government in conjunction with other national public administrations and the European Commission.

In this chapter, I want to explore how the Portuguese public administration internalized these new developments and integrated them into the overall discourse of modernization of the state and of public administration, which has been dominant since the early 1990s. This also will show the strength of the impact of the *vincolo esterno* (external link)[1] in the Portuguese case.

In the next section, I will attempt to delineate the development towards a Europe of Administrations/European Administrative Space and report on the latest developments of this growing cooperation. This is relevant because it is a collective effort of national public administrations in implementing international trends of modernization, reform, and democratization. Most of these latest developments are linked to the initiatives coming from the Organization for Economic Cooperation and Development (OECD). As such, Europeanization is closely linked to the internationalization of such administrative trends. The subsequent sections are devoted to the main problems of public administration since 1974. Although the democratization and modernization of the public administration is an integral part of the discourse of all governments since the Portuguese Revolution of Carnations, it was only after accession to the European Community (EC) in 1986 that such a modernizing and democratizing reform began.

After this overview, the major elements of state and public administration reform will be addressed. One particular integrative element of this transformation is the Common Support Frameworks established since 1989 and which have a global effect on the Portuguese political system. The internalization of the new public management philosophy and the total quality language in the overall efforts of Portuguese administrative reform will be discussed.

And lastly, this chapter will present some conclusions related to the "Europe of Administrations" and how they affect the developmental priorities of semiperipheral administrations.

The Context: The Emerging "Europe of Administrations"

In the past fifty years, the role of public administrations has been growing within the European Union multilevel governance system. The paradigm of "closed national government" is being replaced slowly by a paradigm of "open shared transnational governance." This transformation has become quite crucial in the past twenty years. The overall multilevel governance system, which had escaped prior reform, became administratively a more complex and differentiated structure. National traditions were more or less hostile to moving towards a system of "shared governance." Governance meant for public administration a growing flexibilization of the state, slimming it down and making it less heavy. The main objective was to make the state more competitive and simultaneously better able to motivate civil society to take part in the political system.

Although contacts among the national administrative systems and the European Commission have been going on for over fifteen years in an informal way, the big bang of stronger cooperation started only recently during the Austrian (1998), German and Finnish EU presidencies (1999). The representatives of the national directors-general of the departments of administrative reform meet twice a year, once during each presidency, to discuss informally issues of interest to all member-states since the 1970s.

Meanwhile, more than thirty-seven meetings of these national directors-general have taken place. This is paralleled by meetings of the national ministers of administrative reform of the member-states. Such meetings started in

1988.[2] A stronger cooperation among the administrations of the member-states became more and more relevant with the incrementalism of EU policymaking during the 1990s. A secretariat of directors-general of administrative reform was established in the European Institute for Public Administration (EIPA) in Maastricht in 1993. There was a permanent need to improve the skills of national civil servants. At the center of this continuous convergence effort in terms of training and skills is the EIPA in Maastricht, founded in 1981 and which is partly financed by the member-states (24 percent), the European Commission (8 percent), and partly by training and consultancy contracts coming mainly from national, regional, and local authorities and other bodies (68 percent).[3] According to the EIPA Annual Report 2000, the number of activities has increased exponentially in the past decade. EIPA provides courses for national civil servants related to the comitology in a presidency scenario and has increased the activity in terms of training civil servants of central and eastern Europe. For our purposes, it can be noted that over 1,000 Portuguese civil servants took part in EIPA courses in 1998 and 1999 as a preparation for the presidency in the first half of 2000.[4]

It is only since the Austrian presidency that cooperation among the national public administrations and the European Commission was established. Conclusions of the meeting of European ministers responsible for the Reform of Public Administration and Public Service, which took place in Vienna, Austria, on 12 November 1998, made it clear that the member-states and the European Commission were prepared to move towards an "European Administrative Space" with a common framework assessment in relation to the quality of delivery of administrative services.

Four main areas of cooperation for reform of public administration in Europe were identified:

> Firstly, the European Union would develop and use performance indicators and international benchmarking to make EU-wide performance comparisons between the individual states' public administrations.
>
> Secondly, dissemination of Best Practices and the creation of a common assessment framework was to be developed. This was to be applied to Europe's public administrations, so that they can learn from each other. A conference presenting examples of innovative administrations was to take place in Portugal in Spring 2000
>
> Thirdly, it aimed at raising the standards of service to the citizen. This would include transparent and accountable procedures that could be taken up by the citizens. If possible more cooperation with business and citizens had to be achieved. Moreover, stronger cooperation among public administrations to ensure best practice was quite central to the success of the "Europe of administrations."
>
> Fourthly, European training initiatives provided by enhanced cooperation among the training institutions of the EU member-states and the European Commission.[5]

In 1998, the Directors-General of Public Administration established a steering group to manage the cooperation between sixteen partners (fifteen national public administrations and the Commission) in the field of international exchanges and cooperation in public administration development (Innovative Public Services). From then on, the steering group monitored the process towards the completion of several projects such as the first European conference on best practices, which took place in Lisbon during the Portuguese presidency, and the development of the Common Assessment Framework.

Influenced by international developments towards new public management and total quality management disseminated by the OECD and the European Foundation for Quality Management (EFQM), the Common Assessment Framework (CAF) was developed throughout the Austrian, German, and Finnish presidency. It was finished and pilot-tested under the Finnish and Portuguese presidencies. Most of the academic work was undertaken by professionals from the EIPA in Maastricht and the German Academy for Administrative Sciences in Speyer. The CAF is a light version of quality assessment in organizations. It seeks to be a bridge between national administrations that tend to use different methodologies for assessing quality assessment. Although CAF is still in development, one can argue that it is an easy instrument to use. Most public services organizations needed only one day to complete the assessment. Basically, CAF is regarded potentially as an instrument to create Europeanwide instruments for international benchmarking and performance indicators.[6]

The first quality conference for public administrations in the EU, *Sharing Best Practices*, which took place in the Lisbon Congress Center, brought together a huge number of diverse examples from all levels of government. The selection of best practices cases was done under the German presidency. In total, thirty-nine cases were selected, which were presented in Lisbon in four parallel sessions (New Millennium, New Management: Emerging Best Practices in Public Management; The Search for Excellence in Public Administration: Quality Management in Action; Public Administration in the Age of Internet: Innovative Uses of New Technology; The Citizen is King: The New Emphasis on Citizen´s Services). This unprecedented cooperation of sixteen public administrations opened up the best practices of the member-states. It created a situation of looking at public administrations in comparative perspective. The Lisbon conference has shown the diversity of experiments, but also the level of convergence of public administrations. This exercise was quite important to foster the development towards a "European Administrative Space."[7]

Indeed, the quest for the creation of a "European Administrative Space" is more ambitious than one would expect. It includes the slow establishment of an open administrative exchange of civil servants within the European Union and also between the member-states, the candidate countries, and the EEA countries. The so-called Karolus program has already been in action for some time and has led to several fixed-term exchanges, which is the reason why CAF and the convergence of recruitment and training are essential to achieve this aim.[8] According to June Burnham and Moshe Maor, the European integration process is a major pressure for converging administrative styles. The opening up of national administrations to civil servants from other member-states will create similarities in the career patterns as well as administrative cultures. The European Commission's DG IX for personnel and administration is pushing the national administrations to move towards this "European administrative space" so that harmonization and implementation of legislation can be achieved more smoothly.[9]

These latest developments towards convergence of public administrative practices coincide with the overall effort of the European Commission to reform their bureaucratic structures towards new public management—a process that has been quite difficult. The damaging report of the independent *Committee of the Three Wise Men* presented to the European Parliament clearly showed that long-standing administrations tend to resist change. Commissioner Neill Kinnock's difficult role of introducing reform in the Commission can be paralleled with problems of reform of the member-states. In spite of programs such as SEM 2000 or MAP 2000 there is still much to be done.[10] A collective effort to create a "European administrative space" may in the end create a new, more dynamic momentum in this field. Today, the European Commission is surrounded by over 1,000 committees (the so-called "comitology") where national civil servants meet regularly with European Commission officials.[11] It is therefore crucial to improve the coordinating interfaces between the supranational, transnational, national, and subnational levels. In the end, the European Union as a "European administrative space" means a better multilevel network-like integration of the diverse administrative structures. New developments towards electronic government may contribute to a stronger integration of administrative structures.

Although some resistance towards change has been exerted by national bureaucracies, as the German example shows,[12] this high level of cooperation and convergence is unprecedented. The diversity of administrative policy styles and efficiency is still highly varied and asymmetrical,[13] but one cannot deny a positive development towards sharing experiences and learning from each other.

This level of communication is beginning to be a crucial exercise with a speedy development towards the charter of fundamental rights and now the constitutional reform.[14] Soon the construction of fair public administration in the multilevel governance system will become an essential element in the emerging new European polity. The constitutional implications of a European administrative space are already being felt and will become increasingly important.[15] The present construction of the Single European Market, the Economic Monetary Union, and the growing importance of Eurowide social and employment policies will be linked to an efficient administration that can be reflexive[16] in terms of a multilevel governance system.

Government as a closed, well-defined structure is moving rapidly towards governance as an open, less-defined space of processes.[17] This transition is complicated by the fact that the transformation is no longer happening in a closed, nationally defined space, but has become a multilevel process of spatial redefinition. It is erosion from above and below the nation-state. New, more blurred boundaries and borders begin to appear on the European Continent, which are created by European public policies such as INTERREG.[18]

Multilevel governance is changing the nature of public administration and transforming it into an integral sustaining part of it. The main characteristic is the capture of government by the dynamics of the market and the growing importance of civil society in the European Union. What seems to be happening is the move towards a light network-state that uses the rationale of the market and citizen-friendliness to reform itself. Governance changes the political dimension of the state. The state is no longer political. Politics merged with the market and became governance. The overall new language of public administration and reform of the state is about delivery, products, customers, and suppliers. It is about public-private partnership, privatization, and regulatory agencies. Governance summarizes the symbiosis between state and market, both of which were distinctive categories until the 1970s.

Indeed, these public administration reforms are spearheaded by the Public Management Committee (PUMA) of the OECD. Their policy brief papers are bringing to the fore the main developments of future government. One crucial aspect is to improve the relationship between citizens and public administration. The overall strategy is to create a policy mix that will fit the needs of a particular country. Instead of having an opportunistic anticipatory policy formulation controlled merely by civil servants, the new public management will focus on strategic policymaking based on consultation and participation of the public. The new information and communication technologies are regarded as crucial for this transformation of public administration. Recent developments towards what is called electronic government (e-Government) can be found across the European Union. This would include electronic voting as well.

Best practices examples, such as the People's Panel of 5,000 randomly selected UK citizens used by the First Service Unit of the Cabinet Office, help to search out the main priorities of future government.

The language of public management reform includes slogans such as "champions of public administration reform," "partnership between citizens and public administration," and the "market and public administration." At some stage, it is recognized that the government is just one player in serving the people. It has to compete with other players in a market-oriented society.

Table 5.1
Guiding Principles for Engaging Citizens in Policymaking

Guiding Principle	Explanation
Commitment	Leadership and strong commitment to information and active participation are needed at all levels—from politicians, senior managers, and public officials
Rights	Citizen's rights to access information, provide feedback, be consulted and actively participate in policymaking must be firmly grounded in law or policy. Government obligations to respond to citizens when exercising their rights must also be clearly stated. Independent institutions for oversight, or their equivalent, are essential to enforcing these rights.
Clarity	Objectives for, and limits to, information, consultation and active participation during policymaking should be well defined from the outset. The respective roles and responsibilities of citizens (in providing input) and government (in making decisions for which they are accountable) must be clear to all.
Time	Public consultation and active participation should be undertaken as early in the policy process as possible to allow a greater range of policy solutions to emerge and to raise the chances of successful implementation. Adequate time must be available for consultation and participation to be effective. Information is needed at all stages of the policy cycle.
Objectivity	Information provided by government during policymaking should be objective, complete, and accessible. All citizens should have equal treatment when exercising their rights of access to information and participation.
Resources	Adequate financial, human, and technical resources are needed if public information, consultation and active participation in policymaking are to be effective. Government officials must have access to appropriate skills, guidance, and training as well as an organizational culture that supports their efforts.
Co-ordination	Initiatives to inform, request feedback from, and consult citizens should be co-ordinated across government to enhance knowledge management, ensure policy coherence, avoid duplication and reduce the risk of 'consultation fatigue' among citizens and civil society (CSOs). Coordination efforts should not reduce the capacity of government units to pursue innovation and ensure flexibility.
Accountability	Governments have an obligation to account for the use they make of citizens' input received through feedback, public

Table 5.1 (cont.)

	consultation and active participation. Measures to ensure that the policymaking process is open, transparent, and amenable to external security and review are crucial to increasing government accountability overall.
Evaluation	Governments need the tools, information, and capacity to evaluate their performance in providing information, conducting consultation, and engaging citizens in order to adapt to new requirements and changing conditions for policymaking.
Active citizenship	Governments benefit from active citizens and a dynamic civil society and can take concrete actions to facilitate access to information and participation, raise awareness, strengthen citizen's civic education and skills as well as to support capacity-building among civil society organizations.

Source: Engaging Citizens in Policy Making. Information, Consultation and Public Participation. *OECD, Public Management Policy Brief* no.10, July 2001: 5.

Although still in a privileged position, public services face more and more competition from the private sector.[19]

What all of this means is that government and public administration were absorbed by the rules of the market and there is no way out. In this new condition, public administration is part of this new governance culture, a new language integrating both politics and the market.

In sum, the "European Administrative Space" is eroding rapidly the boundaries among national administrations. A reconstructionist process of public administration within the multilevel governance is taking place. This is still far from being recognized, but in long-term perspective it will become more salient. In this context, the Portuguese case is quite interesting, because it still features elements of a lagging behind modern public administration, although it is already involved in the present transformation of European public administration. Before assessing the transformations of Portuguese public administration, it is a good idea to give a brief account of the development of Portuguese administration since the transition to democracy in the mid-1970s.

From Democratization to Europeanization of Portuguese Public Administration (1974-2001)

One of the more salient factors in the development of Portuguese public administration is that it was characterized by a lack of direction of reform up until the mid-1980s. In some way, Portugal lived through a period of post-

Salazarism,[20] meaning that in spite of the Revolution of Carnations in 1974-75, the political administrative culture of the previous authoritarian regime was able to resist any attempts of change. In this section, it is important to delineate the main developments before and after accession to the European Union.

Overcoming Authoritarian and Revolutionary Legacies (1974-1985): The Vicious Cycle of Patrimonial Behavior

Public administrative reform has been a major priority for Portuguese government since the transition to democracy in 1974 and 1975. The main problem was to decide upon the direction this public administration should take. During the revolutionary process, several purges were conducted within public administration by the left-wing transitional governments under the leadership of General Vasco Gonçalves, who seemed extremely connected to the Communist party. The colonization of public administration by the Communist party was regarded as a danger to the future development of democracy in Portugal. According to estimates by Antonio Costa Pinto, by end of the revolutionary process over 20,000 persons had been purged from senior or important positions within the public administration. The main reason for these purges was that the successive left-wing governments wanted to get rid of civil servants attached to the former authoritarian regime and replace them with their own people. This naturally led to abuses in a period of transition and lack of legal framework. Similar purges occurred among public enterprises, the military, the judiciary, and major private enterprises.[21]

The restoration of democratic legitimacy after the approval of the Constitution of 2 April 1976 was a crucial step towards the normalization of political, economic, social, and administrative life in Portugal. The main problem for the public administration was that governments did not stay in power long enough to undertake major reforms of the public administration. Between 1976 and 1985 there were ten governments in power. Their average time in power was below one year. Governments were not only of a short duration , but they were unstable due to the fact that they were minority governments with fragile support in Parliament or coalition governments, which were characterized by internal infighting among the main coalition partners or within the parties. This situation prevented the development of a long-term strategy of reform.[22]

One could say that the political class, traumatized by the revolutionary process, was unable to work consensually towards an agreed postfascist administrative reform. Therefore, administrative reform was postponed to a later date, in which political stability would contribute to a more long-term reform.

Until 1986, the political inertia in relation to public administration reform contributed to the persistence of neopatrimonial forms of behavior, the main purpose of which was to give employment to supporters of the respective parties.[23] This situation further undermined the reform of public administration in Portugal. The reintegration of several civil servants who were purged during the revolutionary process also contributed to a resistance to public administrative reform. As Walter C. Opello found, most of the director-generals in the early 1980s were selected before 1974 and were advanced in age. Most had been recruited from the rural areas of Portugal, meaning that part of the administrative elite that supported Salazarism/Caetanism was still intact until the mid-1980s.[24] Actually, it was the civil servants that were the majority of MPs in Salazar´s rubber stamp parliament, The National Assembly (*Assembleia Nacional*).[25] The strong linkage of civil service and economic elites at the local level further undermined the development of a neutral Portuguese public administration before 1974.[26]

Prior to 1985, the successive governments were slow in overcoming this authoritarian legacy. One of the chief problems continued to be the high concentration of public administration in the two main cities of Lisbon and Porto. Some reform was undertaken by the introduction of regional Bureaus for Technical Assistance (*Gabinetes de Apoio Técnico*-GAT) in 1977 and later, the Commissions of Regional Development (*Comissões de Desenvolvimento Regional*-CCRs). However, the chronic problems of public administration could only be solved by a radical change of the culture.

Portuguese public administration was also characterized by a lack of highly skilled human resources. Most civil servants were poor educated, which was characteristic of a country that still had a high level of illiteracy (between 15 and 20 percent) in the mid-1980s. Moreover, the lack of a privatization of a huge sector of public enterprises created major fiscal problems for the state. The huge sector of public enterprises accumulated during the revolutionary process, when many firms were not able to survive and the state intervened to protect jobs.[27] By the mid-1980s this had become a huge burden for a poor inefficient public administration. Such reform would require a change of the constitution, which took only place in 1989.

Breaking the Patrimonial Cycle: The European Union as Vincolo Esterno of Modernization, Democratization, and Decentralization since 1986

Any administrative reform would need to achieve a higher level of deconcentration of public services, which was imperative to attaining a higher level of democratization in Portuguese society. All reform attempts tended to end in failure due to the vicious circle of neopatrimonial behavior inherent in politics and public administration.[28] The Portuguese state lacked the strength

Figure 5.1
Public Administration in Portugal 1968-1989

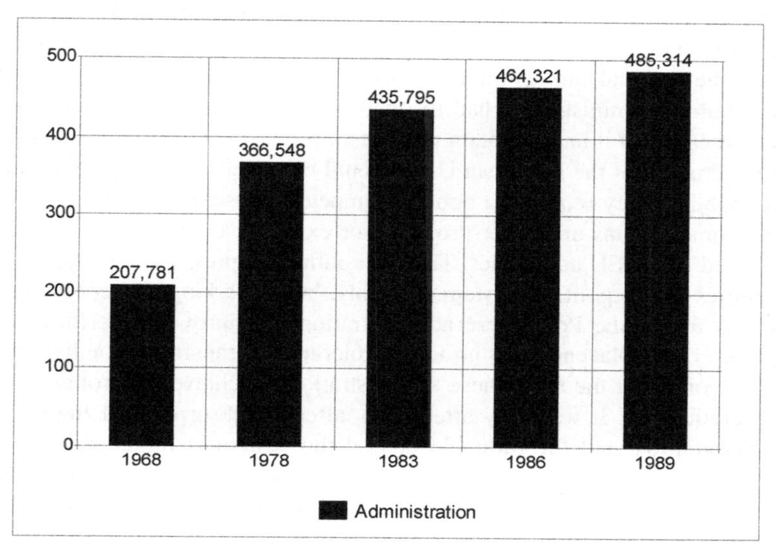

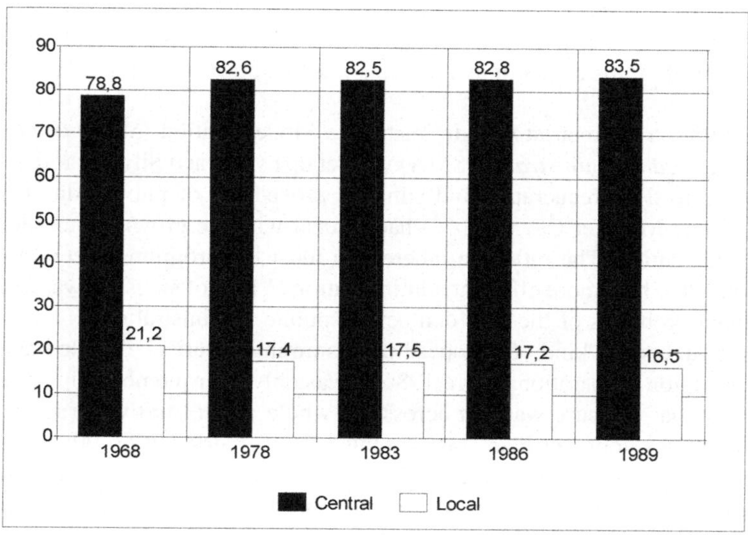

Source: Lawrence S. Graham, "Administração publica central e local: continuidade e mudança." In *Analise Social*, vol. 21 (87-88-89), p. 912; António Barreto, Clara Valadas Preto, "Indicadores Sociais: Portugal, 1960-2000." In António Barreto (ed.), *A Situacao Social em Portugal 1960-1999, Vol. II. Indicadores Sociais em Portugal e a União Europeia* (Lisbon: Instituto de Ciencias Sociais 2000), p. 225.

to do it on its own. The European *vincolo esterno* (external link) became a major way out of the crisis that existed with both the political class and public administration. As with Greece, Spain, and Italy, the European Community meant modernization and democratization simultaneously.[29] The EC/EU as the external link to modernization had varied effects. Firstly, Portuguese public administration had to open up and become more transparent, which meant that it had to obtain reliable empirical data, so that adjustments to the demands of the European Union could be undertaken. Secondly, European public policy required a pool of competent personnel so that Regional Development Plans and other projects, for example, could be designed and presented to the EU authorities. Thirdly, continuous pressure was exerted on all entries of the political system. Fourthly, benchmarking and comparative analysis forced the Portuguese administration to improve its performance. And lastly, complacency was no longer tolerated; a transformation had to be made in order for the Portuguese administration to achieve the promises of a democratic state. It was only after 1986, after the absorption of the *acquis communautaire* and the rationale behind the structural funds, that Portuguese public administration was able to change from a neopatrimonial static organization to a modernizing one. The discourse of administrative reform became salient with the election of Prime Minister Anibal Cavaco Silva in 1985 and his achievement of an absolute majority in 1987. From then on until 1995 there was a frenzied struggle against time to catch up with the rest of the world. At the center of this struggle was the reform of public administration.

In 1987, a Secretariat of Administrative Modernization (*Secretariado de Modernização Administrativa*-SMA) was set up by Cavaco Silva, whose main aim was to de-bureaucratize and simplify procedures of public administration. Prime Minister Cavaco Silva had to deal with the growing pressure of Europeanization. The rationale inherent in most EC programs needed to be responded to by a more efficient administration. A lack of statistics was one of the main problems of the new democratic public administration.

Although some kind of European programming experience existed during pre-accession preparation before 1986, it was only after membership became a reality that pressure was felt across the whole administrative structure. A Regional Development Plan was presented for the period 1986-90, but only after the reform of the structural funds in 1988 did Portugal make a great effort to modernize. The crucial agent of change in this respect was the Common Support Framework (CSF) programming, which required previous negotiation of a regional development program (PDR). It was with difficulty that the unprepared and inefficient Portuguese public administration delivered the first PDR, which led to a comprehensive CSFI. The whole of Portugal was declared objectively one region and programs were interlinked to assure maximum impact of the structural funds.

The CSFI (1989-93), CSFII (1994-99), and CSFIII (1999-2006) became catalysts along with the Single European Market (SEM) and Economic and Monetary Union (EMU) for the modernization of public administration and the country. Several reforms including auditing practices and privatization were undertaken until the early 1990s under the Cavaco Silva government.[30]

In spite of all the reform, public administration continued to be heavily concentrated in Lisbon and Oporto. Attempts to create deconcentrated services were made, but the imbalances continued. While the inner parts of Portugal were affected by desertification, over 70 percent of the population was concentrated along the coastal line from Lisbon to Oporto. The CSFs were designed to reverse this process by improving infrastructures within the country, investing in and promoting industry in the regions. Without a culture of project most of the small and medium-sized enterprises had difficulty in presenting projects to the programs established within CSF.[31]

One of the major problems the Portuguese political system had to face was the fact that regionalization was an integral part of the constitution, but it was never implemented. As a provisional structure, five Commissions of Regional Coordination (*Comissões de Coordenação Regional*-CCRs) were set up in 1979, which were designed to help with the implementation of national policies and later on the European programs. The problem of the CCRs was that they were strongly dependent on decision-making from Lisbon, which naturally delayed and bureaucratized the entire process of decision-making. Indeed, the reform of public administration was always linked to this unfulfilled implementation of administrative regions. Although on the agendas of several governments in the 1980s and 1990s, it remained unfulfilled.[32] Cavaco Silva opposed the implementation of administrative, directly elected regions in Portugal, believing that this would weaken the negotiating position of Portugal vis-à-vis the European Union.[33] His preferred option was to achieve the highest level of deconcentration of the central services. Indeed, during his premiership several services were deconcentrated in 1992. The ministries of Health, Social Security, Environment, Education, and Industry established bodies in the five regions.[34]

When the Socialist government came to power in October 1995 it had as its central aim the implementation of administrative regions after a successful referendum. If we look at publications of the Socialist party before the referendum, they clearly show its strong commitment to the regionalization process. Indeed, the socialists saw this as the central issue for the overall administrative reform that they intended to achieve.[35] In reality, the overall project of regionalization was more or less delayed by the opposition during the process of design and opposed during the referendum, which took place in November 1998. After more than two decades of discussion, the project of regionalization was shelved, because two-thirds of the weak turnout was against it. The whole strategy of the Socialist government related to the modernization and democratization of the country collapsed on that day. For several days, Antonio Guterres would not be able to speak to anyone, disappointed about a result that was central to his own reform plans. More than half of the electorate decided not to vote, so that the results of the referendum were not valid, which was a major blow to the overall regionalization project. The main argument against the regionalization was a bit far-fetched, but it influenced the population.

Apart from the question of the unnecessary division of a small country into eight administrative regions, there was the argument that it would lead to the duplication of bureaucracies and to the collapse of national cohesion.[36] The referendum on 8 November 1998 illustrated two points. First, the population did not see the advantages of regionalization as democratization and decentralization of central power from Lisbon and Oporto to the regions and, more importantly, they felt alienated from a political class that only after twenty-four years was introducing mechanisms of consultation. These viewpoints contributed to abstention and passivity in relation to the regionalization question.[37]

This caused major problems for a government that was convinced it could win the population for regionalization, which was part of the constitution. The reelection of Antonio Guterres in October 1999 showed the problem the government in dealing with the popular verdict. Only after the Portuguese presidency of the European Union, which took place in the first half of the year 2000, did some major reform of the government structure take place. The upgrading of the issue of modernization of public administration and state reform to a ministry and the rearrangement of all related departments in this direction, showed again how important it was to improve efficiency in public administration. Major restructuring took place during 2001. This restructuring became a priority due to the fiscal problems that the public sector was causing for the government. As already mentioned, Portugal passed the allowed 3 percent margin of budget deficit in 2001. Public administrative reform is essential, so that the Portuguese government can gain again more maneuverability in its policy choices. The present coalition government had to undertake drastic measures, including the centralization of all finances under Superminister Manuela Ferreira Leite, so that budget 2002 until 2004 does not cross the 3 percent margin.

A Profile of Portuguese Public Administration

In spite of many declarations, the Portuguese civil service continued to rise throughout the 1990s. Between 1968 and 1999 the civil service increased by 345 percent. This number shows the problems that the Portuguese government is facing in terms of sustaining this large corps of civil servants in relation to the population. At the moment, the ratio is one civil servant to

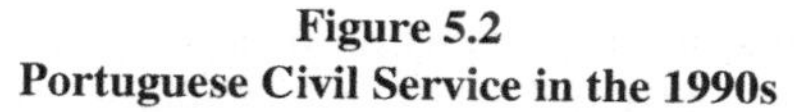

Figure 5.2
Portuguese Civil Service in the 1990s

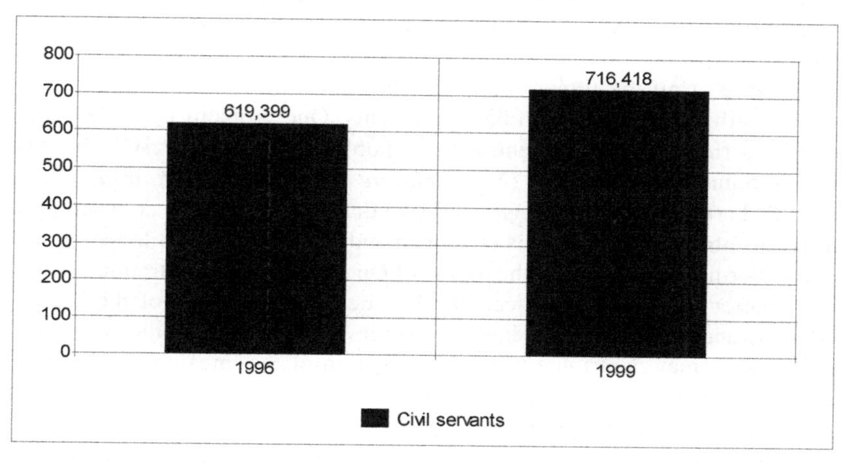

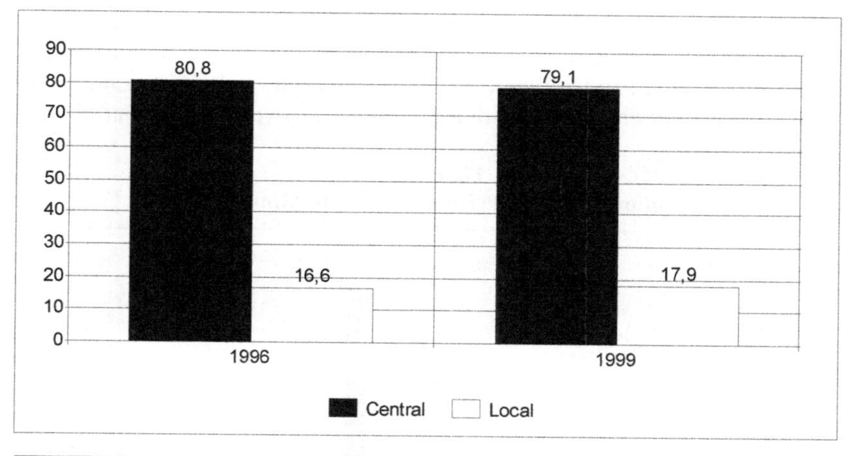

Source: Ministry of State and Public Administration Reform (MREAP), Public Administration in Figures (Lisbon: DGAP, 1996); MREAP, *Administração Pública em Números. II Recenseamento da Administração Pública* (Lisbon: MREAP, 2000).

fourteen citizens. As in most other West European countries, the civil service is concentrated in the areas of health and education. Employment in Portuguese civil service does not fare badly in relation to other European countries. The average ratio of public employment in overall employment in the OECD countries is 15.15 percent. The Portuguese figure is slightly below it, coming to 14.2 percent of the active population and 14.8 percent of the employed population.[38] Education, in particular, occupies a privileged place in Portuguese administration. Expansion of the education sector to the regions throughout the 1980s and 1990s was a major priority of the government, as was the Portuguese National Health Service, which is universal and has been expanded considerably in the past decades (see figure 5.3).[39]

In spite of all the transformations and improvements, Portuguese civil service still suffers from two basic problems. One problem is the fact that despite a rhetoric of deconcentration of public service, most civil servants can be found in two NUTSII (*Nomenclature of Statistical Territorial Units*), so-called artificial regions (*regiões*). More than one-third of all civil servants are concentrated in the regions of Lisbon and Vale do Tejo, while the region of the North, which includes the region of Oporto, has a concentration of only one-quarter of the civil service. The less developed regions of the center, Alentejo and Algarve, clearly have a lower level of presence of the state. This discrepancy may contribute to the perpetuation of the imbalances in Portugal. Over 65 percent of civil servants are still concentrated in the regions of Porto and Lisbon. The previous Socialist government wanted to overcome this persistence towards heavy concentration in the two regions by introducing new laws on the Deconcentration of the State and Territorial Administration. This move may lead to a gradual deconcentration of the central service towards local civil service functions. Reducing central administration is the main dilemma of public administration.[40] Presently, over 51.1 percent of civil

Figure 5.3
Distribution of Civil Service According to Ministries (1999)

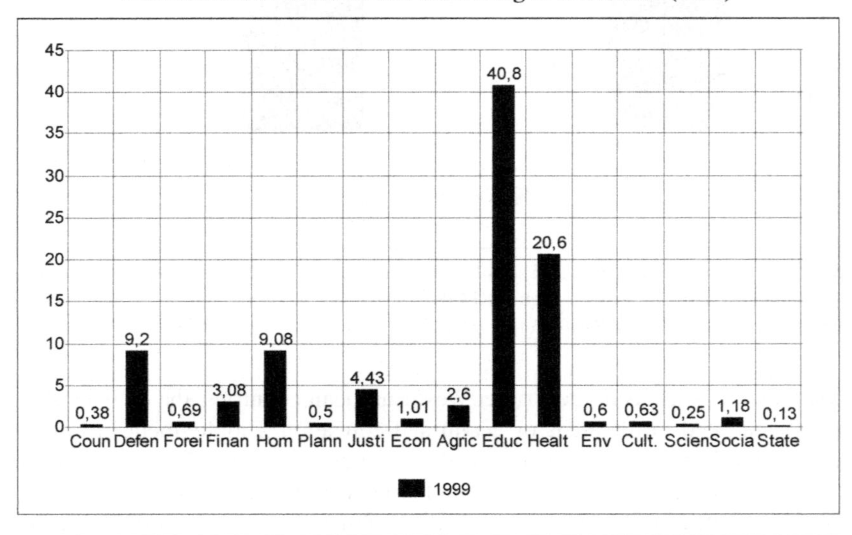

Source: MREAP, *Administração Pública em Números. II Recenseamento da Administração Pública* (Lisbon: MREAP, 2000).

service is in the central administrative services, while 28 percent is regionally deconcentrated. This means that 79.1 percent is central administration and only 21.9 percent is actually local or regional autonomous administration. The coalition government under Durão Barroso wants to reinforce the autonomy of local government; thus, it is expected that further deconcentration processes to the local level will continue to take place in the next couple of years.

The second major problem of public administration is the level of qualifications. As figure 5.5 documents, the majority of civil servants has only a secondary education or less, while about one-third has a higher degree of education. Still, in spite of attempts at reform, very few have achieved a Master's degree or a Ph.D., which require a lengthy period of study in Portugal compared to other countries (see figure 5.5).

Nevertheless, the majority of higher education degree holders can be found in the education and health sectors, which tends to relativizes this figure. In reality, excluding the health and education sectors, we come to a more realistic figure of a lower level of qualifications. The predominant qualifications of an average civil servant are mid-secondary school qualifications, accounting for 25.1 percent of all civil servants. People with a less than primary school education are a disappearing minority within the civil service.

If we look at the periods of employment, we can recognize the fact that today's civil service has already achieved a generational change. The over-

Figure 5.4
Distribution of Civil Service According to Nuts II Regions

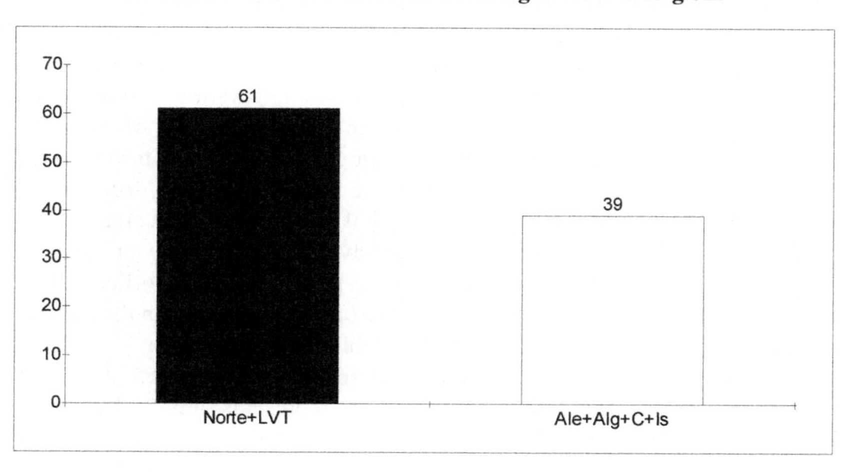

Source: MREAP, *Administração Pública em Números. II Recenseamento da Administração Pública* (Lisbon: MREAP, 2000). Regions Norte, Lisboa and Vale do Tejo (LVT), Alentejo (Ale), Algarve (Alg.), Centro (C), islands of Madeira and Azores (Is.).

Figure 5.5
Educational Background of Portuguese Civil Service (1999)

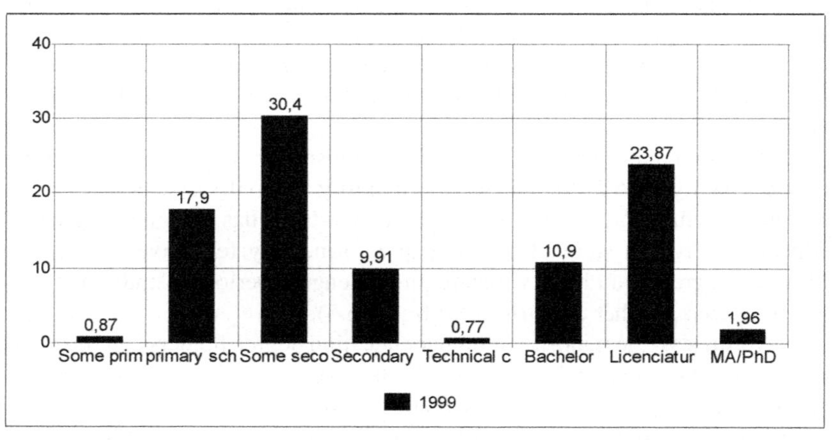

Source: MREAP, *Administração Pública em Números. II Recenseamento da Administração Pública* (Lisbon: MREAP 2000).

whelming majority of civil servants was hired after the Revolution of Carnations in 1974. Moreover, it is expected that one-fifth of the civil service may retire in the next few years because they are approaching or have approached retirement age. This fact may free up places for more investment in the deconcentrated services. Quite interesting is the fact that over 52 percent of the civil service was hired after accession to the EC in 1986, which means that European integration contributed somewhat to the integration of more staff. This becomes particularly salient in terms of the employment of local authorities, which hired over 70 percent of their staff after 1986. This evidence points to the continuing effort of Portuguese administration to decentralize and shift the priorities to a deconcentrated civil service. The main areas where employment increased above or around the average after 1986 were justice, education, health, and culture as well as the prime minister's office, all of which appears to confirm some impact of European integration on the recruitment of public administration (figure 5.6; table 5.2).

In terms of gender, central public administration consists of 55: 2 percent women, while in local public administration it represents only 32.2 percent. Portuguese public administration also has a low number of young persons aged 25 or younger with a percentage of 4.9 percent. Most of the public administration consists of civil servants who are over forty years old.

In sum, Portuguese public administration still has a long way to go in regard to its long-term restructuring program. In spite of a rhetoric of

Figure 5.6
Seniority in Portuguese Civil Service According to Tiers of Government (1999)

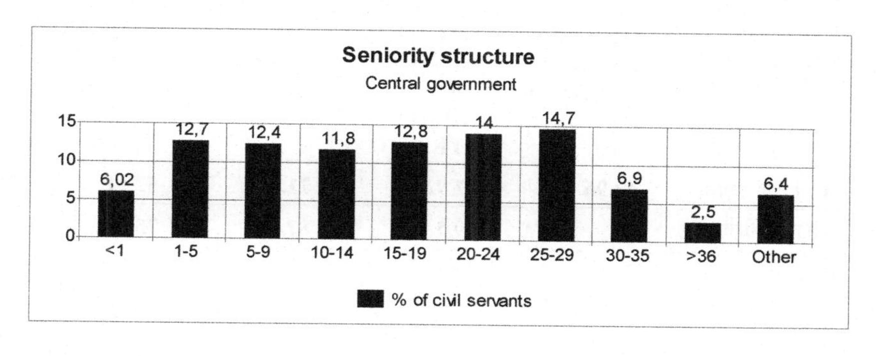

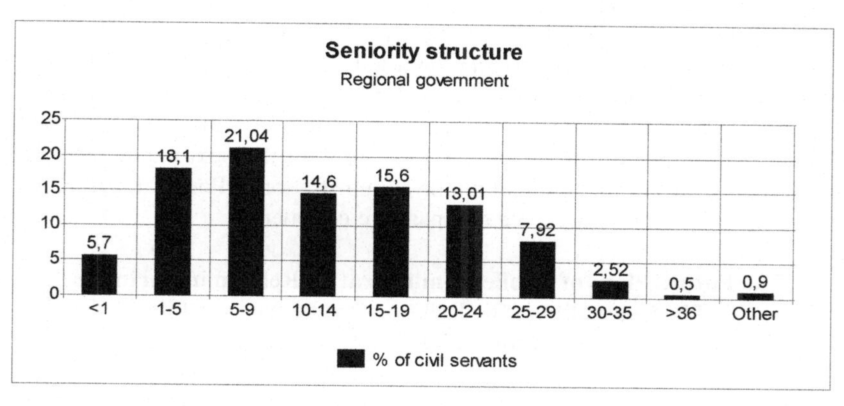

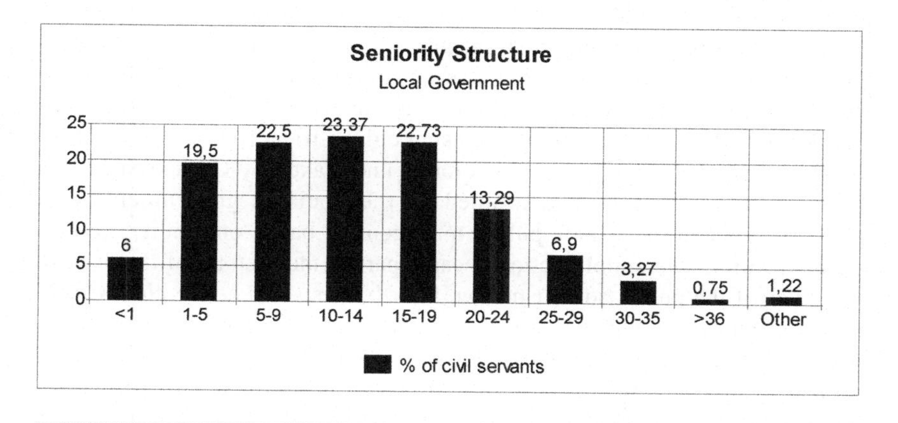

Source: MREAP, *Administração Pública em Números. II Recenseamento da Administração Pública* (Lisbon: MREAP, 2000).

Table 5.2
Employment Longevity

TIME OF ENTRANCE	CENTRAL ADMINI-STRATION	REGIONAL AUTONO-MOUS ADMINI-STRATION	LOCAL ADMINI-STRATION	AVERAGE
AFTER 1986	**42.96**	**42.92**	**71.37**	**52.41**
AFTER 1974	70	69.5	87.86	75.8
BEFORE 1974	24.1	24.1	10.92	19.71

deconcentration, the major problems of public administration have yet to be solved. The two main problems are the high level of civil service concentration around Lisbon and Oporto and the low level of qualifications. Through pressure from Europeanization and the Economic Monetary Union macroeconomic plans, different policy areas, for the sake of democratization, will continue to push towards considerable reforms. In the next pages, we will discuss the plans for the future of public administration in Portugal, before we arrive at conclusions with some comparative comments.

The Future Plans of Public Administrative Reform in Portugal: The Centrality of the Relationship between Public Administration and Citizens

The past seventeen years have been years of continuing the transformation of Portuguese public administration. Since 1986 the whole approach of public administration changed, from public administration as an institution of power to public administration as an institution serving the public. This shift led to major transformations and changes in behavior. The main task was to open up public administration to make it citizen-friendly in view of fulfilling the change of paradigm.[41] The reforms undertaken by Cavaco Silva between 1985 to 1995 were continued by the Socialist government. The philosophy/ideology of new public management based on quality, de-bureaucratization, and simplification became part of the rhetoric of the overall workings of the public administration. New bodies, such as the *citizens-administration forum* and the *enterprises-administration committee,* became important interfaces in relations with the outside world. Both bodies were formed to advise public administration in terms of improving and simplifying administrative practices.[42] Despite the rhetoric, however, there is a general feeling that the actual consultation process, in particular that of citizens' or organized civil society organizations, is taking place at a very late stage of the decision-making process. Citizens and organized civil society are provided with pre-selected information that is formulated in a highly technical language so as to prevent a closer relationship and cooperation.[43]

Several documents were finally produced to regulate the relations of public administration and citizens and disseminate the practice of quality enhancement and control throughout public administration from a macro-, meso-, and microperspective. Most publications advocated a continuing effort of simplification of procedures, de-bureaucratization, and growing deconcentration and decentralization of services from central and regional to the local authority level. Theoretical and empirical documents were produced in view of becoming more knowledgeable about public administration. The best example is the excellent report of the ad hoc Commission for quality and rationalization of the public administration (*Comissão para a Qualidade e Racionalização da Administração Publica*) set up by the Council of Ministers in 1993. In March 1994, the Commission produced a report that gave a general overview of the public administration and its main problems. It recognized three main challenges for public administration in the future: quality, rationalization, and convergence. The third aspect is particularly relevant here. It is a challenge that has been mentioned since 1986 and is related to the need to adjust to the overall European administrative space. The aspect of convergence to Europe is clearly linked to the idea of *vincolo esterno,* which emphasizes the symbiosis of modernization with Europeanization. The Commission's recommendations concentrated on achieving a long-term plan of desintervention of the state in the economy and society by subcontracting services and by greatly improving the quality of service to the citizens.[44] As mentioned in many other publications, deconcentration and decentralization from central to regional and local government is regarded as an important structural measure to achieving these aims.[45]

In the second half of the 1990s, the mere pursuit of quality enhancement became an addition to the important challenge of achieving convergence to the European Union. Several documents gave as rationale the need to become part of the European administrative space.[46]

This rhetoric of total quality, rationalization, simplification, and decentralization has contributed to an improvement of public services, although there is still a long way to go towards a more citizen-friendly public administration. Major efforts were made in the past decade to inform citizens about their rights according to the Portuguese constitution, particularly vis-à-vis public administration.[47] Moreover, the establishment of a Code of Administrative Procedures and the production of an ethical charter of public administration improved relations between the public and public administration. In addition, an online information database on the main issues related to citizenry was created, forming a network of support for citizens based on the principle of electronic government, and a decentralized, so-called citizen's shop (or one-stop shops—*lojas do cidadão*) was established. The citizen's shop concentrates in one place all the major public services that citizens may need (such as identity cards, ability to pay bills, passport renewal, registration of vehicles, driver's licenses, and so on).

This project, begun in 1997 in Lisbon and Oporto, was expanded to other cities such as Aveiro, Viseu, Setubal, and Braga. Moreover, smaller units of facilitation of access to public administration were to be deployed in smaller towns and villages.[48] According to a 2001 opinion poll conducted by the then Ministry of Administrative Reform, 48.3 percent of respondents were happy with public services, but 43.9 percent were not. Discontentment with the justice system has risen to 51.9 percent of respondents, clearly indicating that any Portuguese government will be under pressure in the foreseeable future to deliver further improvements in the quality of public services.[49]

Further internal reforms were initiated by the outgoing government to include a more rigorous impartial code for recruitment of senior personnel, which is being monitored by an internal accompanying and observing committee of competitions for senior positions (*Comissão de Observação e Acompanhamento de Concursos para Cargos Dirigentes*) and the establishment in 1997 of an Interministerial Network for Administrative Modernization (*Rede Interministerial para a Modernização Administrativa-RIMA*) which aimed at integrating all services to achieve modernization, simplification, and de-bureaucratization of public administration. The interministerial network consists of units of administrative reform in each ministry that is in direct dependency to the Ministry of State Reform and Administrative Reform.

The linkage between administrative reform and regional development was further strengthened by the inclusion in the most recent Community Support Framework (CSF III) of two areas of investment to modernize public administration. The programs, "Open State- Modernizing Public Administration" and "Improve Qualifications to Modernize Public Administration," clearly were created in an effort to improve and simplify relations between public administration and its users (citizens and enterprises). It is hoped that they will target the extension and improvement of information society services and the improvement of job opportunities in the regions.

After the presidency of the European Union in the first half of 2000, the Portuguese government started a major restructuring of its administrative reform structures. The Ministry was reorganized. Services were amalgamated and new strategic structures put in place. The Secretariate for Administrative Reform was abolished and replaced in November 2001 by an Institute for Innovation of the State Administration (*Instituto de Inovação da Administração do Estado*-IIAE), which more or less retains the function of monitoring processes of administrative reform. A first document was pro-

Table 5.3
The Ethical Chart of Portuguese Public Administration

PRINCIPLES	EXPLANATION
Principle of public service	Civil servants are at exclusive service of the community and citizens, the public interest before individual or group interests.
Principle of legality	Civil servants act according to the constitutional principles and according to the law.
Principle of justice and impartiality	Civil servants in their acting duty shall treat all citizens in an equal and impartial way, acting according to rigorous principles of neutrality
Principle of equality	Civil servants cannot discriminate citizens according to their social origins, gender, race, language, political, ideological or religious convictions, economic or social situation.
Principle of proportionality	Civil servants exercising their duty can only ask from the citizens the indispensable for the fulfilment of the administrative activity
Principle of cooperation and good	Civil servants exercising their duty, faith shall cooperate with the citizens according to the principle of good faith, so that the interest of the community is fulfilled and their participation in the administrative activity is encouraged.
Principle of information and quality	Civil servants shall inform or clarify citizens in a clear ,simple, courteous and fast way.
Principle of loyalty	Civil servants exercising their duty, ought to act loyally, solidarously and cooperatively
Principle of integrity	Civil servants are regulated by principles of personal honesty and character integrity
Principle of competence and responsibility	Civil servants act responsibly and competently, dedicated and critically, in view of their professional self-enhancement

Source: SMA, *Carta Ética. Dez Principios da Administração Publica* (Lisbon: SMA, 1999).

duced, setting out clearly the main objectives for the future. The Mission Statement and Strategic Measures emphasize the continuity of the reform. Deconcentration and decentralization of public administration to the local level and the improvement of the qualifications of staff continue to be crucial items. Naturally, the total quality management philosophy is already an integral part of the overall process of modernization.[50] Although it is too early to say whether it will continue, the Durão Barroso government has committed itself to continue on the path of administrative reform. While the present government reduced the number of ministries, it has kept the Institute for Innovation of the State Administration (IIAE) in order to continue the reform of the administration, which consists of two main priorities: (1) reduction of personnel by targeted freezing of further employment in targeted sectors and the reemployment of surplus personnel to services where there is a lack of personnel, and (2) the devolution of finances, competences, and personnel to local authorities, because it is felt that there is more value-added productivity if funding is spent at the local rather than the central level.[51] One positive aspect is that finally a reform of administrative law was undertaken. It took fourteen years to make this major reform, far too long if modernization is to be achieved at a faster pace than that of the rest of the European Union. The main rationale is one of revolutionary change from the French to the German model.[52] Hopefully, it will contribute to creating more certainties in the administrative system and to the restoration or establishment of full administrative cycles, which will allow administrative memory to become part of the process of reform.[53]

In sum, the politics of administration reform in Portugal has translated into a continuing process based on the principle of good governance since 1986. It became a serious attempt after 1991. The importance of a *vincolo esterno* in pushing reforms forward and opening up the former patrimonial state cannot be emphasized enough. It appears that the European Union and a convergence towards the European administrative space helped to break the cycle of mere rhetoric towards concrete processual transformation. Despite the progress, Portuguese public administration still faces the challenge of decentralizing the administration from the central to the local level and improving the qualifications of civil servants.[54] The *vincolo esterno* will be used to further democratize and decentralize the Portuguese public administration in the next decade.

Conclusions: Portugal and the European Administrative Space

Portugal's legacy of an authoritarian regime until 1974 conditioned its strategies towards a more democratic and decentralized state after transition to democracy. The main difficulty was overcoming the patrimonial vicious cycle of rhetoric and political instability. Accession to the EC in 1986 may be considered the turning point for administrative reform and democratization of public administration in Portugal. What began as a quest for catching up with the more advanced member-states, became an integrated effort of all fifteen public administrations and the European Commission. This naturally was linked with the continuing preoccupation with regional development. The Europeanization of public administration in Portugal means not only modernization, democratization, and decentralization; beyond that, it means interdependent integration into a European administrative space, which naturally changes the logics of administrative reform and regional development from one of nationhood to one of multilevel governance and Single European market building. The harmonization of the languages of the fifteen public administrations towards total quality enhancement based on principles of new public management clearly indicate that Europeanization is only one factor of the overall European integration process. In reality, Europeanization has to be complemented by an ongoing process of creation of a European public space, what I would call a domestication of European Union politics in different fields, including administration.

Notes

1. Term borrowed from Kenneth Dyson, Kevin Featherstone, "Italy and EMU as a 'Vincolo Esterno': Empowering the Technocrats, Transforming the State," in *South European Society and Politics*, 1, 2, Autumn 1996: 272-299.
2. Republique Francaise, Ministére de la fonction publique de la reforme d'Etat et de la decentralisation, *Rapport annuel de relations internationales et de la cooperation administrative.1998-99* (Paris: MFPRED, 1999), 9-11; European Institute for Public Administration, *Annual Report 2000* (Maastricht: EIPA, 2001), 8.
3. Republique Francaise, *Rapport Annuel*, 14.
4. European Institute for Public Administration, *Annual Report 2000* (Maastricht: EIPA, 2001), 5.
5. OECD, Reform of the Public Administration in Europe (http: //www.1.oecd.org/puma/focus/compend/eu.html).
6. Ministério da Reforma do Estado e da Administração Publica, *CAF: Common Assessment Framework* (Lisbon: MREAP, 2000), 1-5. The nine assessment criteria are (1) Leadership; (2) Policy and Strategy; (3) Human Resource Management; (4) External Partnerships and Resources; (5) Process and Change Management; (6) Customer-Citizen Oriented Results; (7) People (employees) Results; (8) Impact on Society; (9) Key Performance Results.
7. Ministério da Reforma do Estado e da Administração Publica, *First Quality Conference for Public Administrations in the EU* (Lisbon: MREAP. 2000), 5-7.
8. Republique Francaise, *Rapport Annuel*, 13. It was established in 1992 and opened to the EEA countries and Central and Eastern Europe in 1998.
9. June Burnham, Moshe Maor, "Converging Administrative Systems: Recruitment and Training in EU Member States," *Journal of European Public Policy* 2:2, June 1995: 185-204; particularly 190-191
10. The European Commission, *Reforming the Commission. A White Paper*, Brussels, 1 March 2000, COM (2000), 200 final, two volumes; see also David Spence,

"Plus ca change, plus c'est la meme chose? Attempting to Reform the Commission," *Journal of European Public Policy* 7, 1, March 2000: 1-25, and Laura Cram, "Whither the Commission? Reform, Renewal and Issue-Attention," *Journal of European Public Policy*, 8, 5, October 2001: 770-786.

11. Robert A. Jones, "The European Union," in J. A.Chandler (ed.), *Comparative Public Administration* (London, New York: Routledge 2000), 173-199; particularly 191-193.
12. See the comparative study of Germany and UK by Christoph Knill, *The Europeanisation of National Administrations* (Cambridge: Cambridge UniversityPress, 2001).
13. One has only to mention the compliance rate of each member state to see the asymmetrical nature of the "European administrative space"; see the excellent study of Tanja Börzel, "Non-compliance in the European Union: Pathology or Statistical Artefact," *Journal of European Public Policy*, 8, 5, October 2001: 803-824.
14. *The Economist*, 23 February 2002, pp. 45-46.
15. Michelle Everson, "Administering Europe?" *Journal of Common Market Studies* 36, 2, June 1998: 195-215. Everson is quite critical of the concept of governance, which does not solve at the all the growing problems of multilevel administration of the market and the constitutional implications attached to it: "Gone is the notion that European administration might do no wrong. With it has disappeared the curious logical detachment of European administrative activity from constitutional considerations about the overall place of delegated legislation within the polity or, more precisely, from theoretical concerns about what administration should and should not doing, and who should define its tasks. Rather, with its efforts to ascertain the best possible means to protect the individual European citizen's law, but limited, political and more general 'human rights,' including the right to 'fair administration,' European administrative law thinking has necessarily begun (albeit implicitly) to address the related questions of where European administration derives its mandate from, what the limits of this mandate are and who may challenge its execution, and under what conditions" (pp. 204-205), and her conclusion, "The process of EU market socialization remains uncertain while the character of the emerging European polity has yet to be settled. Under such conditions, administrative law's traditional role of ensuring the accountability and fidelity of delegated legislation is obsolete: accountable to whom, faithful to what? EU administrative law accordingly has no choice but to develop new models of administration and its oversight and to admit the fact the delegated market management is far more than a simple matter of transmission" (p. 215).
16. A governance approach towards public administration will overcome the boundaries between public and private and between civil service and citizens. New spaces have to be created to assure governance processes of consultation, cooperation, transparency and accountability. See Charles J. Fox, Hugh T. Miller, *Postmodern Public Administration. Towards Discourse* (London: SAGE, 1995); see also Anthony Giddens, *Modernity and Self-Identity. Self and Society in the Late Modern Age* (Cambridge: Polity Press, 1991): Institutional reflexivity is "the regularised use of knowledge about circumstances of social life as a constitutive element in its organisation and transformation" (p.20).
17. Thomas Christiansen, "Tensions of European Governance: Politicized Bureaucracy and the Multiple Accountability in the European Commission," *Journal of European Public Policy* 4, 1, March 1997: 73-90; Andreas Maurer, Jürgen Mittag, Wolfgang Wessels, "Theoretical Perspectives on Administrative Interaction in the European Union," Thomas Christiansen, Emil Kirchner (eds.), *Committee Gover-*

nance in the European Union (Manchester: Manchester University Press, 2000), 21-44.

18. Thomas Christiansen, Knud-Erik Jorgensen, "Transnational Governance 'Above' and 'Below' the State: The Changing Nature of Borders in the New Europe," *Regional Studies* 10, 2, Summer 2000: 62-77; L. Hooghe, G. Marks, *Multilevel Governance and European Integration* (Lanham: Rowman and Littlefields, 2001); M. Jachtenfuchs, "The Governance Approach to European Integration," *Journal of Common Market Studies* 39, 2, 2001: 245-64.
19. The Government of the Future, *OECD Public Management Policy Brief*, no. 9, June 2001; Engaging Citizens in Policy Making Information, Consultation and Public Participation, *OECD, Public Management Policy Brief*, no.10, July 2001.
20. Joaquim Aguiar, *O Pós-Salazarismo. 1974-1984* (Lisbon: Dom Quixote, 1985), who clearly ends his book with a critical voice about the limits of any internationalization if the Portuguese political elites do not recognize that the problems of the Portuguese patrimonial state are nationally made and need really a break from the patrimonial cycle; see pp. 200-205.
21. António Costa Pinto, "Dealing with the Legacy of Authoritarianism: Political Purges and Radical Right Movements in Portugal´s Transition to Democracy 1974-1980," in Stein Ugelvik Larsen (ed.), *Modern Europe After Fascism. 1943-1980s* (New York: Columbia 1998), 1679-1717; particularly 1683-84 and 1686-88. See also Lawrence S. Graham, "Bureaucratic Politics and the Problem of Reform in the State Apparatus," in Lawrence S. Graham and Douglas L. Wheeler (eds.), *In Search of Modern Portugal: The Revolution and Its Consequences* (Madison: The University of Wisconsin Press 1982). This happened also among the judiciary. The revolutionary process led to the establishment of People's Tribunals challenging the justice of the bourgeoisie; see A. M. Hespanha, "As Transformações Revolucionárias e o Discurso dos Juristas," *Revista Critica de Ciencias Sociais* 18/19/20, February 1986: 311-341.
22. José M. Magone, *European Portugal. The Difficult Road to Sustainable Democracy* (Basingstroke: Macmillan, Palgrave, 1997, 2001), 27-33; 46; José M. Magone, "Portugal: The Rationale of Democratic Regime Building," in Wolfgang C. Müller, Kaare Strom (eds.), *Coalition Governments in Western Europe* (Oxford: Oxford University Press, 2000), 529-558.
23. It is estimated that public administration provided 35,000 to 45,000 people with jobs when they came from the former colonies or became unemployed. See Lawrence S. Graham, "Administração publica central and local: Mudança e continuidade," *Analise Social* XXI (87-88-89), 1985: 903-924; particularly 913.
24. Walter C. Opello, Jr., "Portugal's Administrative Elite: Social Origins and Political Attitudes," *West European Politics* 6, 1, January 1983: 69.
25. Philippe C. Schmitter, "The 'Regime d'Exception' That Became the Rule: Forty-Eight Years of Authoritarian Domination in Portugal," in Lawrence S. Graham and Harry M. Makler (eds.), *Contemporary Portugal. The Revolution and Its Antecedents* (Austin: University of Texas, 1974), 3-46; particularly 19; see also Manuel Braga da Cruz, *O Partido e o Estado no Salazarismo* (Lisbon: Editorial Presença, 1988), 210.
26. Schmitter, "The 'Regime of Exception,'" 22-23; Harry M. Makler, "The Portuguese Industrial Elite and Its Corporative Relations: A Study of Compartmentalization in an Authoritarian Regime," in Lawrence S. Graham and Harry M. Makler (eds.), *Contemporary Portugal. The Revolution and Its Antecedents* (Austin: University of Texas, 1974), 123-145; particularly 140-141.

27. It corresponded in 1982 to 7.8 percent of employment among the active population; for an assessment, see J. M. Torres Campos, Empresas Públicas," in Manuela Silva (ed.), *Portugal Contemporaneo. Problemas e Perspectivas* (Lisbon: INA, 1986), 437-459; particularly 443. In comparison Germany employed 7.8 percent, Belgium 8 percent, France 14.6 percent, and Italy 26.8 percent.
28. Here is not the place to discuss the nature of the patrimonial state in Portugal, see for that Boaventura de Sousa Santos, *O Estado e a Sociedade em Portugal* (1974-1988) (Porto: Afrontamento, 1990) and Joaquim Aguiar, "Partidos, estruturas patrimonialistas e poder funcional: A crise de legitimidade," *Análise Social* 21, 1985: 759-783.
29. "Vincolo esterno" stands for external link, meaning here the impact of the EU on modernization of public administration. See Kenneth Dyson, Kevin Featherstone, "Italy and EMU as a 'Vincolo Esterno': Empowering the Technocrats, Transforming the State," *South European Society and Politics* 1, 2, Autumn 1996, 272-279.
30. For an assessment of the Common Support Frameworks, see José M. Magone, "The Transformation of the Portuguese Political System: European Regional Policy and Democratization in a Small EU Member State," *South European Society and Politics* 5, 2, Autumn 2000: 119-140; Luis Madureira Pires, *A Politica Regional Europeia e Portugal* (Lisbon: Fundação Calouste Gulbenkian, 1998); Isabel Mota, "Application of Structural Funds," in Alvaro de Vasconcelos, Maria Joao Seabra (eds.), *Portugal. A European Story* (Cascais: Principia, 2000), 131-152; António Covas, *Integração Europeia, Regionalização Administrativa e Reforma do Estado-Nacional* (Oeiras: INA, 1997). See chapter 8.
31. M. Eaton, "Regional Development Funding in Portugal," *Journal of the Association for Contemporary Iberian Studies* 7/2, Autumn: 36-46.
32. César Oliveira, "A questao da regionalização," in César Oliveira (ed.), *História dos Municipios e Poder Local* (Lisbon: Temas e Debates, 1996), 495-509, particularly 499-503.
33. José M. Magone, *European Portugal. The Difficult Road to Democracy* (Basingstroke: Macmillan 1997).
34. OECD, *Managing Across Levels of Government* (Paris: OECD, 1997), 376.
35. Grupo Parlamentar do Partido Socialista, *Regionalizar. Cumprir a Constituição e Concretizar uma Reforma* (Lisbon: PS 1998); Ministério do Equipamento, do Planeamento e da Administração do Território, *Descentralizacao, Regionalização e Reforma Democrática do Estado* (Lisbon: MEPAT 1998), 21-24.
36. Articles on arguments from both sides can be found in António Barreto, *Regionalização. Sim ou Não* (Lisbon: Publicações Dom Quixote, 1998).
37. On the referendum results, see Tom Gallagher, "Unconvinced by Europe of the Regions: The 1998 Regionalization Referendum in Portugal," *South European Society and Politics* 4, 1 (Summer 1999): 132-148; Alvaro Xosé López Mira, in *Regional and Federal Studies*, 9, 2 (Summer 1999): 98-105; David Corkill, "Portugal´s 1998 Referendum," *West European Politics* 22, 2: 186-192; José M. Magone, Maria José Stock, "Portugal," *European Journal for Political Research* 34 (1998): 507-511; particularly 508-509; José M. Magone, "Portugal," *European Journal for Political Research* 38 (2000): 499-510.
38. Ministério da Reforma do Estado e da Administração Pública, *Intervencao do Senhor Ministro da Reforma do Estado e da Administração Publica, Sessao de apresentacao do 2°Recenseamento Geral da Administração Publica*, Centro Cultural de Belém,19 de Setembro de 2001(http: //www.mreap.gov.pt/docs/resenc.html).
39. One can argue about the quality of the services which has deteriorated in 2001. Rising waiting lists, lack of doctors, nurses and specialists and a growing deficit

are some of the problems. The former Socialist government had to recruit doctors in Spain. Over 40 percent of doctors are too old and will retire within the next decade (*Expresso*, 13 April 2001); for a summary of health policy in Portugal, see Carlos Gouveia Pinto, Saúde e Cuidados de Saúde," in *Portugal Hoje* (Oeiras: INA, 1995), 162-178.

40. Ministério da Reforma do Estado e da Administração Pública, *Intervenção do Senhor Ministro da Reforma do Estado e da Administração Publica, Sessão de apresentação do 2°Recenseamento Geral da Administração Publica*, Centro Cultural de Belém,19 de Setembro de 2001(http: //www.mreap.gov.pt/docs/resenc.html). Accessed in November 2001.
41. Laura Lampreia, *Contributos para uma nova Cultura da Gestão Pública* (Lisbon: SMA 1997), 9-12; 18.
42. Secretariado para a Modernização Administrativa, *Comissão de Empresas-Administração. Plano de Actividades 1997/99,Regulamento de Funcionamento* (Lisbon: SMA 1998); Secretariado para a Modernização Administrativa, *Forum Cidadãos-Administração. Regulamento e Funcionamento* (Lisbon: SMA 1998).
43. João Salis Gomes, "Perspectivas da Moderna Gestão Pública," in Juan Mozzicafreddo, João Salis Gomes (eds.), *Administração e Política. Perspectivas de Reforma da Administração Pública na Europa e nos Estados Unidos* (Oeiras: Celta 2001), 77-102; particularly 93.
44. Relatório da Comissão para a Qualidade e Racionalização da Administração Pública, *Renovar a Administração* (Lisbon: Secretaria do Estado da Modernização Administrativa, 1994), 8; 47-48; 80; 108-113.
45. Relatorio da Comissão para a Qualidade e Racionalização da Administração Pública, *Renovar*, 125-127.
46. Secretariado para a Modernização Administrativa (SMA), *Gestão da Qualidade. Conceitos, Sistemas de gestão, Instrumentos* (Lisbon: SMA 1995); Júlio da Mesquita Goncalves, *Desburocratização. Uma administração para o século XXI* (Lisbon: SMA, 1997); SMA, *Qualidade em Servicos Publicos* (Lisbon: SMA, 1998); SMA, *Carta de Qualidade.Um Compromisso com o Cidadão* (Lisbon: SMA, 1998); SMA, *Servicos Publicos,Da Burocracia à Qualidade* (Lisbon: SMA, 1999); SMA, *Auto-Avaliação da Qualidade em Servicos Publicos* (Lisbon: SMA, 1999).
47. SMA, *Os direitos do cidadão face à Administração Pública* (Lisbon: SMA, 1996).
48. Ministério da Reforma do Estado e da Administração Pública, Grandes Opções do Plano 2002. (http: //www.mreap.gov.pt/docs/gop2002.html); Ministério da Reforma do Estado e da Administração Publica, *First Quality Conference for Public Administrations in the EU*, 118-122.
49. *Expresso*, 5 October 2001.
50. Instituto para a Inovação da Administração do Estado, *Missão e Linhas Estratégicas.Iniciativas a desenvolver em 2002* (Lisbon: IIAE 2001)
51. *Expresso*, 17 August 2002.
52. See Law 13/2002 on Administrative and Fiscal Courts and Law 15/2002 on Judicial Proceedings in Administrative and Fiscal Courts. Both published in João Caupers, João Raposo, *A nova justica administrativa* (Lisbon: Ancors editoras, 2002).
53. Juan Mozzicafreddo, "Modernização da Administração Pública e Poder Politico," in Juan Mozzicafreddo, João Salis Gomes, *Administração*, 1-33; particularly 13.
54. One cannot deny that public administration has made major efforts to improve the qualifications of their staff through staff development courses offered by the National Institute of Administration (*Instituto Nacional de Administração*-INA) and other courses in the European Institution for Public Administration (EIPA) in Maastricht.

6

National European Union Policy Coordination in Portugal: The Establishment of a Simple System

Introduction: A Comparative Note on the Systems of EU Policy Coordination

One of the most important parts of the Portuguese administration is its interface with the European Union decision-making structures. The quality of such interface, which is mainly in charge of coordination of European Union policy, is of vital importance for the influence possibilities of a small state. The Portuguese European Union policy coordination system was built over the past three decades, particularly after accession to the European Union. One of its chief characteristics is that it is a simple, down-to-earth system that corresponds to the ambitions of a small state within the European Union. It differs from the systems established by the larger countries such as France, Germany, and the United Kingdom, which clearly have allocated the interface closer to the Prime Minister's Office.

Over the years Portugal's system has differed from the Spanish model, which is more integrated and more in line with regional governments in the EU policy coordination system. Both the Italian and Greek coordination systems were regarded as negative examples, due to the fact that they are the two laggards in compliance with EU legislation implementation into national law. The Portuguese coordination system is closer to systems of other small states such as the Netherlands, Denmark, Sweden, Luxembourg, and Finland, which still retain a unitary state structure, and differ immensely from Belgium and Austria which integrate the subnational level into the overall decision-making process. In comparative terms, the Portuguese system has learned to estimate accurately its ability to influence policy and in adjusting its coordination structures accordingly. These structures are most of the time peripheral to the supranational decision-making, but may be extremely active in matters of national importance such as the structural funds or during presidencies. As a learning process in the early stages of accession to the EC/EU, the Portuguese administration carefully studied all other coordination systems, before it put its system in place. Such a learning process has become a permanent one, as the recent presidency of 2000 has shown. In part, the Portuguese coordination system has been quite successful in achieving the main aims of the Portuguese government, which are related to ensuring that structural funds continue to flow into the country. Nevertheless, one has to acknowledge that the Portuguese government and public administration have gained enough self-confidence to venture into developing their own proposals in new policy areas, which is evident in the case of employment policy coordination and in the creation of the Lisbon employment strategy, which will continue until 2010.

The Development of EU Policy Coordination

It takes a few years to create the institutionalization of a culture. The Portuguese case clearly highlights this point, where before the final construction of the EU policy coordination was undertaken, there was a period of diplomatic, administrative and political learning about how other, more experienced countries dealt with the same phenomenon. Portugal shares one special feature with Spain and Greece—that their relationship to the European Community/European Union happened simultaneously to the process of consolidation and institutionalization of democracy in these countries. This parallel process of democratization and Europeanization makes these three countries distinctive from the experience of other EU member-states, which were already established democracies when Portugal, Spain, and Greece joined the EC/EU. For certain, one can say that Europeanization has been a positive factor for democratizing the administrative structures and culture in Portugal. Another special feature is Portugal's ability to overcome the policies of the past that led in certain periods to the Salazarist attitude, "we are proudly alone."

The European integration process required an attitude of continuous convergence of positions and administrative cultures. In this changing experience Portugal is not unique, for the same experience can be found among other countries. Between the maximalist position of Belgium, the most European of all member-states,[1] and the minimalist position of the United Kingdom, there is a continuous search for each golden decision for the specific subject. EU policy coordination in the Portuguese case soon discovered that the best position within the EU framework was twofold: (1) that the definition of the Portuguese position has to be adequate to a middle-size member-state and therefore very realistic and pragmatic; and (2) that the key to success is to have well-trained political, administrative, and diplomatic negotiators, who are able to defend the vital interests of Portugal (particularly the structural funds) but leave the negotiating table, along with the other partners, as a winner as well. It is this twofold aspect of Portuguese EU policy coordination that makes the Portuguese case so interesting.

This chapter is divided into three parts. The first part deals with the making of the EU policy coordination machinery in Portugal; the second part analyzes thoroughly the structure and culture of the present EU policy coordination machinery; and the last part focuses on the interaction of the EU policy coordination machinery and the political and administrative environment. Some conclusions will be drawn at the end of this chapter.

The Authoritarian Regime: EC Membership Denied

The integration of Portugal into the European Community/European Union on 1 January 1986 was prepared essentially by the political and administrative elites. The relationship between Portugal and the EC/EU had already begun in the 1960s while Portugal was still in the heydays of the authoritarian regime of dictator Antonio Oliveira Salazar; nevertheless, it was only during the 1970s that this relationship became more intense.[2] In the late days of the authoritarian regime, the Portuguese political elites attempted to join the European Union without having to pay the price of democratization. Even the initial attempt of Salazar's successor Marcelo Caetano to introduce liberalization and democratization into the authoritarian corporatist regime was prematurely halted by the ultraconservative elites around former foreign minister Franco Nogueira[3] and Americo Tomaz. Negotiations for the entry of Portugal into the EC/EU started on 27 November 1970 and ended on 22 July 1972 with the signature of trade agreements with the EC and the ECSC. The two ministries responsible for the negotiations were finances and economy, but they were coordinated by foreign minister Dias Rosas, who was replaced later by Rui Patricio. In this sense, the Portuguese tradition allocated from the very beginning a coordinating role to the foreign ministry in the relationship with the EC/EU.[4] The purely economic relationship was partly related to the fact that the main pressure groups asking for a closer relationship with the European Union were the modernizing economic groups that had an interest in improving access to the main market for Portuguese products.[5] However, the commitment of the EC/EU was only to accept democracies as members of this new supranational organization. The so-called Birkelbach report of 1962, formulated in the European Parliament, continued to be the guiding document for the integration of new member-states in the EC. The definition could be found already in Article 237 of the Treaty of Rome, in which the precondition for the accession was to be a parliamentary democracy of West European style. The Birkelbach report further specified: "Only states which

Figure 6.1
National EU Policy Coordination in Portugal (domestic and supranational levels)

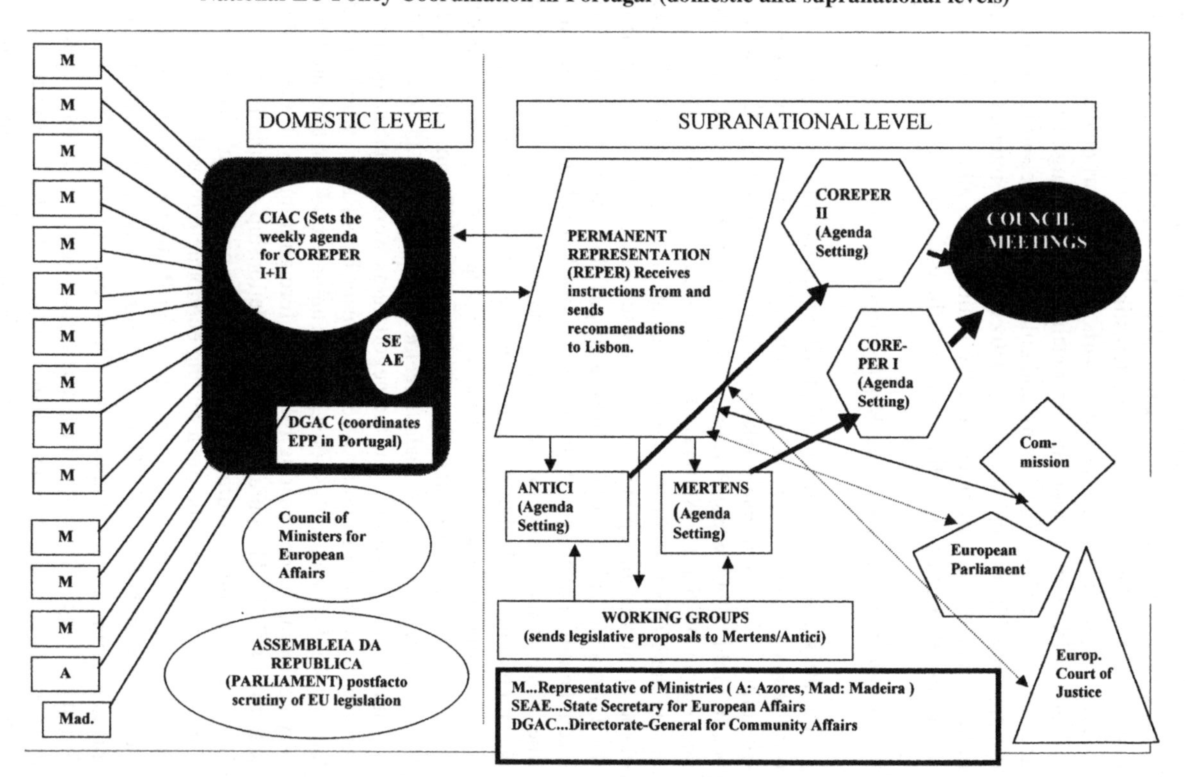

guarantee on their territories truly democratic practices and respect for the fundamental rights and freedoms can become members of our Community."[6]

The Revolutionary Period (1974-75): Monitoring Portuguese Democratic Transition

After the collapse of the authoritarian regime on 25 April 1974, the Birkelbach report continued to be the main document measuring Portugal's ability to become member of the EC. The coup d' etat staged by the colonels against the authoritarian regime developed throughout 1974 and 1975 into a revolutionary situation, which led to a situation of radicalization. Some factions of the Movement of the Armed Forces (*Movimento das Forças Armadas*-MFA) actually wanted to transform Portugal into a socialist democracy following the model set up by the Soviet Union and other countries of the third world. The options varied between Portugal being the last in the first world or the first in the third world. The EC was an important external actor monitoring the development towards democracy in Portugal. EC support was made conditional on Portugal's adoption of a parliamentary democracy west-European style. Several EC delegations went to Portugal to make officials aware of this condition. In this sense, the EC was an important regional monitoring agent in channeling the options of the political elites towards a European-style democracy. The last provisional government of the revolutionary period complied with this condition of the EC, in spite of the continuing radicalization and instrumentalization of the masses against their policies by extreme left-wing groups and the Communist party.[7]

The Postrevolutionary Period since 1975: The Making of Democratic EU Policy Coordination

It was only after the adoption of the constitution on 2 April 1976 that the relationship between Portugal and the EC became more normalized. Application for membership was submitted by the first Socialist minority government under the leadership of Mário Soares on March 28, 1977. The positive response of the Commission, forwarded to the Council of Ministers on 19 May 1978, established the conditions to start the negotiations of accession.[8] The negotiations between Portugal and the European Community were officially opened in Luxembourg on 17 October 1978. It was during this period that co-ordination between the different ministries took on importance. In August 1977, a Commission for European Integration (*Comissão para a Integração Europeia*) was established within the Presidency of the Council of Ministers, and was in close relationship and contact with the permanent members of the Portuguese mission to the EC. The positive opinion of the Commission and the negotiations with the EC led to the creation, in July

1979, of the Council of Ministers for European Integration (*Conselho de Ministros para a Integração Europeia*), which would meet monthly, acting as the whole administrative apparatus of policy coordination in relation to the negotiations with the EC, which began to grow and differentiate steadily. Until the accession to the EC policy, coordination would grow and gain overwhelming importance in the process of negotiations. The creation of a proper administrative service dedicated to European affairs in 1979 and its actual functioning in 1981, the so-called Secretariate for European Integration (*Secretariado de Integração Europeia*) became the stable element of the construction of the Portuguese system of EU policy coordination before and after accession.

A second feature was that during accession negotiations the Secretariate was partly integrated into the structures of the Presidency of the Council of Ministers and the Finance Ministry; however, in 1985, shortly before the membership came into force, the Secretariate was transferred to the Ministry of Foreign Affairs. The main reason presented in the decree law no. 526/85 of 31 December 1985 is that "looking at the experience of the current member-states in the conduct of EC affairs, they clearly give the responsibility to the corresponding Ministry of Foreign Affairs in coordinating internally and presenting externally the positions of the different sectoral interests of the state." At the same time in order to fulfill the tasks of coordination it received administrative autonomy within the Ministry of Foreign Affairs. As one can see from the date, this was a last minute adjustment of the Portuguese coordination structures before becoming members of the EC/EU the day after. In spite of that, the structure was well thought-out and based on lessons learned from other member states.

Despite governmental instability and ideological conflicts between left and right, the European integration process and its administrative structures were not questioned by the various parties coming to power. Although overall, despite the administrative discontinuities that existed in the different Ministries, the *Secretariado* was able to increase and improve its position within the government, mainly due to the fact that accession negotiations, as well as the period of membership, required a stronger effort of coordination and expertise.[9]

Portugal in the European Community/European Union: The Challenge for Portuguese Administration

After 1986, the whole institutional administrative framework, policy coordination, and policy processes became more stable and were dominated by long-term planning. On the one hand, this was due to the fact that Prime Minister Anibal Cavaco Silva was able to win three consecutive elections in 1985, 1987, and 1991. For a decade, the Portuguese experienced a strong stable government that had a positive impact upon the administrative structures and the policy formulation, policymaking, and implementation processes. Such a long-term approach was taken up by the Socialist government under Antonio Guterres, who clearly was determined to emphasize the continuity of policymaking in EU affairs. The Cavaco Silva decade led to a stabilization and institutionalization of the former Secretariate of European Integration, which changed its name in 1994 to State Secretariate for Community Affairs (*Secretariado de Estado para Assuntos Comunitarios*-SEAC), supported by the administrative unit General-Directorate for Communitarian Affairs (*Direcção-Geral para Assuntos Comunitarios*-DGAC).

In the past thirteen years, the DGAC has increased in terms of administrative personnel and in dealing with the widening scope of EU Policy. It took four to six years to learn to coordinate all the different ministries and create a culture of dialogue and consensus. Between 1986 and 1990, Portuguese administrators dealing with EU affairs had to cope with a substantial amount in the workload of EU policy coordination. According to the first report on Portugal's membership in the European Community in 1985-1986, the Portuguese government completely restructured its interface vis-à-vis the European Community by creating the Interministerial Commission for the European Communities (*Comissão Interministerial para as Comunidades Europeias*-CICE), as well as the General-Directorate of European Communities. At the same time, the various ministries that had an interest in community affairs established specialized units to communicate with the CICE. Quite relevant was the fact that within one year Portugal had to nominate representatives for the committees and working groups that labored in support of the council and commission. Moreover, it had to guarantee Portuguese participation in the various structures of the Community as well as in about 250 committees and 500 expert groups that worked in the Commission. In conclusion, the report estimated that Portuguese administration via the coordination of the State Secretariat of European Integration was able to guarantee participation of Portuguese representatives in over 2,500 meetings.[10] The Portuguese experience clearly demonstrates that the structures of the EC/EU were a major factor in restructuring the administrative machinery, which had been, until 1985, still searching for its own identity within the new democratic structures. The effort of adjustment required not only changed, but dynamized, mentalities, and gave orientation to the whole policymaking culture in Portugal. Indeed, one could say that after 1986 one witnessed the steady institutionalization of a reflective postmodern culture emphasizing administrative learning through participation.[11]

The Institutionalisation of EU Policy Coordination: The 1992 Presidency and the Intergovernmental Conferences of the Second Half of the 1990s

Events such as presidencies or intergovernmental conferences are taken very seriously by the Portuguese government because it believes that it is important to ensure that the national prestige is not undermined by an ill-prepared Portuguese representation. Therefore, the Portuguese administration attempted to be extremely well-prepared and updated during such sporadic events, which was one of the reasons that Portugal decided to give up on its first presidency, which occurred within such a short period after becoming a member of the European Union. This serious attitude has become an institutionalized element in the behavior of civil servants dealing with EU affairs for it is evident that Portugal believes it is of utmost importance for a small country to perform well in representing all member-states of the European Union as a collective identity. Indeed, the first Portuguese presidency took place only in the first half of 1992.

The 1992 Presidency of the European Communities: Learning by Doing

Preparation for the big event had begun already in 1988, four years prior. It started with a general assessment of the presidency and what kind of functions it had to fulfill in this period. For this purpose, an internal report of over hundred pages was produced, called "Preparation for the First Portuguese Presidency of the Council of the European Comunities" (no. 45/MNE/88). The report included information on the experiences of other presidencies as well as constraints and opportunities of the presidency. At the same time, it was decided to construct a new building that would be used by the presidency for council meetings: the so-called *Centro Cultural de Belém* (Cultural Centre of Belém-CCB). A general assessment of the resources needed both in Lisbon as well as in the representations in other member-states was undertaken, while at the same time, contacts and missions to other member-states were intensified and the liaison to the General-Secretary of the Council was strengthened.[12] During 1989, several civil servants dealing with EU affairs were trained for the big event. The main institution undertaking this training was the National Institute of Administration (*Instituto Nacional de Administração*-INA), which created training modules tailored to the needs of the Portuguese civil servants. Moreover, several civil servants were sent to France, the United Kingdom, and the Netherlands for training courses. At the same time, working groups were created to study the Spanish presidency in the first half of 1989, the French one in the second half, and contacts were intensified with the responsibles preparing the Dutch presidency and the British presidency that would take place before and after the Portuguese presidency, respectively, so that there would be continuity of policymaking and formulation among the three presidencies.[13]

It was during 1990 and 1991 that the final preparations took place for the presidency. In 1990 and 1991, the training effort of civil servants who would be involved in the presidency was reinforced. Several courses on the Presidency of the Council of the European Communities, related to techniques of negotiation, were organized in the European Institute of Public Administration in Maastricht. Linguistic training was also reinforced and several civil servants were sent to the United Kingdom and the Netherlands to reinforce the coordination of the three presidencies. The government created the Council of Ministers for Community Affairs (*Conselho de Ministros para Assuntos Comunitarios*-CMAC), which dealt exclusively with coordination issues related to European affairs.

In terms of the final structure of coordination for the presidency, three working groups were organized within the overall structure to coordinate EU affairs prior to and during the presidency:

1. *Working Group on Organization and Logistics* (*Grupo de Trabalho de Organização e Logistica*-GTOL), presided over by the secretary-general of the Ministry of Foreign Affairs, was in charge of promoting, coordinating, and supervising the necessary actions in terms of organization, logistics, and promotion of the preparation, organization, and exercise of the presidency.
2. *Working Group of Community Affairs* (*Grupo de Trabalho de Assuntos Comunitarios*-GTAC), presided over by the general-director of the General-Directorate for the European Communities, was in charge in dynamizing and coordinating the training program for civil servants, in identifying priorities and delineating the strategic approach to the dossiers; and in proposing decisions that permitted the functional organization of the Presidency of the Council of the European Communities.
3. *Working Group of European Political Cooperation* (*Grupo de Trabalho Cooperação Politica*-GTCP) was in charge of identifying and studying the national priorities related to the European Political Cooperation, of proposing a calendar for the different meetings of the European Political Cooperation, and of coordinating and articulating the Secretariat of Political Cooperation and the previous and subsequent presidencies of the Council of European Communities to the Portuguese one.

Beyond that the Ministry of the Interior established a working group on Security (*Grupo de trabalho Segurança*) to prevent any security problems during the presidency. A subcommittee of CICE, the interministerial commission, was established to support the preparation of the presidency. This subcommittee functioned as a supervisory body for the preparations of the presidency of the European Comunities. It was required every three months to submit reports to the CICE regarding progress made in these preparations of the presidency until June 1991.[14]

During 1991 the entire structure developed for the presidency of the European Communities intensified its work. The CMAC began to have weekly meetings instead of monthly, as did the Governmental Commission for Community Affairs (*Comissão Governamental para Assuntos Comunitarios*-CGAC) supporting CMAC. At the same time, both Prime Minister Cavaco

Silva and the State Secretary for European Integration, Vitor Martins, were equipped with a small coordination staff to accompany systematically the presidency. Each ministry nominated a liaison officer for affairs related to the presidency as support in dealing with the dossiers as well as reinforcing the logistics of the presidency. Training programs, the distribution of a Guide for the Conduct of the Presidency (*Guia para o exercicio da presidencia*),[15] a vademecum of 158 pages on how to deal with aspects of the presidency, and a document called "Towards the European Union" (*Rumo á União Europeia*) defined the main aims of the Portuguese presidency which were (1) the consolidation of the Maastricht treaty, (2) the preparation of the Delors II package and reinforcement of ties with the world, and (3) the preparation of the Nordic enlargement.[16]

The presidency of the European Communities was, in spite of unexpected occurrences, well coordinated. If there was a lack in success in completing most of the dossiers it was because of the complexity of the areas with which the Portuguese presidency had to deal. The ratification of the Maastricht treaty by the member-states was slowed down by the negative first referendum in Denmark on 3 June 1992. Other countries such as the United Kingdom and France faced difficulties in achieving an overwhelming majority for the adoption of the treaty. Moreover, the decision on the Delors II package, which was quite important for the Portuguese government, had to be postponed to the British presidency. Some success would be achieved in closing at the end of the presidency the reform of the Common Agricultural Policy (CAP) by the Agricultural Minister Arlindo de Carvalho. A climax to the Portuguese presidency was Prime Minister Anibal Cavaco Silva's representation of the European Communities in the Rio de Janeiro Conference, in which a strong amount of coordination was required to succeed in having the European Community speak with one voice.[17] The Portuguese government was the incumbent in the presidency of the EU in the first half of 2000. In 1998, the relevant diplomatic services started to prepare such a small country as Portugal for this important event. Many lessons that were learned from the 1992 presidency were applied to the 2000 presidency. Indeed, a somewhat more relaxed attitude due to this institutional memory dominated preparations for and the organization of the presidency 2000. The positive experience of 1992 was repeated and even superceded by the very successful 2000 Portuguese presidency (see chapter 7).

Intergovernmental Conferences in 1990s: From a Defensive to an Assertive Realistic Position

Portugal was involved in two Intergovernmental Conferences. The first related to the Treaty on the European Union, which aimed essentially at establishing the convergence criteria for the fulfillment of the Economic

Monetary Union, a crucial piece in the whole design of the Single European Market. The Portuguese delegation was close in position to that of the Spanish delegation, both of which were willing to support the Economic and Monetary Union and the overall Treaty, if they could achieve an increase of structural funds for the adjustment of their economies to the SEM and the impact of the Economic and Monetary Union. During the Edinburgh European Council in December 1992, Portugal and Spain were eager to secure this doubling of structural funds as well as for the creation of a new cohesion fund for all the countries that would have an average GDP/per person of less than 80 percent of the EC/EU average. In the end, they were successful in achieving this aim. Indeed, after the end of the Portuguese presidency, the Portuguese government became more self-confident in defending its interests, searching for alliances with Spain and other countries.[18]

In the Intergovernmental Conference 1996, the Portuguese government kept to a more reserved and realistic position. According to several articles by the present State Secretary of European Affairs (*Secretario de Estado de Assuntos Europeus*), Francisco Seixas da Costa, in the 1996 Integovernmental conference, the position of Portugal was highly defensive and uncoordinated in many aspects. The presidency clearly helped to change this defensive perspective. In the Intergovernmental Conference of 1996, Portuguese administration was avid to improve the coordination of the Portuguese position, internally and externally. Preparatory work started as early as October 1994 in the General-Directorate for Community Affairs (DGAC). Nevertheless, until the autumn 1995 no document was made official that would help Portuguese diplomats to explain the Portuguese position. Early in 1995 a working group, consisting of three civil servants from DGAC and one from the national structure of the CFSP, was able to produce a document, which was used subsequently by Prime Minister Anibal Cavaco Silva to write an article for the daily newspaper *Publico* on 2 June 1995. This newspaper article was then handled as the official position of the government in relation to the forthcoming IGC. The nomination of the Portuguese representative André Goncalves Pereira to the Reflection Group of the IGC and the integration of Seixas da Costa to the team clearly led to a closer relationship with the DGAC. After the change of government in October 1995, Seixas da Costa replaced Vitor Martins as the new secretary of state for European Affairs. After approval of the report of the Reflection Group, Seixas da Costa created five working groups, which were organized and supported by the corresponding subdirectorates inside DGAC. The five working groups were concerned with (1) institutional questions, (2) juridical questions, (3) questions related to justice and internal affairs, (4) economic and financial questions, and (5) CFSP questions. They were linked to the permanent structure of mediation among the different ministries, the so-called Interministerial Commission for Community Affairs (*Comissão Interministerial para Assunto Comunitarios-*

CIAC), which met weekly in the State Secretariate for European Affairs.[19] Before March 1996, the government was able to present a realistic document of the possible outcome of the IGC called "Portugal and the Intergovernmental Conference for the Revision of the Treaty on the European Union" (*Portugal e a Conferencia Intergovernamental para a Revisão do Tratado da União Europeia*).[20] The representative document was interested in protecting the interests of the small- and medium-sized member-states, particularly in questions related to representation and voting rules, without adventuring into ambitious plans for further European integration such as was done by Belgium and Luxembourg. The particularly flexible composition of the working groups was kept throughout the IGC and fulfilled its role as supporting structure. Links with the Permanent Mission of Portugal in Brussels did work without problems. Occasional difficulties were overcome by informal contacts between the Secretary of State and/or the Ministry of Foreign Affairs and the corresponding members of government. There was also a close cooperation with the Committee of European Affairs (*Comissão de Assuntos Europeus*) of the Assembly of the Republic (*Assembleia da Republica*-AR), the Portuguese parliament, under the chairmanship of José Medeiros Ferreira, which conducted several conferences and meetings with interest groups and representatives of other institutions and were put forward to the Secretary of State Seixas da Costa.[21] Moreover, the government kept the public informed about the negotiations throughout the period, particularly targeting nongovernmental organizations, universities, trade union confederations, and the business confederations. There was also an attempt to involve the Portuguese members to the European Parliament in this process, but with limited success.[22]

The experience of the IGC 1996 gained particular importance in the follow-up IGC 2000, which led to the Treaty of Nice. Indeed, the Portuguese government had a much clearer picture of what it wanted to achieve in the Nice Treaty. The role of Francisco Seixas da Costa cannot be underestimated here. He was president of the IGC Reflection Group throughout the Portuguese presidency. At some point, the Portuguese government asked for commitment by the larger countries in terms of their positions for the Nice Treaty, which led to the well-known discussion between German foreign minister Joschka Fischer and his French counterpart Hubert Védrine. On one hand, full-fleshed federalism was advocated; on the other, a more advanced Gaullist confederation of nations. The negotiations leading up to the Nice Treaty were designed to prepare the EU for enlargement. The Portuguese position was quite modest. Indeed, Seixas da Costa had already in 1998 begun to present the Portuguese position on the forthcoming negotiations. He particularly emphasized that Portugal wanted to preserve equality among all member-states and not permit some larger countries to take over the decision-making process of the European Union.[23]Indeed, during the French presidency, in preparations towards the Treaty of Nice, Portugal became a pivotal player in shaping the weight of votes in the Council after enlargement. Indeed, Portugal coordinated the position of the smaller countries vis-à-vis the position of the larger countries, achieving in the end a satisfactory position for the country. This assertive position of Portugal can be understood as a maturing of the learning processes of the Portuguese diplomatic service within the EU institutions.[24]

On the whole, one could say that sporadic events such as the presidency of 1992 and 2000 and the IGCs 1996 and 2000 were important in making EU policy coordination more salient within the Portuguese institutional framework. It appears that after more than sixteen years of EU membership Portuguese administration was able to find its own style in dealing with the processes of European integration. The Portuguese style of EU policy coordination seems to emphasize the institutionalization of a minimalist, highly flexible style, but one simultaneously based on strong permanent structures of policy coordination, which may be complemented by other temporary structures (such as working groups, subcommissions, temporary coordination staff allocation, and so on) during events.

The Portuguese EU Policy Coordination System

EU policy coordination needs a system that is compatible with each respective country. Portugal, being a small country, developed a system that was more or less adequate to its needs. In a situation where the political and social environments are quite simple, administration was able to monopolize the whole coordination process. This system, similar to that of other members of the European Union, is divided into two parts that are in permanent contact: the coordinating unit dealing with EU affairs attached to the Ministry of Foreign Affairs in Lisbon (the domestic level) and the Permanent Representation located in the European Union capital of Brussels (the European level).

The Domestic Level

The structure of EU policy coordination in Portugal achieved its stability only after the signature of the Treaty of Accession on 12 June 1985. The transfer of the administrative-bureaucratic structure from the presidency of the Council of Ministers and the Ministry of Finances to the Ministry of Foreign Affairs took place after 1985. One of the main reasons was that it was more efficient to have the whole administrative structure related to EU policy coordination in the Ministry, which had the best communication infrastructure to the outside world of the overall administration, in order to achieve a more efficient internal and external coordination.[25] Moreover, after careful study, the Portuguese government decided to follow the general approach with most other West European countries that tended to locate their EU policy coordination machinery in the Ministry of Foreign Affairs.[26] Today the primordial position of the Ministry of Foreign Affairs in leading the EU policy coordination machinery is uncontested in Portuguese public administration, a fact that provides stability and routinization to the whole process of EU affairs. In spite of the restructuring of the Ministry of Foreign Affairs since the democratic transition from authoritarian regime, the administrative bureaucratic structure of EU policy coordination has been characterized by continuity of existence and competence. Such institutionalization has been reinforced by the stability of the government since 1987.

The main administrative unit in charge of EU policy coordination is the General-Directorate for Community Affairs (*Direcção-Geral para Assuntos Comunitários*-DGAC), which supports the work led by the State Secretary for European Affairs (*Secretario de Estado de Assuntos Europeus*) with junior minister status and is appointed by the government. Although the State Secretary has a small support staff in the State Secretariate, most of the research and coordination work is done by officials of the DGAC. The DGAC is actually the filter between the EU coordinators of all other ministries and the permanent mission as well as the European institutions. According to an information sheet distributed by the DGAC, it is this unit that ensures all links with the Portuguese Permanent Representation in Brussels and the institutions in the Union. Furthermore, it disseminates the information coming from the Permanent Representation as well as the institutions and organs of the Union and ensures the transmission of instructions and documents to the Permanent Representation. The DGAC is also the unit dealing with the technical coordination of the community dossiers. Moreover, it is the supervisory body for the implementation of European law and any contentious issues that may emerge in this process.

The DGAC consists of twelve departments (*direcções de servico*-DS) dealing with different aspects of the European Union. Each department is headed by a director (*director/a de serviço*), who coordinates the work within that department. This structure has been, with minor exception, quite stable since 1984 when the government began to upgrade the State Secretariate for European Integration (*Secretariado de Estado para a Integração Europeia*-SIE). Between 1998 and 2000, the former department of external relations was split in two; one area would deal with multilateral external relations and the other with regional external relations. Moreover, a new department was created after the Amsterdam Treaty, which was simply the inclusion of the former national coordinator for affairs related to free movement of persons in the European space (*coordenador nacional para os assuntos da livre circulação de pessoas no espaco europeu*) into the DGAC after 1999.[27] On the whole, the DGAC has about 165 staff members, of which more than two-thirds are actually administrative and one-third diplomatic staff. Many members of the technical staff are seconded from the individual ministries.[28]

Table 6.1
Departments of the General-Directorate for Community Affairs (DGAC)

Department	Description of Functions	Staff
Community Institutions	This department is probably the most important one in terms of internal EU policy coordination. It is in charge of organizing the weekly meetings of the Interministerial Commission for Community Affairs (*Comissão Interministerial para Assuntos Comunitarios*-CIAC), which includes representatives from all the other ministries and aims at sorting out policy formulation problems as well as competence disputes between the different ministries. This department also allocates the representative of the corresponding ministry to the meetings of the Council of Ministers at European Union according to issues.	15
Intra-European Relations	It is in charge of coordinating in the DGAC all issues related to the relations of the European Union with the European countries outside of the European Union, as well as to the implementation of the Economic European space and enlargement.	18
Bilateral Relations	This department deals with bilateral relations with the other member-states. It collects all information of an economic character which is related to other member-states. It analyzes the position of Portugal in relation to other member-states as well as the position of other member states within the European Union, and as well assures interdepartmental coordination so that one can act outside with one voice externally. It has to guarantee a continuous flow of information to the diplomatic missions about the latest developments in the European Union. It is also in charge of monitoring agreements, treaties of economic nature.	6
Regional External Relations	It deals with all relations of the EU with third countries without interferring with the competency of other departments of DGAC.	9
Multilateral External Relations	It deals with all relations of the EU with International organizations.	11
Department of Juridical Affairs	This is the main department dealing with the transposition of European law into Portuguese law. It is the main addressee to deal with legal issues that are pre-contentious or contentious. It advises both public as well as private actors how to deal with trials before the European Court of Justice. It also issues reports and opinions about the way European law was implemented in certain cases in Portugal.	9

Table 6.1 (cont.)

Economic and Financial Questions	This department has become quite important in the past ten years, due to the fact that is in charge of advancing dossiers such as the allocation of structural funds to Portugal as well as the recent need to adjust to the requirements of the Economic and Monetary Union.	14
Agriculture and Fisheries	This department deals with all issues related to CAP and Common Fisheries policy.	9
Internal Market	It accompanies the implementation of the SEM-Program in all sectors so that the free movements of persons, goods, services and capitals can be guaranteed.	10
Scientific, Technological and Industrial Questions	It supports and acompanies the issues related to industrial policy and energy policy of the European Union, the elaboration and implementation of trade agreements related to scientific, technological, and industrial issues, and all topics related to science and technology developed within the European Union.	7
Information, Training and Documentation	It focuses its attention on providing the other departments with documentation and training. It acompanies all topics in the field of culture, education, information, health, and youth of the presidency.	12
Justice and Home Affairs	It deals with all issues related to third pillar. It coordinates the Portuguese position in relation to the Schengen agreement and adjacent initiatives.	6

Source: http://www.min-nestrangeiros.pt/mne/portugal/dgac.html. Accessed on 5 January 2002.

The DGAC is chaired by the Secretary of State for European Affairs (SEAE), who works within the general policy objectives established by the Minister of Foreign Affairs. The state secretary has also competency in questions related to the Council of Europe and the Organization for Cooperation and Economic Development (OECD) which are allocated to other General-Directorates within the Ministry of Foreign Affairs such as the Directorate-General for Bilateral Relations and the Directorate-General for Multilateral Relations. The state secretary has a small staff of assistants and advisers and he is supported by a chief of cabinet. Both former state secretaries Vitor Martins and Francisco Seixas da Costa could be described as experienced professionals who are always crossing the world of diplomacy, administration, and politics. Such a mix of experiences makes them excellent professionals to deal with the very difficult task of coordination. About sixteen persons are attached to the SEAE, of which two-thirds are administrative and one-third administrative staff.[29]

The Interministerial Committee of Community Affairs (CIAC)

The central piece of EU policy coordination in Portugal is naturally the CIAC. This interministerial committee is the main institution where conflicts between ministries, policy decisions as well as administrative cohesion, are handled so that sectorialization is reached. The CIAC used to meet every Friday morning in the Palace Cova da Moura, the actual address of the DGAC. However, since the government of Manuel Durão Barroso came to power, the new State Secretary for Community Affairs, changed the meetings to Thursday afternoon. Attending are the representatives of all ministries and the representatives of the governments of the autonomous regions of Madeira and Azores. On the whole, there are around twenty participants at each meeting of CIAC. The CIAC is formally chaired by the Minister of Foreign Affairs and most representatives are at Secretary of State level. In reality, it is the State Secretary for European Affairs that chairs the meetings and most representatives are only delegates of the actual EU liaison officers in the individual ministries. Due to its routinization and institutionalization, it seems that the CIAC during the previous government held more of a pro forma meeting, a kind of ceremony that had to be fulfilled every Friday morning, with most of the exceptional problems of EU policy coordination resolved by informal telephone calls or personal bilateral meetings that helped smooth the most difficult problems. Carlos da Costa Neves, the successor of Seixas da Costa, has changed the attitude towards it considerably. Although sometimes it is not possible to have meetings every Thursday afternoon, his presence and commitment has changed the overall culture of the exercise.

During the Guterres government, at some stage, the CIAC was more or less attended by officials lower than the state-secretary level while under Costa Neves counterparts of similar rank in the other ministries are now attending. This naturally gives more weight and importance to CIAC.[30] Therefore, CIAC continues to be the most important piece of machinery that in times of crisis or during sporadic events such as presidency and intergovernmental conferences is able to solve all policy coordination problems. Its flexible nature allows for the creation of temporary subcommittees to prepare, discuss, or monitor certain aspects that are relevant to the position of Portugal in the European Union. The CIAC is the focus point for all departments of the DGAC in the creation of specialized committees for certain issues, such as the ongoing discussion about the allocation of the structural funds, the single European currency, or the implementation of EU legislation in Portugal.[31] It appears that the relationship between DGAC and the Permanent Representation of Portugal in Brussels is quite excellent. Normally, members of the Permanent Representation receive instructions from the DGAC. In reality, they receive more informal detailed technical instructions or advice from the liaison officers in the individual ministries. Thus, before any meetings in Brussels Portuguese members of the Permanent Representation may receive both formal general as well as informal technical instructions to speed up the information process.

This demonstrates that DGAC aims at including the other ministries to smooth and keep flexible the information channels between the Permanent Representation members and the national institutions. Members of the Permanent Representation are requested to write reports after each meeting, which normally include additional comments or suggestions on how to deal with certain issues. This in-put is appreciated by DGAC because it helps the decision-making process in Lisbon. The relationship between DGAC and the Permanent Mission in Brussels resembles a partnership more than submission to the decisions in Lisbon.[32]

If neither the CIAC nor the bilateral informal contacts can sort out the problems of EU coordination, the issue is discussed in the Portuguese Council of Ministers for European Union Affairs (*Conselho de Ministros para Assuntos da União Europeia*), which consists of the prime minister and all ministers. Moreover, if the prime minister does not disagree, the state secretary of the Presidency of the Council of Ministers, the secretary of state allocated to the prime minister, and the secretary of state for European Affairs can participate without voting rights. Other state secretaries can take part, if the prime minister so wishes. The Council of Ministers for European Union affairs is in charge of global policy coordination, internally and externally, in the framework of Portugal's participation in the European Union. The main tasks of the Council of Ministers for European Union affairs are: (1) to establish the general lines of orientation in the respective field; (2) to assure coordination at the political level, in the most relevant dossiers in the framework of the Portuguese participation in the Union; (3) to acompany, in general terms, the evolution of the Union and that of the European integration; (4) to approve the annual report related to Portugal's participation in the European Union; and (5) to discuss all matters submitted by the prime minister.[33]

One can note that this route is seldom used. The Portuguese EU coordination policy process is characterized by a culture of consensus, negotiation, and informality. After more than a decade of EU policy coordination the more or less two to four hundred civil servants, diplomats, and politicians know each other and respect each other in their commitment to achieve the best solution to the problems that may arise. One has also to emphasize that the location of DGAC in the Ministry of Foreign Affairs has created a culture of internal and external diplomacy that is targeted towards negotiation and consensual bargaining where all can be winners and there are no losers.[34] It can be noted that Portuguese EU Policy coordination tries to find the golden point between formal and informal, bureaucratic and political, closed and transparent, and centralized and diffused. It is this flexible in-between structure that shapes also the nature of the processes.

The European Level: The Important Role of the Permanent Representation

The Development of the Permanent Representation

The Portuguese Permanent Representation (*Representação Permanente*-REPER) is a follow-up to the Portuguese Mission to the European Communities, which was established originally in 1977 after application for membership on 14 March. Decree law nr.185 on 20 June 1979 defined the Mission as a supporting organ of the Commission of European Integration based in Lisbon. It was the supporting organ at the European level, while the Secretariate of European Integration (*Secretariado de Integração Europeia*-SIE) was the core supporting organ for the coordination of negotiations with the European Community. After the positive opinion by the Commission of the European Communities on Portugal's membership application, negotiations were started formally on 17 September 1978. The establishment of a Mission to the European Community was regarded as an important step in coordinating the Portuguese position in relation to different issues in the negotiations. The substantial negotiations began in 1980, but already by 1979 the Portuguese administration wanted to put in place the structure for a successful negotiation towards European integration.

According to the decree-law, the Mission received instructions from two ministries. In aspects dealing with foreign policy issues related to European integration and the respective consequences for adjustment for the planning and implementation by Portuguese foreign policymaking the Mission received instructions from the Ministry of Foreign Affairs (*Ministro de Negócios Estrangeiros*-MNE), while in all technical aspects linked to European integration, from the vice prime minister for Economic and European Integration Affairs, directly or indirectly through the Commission of European Integration. The vice prime minister was obliged to let both the minister of foreign affairs as well as the president of the Commission on European Integration know about the technical instructions given to the Mission.[35] Shortly, before Portugal's accession to the European Community, the Mission became then the Permanent Representation in Brussels. Decree-law 526 of 31 December 1985 reformulated the entire structure of the institutions of national EU policy coordination in Portugal. The Portuguese REPER was then completely integrated into the Ministry of Foreign Affairs and all instructions to the REPER had to go through the General-Directorate of the European Communities

(*Direcção-Geral das Comunidades Europeias*-DGCE).[36] This formal monopoly was naturally complemented by a wide range of continuing informal relationships between the REPER and individual ministries.

Nevertheless, the new decree-law ended the bicephalous nature of the institutions of policy coordination by following the most common model of all other member-states that had integrated their national EU policy coordination institutions in the Ministry of Foreign Affairs. The Portuguese REPER had time to learn from the various models of Permanent Representations of other member-states and decided in favor of a flexible structure dominated by civil servants and a diplomatic head. This flexible structure enhances the teamwork and is characterized by non-hierarchical relations. Only two tiers are visible in the Portuguese REPER: the Diplomatic Permanent Representative and the technical staff, consisting mostly of civil servants. The assistant of the Diplomatic Permanent Representative is normally the liaison between the two levels as well as the coordinating liaison figure. The division of responsibilities may change according to the different topics discussed in COREPER or other institutions of the European Union. The flexibility and quality of response is the most important aspect emphasized in the Portuguese REPER. Due to the amount of questions with which the REPER is confronted, the teamwork and non-hierarchical approach helps to strengthen the Portuguese position. Such a position can be a non-position as well, meaning that Portugal in conjunction with other countries may block proposed legislation or other aspects for years. The work of the REPER is extremely difficult to assess because of its interface nature, its Janus face between national and supranational levels. Sometimes the work may be very positive, but in controversial questions the REPER may use the negative strategy of delay or blockage for new legislative proposals. In this sense, the flexible non-hierarchical structure prevents the establishment of an organigramme.[37]

Organization and Resources

The Permanent Representation is located closely to the main building of the Council. It is a modern building of seven floors in the avenue Corthenberg, owned by the Portuguese government, and is within two minutes walking distance of the Council main building located in the Robert Schuman Roundabout. This move is recent; before 1998 the REPER was in the rue Marie-Therese, close to the Palais Royal, quite far away from the Council. This attempt at proximity means that Portugal intends to play a role in the overall decision-making process by investing in coordination structures.

Central to any ambition to influence European policies, this outpost of the Portuguese policy coordination system is well resourced. The REPER is in continuing contact with the DGAC and informs it of all new processes of decision-making in the working groups, in the Committee of Permanent Representatives (COREPER), and in the Council meetings. It clearly is a team of highly experienced diplomatic and technical negotiators. Staff members are seconded from the individual ministries, and they are among the best civil servants in terms of skills that the Portuguese public administration can offer. The REPER is, in comparison with its counterparts, one of the largest, which naturally has to do with the fact that Lisbon is so far away from Brussels. This means that the Permanent Representation is well resourced both in terms of human as well as material resources, so that it can do a good job in the bodies of the Council.

At the very beginning, the size of the Portuguese REPER was small, comprising only twenty-four persons. The number of people working for the Permanent Mission more than doubled between 1986 and 1992, with the absolute climax occurring during the Portuguese presidency of the European Union, with fifty persons working in the REPER. After 1992 the number of persons working for the REPER stabilized at forty-seven, which is a large number compared to other permanent representations. In terms of sectional organizations, the REPER had eleven departments in 1986 and increased to fifteen departments in 1988. The restructuring of portfolios inside the REPER continued until the Portuguese presidency in 1992, but already in 1991 one could observe a stabilization of the structure and a certain level of continuity of the different departments. Some minor restructuring happened after 1992, but the overall structure seemed to have achieved stability by then. Some policy areas, such as regional, agricultural, and environmental policy, were able to become more autonomous over time. After 1992, one can observe an increase in personnel dealing with regional policy, which may be related to the importance attached to the structural funds by Portugal. Already in 1988, a department to deal with Internal Market questions was established to prepare Portugal for the forthcoming SEM. This department still exists today and plays a role in supporting the coordination of SEM related matters. One aspect that becomes apparent is that the growth in complexity of EU policy coordination led to a strengthening of the REPER over time. An increase in the number of personnel and the singling out of certain policy areas that were relevant for the Portuguese economy became the most salient features of the adjustment of this interface between the Portuguese government and the European institutions. Several officials of the REPER became specialists in certain areas such as Schengen or relations with the ACP States and the Lomé Convention (existing since 1996). In many ways, the Portuguese REPER bears strong similarities with the UK Permanent Representation in terms of its organization.

The normal year by year renewal of personnel reaches 5 to 6 percent; only after a cycle or a particular important event such as the presidency does the rate of renewal increase substantially. After the presidency of 1992 and before the presidency of 2000, in 1998, there was a renewal of 34 and 20 percent, respectively. This stability of personnel is particularly evident in certain policy areas such as internal market, regional policy, social policy, education and health, and particularly agriculture and fisheries. Expertise is a major criterion for preventing a fast renewal of personnel. Generally, most civil servants in REPER stay for a period of five to six years, but about one-third of the officers are already more than nine years in the REPER. They entered in second half of the 1980s and still have not been replaced by newcomers. This is particular the case in the section dealing with agriculture and fisheries which has remained quite stable since 1986.

Other sectors are the internal market, social affairs, legal affairs, and transport and communication. The highest level of renewal can be seen in the largest department dealing with political and foreign affairs, which had a major renewal in 1993 after end of the Portuguese presidency. A high level of stability increases the conditions to create a pool of expertise in the REPER, without disrupting long-term strategies adopted in the COREPER and different other committees. Portuguese civil servants tend to remain in public administration after leaving the REPER. Their expertise is regarded as an important asset for the different ministries, so that the Brussels' experience

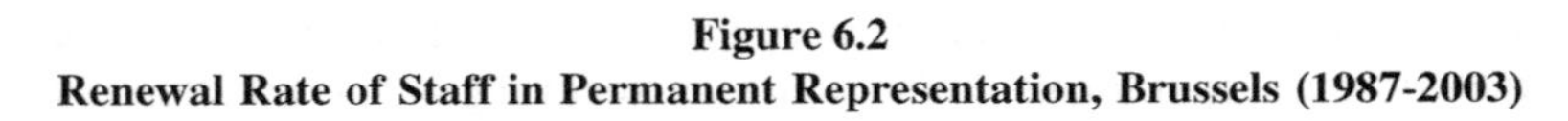

Figure 6.2
Renewal Rate of Staff in Permanent Representation, Brussels (1987-2003)

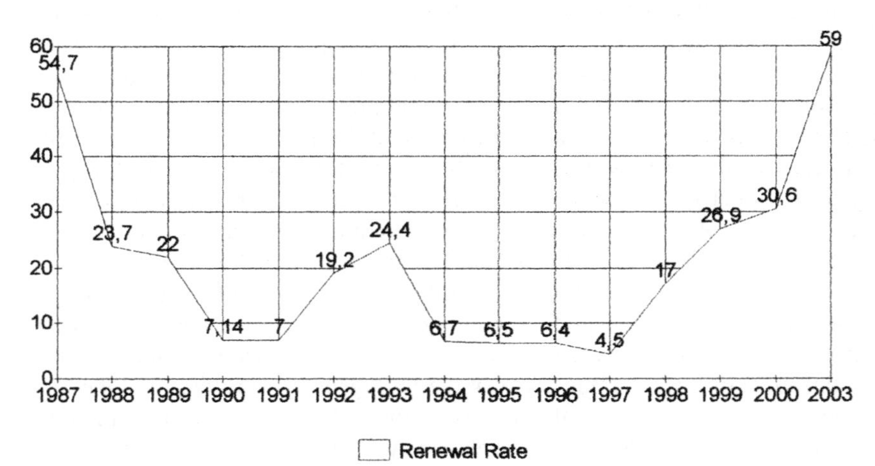

Source: Author's own calculations and graph based on data provided by General Secretariat of the Council, *Guide to the Council of the European Communities* (Brussels, 1989-1993), *European Commission, Who's Who in the European Union. Inter-institutional Directory 1995 and 1998* (Luxembourg: Office of the Official Publications of the European Union 1995), *Vacher's European Companion* (Berkhampsted: Vacher's Publications) No. 100, June 1997, pp. 12-13, nr. 106, and December 1998, pp. 13-14.

may pay off in terms of career. Moreover, they may come back at a later stage to reinforce some of the departments within the REPER. The possibilities of leaving public administration and applying its expertise in a job in the private economy are extremely reduced in the context of the Portuguese market, which is still learning to introduce lobbying and information-related skills into its marketing strategies. Generally, civil servants remain in public administration, which is regarded as prestigious in the Portuguese context, particularly if it is related to European integration issues.[38]

While technical civil servants tend to stay for a lengthier period in Brussels, the positions of the diplomatic permanent representative as well as the deputy permanent representative, both members of COREPER II and COREPER I, respectively, are renewed more frequently.

It seems that renewal occurs after two years for the permanent representative, while the deputy permanent representative tends to stay longer and acts as a kind of stability element between the technical staff and the permanent representative. During the 2000 presidency, the permanent representative already had previous experience in the REPER. Ambassador Vasco Valente was deputy permanent representative between 1987 and 1993 and was a crucial, pivotal figure in the preparation for the Portuguese presidency of the European Union. Ambassador Valente was fifty-five years old in 2000; his diplomatic trajectory had begun during the authoritarian regime. He had rich diplomatic experiences in London and Africa. Most of his time was spent in the Ministry of Foreign Affairs where he worked in the Asian and African departments. In the second half of the 1980s, he was then seconded to the Permanent Representation as deputy permanent representative.[39]

During the 2000 presidency, the deputy permanent representative was Maria Margarida de Araujo Figueiredo who had been in the REPER since 1994 as a minister plenipotentiary working in the department of political and external affairs. This promotion to deputy representative shows that the diplomatic group dealing with European Union affairs has become more integrated and defined since its beginning. De Araujo Figueiredo also had some professional experience in the Commission as assistant of Commisssioner João Deus Pinheiro between 1992 and 1994.[40] The former deputy permanent representative João de Vallera was born in 1950 and is a representative of the new generation of Portuguese diplomats. He began his diplomatic career in the Ministry of Foreign Affairs in 1974 and, after serving as secretary in the Portuguese Bonn embassy, he became a member of the Portuguese mission to the EEC between 1979 and 1984. He returned in 1991 to the position of assistant to the permanent representative and Portuguese representative in the Antici group of the Council.[41]

In general terms, it appears that the core of specialists on European affairs was already established by 1993. Today, the Permanent Representation consists of markedly experienced persons who have already been in the REPER an average of six years, some even longer. Also the recruitment patterns have become more stable and structured. A core of diplomats and technical civil servants, because of their expertise, are able to socialize newcomers in an incredibly short period of time. Such a fact makes the REPER more efficient and particularly professional in its tasks.

The REPER as Actor at the European Level: Patterns of Negotiation and Behavior

In a recent, much acclaimed book by former Belgian permanent representative Philippe de Schoutheete, the present European Union has to be perceived as a network that is permanently changing. This web of relations and flows is charaterized by an asymmetrical density and thickness of relationships in some parts and less so in others.[42] The transnational Janus nature of COREPER, which transmits, mediates, and negotiates between national governments and the supranational institutions, makes this a privileged area of study. The COREPER may be regarded as an interface between the national network systems and the supranational ones, creating itself a convergence of the two into a transnational one. In recent studies on COREPER, the network approach has been examined in more detail leading to an assessment of the influence and importance of certain actors over others in this context. The studies clearly assign a subaltern actor capacity to the Portuguese REPER and tend to emphasize that the larger countries are really the major players in this web of relationships.

Indeed, in an empirical study conducted by Jan Beyers and Guido Dierickx during the Belgian presidency in 1993, they attached a high level of importance to the working groups that exist in the Council preparing and discussing legislation for COREPER. These working groups, consisting of diplomats and civil servants, amounted to 170 in 1993. In 1994, there were 2,580 meetings of these working groups, while the Council had only 125 and COREPER 117.[43] Therefore, Beyers and Dierickx feel that the working groups are creating a common culture among the members of the working groups, a kind of *esprit de corps*. Between 90 and 70 percent of all decisions are taken informally at this level, while the rest is agreed in COREPER and the Council. This growth in complexity increased the formalization of the working groups in relation to COREPER and the Council.[44] According to the authors, Portugal is regarded as a peripheral actor within this spiderweb. Indeed, the core actors in these different stages of legislation are Germany, France, and the United Kingdom. Only Germany is interested in keeping strong linkages to the periphery, while France and the United Kingdom tend to neglect the periphery and work closer with other northern European countries or together. The second group is labeled as the northern European small states, which is still in the making, comprising the Benelux countries, Ireland, Denmark, and probably Finland, Sweden, and Austria since 1995. The third group of southern European member-states consists of Italy, Spain, Greece, and Portugal. Their weak linkages to the center make them appear peripheral.[45]

This categorization of member-states based on communication flows during the Belgium presidency can be regarded as only a small part of the story in this complex spiderweb. The configurations may differ from presidency to presidency, and also in different periods depending on dossiers to be approved or issues to be raised. Another aspect is that Portugal until 1992 and 1993 was still learning to deal with the spiderweb and adjusting its public-administrative structures (including REPER) to the growth in complexity. This included also the set-up of telecommunications among the different Portuguese embassies and the ministry of foreign affairs.[46] The recent Portuguese presidency has shown that this peripheral position of Portugal may change considerably, if national interests are at stake. Indeed, the presidency has shown a high level of engagement to achieve a compromise in the extradionary Council of Lisbon towards the Lisbon Strategy. The hard work of Professor Maria João Rodrigues led to the establishment of a new, open method of coordination as well as a stronger, more independent engagement of the Council vis-à-vis the Commission. Moreover, Portugal assumed an informal coordinating role on the position of the ten small- and medium sized members vis-á-vis the larger member-states in relation to the weighting of the voting system in the Council and the new arrangements in the other institutions in the negotiating process towards the Treaty of Nice. The REPER was quite central to these efforts of former foreign minister Jaime Gama and State Secretary for European Affairs Francisco Seixas da Costa. Actually, one could find Portugal and Belgium sometimes defending the same principles collectively.[47]

The Portuguese REPER is one of fifteen that have formed a transnational community. In this sense, their allegiances although formally attached to the national administrations, informally are transnational dealing with three, and in some cases even more network systems. The accumulated knowledge of former permanent representatives such as ambassador Philippe de Schoutheete, the French ambassador Pierre de Boissieu, or the German deputy Jochen Grünhage socialize the newcomers in formalized common practice.[48] Indeed, the Portuguese Permanent Representation is no longer an inexperienced transmission belt of instructions coming from the national capitals. After more than sixteen years of existence, it has gained a reputation in the national capital and sometimes transmits options of decision-making to the main interministerial committee, the CIAC, which meets now every Thursday afternoon in the Ministry of Foreign Affairs in Lisbon. Thus, making the REPER no longer different from the Permanent Representations of other countries. Although in theory the REPER is completely under instruction from the national capitals, in reality they are actors in their own right in shaping the decision-making process. During the presidency 2000, for example, the Permanent Representation was the real center of decision-making, which had to manage most of the tasks required to make it work. Only in strictly political decisions, was there a stronger involvement of Lisbon.[49] Like other Permanent Representations, the Portuguese REPER tends to follow the four generic patterns recognized by Jeffrey Lewis:[50]

1. *Departing from recommendations and making "recommendations"*: In some cases the instructions do not reflect the necessary approach in the process of negotiation, so that the REPER may send recommendations to change the instructions. This seems to have become more and more *common practice* leading to a dialogue, sometimes very informal, about the approach to take in a particular situation.

2. *The national capital signals that a margin of manoeuvre exists:* The REPER consists of the most competent civil servants and diplomats of Portuguese public administration. Their expertise in negotiations and discussions gives them a special status in the coordination of EU policy. They are able to deal with a margin of manoeuvre and to achieve a realistic outcome for the Portuguese delegation.

3. *There is a political need to minimize confrontation:* For Portugal the general approach is to be consensual. The avoidance of confrontation has been the general pattern in the Portuguese case. As a small state, the Portuguese public administration through REPER prefers to come to a compromise than to bring issues to the Council.

4. *The national capital cannot make up its mind:* The distance to the negotiating arena and to the dynamics among the different COREPER actors leads to a strengthening of the position of the REPER as the actual giver of instructions to themselves. The reports received in Lisbon from REPER may come back to Brussels as instructions, because the Portuguese CIAC trusts the expertise and knowledge of the REPER.[51]

In this sense, the package of issues to be presented at the national CIAC is normally organized by the REPER in relation to what it may discuss in the next COREPER meetings. The dialogue between Brussels and Lisbon is overwhelmingly dominated by Brussels, which asks for instructions or makes recommendations. In the Council fora, Portugal is more reactive than proactive. Portugal has no capacity of agenda-setting; this is left normally to the larger countries. In relation to the capital, the REPER has the power of knowledge, so that the flow of information tends to be dominated by Brussels rather than Lisbon. This power of knowledge is also used informally by the individual ministries. The main task is to support the ministers and officials who come for meetings in Brussels before the Council meetings. This prestigious position of the REPER within Portuguese administration is also due to the fact that they are aware of their realistic position within the spiderweb of the COREPER. The Portuguese REPER becomes more active in aspects related to structural funds, regional policy, social policy during the presidency or

IGC negotiations. The discussion about the financing of Agenda 2000 led to a tougher negotiating position by Portugal to assure that it was able to retain a maximum of the structural fund amounts until 2006.[52]

The Environment of EU Policy Coordination

In comparison to other national EU policy coordination systems such as Germany, Netherlands, France, UK, Denmark, Sweden, and Austria, the Portuguese system monopolizes more or less the whole decision-making process. The Portuguese coordination system has to deal with a very simple political, social, and economic environment. One of the characteristics of the Portuguese political system is that it is highly centralized. It does not have to deal with any regionalized tiers of government such as in Spain, Belgium, Germany, Austria, and more recently the United Kingdom. It controls the whole decision-making process; it does not consult any council of the regions. The local authorities in Portugal are too weak and fragmented to play a major role in the decision-making process (see chapter 5).

In relation to the Assembleia da Republica, the executive is also able to monopolize the whole decision-making process. In spite of the protocol in the Treaty of Maastricht and the Treaty of Amsterdam, the Portuguese Parliament remained quite weak in the system of policy coordination. In the so-called decision-making process it is seldom consulted and the lack of resources prevents an ex ante scrutiny as exists in Denmark, Sweden, Finland, UK, Germany, and France.[53] The role of Parliament has remained one of information and the mobilization of civil society. It fulfills a role of scrutinizing ex post the transposition of directives, but this is done in a superficial fast-track way, further strengthening the role of the executive. Among the parties, only the Communists and the new Block of the Left have been more critical in relation to European integration. The two main parties are strongly committed to the European integration process. The center-right People's Party is normally an anti-Maastricht party and for the Europe des Patries, but tries not to be too dogmatic about it. It is presently sharing a government with the social democrats (see chapter 3).

This lack of pressure coming from the institutional environment is helped also by a weakly organized civil society. First of all, the majority of the population supports European integration and tends to accept uncritically the Europeanization process of the Portuguese political system, economy, and society. Secondly, the long night of fascism was a major obstacle to the development of a pro-active organized civil society. This may change in the future, but it is still too weak. The strongest economic lobbies come from the agricultural sector, which have been the losers in European integration. They tend to target the Ministry of Agriculture. Moreover, environmentalist associations have been highly critical of governments in relation to a lack of commitment to protection of the environment when developing new projects with the EU structural funds. Indeed, the manufacturing of positive environmental impact assessments has been exposed by the environmentalist associations in Portugal.

Conclusions

The Portuguese EU policy coordination system is quite simple in comparison with other countries. It is highly centralized and monopolized by public administration. It works in a very simple environment without serious challenges coming from the Parliament, interest groups, or subnational tiers of government. In this sense, policy coordination works smoothly and quite efficiently. The best civil servants, specializing in different policy areas, are sent to Brussels because the Portuguese government regards the Brussels outpost as an important piece of the overall policy coordination. Indeed, the REPER has a high level of autonomy and credibility in Lisbon. Their daily recommendations are normally transformed into instructions by Lisbon. Since 1985, the EU policy coordination system has been more or less the same, which suggests that the Portuguese were able to create a system that works efficiently and smoothly for them. The system is highly flexible. This contrasts heavily with Italy, which today still struggles to find the adequate structures for its policy coordination system. In sum, the EU policy coordination system can be regarded as one of the best areas in which civil servants and diplomats are operating. This shows the commitment of successive Portuguese governments to invest in this important filter structure between the national and the European levels. It led to the creation of a pool of highly qualified experts, who are determining and negotiating successfully the position of Portugal in the present and future of the European Union.

Notes

1. Liesbet Hoeghe, "The Dynamics of Constitution Building in Belgium," in Patrick Dunleavy, Jeffrey Stanyer (eds.), *Contemporary Political Studies 1994, Volume 1. Proceedings of the Annual Conference Held at the University of Wales, Swansea, March 29-31, 1994* (Belfast: PSA, 1994), 314-324, even asserts that today's Belgium can only exist as a member of the European Union. The European Union is the main cohesive factor of a highly heterogeneous, complex state trying to accommodate the interests of all the different communities and regions (322-323).
2. Portugal followed very much the approach of the United Kingdom to the EC in the 1960s; it became one of the founding members of the European Free Trade Area and used it as a plattform to come closer to the EC. Salazar was willing to allow strong intergovernmental relations within European institutions, but extremely opposed to any supranational European organization (Maria Fernanda Rollo, "Salazar e a construção europeia," in António Costa Pinto, Nuno Severiano Teixeira (eds.),

"Portugal e a Unificação Europeia," Special Issue of *Penélope*, 18, 1998: 51-76; particularly 70).

3. In April 1970, Franco Nogueira, deputy for the Lisbon constituency, argued in the National Assembly (the façade legislative chamber of the authoritarian regime) on Portugal's intention to enter the European Community that "on the terms in which the proposition is set before us, we should become colonized by Europe, and then Europe would colonize the overseas territories. We can be certain that Europe would not look after our prosperity." By comparing the present Portuguese situation with the possible integration of Portugal into the European Community, he declared that Portugal's strength lay in the indissoluble whole "made with the overseas provinces, which gives us strength, economic potentiality, and political dimension." He ended by defending those who advocated a seemingly conservative global national policy as "much more daring, much more revolutionary, much more ambitious than those who put forward a limited and bourgeoisly European policy" (quotation from the *Times*, 9 April 1970, quoted from José Magone, *The Changing Architecture of Iberian Politics: An Investigation on the Democratic Structuring of Political Systemic Culture in Southern Semiperipheral Societies* (Lewiston, NY: Edwin Mellen Press, 1996), 465.
4. José Manuel Castilho, *A Ideia da Europa no Marcelismo (1968-1974)* (Lisbon: Edições Afrontamento, 2000), 157-166.
5. More than half of all the exports and imports went to and came from the European Community in the early 1970s. Such a structure of import-export continues to prevail until today. Pedro Ordaz, "Portugal and Trade Policy," in José da Silva Lopes (ed.), *Portugal and EC Membership Evaluated* (London: Pinter, 1994), 108-123. According to Thomas Bruneau, *Politics and Nationhood. Postrevolutionary Portugal* (New York: Praeger 1984), 25, the different economic groups were split into two factions: the Europeanists (industrial elites) and Africanists (agrarian elites). This is confirmed by other authors such as Santos Boaventura Sousa Santos, "A Crise e a Reconstituição do Estado em Portugal (1974-84)," *Revista Critica de Ciencias Sociais* 14, 1984: 7-27; particularly 16, and Nicos Poulantzas, *Die Krise der Diktaturen. Portugal, Griechenland und Spanien* (Frankfurt A. M.: Suhrkamp, 1977), 8-9; particularly 14. This was also quite evident during the early sixties; see Luis Nuno Rodrigues, *Salazar e Kennedy: A crise de uma alianca* (Lisbon: editorial noticias, 2002), 171-181. Marcelo Caetano was not able to keep the different groups under control as predecessor Salazar had done for four decades; see Lawrence Graham, *Portugal. The Decline and Collapse of an Authoritarian Order* (London, Beverly Hills: SAGE, 1975).
6. Geoffrey Pridham, "The Politics of the European Community. Transnational Networks and Democratic Transition in Southern Europe," in Geoffrey Pridham (ed.), *Encouraging Democracy: The International Context of Regime Transition in Southern Europe* (London: Leicester University Press, 1991), 211-54; particularly 215.
7. José Magone, *The Changing Architecture*, 465-470; Rainer Eisfeld, *Der sozialistischer Pluralismus in Europa. Ansaetze und Scheitern am Beispiel Portugal* (Koln: Verlag Wissenschaft und Politik, 1984), 118-120.
8. Kommission der Europaeischen Gemeinschaften, 1978: Stellungnahme zum Beitrittsantrag Portugals (von der Kommission am 19. Mai 1978 dem Rat vorgelegt), in *Bulletin der Europaeischen Gemeinschaften*, Beilag 5/78.
9. On the problems of administrative discontinuity during the early phase of the consolidation period 1976-1986, see José Magone, *European Portugal. The Difficult Road to Sustainable Democracy* (Basingstroke, New York: Macmillan, St. Martin's Press, 1997), 53-57; José Magone, "The Rationale of Democratic Regime

Building in Portugal." In Wolfgang C. Müller and Kaare Strom (eds.), *Coalition Government in Western Europe* (Oxford: Oxford University Press, 2000), and Graham Lawrence, "A Administração Publica central e local: Continuidade e mudanca," *Analise Social* XXI, 87-89, 1985: 903-24; Graham Lawrence, *The Portuguese Military and the State. Rethinking Transitions in Europe and Latin America* (Boulder, CO: Westview Press, 1993). Between 1976 and 1985 there were nine different governments with an average of 328 days. For a short period there was a Ministry for European Integration during the government of Prime Minister Pinto Balsemão, between 9 January 1981 and 14 August 1981, in the hope of reinforcing what was hoped at that time to be the last phase of negotiations (Programa do VII Governo Constitucional, DAR, II-Serie-Number 20, 17.1.1981, pp.345-346). Due to the fact that the optimistic view of the government did not materialize the Ministry was downgraded again to a mere administrative unit under both the presidency of the Council of Ministers and the Ministry of Finances under the successive Pinto Balsemão government. During the first government under Prime Minister Anibal Cavaco Silva, between 4 November 1985 and 17 August 1987, the Ministry of European Integration was reinforced once again to cope with the early phase of membership. Indeed, the Portuguese administration was taken by surprise at the amount of issues in which the EC institutions and the large number of committees asked for positions in the Portuguese government or even representation in committees (Interview with Dr. Rui Marques, DGAC, on 23 September 1998).

10. *Ministério dos Negócios Estrangeiros, Portugal nas Comunidades Europeias. Primeiro Ano 1986* (Lisbon: MNE, 1987), 181-182. According to one witness, it seems that after the signature of the membership act to the European Community in the Monastery of the Jeronimos on 12 June 1985, which was followed by the 13 June, a national holiday celebrating Saint Anthony, the saint of Lisbon, the Portuguese secretary for European integration was bombarded with requests by fax from different working groups and committees of Council of Ministers, Commissions and other institutions and agencies to send Portuguese representatives or state the Portuguese position on certain policy affairs (Interview with Rui Marques, DGAC, 23 September 1998). Norway experienced a different attitude from the European Union after the negative outcome of the referendum, leading to a closing down of the informal information channels (see Fredrik Sejersted, "The Norwegian Parliament and European Integration-Reflections from Medium-Speed Europe," in Eivind Smith (ed.), *National Parliaments as Cornerstones of European Integration* (London: Kluwer, 1996), 124-156, particularly 140.
11. The ideas on reflective postmodern administrative culture are taken from Charles J. Fox and Hugh T. Miller, *Postmodern Public Administration. Towards Discourse* (London: SAGE, 1995). What started as one-sided pressure from the European field towards Portugal later became an integrated whole which led to a two-way relationship that was reinforced by learning how other member-states adjusted to the European Community, particularly Spain, Italy, and France, as well as Greece.
12. Ministério dos Negocios Estrangeiros, *Portugal nas Comunidades Europeias, Terceiro Ano,1988* (Lisbon: MNE, 1989), 331-333.
13. Ministério dos Negocios Estrangeiros, *Portugal nas Comunidades Europeias, Quarto Ano, 1989* (Lisbon: MNE, 1990), 351-353.
14. Ministério dos Negocios Estrangeiros, *Portugal nas Comunidades Europeias,Quinto Ano, 1990* (Lisbon: MNE, 1991), 381-386.
15. Secretaria do Estado da Integração Europeia, *Guia para o Exercicio da Presidencia* (Lisbon: SIE, 1992).

16. Ministério dos Negocios Estrangeiros, *Rumo á União Europeia* (Lisbon: MNE, 1991).
17. José Magone, *European Portugal. The Difficult Road to Sustainable Democracy* (Basingstroke: Macmillan, 1997), 164-167; Vitor Martins, "Introdução," in Ministério dos Negocios Estrangeiros, *Portugal nas Comunidades Europeias 1992, setimo ano* (Lisbon: MNE, 1993), I-XI; Ministério dos Negocios Estrangeiros, *Presidencia Portuguesa no Conselho de Ministros das Comunidades Portuguesas* (Lisbon: Casa da Moeda, 1992).
18. Vitor Martins, "Introdução," op.cit.
19. Francisco Seixas da Costa, "Tratado de Amsterdão: Historia de uma negociação," *Politica Internacional* 1, 15/16, Outono-Inverno, 1997, 23-47; particularly 25-27.
20. Ministério dos Negocios Estrangeiros, *Portugal e a Conferencia Intergovernamental para a Revisão do Tratado da União Europeia* (Lisbon: MNE, 1996).
21. Seixas da Costa,"Tratado de Amsterdao," 28-30; Assembleia da Republica, *Acompanhamento Parlamentar da Revisão do Tratado da União Europeia na Conferencia Intergovernamental de 1996*, 2 vols. (Lisbon: Comissão de Assuntos Europeus, 1996).
22. Seixas da Costa, ibid., 30.
23. Francisco Seixas da Costa, "Portugal e o Desafio Europeu," *Nação e Defesa*, no. 85, *Primavera* 98, 2 Serie, 17-28; particularly 25.
24. See the excellent detailed account of the position of Portugal during the Intergovernmental Conference 2000 by Francisco Seixas da Costa, "Portugal e o Tratado de Nice. Notas sobre a estratégia negocial portuguesa," *Negócios Estrangeiros* 1, March 2001: 40-70; see particularly the last days of negotiation in Nice, 61-68.
25. Interview with Luis Inez Fernandes, director of the juridical issues department of DGAC, 22 September 1998.
26. Decree-Law no.526/85, *Diario da Republica*, I Serie, no. 301, 31.12.1985: 130. The current name of the DGAC is used since 1994, after a major restructuring of the Ministry of Foreign Affairs under Minister Manuel Durão Barroso, which did not affect at all the DGAC (see decree-law no. 48/94, Art. 8, *Diario da Republica*, I-A Serie, 24.2.1994: 831). Until 1994, the DGAC was called General-Directorate for the European Communities (*Direcção-Geral para as Comunidades Europeias*-DGCE). In 1991, in view of the forthcoming presidency of the European Communities the overall position of DGCE as a liaison and filter unit was considerably improved (see decree-law no. 344/91, *Diario da Republica*, no. 214, I-A Serie, 17.9.1991: 4901-4908). According to the decree-law the DGCE was given administrative autonomy in terms of dealing with its resources to assure a high level of flexibility. Moreover, the decree-law approved a staff of 198 members. Before the 1985 decree-law, the name of the administrative unit was Secretariate for European Integration (Secretariado da Integração Europeia-SIE) (see decree-law, no. 306/77, *Diario da Republica*, I-Serie, no. 178, 3.8.1977: 1882; decree-Law no. 185/79, *Diario da Republica*, I-Serie-Number 140, 20.6.1979: 1346; Regulatory Decree no. 36/84, *Diario da Republica*, I Serie, no. 93, 19.4.1984: 1294-1298). The regulatory decree created the working structure for the subsequent DGAC by dividing the different EC issues among different departments. Moreover, the number of members of staff was defined in the decree as 109. The SIE does not appear to have become the political structure of DGAC liaisoning with the Council of Ministers in EU matters. Today it is called State Secretariate for European Affairs (*Secretariado de Estado para Assuntos Europeus*-SEAE).
27. The national coordinator position was created in 1996 (Presidencia do Conselho de Ministros, Resolucao no. 31/96, 2 Serie, *Diario da Republica*, no. 139/96, II Serie, 18.6.1996: 8004) and abolished after ratification of the Treaty of Amsterdam.

28. Author's own calculations based on the Ministério dos Negócios Estrangeiros, *Anuário Diplomático e Consular Portugues*, Vol. 2, 67-75 (Lisbon: MNE, 2000).
29. Author's own calculations based on Ministério dos Negócios Estrangeiros, *Anuário Diplomático e Consular Portugues,* Vol. 2, 47 (Lisbon: MNE, 2000).
30. Interview with Heloisa Cid, 10 July 2002, GAERI, Ministry of Cities, Planning and Environment.
31. Interviews with Josefina Carvalho, CIAC, 22 September 1998; Luis Inez Fernandes, Department for Juridical Affairs, 21 September 1998, and Alzira Cabrita, Department of Financial and Economic Questions 24 September 1998. The name CIAC was established in the organic law of the Ministry of Foreign Affairs during its restructuring in 1994; (see decree-law, no. 48/94, *Diario da Republica*, I-A, no. 46, 24.2.1994, Art. 8). Before that it was called Interministerial Commission for the European Communities (Commissão Interministerial para as Comunidades Europeias-CICE) (see decree-law no. 345/91, no. 214, I-A Serie, 17.9.1991). This decree-law increased the position of CICE inside public administration; it replaced decree-law no.527/85, I-Serie, no. 301, 31.12.1985, which originally created CICE. Until 1985, the main interministerial body in the negotiation period was the Comission for European Integration (*Comissão de Integração Europeia-CIE*), supported by the State Secretariate of European Integration (see decree-law no. 306/77, *Diario da Republica*, I-Serie, no. 178, 3.8.1977).
32. Interview with Dr. Josefina Carvalho, CIAC, 22 September 1998.
33. See decree-law, no. 55/98, *Diario da Republica*, I-A Serie, no. 63, 16.3.1998, Art. 32: 1086 and 1091; until 1998 it was called the Council of Ministers for Community Affairs (*Conselho de Ministros para Assuntos Comunitarios*-CMAC) (Ministerio dos Negocios Estrangeiros, 1992: 331). Between 1985 and 1991 it was called Council of Ministers for the European Communities (*Conselho de Ministros para as Comunidades Europeias*-CMCE) and before that Council of Ministers for European Integration (*Conselho de Ministros para a Integração Europeia*-CMIE) (see decree-law no. 185/79, *Diario da Republica*, I-Serie, no. 140, 20.6.1979). Portugal has been searching for an adequate model of policy coordination for the past thirty years with mixed success; see Antonio Correia de Campos, "Coordenação de Trabalho Governamental," *Revista de Administracão e Politicas Publicas* 1, 1 (2000): 51-69; particularly 55-59.
34. Alzira Cabrita, department of finance and economic questions, DGAC, 24 September 1998; Josefina Carvalho, CIAC, 22 September 1998.
35. DAR, 20.6.1979, I-Serie, no. 140: 1347.
36. DAR, 31.12.1985, I-Serie, no. 301: 130.
37. Interview with Manuel Carvalho, REPER, Brussels, 8 February 1999.
38. Interview with Manuel Carvalho, REPER, 8 February 1999.
39. *The European Companion*, 1992 (London: Dod's Publishing and Research Limited, 1993), 449-450.
40. Interview with Manuel Carvalho, REPER, 8 February 1999.
41. *The European Companion*, 1994 (London: Dod's Publishing and Research Limited, 1995), 139-140.
42. Philippe Schoutheete, *Una Europa para todos. Diez ensayos sobre la construccíón europea* (Madrid: Alianza Editorial, 1998), 53-74.
43. According to Wolfgang Wessels, in 1994 there were 1,150 committees, working groups of the Commission (600), working groups of the Council and the Council (270) and the implementation committees of the Commission (280). In 1990, over 1,000 German civil servants were involved in these committees, sometimes two or three committees at the same time (Wolfgang Wessels and Dietrich Rometsch,

"German Administrative Interaction and European Union. The Fusion of Public Policies," in Yves Meny, Pierre Muller, and Jean-Louis Quermonne (eds.), *Adjusting to Europe. The Impact of the European Union on National Institutions and Policies* (London: Routledge, 1997), 73-109 (FN 58, pp.105-106). According to the Council Guide there were 287 Council working groups and committees (General Secretariat of the Council, 1996, *Guide to the Council of the European Communities*, Vol. I (Luxembourg: Office of the Official Publications of the European Communities, 1996), 91-104).

44. Jan Beyers, Dierickx, "The Working Groups of the Council of the European Union: Supranantional or Intergovernmental Negotiations?" *Journal of Common Market Studies* 36, 3, 1998: 289-317; particularly 289-317, 290-291.
45. Ibid., 305-306.
46. Pedro Sanchez da Costa Pereira, "Portugal: Public Administration and EPC/CFSP—A Fruitful Adaptation Process," in Franco Algieri, Elfriede Regelsberger (eds.), *Synergy at Work: Spain and Portugal in European Foreign Policy* (Bonn: Europa Union Verlag, 1996), 207-229, particularly 210-217.
47. As mentioned before, this story was told by Francisco Seixas da Costa in his detailed account. Quite a highlight was the coordinating meeting of the ten small- and medium-sized members in the Portuguese REPER on 24 November 2000. See Francisco Seixas da Costa, "Portugal e o Tratado de Nice," 60.
48. Jeffrey Lewis, "Is the 'Hard Bargaining' Image of the Council Misleading? The Committee of Permanent Representatives and the Local Elections Directive,"*Journal of Common Market Studies* 36, 4, 1998: 479-504.
49. Interview with Dr. Pedro Lourtie, REPER, Brussels, 13 September 2002.
50. Lewis, op. cit., 490-491.
51. Interview with Dra. Josefina Carvalho, DGAC, 22 September 1998.
52. Manuel Carvalho, REPER, Antici Group, 8 February 1999.
53. Some comparative studies are Ana Fraga, *Os Parlamentos Nacionais e a legitimidade da construção europeia* (Lisbon: Cosmos, 2002); Andreas Maurer, *National Parliaments in the European Architecture: Elements for Establishing a Best Practice Mechanism.* Working the European Convention, The Secretariat, Group IV-Role of National Parliaments, Brussels, 9 July 2002; Torbjorn Bergman, "National Parliaments and EU Affairs Committees: Notes on the Empirical Variation and Competing Explanations," *Journal of European Public Policy* 4, 3, 1997: 373-87; Tapio Raunio, "Always One Step Behind? National Legislatures and the European Union," *Government and Opposition* 34, 2, 1999: 180-202.

7

The Portuguese Euro-Elite and the Presidency of the European Union 2000. A Study of the Network of Interactions within the European Union Multilevel Governance System

Introduction

Institutions and institutionalism have been at the forefront of European integration studies since the early days. This naturally has led to the assumption that the construction and reconstruction of these institutions are the crucial factors shaping the European integration process. In reality, institutions are artefacts constructed by political, administrative, and civil society actors. The neglect of studies on the actors of European integration has created a feeling that all processes and institutions had reached a systemic level in which actors no longer matter. The Intergovernmental Conferences (IGCs) of the 1990s and the IGC leading up to the Treaty of Nice showed that political, administrative, and civil society actors within the institutions are the ones who move the European integration process forward.

This chapter attempts to offer some insight into the development of national Euro-elites that work together within a multilevel EU governance system. This chapter intends to study the formation of the national Euro-elites of the European Union, in general, and the Portuguese national Euro-elite, in particular. For this purpose, it is important to look at the national Portuguese Euro-elite as having national, transnational, and supranational traits. In some way, the national Euro-elites based in Lisbon and Brussels are present at all these levels and they shape the nature of all these decision-making arenas.

One of the most intense periods for the national Portuguese Euro-elite as well as any Euro-elite of a EU member-state is the presidency of the Council of Ministers of the European Union. In this period, the member-state organizing the presidency has to mobilize all their human and material resources to make the enterprise a success.

This chapter will first identify the main trends towards convergence of national Euro-elites. In terms of definition, Euro-elite is conceptualized in broad terms comprising both administrative and political elites dealing with aspects of European public policy or European affairs. Afterward, a short discussion of Euro-elites in action during the presidency will follow. The third part of the chapter deals with the making of the Portuguese Euro-elite during the 1980s and 1990s. The last part is dedicated to the study of the network of interactions that existed during the Portuguese presidency in 2000. The chapter will be closed with some conclusions on the Portuguese Euro-elite formation, in particular, and the national Euro-elites, in general.

Some Theoretical Notes on Elites in the European Multilevel Governance System

The Making of the European Union Multilevel Governance System

The concept of the EU multilevel governance system was first devised by Gary Marks in the early 1990s and it has since then caught the mood among political scientists. The very charming concept tries to show that there is a growing fusion of the different decision-making tiers of regional, national and supranational political systems. This thrust towards integration of the different levels can be observed already, although the concept itself has to be defined as a heuristic device to enable people to understand better the processes of European integration of the 1980s and 1990s. This concept of Gary Marks is certainly a useful tool to understand the European Union as a system of interactions of institutions and actors within and among the different levels of the European Union. Governance means, therefore, the dynamics of the whole evolving new European Union system; it is more than the sum of its parts.[1]

One characteristic in the multilevel EU governance system is the incompleteness of the project. The so-called Europolity has reached a high level of complexity in certain areas, while in others integration still lags behind. There is also the fact that some countries may be more integrated than others into the overall EU multilevel governance system. Comparisons can be drawn between Belgium as an extremely integrated country and Italy, which, in some fields, is still lagging behind. The incomplete Europolity lacks also a final design. Despite many scenarios, one is not sure about the final outcome of the Europolity.[2] Therefore, some scholars define the multilevel governance system as a *political system sui generis*, which will overcome the past forms of institutional and political organization and create a new innovative one. This political system sui generis may include several elements of past forms of political and institutional organization, but in the end it will combine all into a new form.[3]

Another aspect is the fact that many of the levels are horizontally and vertically mismatched. This can be found particularly when regions want to create Euro-regions. Normally, the regions or regional tiers of different countries are faced with the problem that their administrative structures do not match. It takes a long period of accommodation to create adequate structures of decision-making that are appropriate for Euro-regions. This can be exemplified with the case of the Saar-Lor-Luxembourg region, which only slowly created its own Euro-regional institutions and corresponding political culture.[4] The good news is that when one becomes aware of these problems it will be easier for other Euro-regions to identify sooner their main problems. As John Loughlin clearly pointed out, all member-states have different forms of multilevel governance; some include three tiers (local, regional, national) and others only two (local, national).[5] There has been some convergence of structures in the past two decades across all countries of the European Union, but differences and divergences still persist. In spite of all this, one assertion can be made with confidence: The spatial organization of the European Union has reduced its rigidity and has become more flexible.

All this affects the EU multilevel governance system. Less studied is the impact of political and administrative elites as well as (regional, national, and European) civil society in creating this multilevel governance system. A study of the operative political and administrative elites on European affairs at all levels can only be achieved by a differentiated approach that will look at elites from various perspectives. For this a typology of European elite formation has to be conceptualized that is broad enough to take into account national, transnational, and supranational elites, which represent the voluntaristic thrust of European integration, or in some cases desintegration.

National, Transnational, and Supranational Elites: Towards a Framework for the Analysis of a European Elite Formation

The introduction of the multilevel governance heuristic device developed by Gary Marks allows us to analyze much better the whole process of European elite formation. In the past two decades, the few studies on European elite formation concentrated on the Members of European Parliaments (MEPs). The direct election of MEPs since 1979 offered an unique opportunity for scholars to study the long-term implications of these new groups of politicians that represent the *demoi* of the European Union at the supranational level. The initial euphoria on the prospects of the making of a new European elite beyond the national elite formations had to be changed by a more down-to-earth approach as it became evident that in terms of professionalization and turnover the whole process would take longer than expected to consolidate and institutionalize.[6] Probably the most comprehensive study was done by Martin Westlake, who, in analyzing the British MEPs from 1979 to 1989, realized that Westminster, the national parliament, continued to be the main point of reference for most British politicians. The European experience was for many of them a way of enhancing their political portfolio in view of receiving a better job within the British system.[7] Although, there is an incomprehensible lack of studies on the MEPs, one can assume that the recent fight against patronage, clientelism, and corruption of the EP against the Commission in 1998 may have changed the perception of the role of the EP in the overall political system.[8]

But a study of the MEPs does not tell the full story of the formation of a Euro-elite. In reality, a study of a Euro-elite has to comprise the three levels in which both political and administrative elites within the EU multilevel governance system operate. Indeed, a study of European elite formation needs to comprise the spatial linkage among the different levels of decision-making: national, transnational, and supranational elements are intrinsic in any conceptualization of a European elite. The whole nature of the European integration process was elitist and technocratic from the very start, so that despite democratization efforts in recent decades the European integration process has been led both by political and administrative elites. The socialization of politicians and public servants at the different levels of the EU political system creates the feeling of belonging to a new future-oriented elite formation, which is still undefined and all over the place, due to the lack of definition of the emerging Europolity.

The most important level of socialization and convergence of atittudes towards the formation of a European political elite is the transnational level. It has both political as well as administrative institutional frameworks, so that both politicians as well as administrators can use these structures to shape European public policy. Interactions can be Brussels-based, but the majority predisposes a continuing traveling of government representatives, interest groups, and politicians from their national capitals to Brussels. In the administrative sector, we can find a huge number of officials taking part in the working committees of the Council of the European Union as well as in the huge number of consultative, management, and decision-making committees attached to the European Commission. According to calculations by Maurizio Bach, about 40,000 civil servants and European Union experts are involved in the decision-making processes in the working committees of the Council of the European Union and the comitology of the European Commission during the year. Moreover, there are on average 150 meetings of the committees of the European Union. In any case, Bach's calculations lead to an estimation that there are about 360,000 travels yearly from the national capitals to Brussels and vice versa.[9]

According to another study in 1996, there were 270 working groups in the council, 400 comitology groups, and about 600 expert committees and adhoc advisory committees attached to the European Commission. In total, there are an estimated 1,300 committees in Brussels that lead to interaction between national and supranational levels. The exponential growth of committees became quite salient in the second half of the 1980s and in the 1990s. This naturally was related to the growth in complexity of legislative processes and the incrementalist agenda of the European Union. Only in the second half of the 1990s, did the incrementalist agenda of the European Union slow down.[10] The core part of this transnational political elite comprises the members of the Permanent Representations in Brussels. In most cases they are permanently based in Brussels and subject to a stronger socialization into the transnational culture dealing with European public policy. They are trained to weigh the national position in relation to options available for new EU legislation. This permanent dialogue in the working groups of the Council of the European Union and COREPER I and II contributes to a culture of compromise and bargaining between the permanent representations of the different member-states.[11]

Political elites on the transnational level can be found among the members of the national parliaments belonging to the specialized committees of European affairs, which meet twice a year in the respective country in which the presidency is held. The COSAC is enshrined in the Treaties since Maastricht. Until now it played a subaltern role in the whole European integration process. It remained an informal institution, in which MPs from the member-states could exchange information on ways to scrutinize better the national governments. There was an attempt in 1989 to achieve a more regular and stronger connection between the COSAC and the European Parliament in Rome, but it failed to become a reality. In spite of the reduced importance of COSAC, these national MPs are engaged in a process of socialization and integration of parliamentary cultures, thus creating the conditions for a Europeanization of parliamentary strategies vis-à-vis the Executive. It is difficult to make an estimation of how many persons are involved in this informal structure, but an educated guess estimates that about 120 persons (parliamentarians and administrative staff) are involved in each meeting.[12]

Quite regular also are the meetings of the Economic and Social Committees of the European Union and similar institutions twice a year. The number of people involved is quite small, not exceeding twenty persons per meeting.[13]

Furthermore, national and Euro-groups play a major role in this transnational level. Their main task is to lobby and influence policymaking in the committees and in the institutions of the European Union. They tend to work at different levels. According to estimations, there are over 2,000 interest groups in the Brussels' arena. Almost 10,000 lobbyists or representatives of interest groups are contributing to the complexity of the political system.[14] They have to be regarded as part of the peripheral Euro-elite in contrast to the central one that comprises the administrative and political policy makers.

While this transnational level can be regarded as the meeting point of two different rationales of governance, the national and supranational, creating a transnational layer of mixed codes among administrative and political elites, this cannot be said about the two other levels.

The political and administrative elites working at the national level have the national interest in mind. This can be said about the process of EU policy coordination concentrated normally in the Ministry of Foreign Affairs. In several ministries there are experts on European affairs that are in permanent contact with the Permanent Representation in Brussels and the corresponding coordinating body in the national capital. The government members are required to make several trips to Council meetings during the year. Some ministries such as the Minister of Agriculture is more engaged than others. In some way, through socialization in the supranational and transnational levels they become socialized into the rationale of the European Union governance. Therefore, in recent years due to growing complexity and interaction between national, transnational, and supranational actors one can say that national governments and administrations are becoming more and more Europeanized. According to Rainer Lepsius, the growing importance of European law and its translation into the different languages of the European Union, further erodes nationally defined policymaking. In reality, European law has become part of our lives, although we do not notice due to the translation into the national languages, which gives the impression that everything is still defined by national law.[15]

Although in some countries there is a resistance to the lack of scrutiny of European legislation, such as in the U.K. and Denmark, in reality the incrementalist, detailed, and complex bulk of legislation has overloaded these parliaments. Most parliaments are bypassed and informed only after legislation has been translated into national law. This again shows that national parliaments have lost power in the past two decades. Some parliaments may have a strong pro-active culture to shape in some way EU legislation such as the German Bundestag and Bundesrat, the Danish Folketing, the UK Parliament, or other Nordic parliaments, but in others, due to a lack of resources and interest, such as in Portugal, Spain, Greece, Belgium, and Luxembourg, they assume a more passive role.[16]

At supranational level, the Euro-elite comprises the administration of all main institutions, the MEPs, and the college of Commissioners. They are naturally representatives of the supranational level, although in the case of the political elite in the European Parliament and at the top of the Commission they again show traits of national, transnational, and supranational ele-

Table 7.1
A Typology of National, Transnational, and Supranational Euro-Elites

	National Section	Transnational Section	Supranational Section
Political Field	Government members (15 member-states), parliamentary Committee of European Affairs (15 member-states)	Specialized Conference of European Affairs of National Parliaments (COSAC)	Commissioners of the European Commission, Council of the European Union (ministers from 15 member-states), Members to European Parliament
Administrative Field	Top civil servants dealing with European affairs in individual ministries and EU policy coordinating body (15 member-states)	Permanent Representations (15 member-states), 270 working council committees, 400 comitology committees, 600 European experts and adhoc advisory committees	Top civil servants of the European Union institutions.
Civil Society	National Interest groups (15 member-states), Economic and Social Committee (ESC)	Euro interest groups, national federations represented in Brussels, meetings of ESC of the EU	Eurogroups, Economic and Social Committee of the European Union, Committee of the Regions and Local Authorities

ments. The MEPs are organized into transnational political groups, which are very loose and in some way influenced by national groups of MEPs that may be particularly strong in a European political group. MEPs also have offices in their countries of origin and thus fulfill an integrative role at the national level. They will also be in connection with their national parties, which contributed to their selection and election as MEPs. In some cases, a specific group of MEPs may be in connection with the corresponding national Permanent Representation and contribute to the national agenda.[17] In this case, we could speak of a nationalization of supranational elites in certain circumstances.

In the case of the Commission, commissioners are still selected by the national government; therefore, ties to the country may still remain despite its supranational status. Some permanent representations try to maintain strong contacts with top civil servants of the same nationality in the European Commission to get inside information.

More peripherally elite are the members of the Economic and Social Committee and the Committee of the Regions and Local Authorities (CoR), which are advisory committees to the European Commission. Their role is not relevant, but in the case of the CoR it gave new impetus to the more peripheral tier of the multilevel governance system, the regional level.

In this sense, the Euro-elite is defined by its involvement in national, transnational, and supranational levels. In most cases, one of these levels is the center of the corresponding section of the Euro-elite, but it may be part of or interact with other sections at different levels at the same time. On the whole, the formation of the European elite is the formation of a elite sui generis that corresponds to the unknown future-oriented Europolity. In mapping out the whole Euro-elite and their subsections, it is easy to proceed towards a definition of nationally based Euro-elite, in general, and the Portuguese Euro-elite, in particular.

The Making of National Euro-Elites

The formation of national Euro-elites is related to the development of the European Union as a political system sui generis in the past fifty years. The entire process of integration clearly led to a blurring of the boundaries between the supra- and national levels. The emergence of the extremely overcrowded transnational level created some kind of symbiosis and filtering of this tension between two different rationales of governance.

After the process of negotiation towards accession, most new members are faced with enormous pressure from the supranational level to adjust political and administrative elites accordingly. The Europeanisation process is mostly related to this adjustment pressure of national public administrations and national political elites to cope with a new more relevant tier of decision-making. It has been recognized that national EU policy coordination[18] has to invest in human and material resources, so that it can play an active and interactive role in the new political system sui generis, due to the fact that the past fifty years did not lead only to an exponential incrementalism of the policy agenda, but as well as to complexity of the issues with which national, transnational, and supranational political elites have to deal.

The core relationship at the national level is between the government and the corresponding Committee of European Affairs. The executive is obliged to inform the parliament about EU legislation and other European initiatives. Both the executive and the Committee of European Affairs are involved in different levels of the EU political system. This naturally makes it imperative to have knowledgeable elites in the area of European integration in these subsections of the national Euro-elite. The central political national Euro-elite would therefore comprise around 40-50 people of each country, leading to an estimation that the 15 political national Euro-elites may comprise a figure of 600-750 members. They are, of course, engaged at different times at Council level or COSAC level or each one in the national arena.

In spite of appearances, the whole decision-making network at the supranational level is quite asymmetrical. Some countries matter more than others. At the center are the "big three," France, Germany, and the UK. This group of countries dominates the political and administrative agenda at Council meetings. These experienced well-established administration and political elites set up the choices of policymaking. A second important tier of states are the northern countries comprising the Nordic countries (Denmark, Sweden, Finland), the Benelux countries, and Ireland. The third tier comprises the periphery of the decision-making process: the southern European countries (Portugal, Spain, Greece, and Italy).[19] The big surprise is the passivity of Italy, which, with the same amount of votes as the big three, has remained peripheral throughout the fifty years of European integration. There are two explanations for this. Firstly, Italians are normally pro-European, advocating further integration towards a federalist state. This can be seen in the Euro-barometer surveys since the 1970s, where Italians tend to trust more the EU political system and institutions than their own national political system and institutions. Secondly, in the past fifty years, Italy has had to face permanent governmental instability. Italy has had over fifty governments with a low duration time over the past fifty years. The recent transition to a new electoral system did not lead to a change of this culture of governmental instability. This naturally debilitates the possibility for Italy to play a long-term professional role at supranational level.

A stronger engagement of the southern European periphery has come from Spain since the late 1980s. The ambition of Spain during the Felipe Gonzalez period (1982-96) and under José Maria Aznar (since 1996) is to acquire superpower status along with the "big three." This ambition is still a far-fetched dream, but informs the activities of Spanish diplomacy.

The formation of a national Euro-elite has only recently become an issue, because the number of arenas of decision-making or cooperation have increased considerably. The support of administrative elites, which are acquainted with all aspects of European affairs, is further evidence of this long-term commitment to the European Union political system. Although some administrations are better than others, they all seem to converge towards some basic principles related to new public management (NPM). Presently, commissioner Neil Kinnock is pushing through a major reform of the Commission bureaucracy based on these principles of NPM.[20] This shows that a "Europe of Administrations" is no longer a far-fetched reality. The convergence of public administration principles clearly opens up the rigidity of national public administrations and forces them to adapt adequately to the new challenges.[21] The European Union public administration comprises, therefore, national, transnational, and supranational elements that more and more follow the same principles, which are set up by shared collective good practice dissemination. In this sense, any national public administration is a reflection of the new political system sui generis and may be a contributor to improvement of public management in certain areas.[22] This naturally requires a complete transformation of administrative law, which is extremely dependent on the evolving political system sui generis[23] (see also chapter 5).

On the whole, the national Euro-elite has transformed over time. The growing public policy agenda of the European Union led to a blurring of the boundaries between the national and supranational level. Fusion and adjustment processes are happening that may transform the whole understanding of the multilevel Euro-elites.

The Presidency of the Council of Ministers of the European Union: Some Comparative Notes on Patterns of Interaction

The highlight for any national Euro-elite is the presidency of the Council of Ministers of the European Union. For a period of six months, a national government has the possibility of being in charge of the policy agenda of the European Union. The agenda-setting, however, is carried out by the European Commission and is related to the work done by the previous presidency. In spite of these restrictions, national governments may be able to shape and promote certain issues of importance to them. This may and may not be pursued with success. The management of the European Union may lead to unexpected problems, such as the Danish "no" vote in the referendum over the Maastricht Treaty during the Portuguese presidency in 1992, or the Danish "no" vote in the referendum on the introduction of the Euro during the French presidency in 2000. In some cases new projects may be launched, such as the Euromediterranean partnership in Barcelona during the Spanish presidency of 1995. This was a prestigious achievement for Spanish foreign diplomacy, which had worked several years to get this project started. In some cases, a project may be successfully started or finalized, but the incumbent of the presidency is delaying its participation in it for a latter stage. This was the case of the UK presidency in the first half of 1998, when the third stage of EMU was agreed upon, but where other countries went ahead without the incumbent of the presidency in the follow-up Austrian presidency.

This most intensive of periods for any national Euro-elite involve a huge managerial capacity. According to Peter Ludlow, the UK presidency in the first half of 1998 comprised twenty-two usable weeks. During this period it presided over forty-five Council meetings, further eight informal meetings of ministers, sixty-five meetings of COREPER I and II, and approximately 1,500 working groups sessions. Moreover, it had to organize several high profile events such as the EU-Japanese meeting in January, the European Conference in March, the EU-Asia meeting in April, and the EU-U.S. summit in May. Other engagements such as meetings with the trojka, ministerial appearances before the European Parliament, participation in parliamentary committees, and meetings within the framework of the Council-Parliament conciliation procedure further give evidence of the complexity and importance of the presidency as a managerial challenge.[24]

Beyond this mere managerial role, some national Euro-elites may use the presidency to promote certain issues, as was the case during the German and Danish presidency, when decision-making related to environmental policy issues was intensified and brought to a conclusion in the whole Council machinery through working groups, COREPER I and II, and in the Council meetings.[25] Other countries such as Portugal and Greece tend to show a more passive role in promoting the issues in which they may be interested.

The Presidency of the European Union has thus been an underresearched subject, particularly the network of interactions. The most thorough description of what the presidency entails has been done by Fiona Hayes-Renshaw and Helen Wallace. According to these political scientists, the main functions of the presidency are:

1. The role of *business manager* in the huge amount of meetings that are taking place.
2. The *Management of European Political Cooperation/Common Foreign and Security Policy* (EPC/CFSP).
3. *Promoter of initiatives* that may or may not be in national interest.
4. *Package-broker* at different levels of the Council system.
5. *Liaison point* for the three main decision-making institutions: Council, Parliament, and European Parliament.
6. *Collective representative* in the system of international relations.[26]

Quite crucial is the ability to organize at least one European Council, which will lead to the drafting of the conclusions of the presidency. The informal nature of the European Council gives the opportunity to look at the achievements and progress made by the corresponding presidency in the individual pillars of the European Union: EC, CFSP, and JHA. This naturally gives structure to an institution that is embedded in a permanent continuum of one member-state replacing another after six months.[27]

A vital support for the country running the presidency is the Council Secretariat, which originally was nonexistent in the treaties, but slowly became an important piece of the institutional framework. The Secretary General of the Council has gained in importance throughout the past fifty years. In the 1950s, the Council had only 200 persons working on different issues; today the complexity of the decision-making process has led to an increase to

2,290 persons assigned to ten Directorate Generals. They are vital for the smooth running of the whole Council system. The former secretary general was the former German permanent representative Jürgen Trumpf. Like his predecessor the Danish Niell Ersboll, he is recognized as being a pro-active supportive secretary general.[28] The present secretary general, Javier Solana, gained new powers as High Representative of the Common Foreign and Security Policy of the European Union (Mr. CFSP).

In the end, each presidency has to deal within a pre-structured agenda, which is set up at its beginning. One can see from the agenda the huge number of formal meetings that the presidency has to organize. A network of interactions, some of them highly formalized, others less so, make it aware of the work done by the national Euro-elite, which is in charge of the presidency. Both the national political Euro-elite as well as the national administrative elite have to work closely together to assure a successful running of the presidency. Some continuity and experience can be retrieved from former presidencies held by a corresponding country. In spite of all this, the nature of the European integration process is one of growing complexity, so that the presidencies of the 1950s,1960s, and 1970s were quite easy tasks in comparison to those in the 1990s and recent ones in the new millennium.[29]

The Making of the Portuguese Euro-Elite

The complexity of a presidency of the Council of Ministers predisposes a well-trained national Euro-elite that is able to deal with this huge network of interactions. As has been stated above, this becomes a huge challenge for any new member-state. In the next two remaining sections, I will try to illustrate empirically, based on the study of the Portuguese case, how much is involved in creating a well-trained, well-organized, national Euro-elite and in the running of the presidency of the European Union. In the third section, I will seek to assess the main characteristics of the national Euro-elite and the process of elite formation. In the subsequent section, I will discuss the Portuguese national Euro-elite in action during the presidency of the European Union.

Administrative Elites

Similar to other countries, the center of Portuguese EU Policy coordination lies in the Ministry of Foreign Affairs. The structures were created in view of having the most efficient communication structures with Brussels. The DGAC is the main body dealing with issues of policy coordination, and is in constant contact with the Permanent Representation (REPER) in Brussels. Both institutions were created in the 1980s and evolved into more mature structures throughout the 1990s, particularly after the first Portuguese presidency in 1992. On the whole, one can estimate that about 500 administrative staff may be involved in EU policy coordination, but not all at the same time. The core is naturally DGAC with 170 administrative staff. Beyond that, one has to count the fifty to sixty members of staff in the Permanent Representation. The other members of this administrative Euro-elite are attached to the individual ministries as well as the regional governments of Azores and Madeira.[30]

The most important liaison point of the Portuguese EU Policy coordination meeting is the so-called Interministerial Committee for Community Affairs (*Comissão Interministerial para Assuntos Comunitários*-CIAC), which meets every week on Thursday afternoon.[31] It consists of all the representatives of the individual ministries, the regional governments of Azores and Madeira and officials from the Secretariat for Community Affairs. The main purpose is to prepare the agenda and decision-making process for the next COREPER I and II meetings with the Permanent Representation. This model of operation is not unique to Portugal; it is, basically, the model adopted across the European Union member-states. A fast-track process of decision-making may be achieved in the technical questions when individual ministries enter in direct contact with the Permanent Representation or vice versa[32] (see chapter 6). The administrative Euro-elite comprises also all the experts sent to the experts committees of the Commission as well as comitology.

Although the tasks of the administrative Euro-elite increased over time, the whole process became routine. The relationship between political and administrative elites has become more organized and coordinated than it was in the late phase of the 1980s. One of the reasons for the success of the Portuguese administrative elites is related to the fact that they never underestimated the "importance of being earnest" about EU policy coordination. Although in 1986, the Portuguese were due to take over the presidency, they decided to postpone this experience to a later date, so that they could concentrate on the process of adjustment of the EU policy coordination process first. The period between 1986 and 1992 was used to train their staff in European languages, European public administration, and EU law through internship or designed courses in Paris, London, and the European Institute for Public Administration in Maastricht.[33]

All of this contributed to a positive image of Portuguese EU policy coordination, in spite of the fact that the Portuguese were regarded as only peripheral to the spiderweb of decision-making dominated by the big three—Germany, France, and the UK.

On the whole, these are the structures that contribute to the successful participation of Portugal in the European Union decision-making process. This naturally is constrained by the fact that Portugal is a small state with scarce resources to play an active or pro-active role in the overall decision-making mechanism. This realistic attitude has helped the Portuguese administrative Euro-elite to find much easier compromises in most issues that other Euro-elites, such as Denmark, Germany, France or the UK, have not.

National Political Euro-Elites (Parliament, Government) and the Supranational Portuguese Euro-Elite (European Parliament)

Here is not the place to make a thorough investigation of the Portuguese political Euro-elite. The task instead is to bring to the fore some findings about what is understood here as the formation of a political elite. For this purpose, the main characteristics of the members of the two governments that dealt with the presidencies of 1992 and 2000 are analyzed. The main purpose is to find out what kind of background these members of the national Euro-elite had when they were presiding over the Council of Ministers of the European Union.

Similarly, we will look at one segment of the parliamentary elites. The members of the Committee of European Affairs (*Comissão de Assuntos Europeus*-CAE) are conceptualized here as part of the national Euro-elite because they are in charge of scrutinizing the performance of the government in EU matters. Moreover, they are also involved in the transnational institutional framework meeting of the committees dealing with EU affairs of the European Union, the so-called COSAC, which meets twice a year and fulfills socializing functions for these MPs into the structures of the European Union as a political system sui generis. Therefore, it is important to analyze their backgrounds as well and compare them to the overall profile of the governments that were in charge with the presidencies of 1992 and 2000.

In general terms, all three segments of the Portuguese national Euro-elite (Parliament, Government, and European Parliament) have similar traits and characteristics. Indeed, there is a high degree of rotation among the three arenas.[34]

Gender

One of the main characteristics is that the Portuguese Euro-elite is dominated by male members. There was an increase in female members at the highest levels of the Portuguese Euro-elite in the 1990s, but in all three partial elite formations female members are in the minority. This is particularly evident in the case of female ministers, while the number of MPs dealing with European affairs has increased considerably. The most woman-friendly party is the Socialist Party. Another characteristic is that the same women tend to move from one arena to the other. The most famous is MEP Helena Torres Marques who accumulated experience in government, national Parliament, and the European Parliament. In spite of all the progress made in terms of coopting more female members into higher positions, however, the vast majority are male members. In some parties, such as the CDS-PP, female members have become quite rare (see figure 7.1).

Age

In all three Euro-elite formations the average MP is between forty and fifty-five years of age. This means that they already have gathered some

Figure 7.1
Gender of the Portuguese Euro-Elite

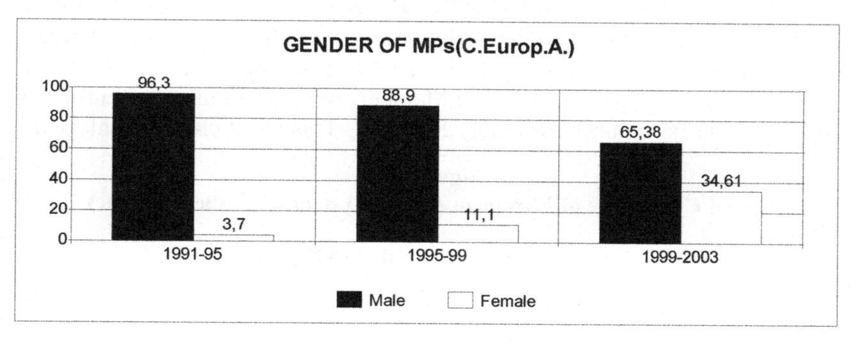

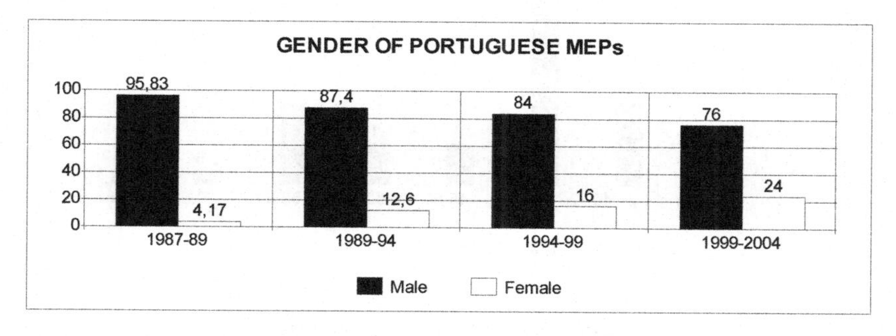

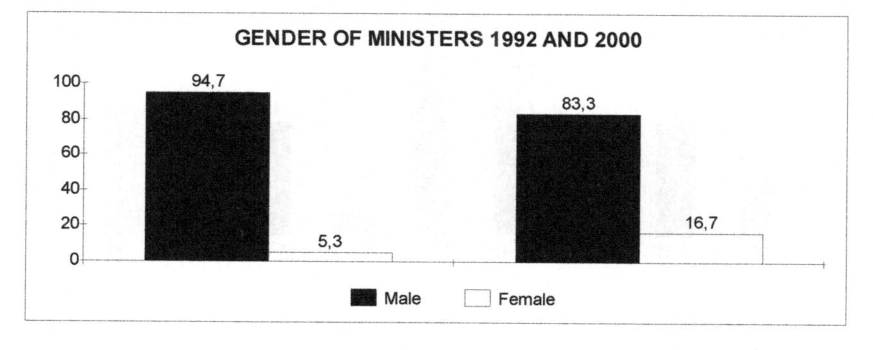

experience before they assumed a position in any of the formations. This can be particularly helpful for incumbents of government positions. Very few members below the age of forty or over fifty-five were coopted to the two governments studied here. This seems the case for the members of the European Parliament after 1989. Less clear is information on members of the national Parliament, but similar conclusions can be drawn about the average age (see figures 7.2 and 7.4).

The Local Origins of Portuguese Euro-Elites

The origins of the members of the different Euro-elites do not show a pattern. The dominance of Lisbon has been replaced by a more heterogeneous outlook. Quite interesting is the fact that at the start of the 1990s many MPs with rural backgrounds became Members of the Committee of European Affairs of the Portuguese Assembly Republic. This trend changed only with

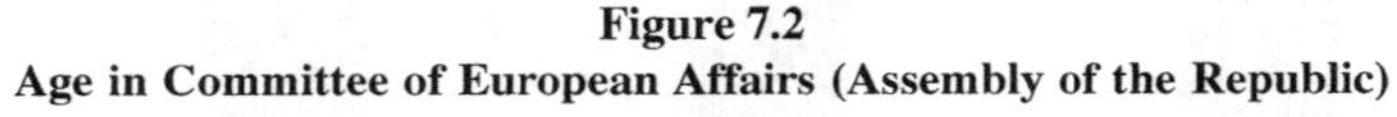

Figure 7.2
Age in Committee of European Affairs (Assembly of the Republic)

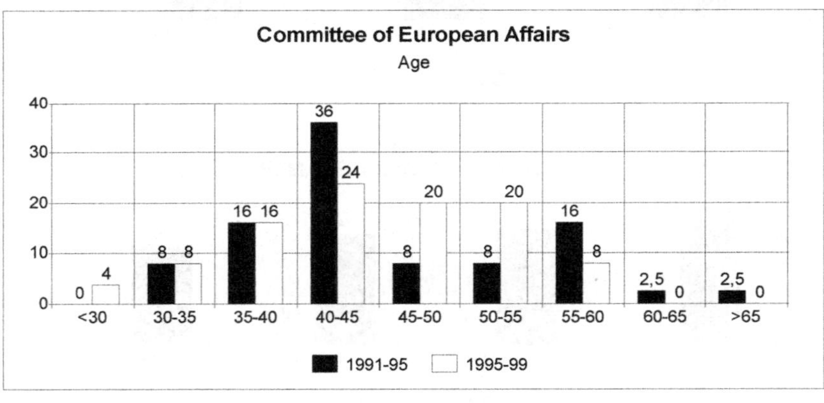

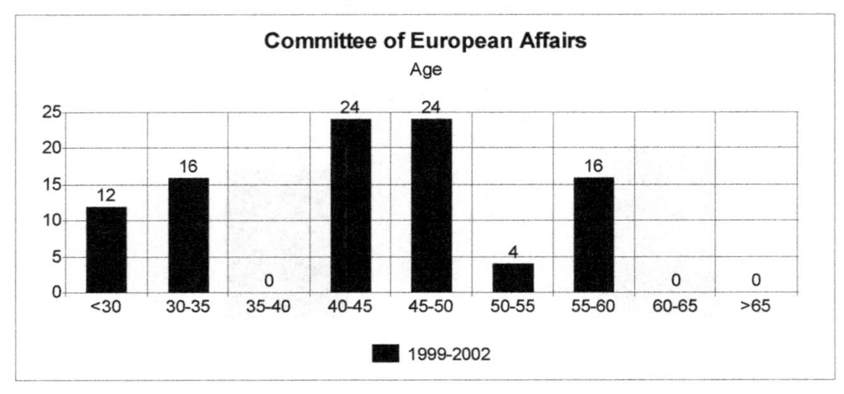

Figure 7.3
Age of Portuguese Members of European Parliament

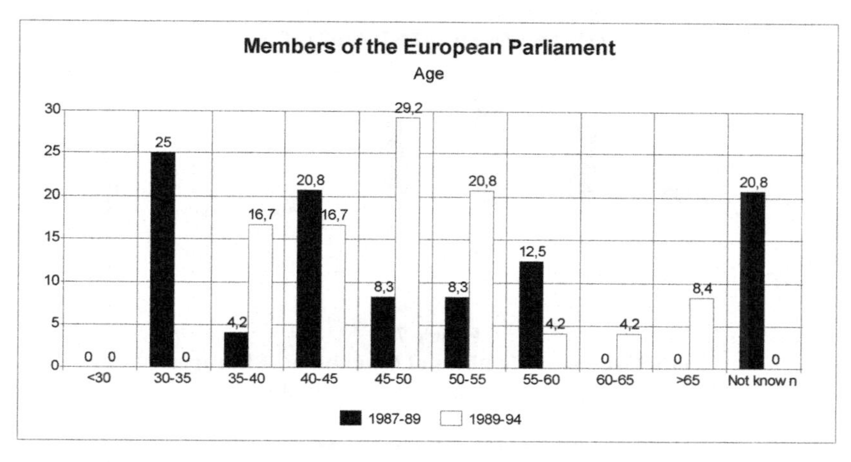

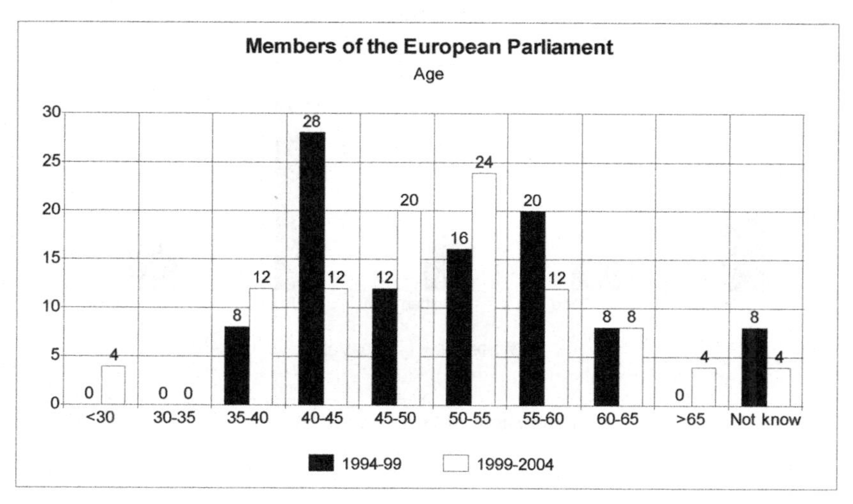

the present legislature, where MPs with urban backgrounds increased in their share. The outlook of the elite formation of the European Parliament is more heterogeneous and balanced, although Lisbon and the urban origins of MEPs is the most salient feature.

In the two governments analyzed here, the rural background of ministers is quite salient. The second largest group comes from Lisbon. This may account for a democratization of the Portuguese Euro-elite. The increase in MPs with rural origins shows that the dominance of Porto and Lisbon is decreasing slightly, although they still represent the most important group (figures 7.5 and 7.7).

Figure 7.4
Age of Government Ministers During the EU Presidency in 1992 and 2000

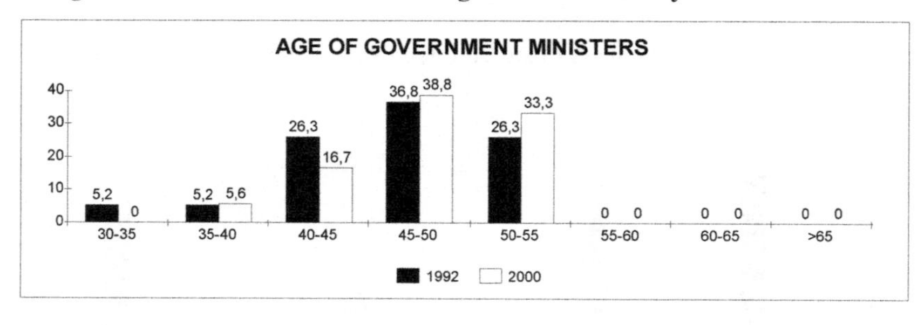

Figure 7.5
Local Origins of Members of Committee of European Affairs in Assembly of Republic

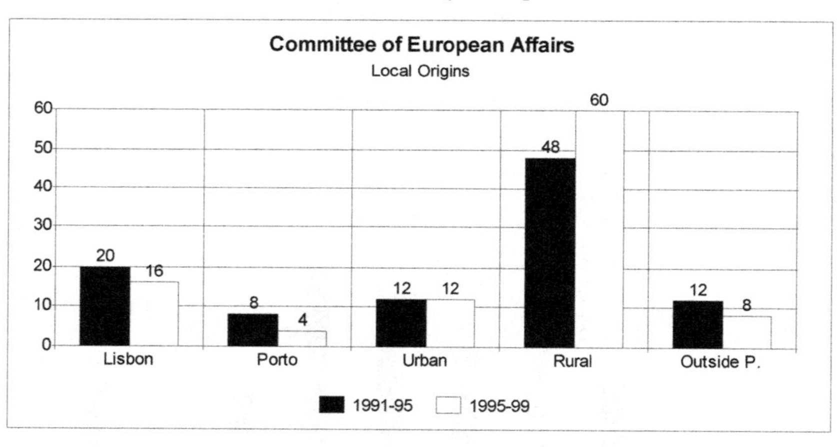

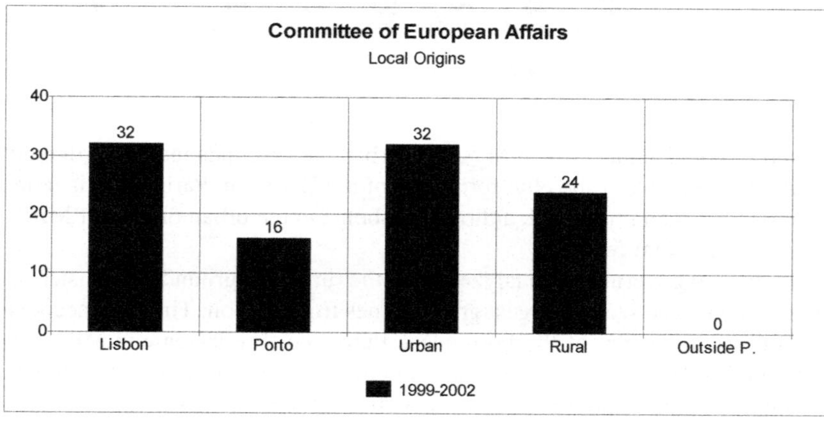

Figure 7.6
Local Origins of Portuguese Members of the European Parliament

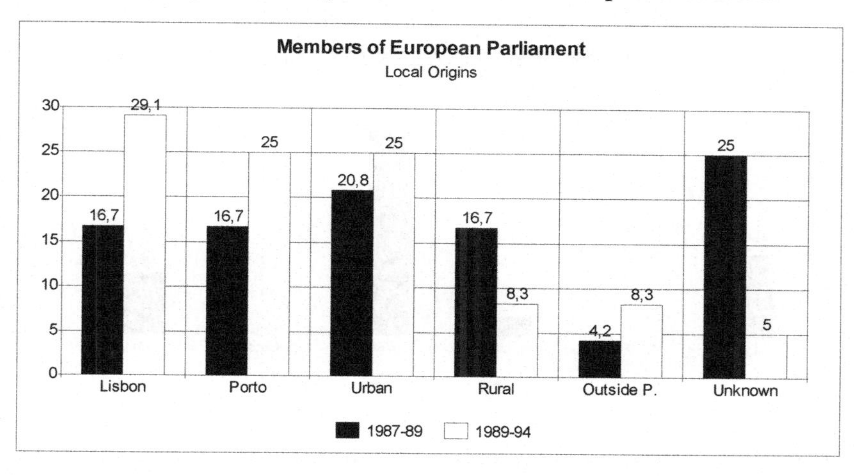

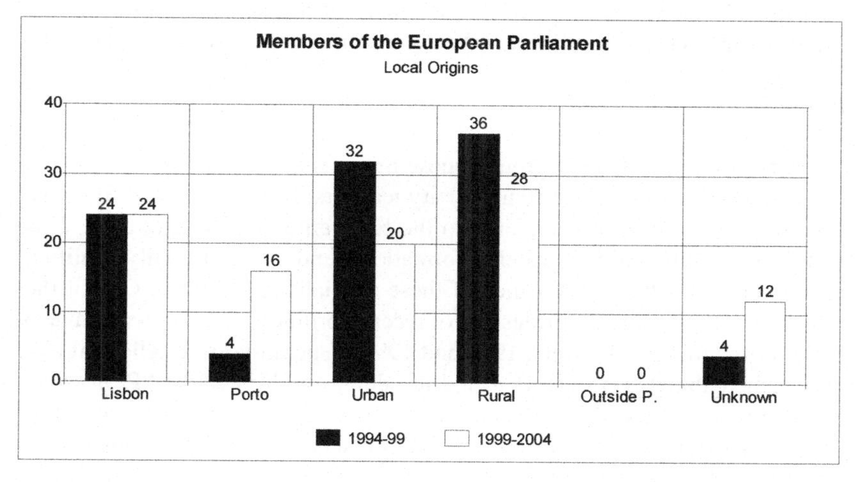

Education Background

In terms of educational background, all three Euro-elite formations are extremely well educated. The vast majority has done some kind of first degree (*Licenciatura*), and some have ventured into Master's and doctorate programs. Most of the incumbents with Master's degrees and doctorates are actually university teachers. Quite prominent is the fact that incumbents with law degrees are highly placed compared to people with a mere licenciatura. Only two MEPs, Elisa Damião (1994-1999;1999-2004) and José Torres Couto

Figure 7.7
Local Origins of Government Members During the Presidency in 1992-2000

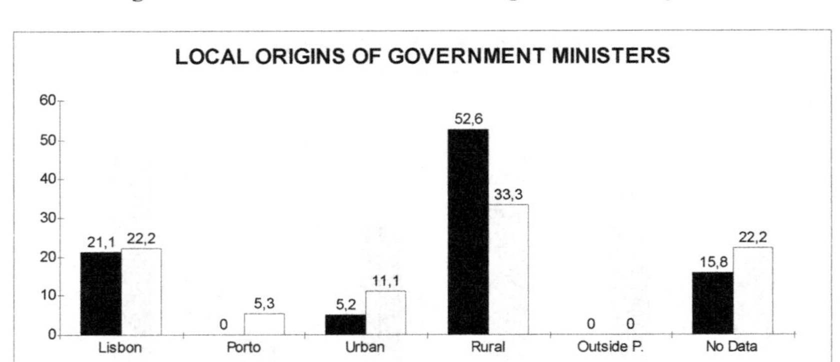

(1989-1994; 1994-1999) have only high school educations. This is more widespread among members of the Assembly of the Republic. An academic degree is quite relevant for the incumbency of a ministry (figures 7.8 and 7.10).

Professional Background

Professionally, all three groups show many similarities. Most of the incumbents of the Euro-elite are university teachers, lawyers, or civil servants. The number of engineers attracted to the Euro-elite is also quite high. This fact shows that the three Euro-elite formations tend to coopt highly qualified professionals for the performance of these specialized positions. One of the most important university professors of recent Portuguese history was Cavaco Silva, prime minister between 1985 and 1995. Veneration from fellow ministers in the cabinet and outside it, led to addressing him as the "Professor." Such approaches towards leaders has changed in the past decade. Prime Minister Antonio Guterres was always a professional politician in the recent democratic period, although he was an engineer before 25 April 1974. He had a strong relationship with the Parliament and parliamentary accountability.

The role of lawyers among the three Euro-elites does not need much explanation. The complexity of the legislative process and the legalistic nature of most issues in the day-to-day running of government politics, requires experts from the legal profession (figures 7.11 and 7.13).

Parliamentary and Public Office Experience (Professionalization)

The parliamentary experience of MPs and government ministers has grown over time. Although in the 1980s the Portuguese political elite was exceed-

Figure 7.8
Educational Background of Members of Committe of European Affairs (Assembly of the Republic)

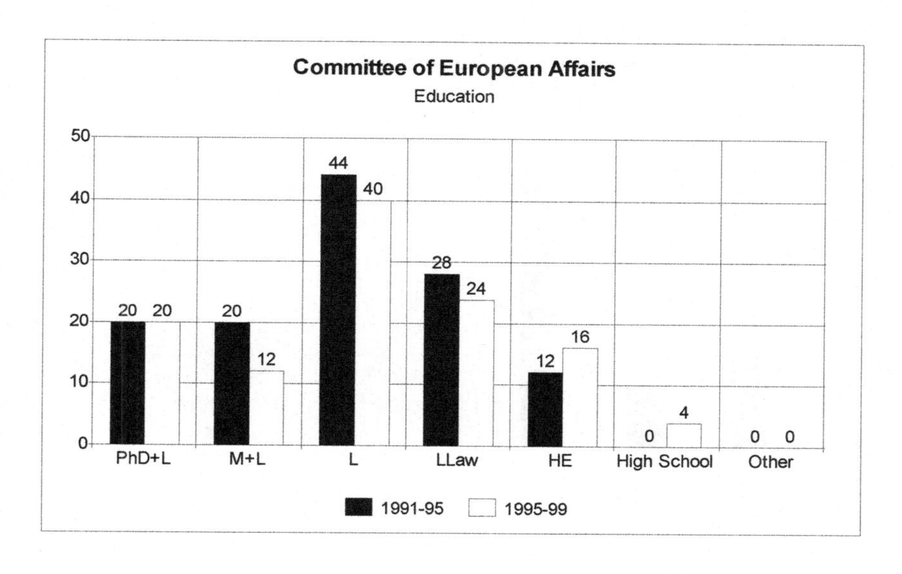

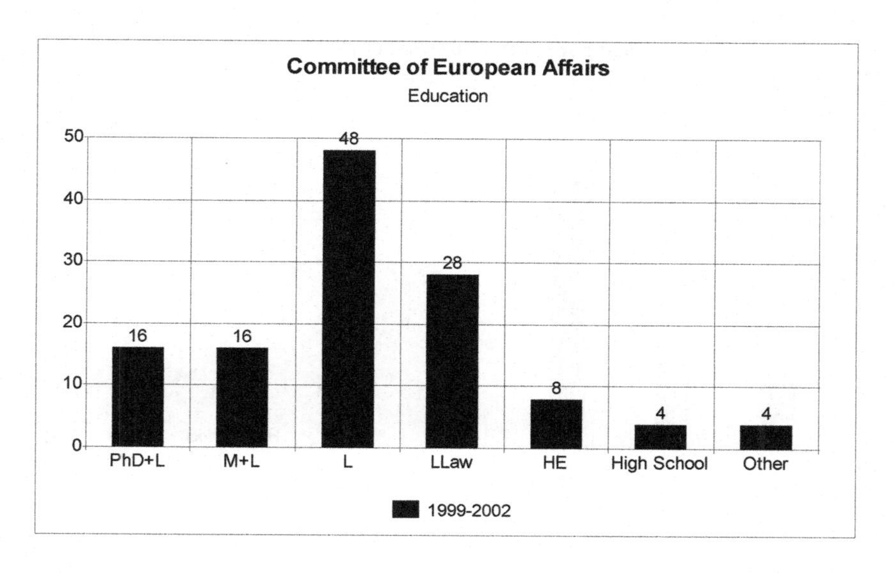

Figure 7.9
Educational Background of Portuguese Members of the European Parliament

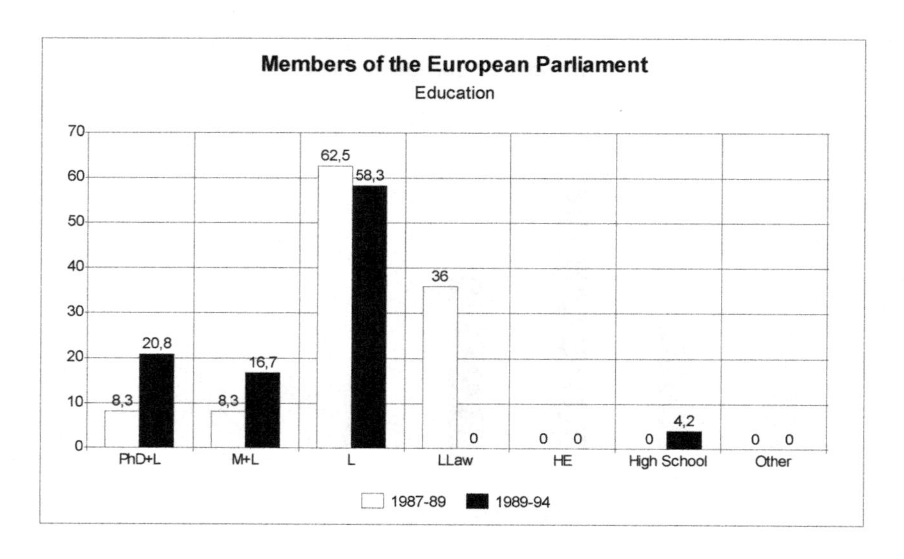

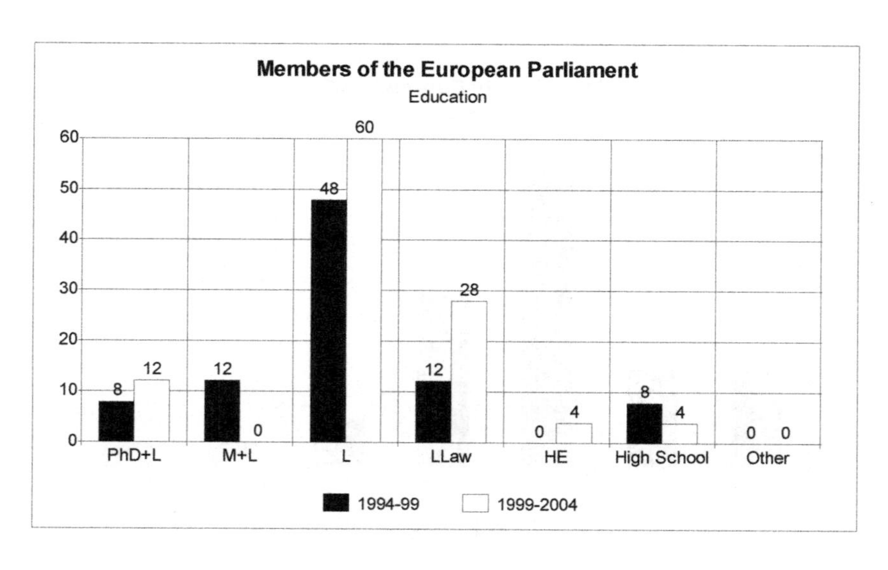

Figure 7.10
Educational Background of Government Members During the EU Presidency in 1992-2000

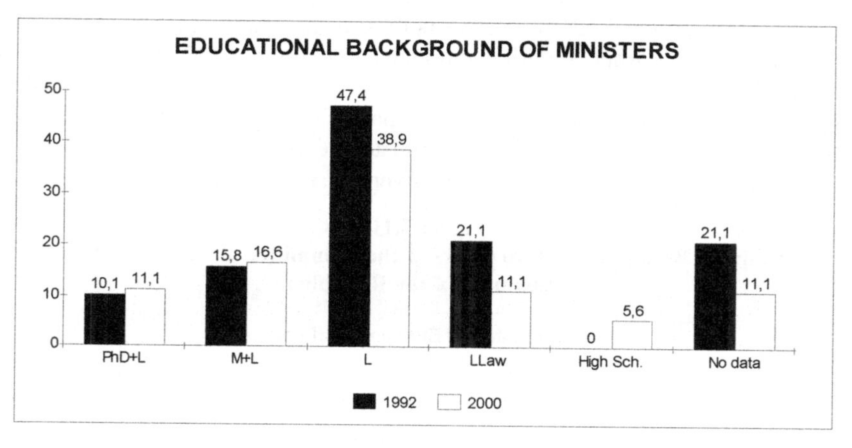

ingly unstable and characterized by a lack of professionalization, today's Euro-elite is more settled and professionalized. This can be said both for the present MPs as well as the government ministers. The Guterres government had a stronger parliamentary experience than the Cavaco Silva government. Indeed, executive-legislative relations during the Cavaco Silva years were at their lowest in the young Portuguese democracy. Most ministers in Guterres' government had an extensive exposure to Parliament and parliamentary politics. This socialization inside the center of Portuguese democracy has to be regarded as a positive trend in Portuguese politics.

The same can be said about the Committee for European Affairs. Until 1993, it was a dormant institution that had no real impact on government policy. It was actually one of Anibal Cavaco Silva's supporters, former Finance Minister Jorge Braga Macedo, who revitalized and revamped the Committee of European Affairs. It clearly followed the recent trend in the Maastricht Treaty adopted in 1993, which allowed national parliaments to take part in the European integration process through such as an institution as COSAC. The Committee of European Affairs has included throughout past years prominent parliamentarians such as José Barros Moura and Isabel Maria Almeida e Castro. In the seventh legislature (1995-1999), José Medeiros Ferreira, a notably experienced parliamentarian, was the president of the Commission and continued the work of Jorge Braga de Macedo. In general terms, one can say that in the 1990s, parliamentarianization of the national Euro-elite was the major feature that united the different parts of the Euro-elite. The Portuguese MEPs also accumulated a strong national parliamentary experience before becoming part of this supranational Euro-elite.

Basically, we can find a strong public office experience in local government and as junior ministers in all groups. Rarely do ministers return or remain in Parliament. Some of them did have experience as civil governors, the extended regional administrative bodies of the central government.

In the recent European Parliament legislature, only one MEP reached the top position of head of state—Mário Soares, who became MEP in the 1999 elections. Very few ministers are actually part of the elite formation related to the Portuguese MEPs. In the case of ministers, experience as state secretary, the label for junior minister, is a major advantage to becoming a minister. This

Figure 7.11
Professional Background of Members of the Committee of European Affairs (Assembly of the Republic)

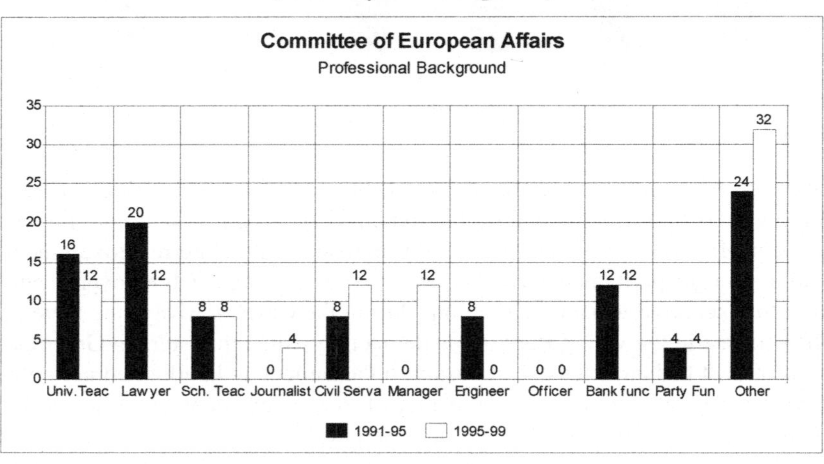

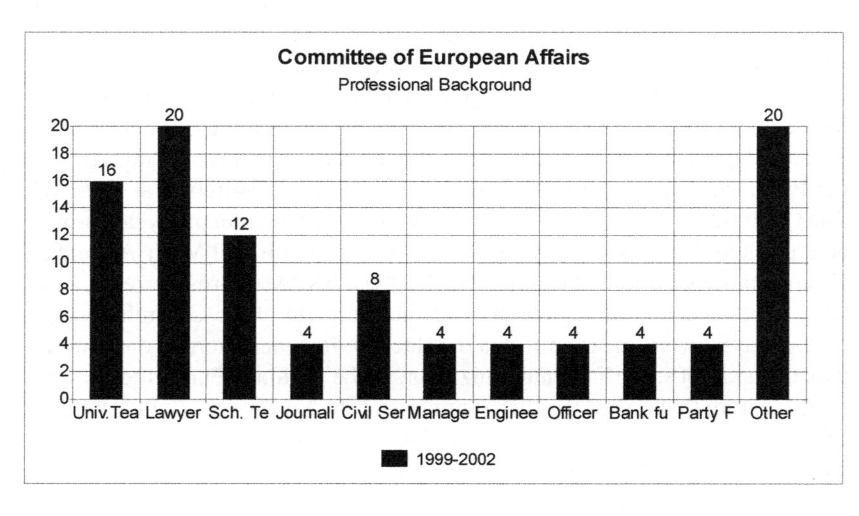

Figure 7.12
Professional Background of Portuguese Members of the European Parliament

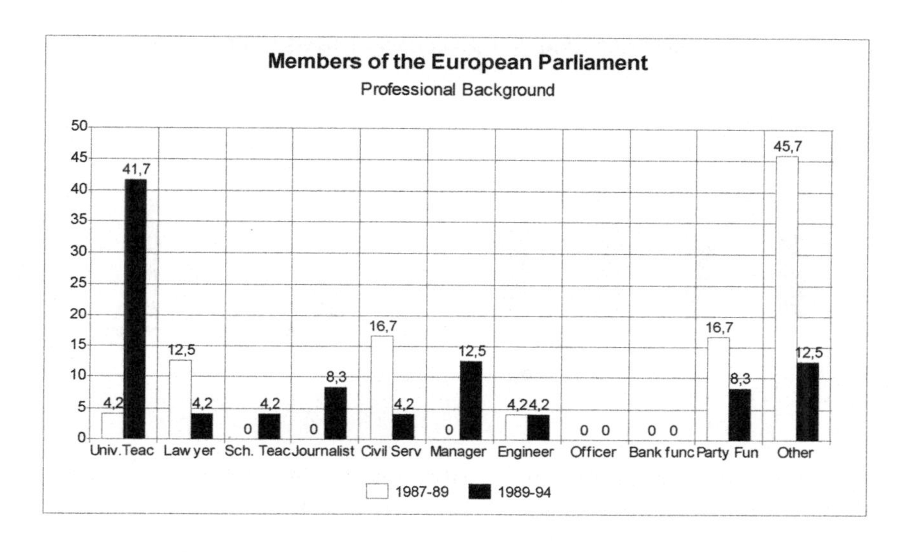

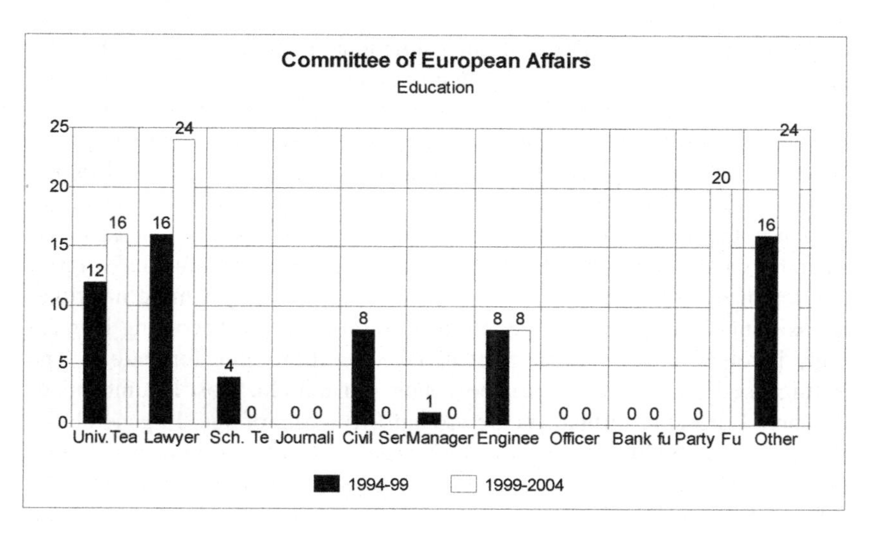

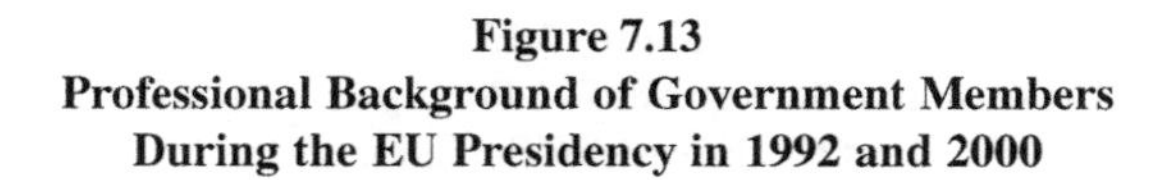

Figure 7.13
Professional Background of Government Members During the EU Presidency in 1992 and 2000

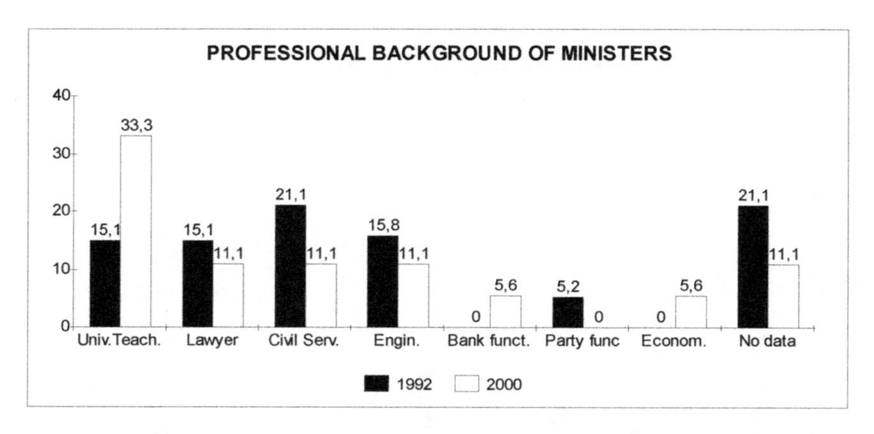

was clear illustrated in the Cavaco Silva government, and became significantly important in the late phase of the Guterres' government after the presidency (figures 7.14 and 7.16).

On the whole, the three formations of the Portuguese Euro-elite are markedly similar in outlook. The centrality of national parliamentary membership must be emphasized. Not only is it an important agency for the Euro-elite, but it is the most likely way of moving upward to government positions or to becoming a MEP. On the whole, the Portuguese Euro-elite is extremely well educated. The main places for recruitment are the universities and public administration. The political Euro-elite is dominated by male members, although in the past decade the number of female members has increased considerably in all three Euro-elite formations. In terms of geographical origins, the dominance of Lisbon and Porto has been replaced by a more heterogeneous outlook. In particular, people from rural areas are becoming increasingly involved in the top positions of the three Euro-elite formations. The Portuguese Euro-elite is neither too young, nor too old; most incumbents of the three Euro-elite formations are around fifty years of age. In general, the Portuguese Euro-elite is exceptionally cohesive in terms of traits and characteristics. One can say that the level of professionalization among the three different Euro-elite formations has grown over time. Experience and professionalization are quite even among all three Euro-formations, which creates the ideal condition for fulfilling successfully the growing tasks assigned by the *European political system sui generis*. One of these tasks is the organization and management of the presidency of the Council of Ministers of the European Union in a period of six months. In the next few pages, I will

Figure 7.14
Public Office Experience of the Members of the Committee of European Affairs (Assembly of the Republic)

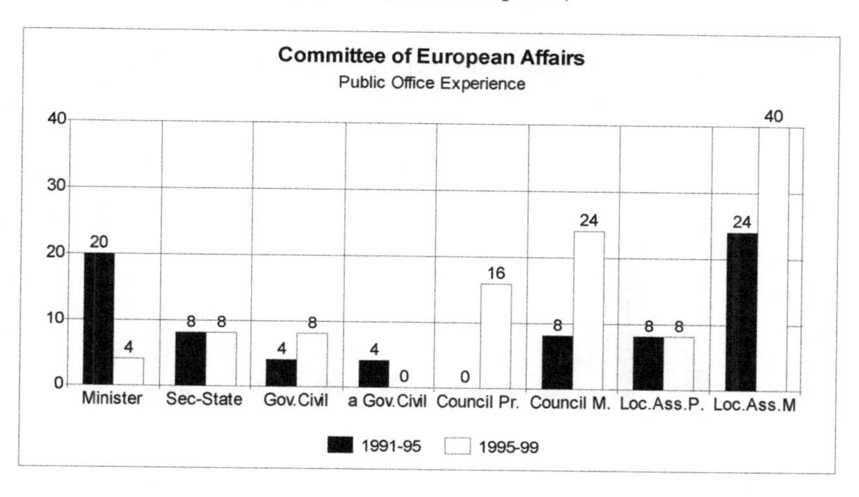

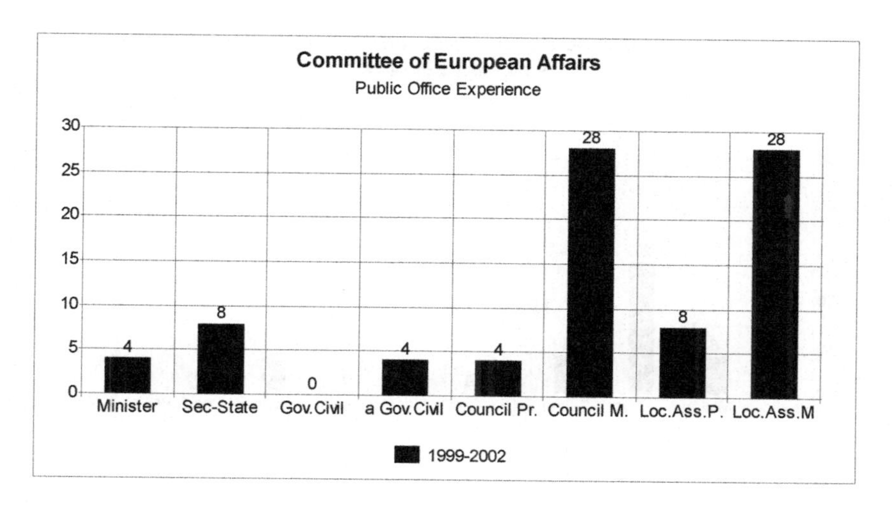

sketch the network of interactions among the national, transnational, and supranational elites. The center point of this analysis is the Portuguese presidency of the European Union, which that took place in the first half of the year 2000.

Figure 7.15
Public Office Experience of the Portuguese Members of the European Parliament (Assembly of Republic)

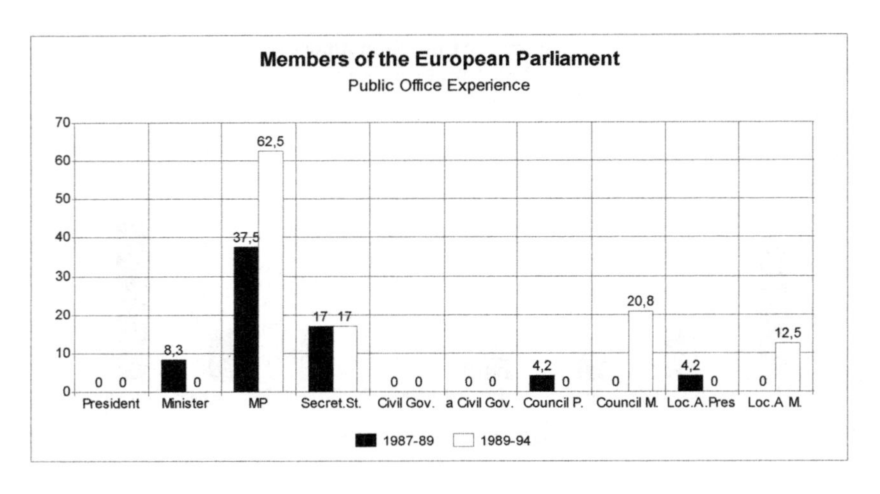

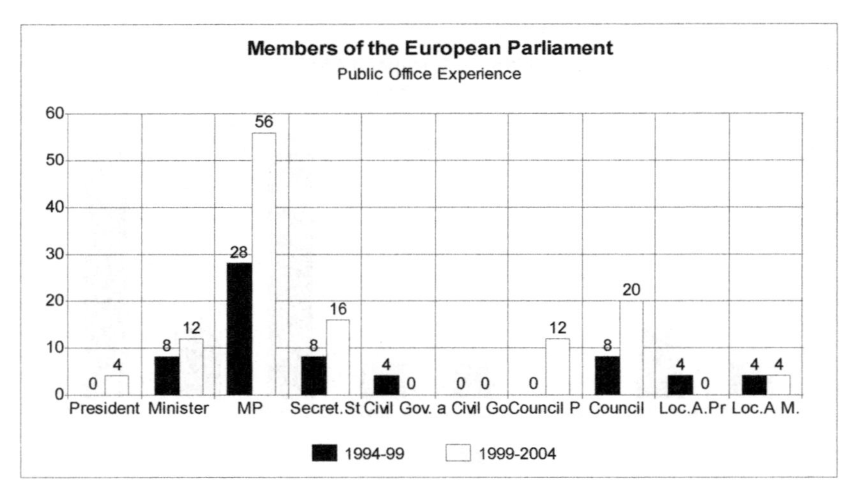

The Portuguese Euro-Elite in Action: The Presidency of the Council of Ministers of the European Union

The Portuguese Presidency of the Council of Ministers of the European Union took place in the first half of the year 2000. It was the first presidency of the new millennium. Despite the fact that from the onset the Portuguese presidency was regarded as a transitional presidency to the French one, it was able to achieve a higher profile due to the Austrian case. French diplomacy was interested in creating momentum for a Treaty of Nice in December 2000; therefore, high on the agenda of the Portuguese presidency was the preliminary preparation of the work related to the final draft of the Treaty of Nice. From the very start, the ambition of the European Commission was modest. It clearly wanted to make small institutional changes to prepare the European Union for enlargement.[35]

Figure 7.16
Public Office Experience of Government Members During the EU Presidency of 1992 and 2000

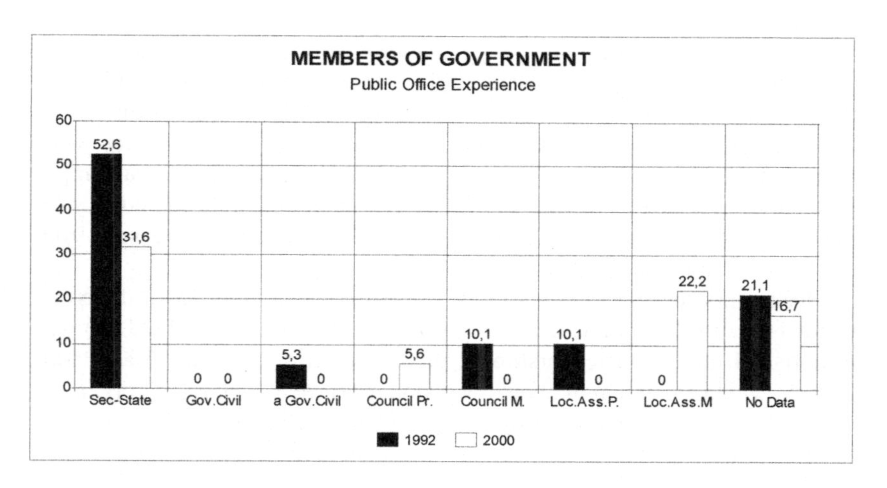

After the Helsinki European Council in December 1999, related to the restructuring of Common Foreign and Security Policy (CFSP), the agenda prepared by the European Commission for the Portuguese presidency was one of an administrative nature. In spite of these restrictions, the Portuguese administrative and political Euro-elite were able to create a momentum for certain policy areas, such as employment, taxation, and external relations with the African Continent, South America, and Russia. On the whole, the presidency was regarded as a big success, in spite of the unpredictible Austrian case. The Portuguese presidency concentrated on six specific areas, of which the most important was the future strategy of the European Union towards Employment.

The presidency was overshadowed by the Austrian problem, to which Portuguese diplomacy found a solution at the end of the presidency. It delegated the decision about lifting Austrian ostracism to an independent Commission of Experts. In this matter, one of the major achievements of Portuguese diplomacy was to de-communitarize the Austrian problem and shift to a bilateral aspect of national foreign policy.[36]

Portuguese diplomacy had already accumulated some experience in running a presidency in the first half of 1992. Indeed, the government of Anibal Cavaco Silva set the example for the 2000 presidency. Although Portugal was due to take over the presidency in 1986 shortly after accession, the Portuguese government decided to delay incumbency until the next opportunity in 1992, which helped to create an efficient administrative Euro-elite that came only into action in the 1990s. In 2000, the Guterres government could refer to this experience of Portuguese diplomacy in running the presidency. Indeed, many civil servants attached to the organization of the presidency felt more at ease and confident about the successful running of the forthcoming presidency.[37]

Similar to preparations made for the 1992 presidency, after November 1998 the Portuguese CIAC created a subcommittee to deal permanently with the presidency. In 1999, weekly meetings of the Council of Ministers on European Affairs (*Conselho de Ministros de Assuntos da União Europeia*-CMAE) took place in view of preparing for the presidency. Additional temporary staff was added to all crucial national liaison points of the presidency, so that the presidency would be able to cope with the increased pressure from the EU institutions and other member-states.

During this period a mission for the organization and logistics of the presidency (*Missão de Organização e Logistica da Presidencia*-E.M.O.L.P.) was established under the leadership of pleni-potentiary minister João Pedro Zanatti, with a core team of about ten people who were in charge of organization matters related to the Portuguese presidency of the EU and West European Union. In Brussels, the personnel of the Permanent Representation was reinforced for the tasks ahead.[38]

According to official data between October 1997 and December 1999, 1,678 civil servants were involved in some kind of training courses. These training courses were organized by the National Institute of Administration (*Instituto Nacional de Administração*-INA) and the European Institute of Public Administration (EIPA) in Maastricht. This training program was directed towards two groups of civil servants. The first group comprised all senior directors or specialized staff that would represent Portugal as president or national delegate in the different working groups of the Council and would be engaged in the coordination of community affairs. The second group consisted of civil servants and secretarial staff that would be involved in the various government departments in functions directly related to the running of the presidency. For the first group, the training program was intensive and demanding, while the second group was trained in basic skills related to the running of the presidency, including general knowledge of the processes of the European Union. More or less, the vast training program was drafted

Table 7.2
Training for the Portuguese Presidency of the European Union (1998-1999)

	ACTION	PCO	Youth	MFA	DoF	Fin	MoI	MEPAT	Just	Econ	Agric	Educ	Health	Labour	Env.	Cult	MCT	AGA	AGM	Total
Group I High Level Managers and Civil Servants	European Institutions And the Presidency Exercise			127																127
	Comitology			220																220
	Team working techniques	4	2	33	-	11	3	14	1	17	20	-	12	9	13	8	-	2	11	160
	Techniques of Conduct and Coordination of Meetings	3	1	52	-	4	5	4	4	5	4	5	5	4	3	3	-	1	2	105
	Sectoral Workshops	-	7	98	6	23	12	70	-	103	65	10	35	4	15	14	-	32	22	516
	Improvement of Linguistic skills	2	2	54	-	5	9	11	5	18	12	-	5	-	18	3	-	-	-	144
Group II Support Staff/ Secretariate	Organisation of Meetings and High Level Meetings	1	1	-	-	1	-	1	-	2	1	1	1	2	2	1	1	2	1	18
	Introduction to the European Union	2	2	13	-	3	3	18	-	9	4	5	4	7	4	-	1	3	2	80
	Secretariate	3	2	36	-	5	4	2	-	11	5	7	4	5	5	2	1	10	4	106
	Languages	2	1	41	-	4	5	2	-	5	3	6	7	4	9	1	-	-	-	90
	Information networks and circuits, e-mail	2	2	35	-	1	2	2	2	8	1	3	3	5	3	2	-	-	-	71
Groups I and II	Computing Skills/ Communication Networks	1	-	19	-	1	1	2	-	5	2	3	3	1	2	1	-	-	-	41
	Total	**20**	**20**	**728**	**6**	**58**	**44**	**126**	**12**	**183**	**117**	**40**	**79**	**41**	**74**	**35**	**3**	**50**	**42**	**1678**

Source: Data kindly provided by the General-Directorate for Community Affairs, Ministry of Foreign Affairs after written request by the author.

based on the experiences of the previous presidency of 1992. The coordinating unit would be the CIAC and the members of the individual ministries in CIAC would be the liaison officers to the overall process. The selection of the trainees was done by the individual ministries according to their needs.

In terms of workload, the team of the presidency had to manage a multitude of meetings. It had to chair over fifty-seven council and other official meetings, sixty-eight COREPER meetings as well as 1,816 working groups (see Figure 7.17). Overall the presidency was estimated to have cost 36 million euros, but in reality it cost 25 million euros.[39] This also included the running of the two parallel presidencies of the West European Union and the Euro-Mediterranean Forum.[40] In several informal and formal international summits and additional meetings, conferences, and seminars that took place in the main center of conferences of the presidency, 13,849 people took part (see Table 7.3.).

The presidency of the European Union offers an excellent opportunity to look at the different networks of interactions between national, transnational, and supranational political Euro-elites. In the next pages, we will see some of these networks of interactions.

The Interaction of the Different Parts of the Portuguese Euro-Elite

During the presidency of the European Union, national politics was secondary only to European Union politics. It is important for any government to assure complete support of the opposition parties during this period, which is so important for the prestige of a country. Antonio Guterres´s government took this challenge seriously. He had regular meetings with the opposition and he exposed himself to parliamentary scrutiny in the first days of the presidency. Moreover, Portuguese government officials were also exposed to scrutiny from the European Parliament. The agenda of the presidency requires regular meetings in front of committees of the European Parliament or reports of the prime minister or other ministers in the plenary session. This clearly shows the growing parliamentarianization of the European Union and national politics. Indeed, one of the reasons for this parliamentarianization at the European Union level was the successful overthrow of the Santer commission in 1998 and its replacement by Romano Prodi´s team. The allegations of corruption, nepotism, and clientelism gave more presence to the European Parliament in the whole framework. Moreover, the European Parliament is a co-legislator in many areas; thus, several meetings of conciliation among Council and the European Parliament are needed to achieve the support for legislative acts initiated originally by the European Commission.

The whole European Union political system is quite complicated, so that a presidency has to adopt a multilevel approach to deal with all the issues.

Table 7.3
Table of Events of Presidency (January-June 2000)

Date	Event	Organization
28-29.1.2000	Informal Council on Development and Cooperation	Min. Foreign Affairs
11.-12.2.2000	Informal Council of Social Affairs	Min. Labour/Solidarity
3-4.3.2000	Informal Council JHA	Min. Justice, Home Office
6.-7.3.2000	Ministerial Meeting on Research	Ministry of Science and Technology
8.3.2000	Preparatory Meeting for European Council	EMOLP
23-24.3.2000	Extraordinary European Council	EMOLP
7-8.4.2000	Informal Council ECOFIN	Min.Finances and Economy
29.2.-1.3.2000	Conference EUROMED Investments	Ministry of Economy
2.3.2000	Ministerial Troika UE/Russia	Min. Foreign Affairs
3.3.2000	Trilateral Meeting EU/Russia/USA	Min. Foreign Affairs
17-18.3.2000	Launch Conference of Programmes Socrates II and Leonardo II	Min. Education
19.4.2000	Conference on Food Security	Secretariat for European Affairs
1-3.5.2000	SOM, ASEM Meeting	Min. of Foreign Affairs
9.5.2000	Ministerial Meeting EU-New Zealand	Min. of Foreign Affairs
12.5.2000	Ministerial Meeting EU-Algeria	Min. of Foreign Affairs
22-23.5.2000	High Level Meeting on Coordination and Cooperation Mechanism in relation to Drug-Trafficking between EU and Latin America	Presidency of the Council of Ministers
25-26.5.2000	Informal Meeting of the Ministries of Foreign Affairs of the EUROMED	Min. Foreign Affairs
7-8.6.2000	Adhoc Meeting of Liaison Committee for West Bank and Gaza	Min. Foreign Affairs
26.6.2000	EU-Canada Summit	Min. Foreign Affairs
28.6.2000	EU-India Summit	Min. Foreign Affairs
9.6.2000	Meeting on European Charter of Fundamental Rights	Min. Foreign Affairs
15-16.6.2000	European Conference on Asylum	Home Office
25.-26.2.2000	VI Euro-Latin American Forum	Institute for Strat. and Intern. Studies
8.3.2000	Meeting with European Presidents of TNCs	EMOLP
30.3.2000	Seminar on Bench-Marking 2000	EMOLP
3.-4.4.2000	Seminar on Non-Military Management	Min. Foreign Affairs
10.-11.4.2000	Seminar on Information and Knowledge Society	Ministry of Science and Technology
10.-11.4.2000	EURASA 2000 Conference	ACDP
13-14.4.2000	Forum of Small and Medium-Sized Enterprises	Ministry of Economy
17-18.4.2000	Working Group Committee 133	Min. of Foreign Affairs
19.4.2000	Conference on Food Security	MNE (SEAE)
2.5.2000	Meeting of Working Group on General Affairs	MNE (Reper)
4-6.5.2000	Seminar on Violence against women	Presidency of the Council of Ministers

Table 7.3 (cont.)

4-5.5.2000	Seminar on Development Financing	Min. of Foreign Affairs
8-9.5.2000	Meeting of Gen. Dir. of Public Administration	DG Public Administration
10-12.5.2000	Conference on the Quality of Public Services in the EU	Secretariat for the Modernization of Administration
1.-2.6.2000	Meeting of European Diplomatic Institute	Diplomatic Institute, Min. Foreign Affairs
5.-6.6.2000	Meeting of the Presidents of the National Parliaments of EU	Assembly of the Republic
5.6.6.2000	Seminar on Maritime Borders	Home Office
23.6.2000	Seminar on Roma Minority in Candidate Countries	Secretariat for European Affairs
23.6.2000	Conference on Maritime Peripheral Regions	Secretariat for European Affairs

Source: Ministério dos Negócios Estrangeiros, Presidencia Portuguesa do Conselho da União Europeia, 1 de Janeiro a 30 de Junho de 2000, 41-43.

The main protagonists of the appearances before the plenary and the committees of the European Parliament were naturally the foreign minister Jaime Gama and the state secretary for European affairs Francisco Seixas da Costa. While Jaime Gama appeared six times before the plenary sessions and two times before committees, Seixas da Costa appeared twenty-two times before the plenary sessions and four times before committees of the EP. All other ministers tended to be called when specific issues related to their field were to be discussed in the European Parliament (see figure 7.18).

Domestically, Guterres was not challenged by the opposition during this period. Regardless of criticisms coming from the leader of the Social Democratic Party (*Partido Social Democrata*-PSD) Manuel Durão Barroso, related to the fact that the Guterres government missed making a case for national issues during the presidency (such as agriculture, structural funds), in general terms there was overall support for the presidency. In the plenary session of the Assembly of the Republic on 5 January 2000, Guterres demonstrated that the importance of Portugal can only be achieved by solidarity with the other member-states. This was reinforced by the final speech given by Jaime Gama, the minister of foreign affairs.[41]

An indication that the government takes national parliament seriously is the continuing information of the Committee of European Affairs before, during and after the presidency. The number of meetings with ministers during the presidency was extensive. The president of the Committee of European Affairs, Manuel dos Santos, was able to gather firsthand information from the government. During this period the Secretary of State for European Affairs, Francisco Seixas da Costa, visited the Committee twice on 26 April and 31 May. On the first occasion, he informed the committee about the consequences for Portugal after finalizing the Intergovernmental Conference.

Figure 7.17
Number of Meetings, Hours, and Days in Council, COREPER, and Working Groups During the Portuguese Presidency 2000

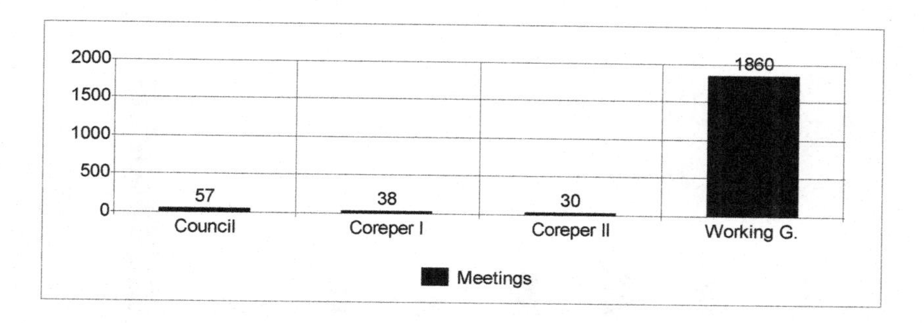

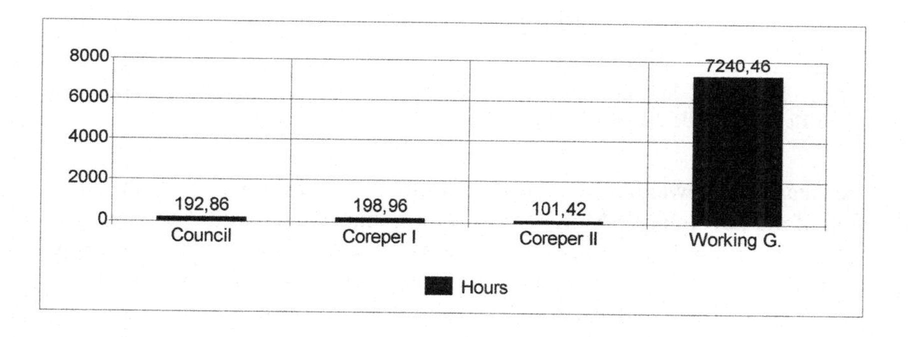

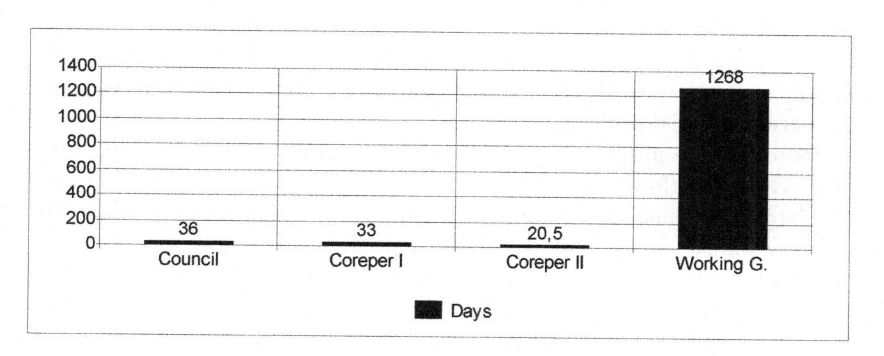

Source: Author's calculations based on Internal Document of the Council kindly supplied by Pedro Lourtie of the Portuguese Permanent Representation.

Figure 7.18
Appearances of Government before Parliament

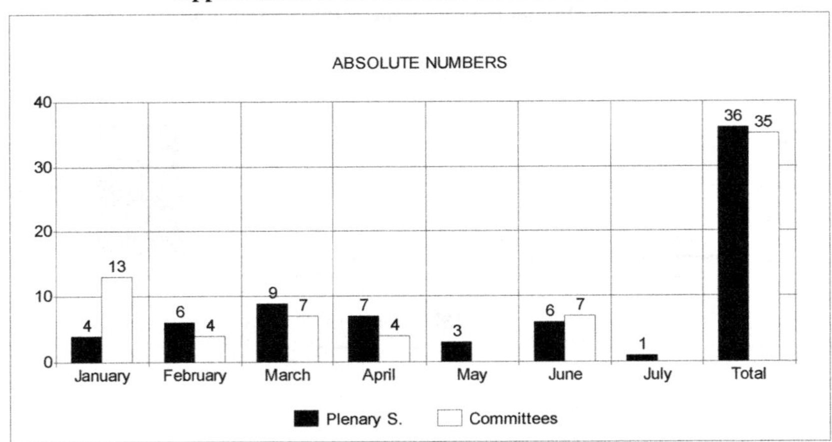

Source: Ministério dos Negócios Estrangeiros, Presidencia Portuguesa do Conselho da umão Europeia, 1 de Janeiro a 30 de Junho de 2000.

He clearly acknowledged that Portugal would lose some power after the adoption of the new treaty.[42] Moreover, several ministers met with the Committee after the Extraordinary Council of Lisbon in March and after the European Council of Santa Maria da Feira in July 2000. The whole network of interactions between national parliament representatives and the government was substantial at the EU level.[43] Several members of the committee met with the Portuguese representative of the Intergovernmental Conference, Professor Pedro Bacelar de Vasconcelos, in February and March. This interaction shows that the overall network of the Euro-elite was extremely active throughout the period of the presidency.

Moreover, the prime minister informed the main leaders of the opposition parties about the forthcoming Extraordinary Council of Lisbon in March and the European Council of the Santa Maria da Feira, a move that contributed to assuring the support of the opposition throughout the whole process.[44] According to official figures of the Committee of European Affairs there were fifteen meetings with members of government during the legislative period, which started in October and ended in July.[45] A special subcommittee was established to accompany the Portuguese presidency and, naturally, the Intergovernmental Conference, leading to a final excellent report by two of the committee members José Barros Moura and Antonio Nazaré Pereira.[46]

This network of interactions was sometimes supported by the Portuguese MEPs, who would turn out to be facilitators in Strassburg and Brussels in light of achieving support from the European Parliament for the work of the

Portuguese presidency. In some cases, they were rather critical and opposed to the work of the presidency, such as in relation to the Intergovernmental Conference. This led even to unity of the Portuguese MEPs across party lines in voting against the report with the proposals of the European Parliament for the Intergovernmental Conference. The main reason for this was that the Portuguese MEPs felt that some proposals to solve the institutional leftovers of the Treaty of Amsterdam were undermining the powers of the small states. In spite of the MEPs vote *en bloque*, the EP accepted the report with 238 votes against 147 and 73 abstentions. The Portuguese MEPs appealed to the representatives of the Intergovernmental Conference asking that they ignore the report.[47]

Portuguese MEPs are also in permanent contact with the MPs of the Committee of European Affairs. A meeting took place on 28 April 2000. These instances highlight the constant cooperation and interaction among the three groups, and point to the Portuguese Euro-elite as having national, transnational, and supranational elements that have become intrinsic to the

Table 7.4
Number of Meetings, Hours, and Days Spent in Different Councils

COUNCIL	MEETINGS	HOURS	DAYS
General Affairs	10	46	8
Economy	6	18	5
Agriculture	4	21	3
Fisheries	1	5.5	1
Internal Market	2	11	2
Trade	2	11	1
Telecommunications	1	3.1	0.5
Research	1	6.5	1
Justice	2	12	2
Education	1	6.5	1
Culture	1	4.4	1
Health	1	6.5	1
Environment	2	14	2
Energy	1	3.2	1
Industry	1	3.7	1
Consumer Affairs	1	4.3	1
Employment	1	3.6	1
Social Affairs	2	5.7	1
Catastrophy protection	1	2.1	0.5

Source: Author's calculations based on Internal Document of the Council kindly supplied by Pedro Lourtie of the Portuguese Permanent Representation.

Table 7.5
Number of Meetings, Hours, and Days Spent in the Busiest Working Groups

	MEETINGS	HOURS	DAYS
Political Committee	16	60	11
Enlargement	40	149	27
Africa	16	690	10
Balkans	47	133	26
Budget	35	151	28
Environment	54	252	47
Social	41	185	35
East	45	157	28

Source: Internal Document of the Council kindly supplied by Pedro Lourtie of the Portuguese Permanent

whole routine. The best examples are the meetings of COSAC that lead to an exchange of information and convergence of practices among national parliaments. The XXII COSAC took place in Lisbon on 29-30 May 2000.[48] Nevertheless, this may be regarded as an exceptional situation related to a successful conducting of the presidency and which may be less visible during normal times.[49] On the whole, the three Euro-elites clearly work in this last instance in the interest of the country and in a manner similar to Euro-elites in other countries.

The Presidency of the European Union: Coordination and Cooperation among National Euro-Elites and the Supranational Institutions

One of the main skills of a successful presidency is the ability to reconcile different points of view before the final decision-making meetings. Most of the technical and less important decisions were discussed in COREPER I and COREPER II. Most of this work was done in the institutions of the Council by a specialized transnational administrative elite that is responsible to the national capitals. During the presidency, Portuguese officials were chairing all Council working groups, COREPER I and II, and naturally the Council meetings. This is already a routine that is easily learned through socialization. More difficult are the meetings where new policy areas will find new definitions or expansion.

The Extraordinary Council of Lisbon on 23-24 March 2000

The Extraordinary Council of Lisbon on employment, economic reform, and social cohesion took place on 23-24 March 2000. Basically, from an early stage, the Portuguese presidency regarded this Extraordinary Council as central to lending importance to the work of Portuguese diplomacy. The final compromise showed the way forward in the European Union: annual coordination and monitoring of national employment policies. Moreover, decisions related to the promotion of new technologies and the information society related to e-commerce were intended to boost the European economy in the new millennium.

The significance of role played by the person in charge, Maria João Rodrigues, cannot not be emphasized enough. Maria João Rodrigues is one of the leading Portuguese scholars in the field of employment policy and already she had had some experience at the supranational level in the formulation of new future-oriented policies.[50] She was minister for employment between 1995 and 1998, but she was replaced by Paulo Pedroso, and followed later by Ferro Rodrigues. During the presidency she became the special consultant to the prime minister and in charge of organizing the Extraordinary Council on employment. Indeed, the whole approach of Maria João Rodrigues was to emphasize the need to articulate and coordinate the employment policies of the fifteen member countries so that a new European economy, based on the new technologies, could be created.[51] In this sense, the Portuguese presidency upgraded the European Council as a monitoring and coordinating institution. This so-called "method of Lisbon" changed the relationship between the European Council and the European Commission. For the first time, the Portuguese presidency was dominant in preparing the Extraordinary Council when compared to previous European Council meetings where the European Commission had the stronger input. This has been interpreted as a pendulum movement from the community method to intergovernmentalism,[52] but, in reality, it may be a further innovative element in the overall political system sui generis. It follows the logic of the Single European Market (SEM) and Economic and Monetary Union (EMU). It wants to move in the direction of a more coordinated, flexible approach towards employment. The Extraordinary Council was markedly successful and set a precedent for continued monitoring and coordinating of economic and social issues in Extraordinary councils in forthcoming years. In this sense, the Portuguese presidency set a precedent for the administrative machinery required by the European Council to deal with this new strategic objective of the European Union.[53]

During the presidency, Maria João Rodrigues had a small office team who worked closely with director-generals and representatives of the other Portuguese ministries. In all, there were eighteen persons in the task force. Moreover, Rodrigues had fifteen persons working on the Extraordinary Council in Brussels. There were meetings of the government (PM, Ministry of Solidarity, and Maria João Rodrigues) every second day and meetings of the "task force," which was in permanent contact with the fifteen ministries of the member-states to find out about the limits of negotiations at the Extraordinary Council. In March, there were fifteen versions of conclusions. These fifteen had to be reduced to one, on the eve of the second day of the Extraordinary Council, 24 March 2000. For the Extraordinary Council on 23-24 March, Maria João Rodrigues had to organize fourteen council of ministers meetings in seven high-level conferences. After the successful meeting, Maria João Rodrigues then had to accompany the progress of implementation of the conclusions in the different countries. There was some margin of maneuver for the individual countries, as was the nature of the *open system of coordination* (OMC) adopted by the Extraordinary Council.[54] The Extraordinary Council also received contributions and representations from the supranational institutions and the main European-wide social European Trade Union Confederation (ETUC) and Union of the Industry and Employers Confederations of Europe (UNICE).[55]

The overall assessment was very positive. It seems that at the beginning most representatives of the member-states were skeptical of whether the Portuguese presidency would be able to do it. According to Guterres, the reason why it turned out to be a success was the hard preliminary work done by Maria João Rodrigues and her team. They read over 40,000 pages of reports before finalizing successfully the guidelines for this new strategic objective. Guterres himself was praised for his negotíation skills throughout the Extraordinary Council.[56]

Starting the Intergovernmental Conference

One of the most difficult tasks for the Portuguese presidency was to start and chair the negotiations of the Intergovernmental Conference, which would end in December in the European Council of Nice. The main task was to discuss the so-called institutional "leftovers" of the Treaty of Amsterdam with a view to preparing the European Union for Central and Eastern enlargement. The so-called leftovers consisted of (1) the question of the weighting of the vote in the European Council, (2) the number of Commissioners, (3) the way they should be coopted, and (4) the extension of majority voting to a large number of areas.

The Portuguese presidency had the task of beginning the preparatory work to the Nice Treaty. Francisco Seixas da Costa, the secretary of state for European Affairs, was in charge of organizing and directing the discussion in the Intergovernmental meetings in Brussels. In total, there were ten meetings, which led to controversies among the different member-states. In particular, France was trying to push the agenda towards a reassertion of the nation-states against the supranationalization of the leftovers. Seixas da Costa was disappointed with the preliminary report of the European Commission issued in January, because it lacked ambition. This lack of ambition for the reform clearly led to a reassertion of the member-states in discussing most issues in national terms. There was a feeling that the European Commission's report was increasing the role of the larger states against the smaller states.[57] The European Council in Nice clearly showed with the final outcome this disappointment of the smaller states. The Portuguese presidency was also confronted with the issue of "reinforced cooperation," meaning that some member-states could move towards more integration, if they so wished. Eight member-states had to adhere to any reinforced cooperation, before such could become a reality. At the end of the presidency, France announced that it wanted to introduce into the discussion a change of the provisions made in the Treaty of Amsterdam and contemplate a possible de-communitarization of the "reinforced cooperation." The Portuguese presidency was annoyed, feeling it had been bypassed after ten meetings of negotiations and a final report presented at the European Council of Santa Maria da Feira in June. This French approach was indeed controversial during the Portuguese presidency and continued to be so during its presidency.[58]

Francisco Seixas da Costa, an extremely dynamic and competent diplomat, had gained his previous experience during the Intergovernmental Conference leading up to the Treaty of Amsterdam, adopted in May 1999. In this IGC of 2000, he had to deal with this reassertion of national representation. In the opening meeting, he had to allow the return of eleven official languages for the IGC, after prior approval of most countries for the use of only three official languages (German, English, and French) to simplify the negotiation process. Countries such as Spain, Italy, and Greece asked for the reinstatement of their languages throughout the IGC.[59]

During the presidency, Seixas da Costa had also to deal with the negative reaction of the Portuguese MEPs, as well as the discussion on federalism between Joschka Fischer, German minister of foreign affairs, and Hubert Védrine, French minister for foreign affairs. Several newspapers carried the story that Fischer advocated a direct election of the president of the Commission and a federalist design for the European Union, while Védrine was eager to preserve an intergovernmentalist approach towards the EU.[60]

The Portuguese presidency attempted a balancing act between these two positions in an effort to achieve compromises in the smaller points, before moving on to the more sensitive ones. Indeed, the more sensitive issues had to be postponed until the highly controversial European Council of Nice on 7-8 December 2000. In the end, the French presidency was assessed negatively by the German press[61] (see chapter 6 for negotiations).

At the some stage, Jaime Gama, Portuguese minister of foreign affairs, expressed his dissatisfaction and disappointment with the IGC model. In a speech at the London School of Economics and Political Science (LSE), he stated that the IGC model was exhausted because the complexity of the European Union no longer allowed for a mere intergovernmentalist approach.

Both the IGC as well as the Community method would have to develop a synthesis of progressing in terms of institutional reform and change; otherwise, the European Union would have difficulty acting as a major global actor at the economic, political, humanitarian and, if necessary, military levels.[62]

On the whole, the IGC was well run by the Portuguese presidency, although the climate in which it took place was constrained by a weakened European Commission that wanted realistic progress but lacked ambition in the preliminary report, and by the reemergence of intergovernmentalism as a misplaced strategy to reform the political system sui generis, which was gaining its own dynamic as a complex structure and which was unlikely to be influenced further by half intergovernmentalist reforms.

Euro-Elites and the Results of the Presidency: An Assessment

This study has shown that there is a pre-established network of interactions in the European Union that thus far has been underresearched. Euro-elites are the dynamic element of the processes of the European Union. The Portuguese presidency is only one case study of the persons and efforts involved in making a project work. Although the duration of a presidency is only six months, it is an important socializing mechanism for the Euro-elites. It transforms national mentalities into transnational ones. During those six months, the national arena is neglected in favor of high supranational politics. This national, regular effort is one of the most positive characteristics of the emerging Europolity. Failure of a presidency is measured on the degree of its organization and coordination ability as well as its ability to overcome the national interest. Although the agenda of the Portuguese presidency was only transitional, it was able to gain momentum with the Extraordinary Council in Lisbon, which led to a positive outcome due to extensive preparations and the allocation of experts in the field.

The IGC conference was well run by the Portuguese presidency, but pursuit of a mere intergovernmentalist agenda by French diplomacy during and after the Portuguese presidency constrained the possibility of achieving a more balanced outcome. Here again the clash of national Euro-elites prevented a more far-reaching reform, which demonstrates again that it is important to study the mentality of each presidency. This mental attitude will also influence outcomes and give meaning to an agenda.

Conclusions

This chapter intended to put the concept of the Euro-elite on the research agenda of European Union politics. A bias towards institutionalism and institutionalisation tended to neglect the role of Euro-elites in shaping the

Table 7.6
The Agenda of the Portuguese Presidency (January-June 2000)

Issues	Outcomes
Employment, Economic Reform, Social Cohesion	Extraordinary Council of Lisbon, 23-24 March 2000: Main agreement about e-commerce, e-learning, and new technologies for employment strategy as well as change from active to proactive policies.
Institutional Reform	Intergovernmental Conference: ten meetings chaired by Secretary of State Francisco Seixas da Costa. Successful preliminary work, taken over by the French presidency (February-June 2000)
Enlargement	Continuing negotiation process: closing of 78 partial dossiers and opening of 52 new ones. Continuing discussions with Cyprus.
CFSP	Implementation of decisions in Finnish presidency. Restructuring of the European security architecture.
Space of Freedom, Security, and Justice	Continuing discussion about strategy to deal with emigration, organized criminality; negotiations and drafting of Charter of Fundamental Rights of EU citizens.
Health and Food Security	Continuing awareness of health and food security issues (January 2000: White Book on Food Security)
External Relations	Euro-African summit Cairo, 3-4 April, Euromediterranean Partnership, European Union-Latin America relations
Other areas (less relevant)	Ultra-peripheral regions; finances and economy; environment and sustainable development; agriculture; internal market; industry; research/society of information; social issues; fisheries; education; culture; transport policy; health; consumers' protection.

whole process. We have made a case for analyzing the Euro-elite in different levels of the multilevel governance system of the EU. The so-called national, transnational, and supranational Euro-elites are interacting with each other all the time. The boundaries among the different Euro-elites are blurred. Moreover, it is relevant to differentiate between administrative and political elites.

As an example, we studied the three main formations of the Portuguese Euro-elite. After analyzing their characteristics we tried to place these findings in the context of the Portuguese presidency as a reinforced network of interactions. In our analysis of the Portuguese presidency we paid particular attention to the study of interactions. Although far from perfect, the dynamics of pre-established and temporary patterns of interaction can be recognized. The Portuguese presidency showed evidence of the necessity to look at Euro-elites to understand success or failure of advancement in the European integration process.

On the whole, the Portuguese Euro-elite is aware of the fact that they come from a small state and their ability to influence is limited. Despite that, however, the quality of the well-trained Euro-elite, reflecting a more transnational mentality during the presidency, shows that the Portuguese administrative and political elites long ago abandoned a rigid national frame of reference. In addition, their flexibility in reconciling national, transnational, and supranational elements makes them an interesting field of research, which may spill-over into the study of other national, transnational, and supranational Euro-elites.

Notes

1. Gary Marks, "Structural Policy and Multilevel Governance in the European Community," in A. W. Cafruny, G. C. Rosenthal (eds.) *The State of the Community, vol. 2: The Maastricht Debates and Beyond.* (Boulder, CO: Lynne Rienner, 1993), 391-410; Gary Marks, Fritz Scharpf, Philippe Schmitter, Wolfgang Streeck, *Governance in the European Union* (London: SAGE, 1996); Helen Wallace, "Politics and Policy in the EU: The Challenge of Governance," in Helen and William Wallace (eds.), *Policy-Making in the European Union* (Oxford: Oxford University Press, 1996), 27-43; Thomas König, Elmar Rieger, Hermann Schmitt (Hg.), *Das europãische Mehrebenensystem* (Frankfurt a. M.: Campus, 1996), 29-45. For a discussion and appraisal, see chapter 2 of José M Magone, *Iberian Trade Unionism: Democratization under the Impact of the European Union* (New Brunswick, NJ: Transaction Publishers, 2001) and José M. Magone, "EU Territorial Governance and National Politics: Reshaping Marginality in Spain and Portugal," in Noel Parker, Bill Armstrong (eds.), *Margins in European Integration* (Basingstroke: Macmillan, 2000), 155-177.
2. The most important theoretical studies have been done by Philippe Schmitter, "Examining the Present Euro-Polity with Past Theories," in Marks, Scharpf, Schmitter, Streeck, *Governance in the European Union*, 1-14; Philippe Schmitter, "Some Alternative Futures for the European Polity and Their Implications for European Public Policy," in Yves Meny, Pierre Muller, Jean-Louis Quermonne (eds.), *Adjusting to Europe. The Impact of the European Union on National Institutions and Policies* (London: Routledge, 1996), 25-40; see also a collection of theoretical papers, Andreas Follesdal, Peter Koslowski (eds.), *Democracy and the European Union* (New York: Springer, 1998); recently, see Fulvio Attinà, "Integrazione e Democrazia: Un´analisi evoluzionista dell´Unione Europea," *Rivista Italiana di Scienza Politica* a.XXX, n.2, agosto 2000: 227-256; Beate Kohler-Koch, "Regieren in der Europäischen Union. Auf der Suche nach demokratischer Legitimität, "*Aus Politik und Zeitgeschichte*, B6/2000: 30-38; J.H.H. Weiler, "European Neo-Constitutionalism: In Search of Foundations for the European Constitutional Order," *Political Studies* 44, 3, 1996: 517-533.

3. This was coined particularly by the German political scientist Rudolf Hrbek, "Nationalstaat und Europäische Integration. Die Bedeutung der Nationalen Komponente für den Integrationsprozess," in P. Haungs (ed.), *Europäisierung Europas?* (Baden-Baden: Nomos 1989), 81-108.
4. Wolfgang Lerch, "Neu in Europa: Der interregionale Wirtschafts- und Sozialauschuß in the Großregion Saar-Lor-Lux," *WSI Mitteilungen* 6/1999: 396-406; particularly 401-405; José Magone, "EU Governance..." op. cit. (fn1), 157-159.
5. John Loughlin, "La autonomia en Europa ocidental: Un estudio comparado," in Francisco Letamendia (coord.), *Nacionalidades y Regiones en la Unión Europea* (Madrid: Editorial Fundamentos 1998), 109-159.
6. In theoretical terms one has to refer still to the classic study by Maurizio Cotta, "Classe politica e integrazione Europea. Gli effetti delle elezioni dirette del parlamento comunitario," *Rivista Italiana di Scienza Politica* X; see also the special issue on the First Direct elections, edited by Karl Heinz Reif and Hermann Schmitt, *European Journal for Political Research* 8, 1980; see the follow-up studies of the European Elections study group Cees Van der Eijk, Mark N. Franklin (eds.), *Choosing Europe? The European Electorate and National Politics in the Face of the Union* (Ann Arbor: University of Michigan Press, 1996); Hermann Schmitt, Jacques Thomassen (eds.), *Political Representation and Legitimacy in the European Union* (Oxford:Oxford University Press, 1999); the very interesting book by Richard Katz, Bernhard Wessels (eds.), *The European Parliament, National Parliaments and European Integration* (Oxford: Oxford University Press, 1999). For a summary of some of the European-level elite studies and a study of the Iberian MEPs for the legislature of 1980-94, see José M. Magone, *The Changing Architecture of Iberian Politics (1974-1992). An Investigation on the Structuring of Democratic Political Systemic Culture in Semiperipheral Southern European Societies* (Lewiston, NY: Edwin Mellen Press, 1996), and José Magone, *The Iberian Members of the European Parliament and European Integration. Their Background, Their Attitudes and the Prospects for Transforming Elite Cultures.* Bristol: Centre for Mediterranean Studies (University of Bristol), Occasional Paper no. 7, June 1993.
7. Martin Westlake, *Britain´s Emerging Euro-elite? The British in the Directly-Elected European Parliament, 1979-1992* (Aldershot: Dartsmouth, 1994).
8. Andrew Macmullen, "Fraud, Mismanagement and Nepotism: The Committee of Independent Experts and the Fall of the European Commission 1999," *Crime, Law and Social Change* 31, 173-192; Brendan Quirke, "1999: Fraud against European Public Funds," *Crime, Law and Social Change* 31, 193-208.
9. Maurizio Bach, *Die Bürokratisierung Europas. Verwaltungseliten, Experten und politische Legitimation in Europa* (New York: Campus, 1999), 72.
10. Andreas Maurer, Jürgen Mittag, Wolfgang Wessels, "Theoretical Perspectives on administrative interaction in the European Union," in Thomas Christiansen, Emil Kirchner (eds.), *Committee Governance in the European Union* (Manchester: Manchester University Press, 2000), 21-44; particularly 36-37; for an assessment and discussion of the incrementalist agenda of the European Union, see Mark Pollack, "Creeping Competence: The Expanding Agenda of the European Community," *Journal of Public Policy* 14, 2, 1994: 95-140.
11. Jaap W. de Zwaan, *The Permanent Representatives Committee. Its Role in European Union Decision-Making* (Amsterdam: Elsevier, 1995); Vincent Wright, "The National Coordination of National European Policy-making: Negotiating the Quagmire," in Jeremy Richardson (ed.), *European Union. Power and Policy-Making* (London and New York: Routledge, 1996), 148-169.

12. Author's own calculations based on the number of representatives sent by the Portuguese delegation to the COSAC in 1997, reported in Assembleia da Republica, *Portugal na União Europeia em 1996 e 1997. Apreciação Parlamentar* (Lisbon: Comissão de Assuntos Europeus, 1998), 185 and 221. Each country is allowed to send a maximum of six representatives and administrative staff.
13. See José Magone, "La construzione di una societá civile Europea: Legami a piú livelli tra Comitati Economici e Sociali," in Antonio Varsori (ed.), *Il Comitato Economico e Sociale nella construzione europea* (Venezia: Marsilio, 2000), 223-242.
14. Oliver Gray, Adapted from Oliver Gray, "The Structure of Interest Group Representation in the EU: Observations from a Practitioner," Paul-H. Claeys, Corinne Gobin, Isabelle Smets, and Pascaline Winand (eds.), *Lobbying, Pluralism and European Integration* (Brussels: European Inter-University Press, 1998), 281-302.
15. M. Rainer Lepsius, "Nationalstaat oder Nationalitätenstaat als Modell für die Weiterentwicklung der Europäischen Gemeinschaft," in Rudolf Wildermann (ed.), *Staatswerdung Europas? Optionen für eine Europäische Union* (Baden-Baden: Nomos Verlagsgesellschaft 1991), 19-40; M. Rainer Lepsius, "Die Europäische Union.Ökonomische-Politische Integration und kulturelle Identität," in Reinhold Viehoff, Rien T. Segers (eds.), *Kultur, Identität, Europa. Über Schwierigkeiten und Möglichkeiten einer Konstruktion* (Frankfurt a. M.: Suhrkamp, 1999), 201-222; particularly 203-206.
16. Torbjorn Bergman, "National Parliaments and EU Affairs Committees: Notes and Competing Explanations," *Journal for European Public Policy* 4:3, September 1997: 373-97; Ana Fraga, *Os Parlamentos Nacionais e a Legitimidade da Construcao Europeia* (Lisbon: Cosmos, 2001).
17. This is the case of France, where there is regular informal contact with French European Commission administrators and MEPs in view of pushing a national position. See Anand Menon, "France," in Hussein Kassim, Anand Menon, Guy Peters (eds.), *The National Co-ordination of EU Policy. The Brussels Level* (Oxford: Oxford University Press, 2001).
18. It is very difficult to calculate the total number of administrative national Euro-elites for all fifteen countries. With the permanent representations one could come to a total number of 500 per country and 7,500 for all countries. Although this may be an underestimation if one compares the figures provided by Wolfgang Wessels and Dietrich Roemetsch, "German Administrative Interaction and European Union: The Fusion of Public Policies," in Yes Meny, Pierre Muller, Jean-Louis Quermonne (eds.), *Adjusting to Europe. The Impact of the European Union on National Institutions and Policies* (London: Routledge, 1996), 73-109, F.58; 105-106. There is naturally an asymmetrical EU policy adjustment and coordination capacity among EU members. See the recent updated article by Vincent Wright, "La coordination nationale de la politique européenne: Le bourbier de la négociation," *Revue Francaise d'Administration Publique* 93, 2000: 103-124.
19. Jan Beyers, Guido Dierickx, "The Working Groups of the Council of the European Union: Supranational or Intergovernmental Negotiations?" *Journal of Common Market Studies* 36, 3, September 1998: 289-317; particularly 301-302; the network nature of the overall decision-making process has been emphasized by former Belgian permanent representative Philippe de Schoutheete, *Una Europa para todos.Diez ensayos sobre la construccion europea* (Madrid: Alianza Editorial, 1998), 53-64.
20. John Barlow, David Farnham, Sylvia Horton, F. Ridley, "Comparing Public Managers," in David Farnham, Sylvia Horton, John Barlow, Annie Hondeghem (eds.),

New Public Managers in Europe (Basingstroke: Macmillan, 1996), 3-25; see particularly 18-23; Charles Fox, Hugh T. Miller, *Postmodern Public Administration* (London: SAGE, 1995); on the Commission, see David Spence "Plus Ca Change, plus c´est la meme chose? Attempting to Reform the European Commission," *Journal of European Public Policy* 7:1, March 2000:1-25; "Les Metcalfe, Reforming the Commission: Will Organizational Efficiency Produce Effective Governance?" *Journal of Common Market Studies* 38, 5, 817-41.

21. See the excellent pioneering work of Heinrich Siedentopf, Jacques Ziller (eds.) *Making European Policies Work? The Implementation of Community Legislation in the Member-States*, 2 vols. (London: SAGE, 1988), and June Burnham, Moshe Maor, "Converging Administrative Systems: Recruitment and Training in EU Member-States," *Journal of European Public Policy* 2:2, June 1995: 185-204.
22. See the excellent volume of Secretariado para a Modernização Administrativa (SMA), *First Quality Conference for Public Administrations in the European Union*, Lisbon, 10-12 May 2000.
23. Michelle Everson, "Administering Europe?" *Journal of Common Market Studies* 36, 2, June 1998: 195-216.
24. Peter Ludlow, "The 1998 UK Presidency: A View from Brussels," *Journal of Common Market Studies* 36, 4, 573-83; see also Douglas Henderson, "The UK Presidency: An Insider´s View," *Journal of Common Market Studies* 36, 4, 563-72.
25. Mikael Skou Andersen and Lise Nordvig Rasmussen, "The Making of Environmental Policy in the European Council," *Journal of Common Market Studies* 36, 4, 585-97.
26. Fiona Hayes-Renshaw, Helen Wallace, *The Council of Ministers* (Basingstroke: Macmillan, 1997), 139-150.
27. Ibid., 159-172.
28. Ibid., 105-109.
29. For an account of the presidencies before 1990, see Colm O´Nuallain (ed.), *The Presidency of the European Council of Ministers. Impacts and Implications for National Governments* (London: Croom Helm, 1985) and Helen Wallace, *National Governments and the European Communities* (London: Chatham House: PEP, 1973).
30. Ibid., 157. A rough estimate may lead to about 200 more people involved in the individual ministerial liaison units.
31. During the Cavaco Silva and Guterres governments it met on Friday morning.
32. Ibid., 149-154.
33. Ibid., 144-145.
34. The biographical data are taken from several sources: Assembleia da Republica, *Biografias dos Deputados.VI Legislatura* (Lisbon: AR, 1993); Assembleia da Republica, *Biografias dos Deputados. VII Legislatura* (Lisbon: AR, 1997); Assembleia da Republica, *Biografias dos Deputados. VIII Legislatura* (Lisbon: AR, 2000); *A Classe Politica Portuguesa* (Lisbon: Edicao, 1989); *European Companion 1990* (London: Dod´s Publishing and Research Limited, 1990); *European Companion 1995* (London: Dod´s Publishing and Research Limited, 1995); José Magone, *The Iberian Members*, op. cit. (fn 6) and José Magone, *The Changing Architecture*, op. cit. (fn 6).
35. The final meeting of preparation of the Commission with the presidency was on 10 January 2000 in Lisbon. See *Diario de Noticias*, 10 January 2000; *O Publico*, 11 January 2000.
36. Interview with Pedro Lourtie, 13 September 2002, Permanent Representation in Brussels.

37. Interview with Pedro Lourtie, 13 September 2002; Permanent Representation in Brussels.
38. http://www.portugal.ue-2000.pt/presidencia_main04.htm. Accessed during 2000.
39. *Expresso*, 31 December 1999; *Diario de Noticias*, 1 January 2000; Ministério dos Negócios Estrangeiros, *Presidencia Portuguesa do Conselho da União Portuguesa.1 de Janeiro a 31 de Julho 2000* (Lisbon: MNE, 2000), 37.
40. Ministério dos Negócios Estrangeiros, ibid., 39.
41. *Diario da Assembleia da Republica*, 6 January 2000, I-Serie, no. 22, pp.838-840.
42. *Diario Economico*, 27 April 2000.
43. A report by president Manuel dos Santos on the work of the committee can be read in http://www.parlamento.pt.
44. *Diario de Noticias*, 21 March 2000; *Diario de Noticias*, 13 June 2000.
45. Relatorio de actividade da Assembleia da Republica referente à 1a sessão legislativa da VIII Legislatura, Diário da Assembleia da Republica, 2 July 2001, II Serie-C, no. 32, p. 328.
46. José Barros Moura, António Nazaré Pereira, *Relatório sobre a proposta de resolução n°59/VIII que aprova para ratificação, o Tratado de Nice que altera o Tratado da União Europeia, os Tratados que instituem as Comunidades Europeias e alguns actos relativos a esses tratados assinado em Nice, em 26 de Fevereiro de 2001* (Lisbon: Comissão de Assuntos Europeus, 24 Outubro 2001), http://www.parlamento.pt. The Committee also asked for several reports from the main Portuguese universities, which were also posted in the website for the wider public.
47. *Diario de Noticias*, 14 April 2000; see also *Diario de Noticias*, 20 January 2000; *Diario de Noticias*, 12 June 2000; *Diario de Noticias*,7 June 2000; *Diario de Noticias*, 4 July 2000.
48. Report of President Manuel dos Santos in http://www.parlamento.pt. Accessed during January 2001.
49. Interview with Ana Fraga, Assembleia da Republica, 13 July 2002.
50. She was a member of the high level group on economic and social implications of industrial change. The group published a report: *European Commission, Managing Change. Final Report of the High-Level Group on Economic and Social Implications of Industrial Change* (Luxembourg: Office of the Official Publications of the European Communities, 1998).
51. Interview in *Expresso*, 4 March 2000.
52. Paulo Sande, "União Europeia: Deriva intergovernmental," *Europa* 7, 2000: 46-52; particularly 46.
53. See for an evaluation a special issue on A Estratégia de Lisboa. A agenda europeia para o desenvolvimento economico e social of *Europa Novas Fronteiras* 9/10, 2001.
54. *Expresso,* 4 March 2000
55. *Diario de Noticias*, 21 March 2000; *Expresso,*10 December1999.
56. *Diario de Noticias*, 28 March 2000;
57. *Diario de Noticias*, 28 June 2000.
58. *Expresso*, 17 June 2000; *Diario de Noticias*, 20 June 2000; The Portuguese presidency felt that the French were impatient to have their presidency. This naturally led to diplomatic disappointments for the Portuguese when the French did not value the ministerial meeting on the WEU in Porto in May 2000 enough to send a minister; they sent only a middle-ranking civil servant. Moreover, the French started to present their presidency program in May when the Portuguese presidency was still on-going; see *Diario de Noticias*, 16 May 2000; *O Independente*,

20 May 2000. Although there were some tensions and overlapping of presidencies and ambitions, it appears that in the end the relationship between the countries did not suffer too much; they regarded this as part of an internalized process of negotiation, which sometimes may assume harder positions. (Interview with Pedro Lourtie, 7 September 2002, Permanent Representation Brussels.)

59. *Publico*, 15 February 2000.
60. *Die Zeit*, 6 July 2000, p. 9.
61. *Die Zeit*, 14 December 2000.
62. *Publico*, 8 June 2000.

8

Catching Up with the European Union: The Strategic Role of the Structural Funds

Introduction: The Structural Policies of the European Union

One major achievement of the Jacques Delors Commission was to change the nature of European public policy. Delorsism clearly had a special agenda of promoting a more offensive role for the Commission in the field of public policy. Indeed, the upgrading of the existing structural funds through the Delors I Package in 1988 and the Delors Package II in the Edinburgh Summit 1992 changed completely the nature of the whole European integration process. The structural funds became a major innovative element in the overall public policy of the European Union, legitimized by the fact that proper implementation of these structural funds would lead to a stronger even more single European market. Indeed, the overall idea was to add to the important notion of competitiveness of the future European market the notion of social and economic cohesion in relation to the American and the Japanese/Asian markets. One characteristic introduced by the Delors Packages was programming, instead of an individual project approach. Moreover, back in 1988, reform of the structural funds furthermore introduced partnership, subsidiarity, and complementarity, which would play a role in the overall funding of the structural funds. The structural funds soon became the second policy area, after the ailing Common Agricultural Policy.[1] The overall rationale of the structural funds was related to the building of the European internal market both in terms of modernization or reconversion of old infrastructures, development of those regions lagging behind, which were and are mostly located in the south, and reconversion of former decaying agricultural and fisheries regions. The so-called structural policies were not directed towards the national governments, which were more or less the monopolistic gateway to the supranational institutions, but to the regions, a fact that increased mobilization of the regions at the European level. They were able to set up offices at the supranational level to exert some influence at the European Union level. Indeed, between 1985 and 1994, one can see an enormous rise of regional offices at the European level, which came mainly from Spain, Germany, Belgium, and France. At a later stage, offices from the Italian northern regions were also set up in Brussels. At the end of the 1990s, all EU member-states had regional offices of some kind in Brussels, with the exception of Greece and Portugal.[2] Some countries, for example, Denmark, tended to send offices from the main cities such as Aarhus. Although the nature of representation was not homogeneous it clearly helped to strengthen the so-called third level of European integration. Indeed, the so-called two-level game[3] that existed until the mid-1980s had been transformed into a multilevel game, which had the relationship between the member-states' national governments and the supranational institutions at the center of the overall decision-making structure; the subnational in all its forms was able to gain direct access to information and play a influencing role both in the supranational and national arenas. Indeed, one can see during this period the emergence of reinforced regionalization in most states such as Spain (1978), France (1984), Belgium (1993), the UK (1997), and Italy (1970, 1999).

There was an unwritten alliance between the European Commission and the regions. The European Commission regarded the region as the main vehicle to weaken and soften the strength of the member-states. Indeed, in the period between 1985 and 1993, we see a strong redefining of the relationship between center and periphery in all member-states.[4] Economically, the region was regarded as a crucial flexible territorial unit to compete in a globalization scenario.[5] The national governments were far too bureaucratic to make the decisions necessary on decentralization of the political system so that a region was competitive enough. A region was regarded as having a strategic interest as ally to the European Commission in order to gain more maneuver in terms of developing its own long-term policies, naturally within the parameters set up by the state. Foreign investors would look at regions in terms of the quality of their infrastructures, human resources, and governmental autonomy. Some regions, such as the four-motor (Baden-Württemberg, Lombardy, Catalonia, and Rhône-Alps), saw themselves as spearheading this movement.[6] The establishment of the Committee of the Regions and Local Authorities further confirmed this renewed power of the regions. Nevertheless, the regions soon came to realize that the Committee of the Regions was a way of controlling this growing importance of the regions at the supranational level.[7]

During this rise of the regions, Portugal, along with Greece, was rather passive. One may attribute this to a lack of strong regional civil societies in these two small countries, or even to complete happiness with the status quo of a unitary state. In Portugal, the democratic state continued to be organized in two-tiers: the national and the local levels. The only regional institutions were the Commissions for Regional Coordination (*Comissões de Coordenação Regional*-CCRs). These are deconcentrated services from the Ministry of the Equipment, Planning, and Administration of the Territory, which changed its name to Ministry of the Cities, Territory Organization, and Environment. This centralization of decision-making and fragmentation at local level in terms of implementation of projects, naturally facilitated any negotiations with the European Union.

Before the Delors Packages I and II came into force, programming had already begun between 1984 and 1988, but it only became more sophisticated and integrated after the 1988 reforms. One of the most important aspects was the definition of objectives of the overall packages. Indeed, five objectives were established back in 1988, which were changed to six objectives to accommodate the Nordic enlargement. In the document on the forthcoming enlargement Agenda 2000 it was proposed to reduce the objectives from six to three.[8] The latest Common Support Framework (CSF) adopted the recommendations of Agenda 2000. Objective 1 remained by far the most important one, which was aimed at improving the infrastructures of lagging behind regions with a GDP per head of less than 75 percent of the EU average. The whole territory of Portugal was identified as being in this situation. Nevertheless, in the latest, CSFIII (2000-2006) the Portuguese had to negotiate heavily to assure that the Lisbon Vale do Tejo region qualified as a transitional region for funding.[9] Indeed, the European Commission imposed a more accelerated implementation of the structural funds for these transitional regions. More than 68 percent of projects had to be approved by 2002. In reality, the delays that occurred are not dramatic, but should further two-year delays occur it may lead to the complete loss of funding.[10]

The structural funds are quite important because they have made the European Union a qualitatively different regional governance system that aims, in some sense, at creating more cohesion and equality of opportunity across the territory. Neglected in the overall discourse of the European Union is the fact that this community of shared sovereignty has achieved a high level of solidarity. Although after Agenda 2000 this process of cross-regional distribution slowed down, most cohesion countries (Portugal, Spain, Greece, and Ireland) were still able to substantially improve their economies. Indeed, all countries came closer to the EU average per head of GDP.

One thing that remains to be seen is if this process of catching up with the rest of the European Union is sustainable. The inclusion of new members with a cheaper and better-trained workforce may become a major worry for the Portuguese development plans. Indeed, the main problem of the Portuguese economy is its lack of innovation and research and technology investment,[11] which is reinforced by the fact that Portugal has the worst qualified workforce of the European Union (see chapter 4).

Despite these negative aspects, Portugal was actually good at absorbing most of the funding related to infrastructures. The outlook of the country changed considerably in terms of high-speed motorways, bridges, and transport infrastructures. Between 1985 and the present, the funds have been used to integrate Portugal into the Transeuropean networks (TENs); nevertheless, there is still a good deal to be done.

In this chapter, I will highlight in more detail the relationship between the European Commission and the Portuguese national administration and then discuss the Common Support Frameworks, which will be followed by a more thorough evaluation. Finally, some conclusions will close the chapter.

The Relationship between the Portuguese Public Administration and the European Commission

The adjustment of public administration to the emerging pressures coming from European regional policy became a major priority. Between 1987 and 1989, Portugal had to submit a Regional Development Plan to the Commission in due time to negotiate a Common Support Framework, which would define the financial participation of the EU in the regional development plan. For this, structural adjustments were undertaken to respond more quickly to problems that might appear between the EU and the Portuguese administration. The new democratic political system had a decidedly fragmented and inefficient structure to deal with regional policy. Indeed, until 1983, the decision-making process was concentrated in the Ministry of Finance and Planning, while the de-concentrated implementation structures, the so-called five Regional Coordinating Commissions (*Comissões Coordenadoras Regionais*-CCR) founded in 1979 were under the control of the Ministry of Internal Administration.[12] This changed with the coming to power of the so-called Central Block (*Bloco Central*) government, a coalition between the PS and the PSD. This coalition was designed to prepare Portugal for its forthcoming membership in the EC. In 1984, the General-Secretariate for Regional Development (*Secretariado Geral para Desenvolvimento Regional*) was created in the Ministry of Internal Administration. Subsequently, an Interministerial Commission for Planning and Regional Development (*Comissão Interministerial para o planeamento e desenvolvimento regional*) was established to coordinate the policies of the various governmental departments in view of achieving maximum impact in regional development. At the later stage, the General-Secretariate was upgraded to a General-Directorate of Regional Development within the Ministry of Planning and Territorial Organization, which has remained in place to the present time.[13] At the same time, the Portuguese Council of Ministers approved a basic document on regional development policy and the means and instruments to implement it. Clearly, this document was general in nature and did not go into detail, but in any case it stated that the regional instruments had to be adjusted to the needs of the different regions of Portugal. Closer to membership, and after a request from the European Commission, the Portuguese government, in 1985, sent a first version of the program for regional development 1986/90, which, in comparison to the regional development plans of the other countries, was largely generic and broad and characterized by a lack of reliable statistics.[14]

This clearly demonstrated that the chief problem of Portuguese public administration was its fight against many decades of underdevelopment imposed by an authoritarian regime that tended to abuse statistics or even to neglect the collection of reliable figures about the Portuguese territory. The main effort, thus, was to present reliable statistics about the five administrative regions in continental Portugal, Azores, and Madeira.[15]

The program of regional development was designed to ensure Portugal's access to the European Regional Development Fund. After negotiations with the European Commission, a more detailed program, called the National Program of Community Interest as Incentive for the Productive Activity (*Programa Nacional de Interesse Comunitário de Incentivo para a Actividade Produtiva*-PNICIAP), was approved, which assured the eligibility of Lisbon for regional development funds.[16]

This first real experience with the decision-making processes of the EC/EU led, after 1987, to better preparation of the Regional Development Plans in order to avoid delays in the decision-making process. The negotiation process became smoother in the first, second, and now third Common Support Framework (CSF). Also in terms of aims and objectives of the CSFs one can see a development towards a concentration around a smaller number of objectives. CSFI contained six axis within Objective 1 funding, comprising economic infrastructure, productive investment, human resources, agrarian development, industrial reconversion, and regional development); CSFII reduced it to four axis—human resources and employment, competitiveness factors of the economy, quality of life and social cohesion, and improvement of the regional economic base. Moreover, the operational programs were reduced from sixty to fourteen.[17] The present CSFIII (2000-2006) shows a high level of continuity to the previous CSFII. Indeed, CSFIII comprises four axis, which are (1) improvement of human resources and employment, (2) change of the productive profile in direction of activities of the future, (3) affirmation of the value of territory and of the geo-economic position of the country, and (4) foster the sustainable development of the regions and national cohesion.[18] This helped to debureaucratize the whole structure by concentrating the funds among fewer operational programs. Moreover, already there was a feeling during the Cavaco Silva government that CSFII may be the last chance for Portugal to receive structural funds from the European Union, in view of the forthcoming enlargement to Central and Eastern Europe, as well as the new eastern Bundesländer in Germany. This led actually to an exceedingly active participation by the entire Portuguese administration. In reality, the delayed enlargement led to the adoption of CSFIII until the year 2006, which is perceived as being the last chance to really make major improvements to the Portuguese economy. After the Portuguese presidency in the first semester of 1992, the government was eager to consult with groups from civil society to counteract the criticisms about the way CSFI was decided in 1989.[19]

Indeed, in CSFI, the Portuguese government was under time pressure to elaborate a consistent regional development plan comprising the whole territory. The Portuguese government also decided to submit the regional development plan even before it was known how much of the funds would be allocated to the individual countries. Portugal was the only country making this early submission. This was both a strategic choice to achieve early approval of the CSFII, and, at the same time, an attempt to show public opinion how efficient the government was in working on behalf of the Portuguese people. Institutionally, the government decentralized many of its implementation structures to the CCRs and to the municipalities. At the same time, it increased its coordinating efforts at all levels of the political system. At the governmental level, a Governmental Commission for the Coordination of the Community Funds, under the chairmanship of the Ministry of Planning and Administration of the Territory, was established, while, at the administrative level, several controlling and coordinating positions were created to ensure optimal use of the funds. The monitoring committee on the structural funds, which consisted of fifty members from the central, autonomous regional governments of Azores and Madeira and the CCRs and twelve members from EU institutions, was not changed at all.[20]

This speedy process towards submission was criticized by the Portuguese Economic and Social Council (*Conselho Economico e Social*-CES), on 30 July 1993, making it known that apart from the fact that civil society was only sparsely represented and involved in the whole decision-making process, the government had to think also about a sustainable strategy after 1999, so that the achieved gains would not be reversed again.[21]

The changeover from a social democratic to a socialist administration after the elections of October 1995 did not change the overall approach towards modernization of the administration. Indeed, the Socialist government under Antonio Guterres emphasized the aspect of continuity in policymaking. In the program of the thirteenth government adopted by the Assembly of the Republic in November 1995, administrative reform towards decentralization, deconcentration, transparency, and accountability was a major aspect. This was linked to the idea of development based on active participation of the population. One of the big objectives was naturally the creation of administrative regions, which would bring the decision-making process closer to the citizens.[22] The referendum of 8 November 1998 led to the rejection of this ambitious project of the Socialist Party. It left the Guterres' government with the five CCRs as the only way to deconcentrate public administration and improve the interfaces between the elected local governments and the extended regional arms of the public administration.

Indeed, the rejection of regionalization was a major blow to the overall manifesto of the Socialist Party. It was difficult for the party leadership to come up with an alternative plan B after the failure of plan A. One of the major problems was the fact that the Socialist government was unable to unite the political elite around a compromise. The overall process towards the design of the regionalization project was accompanied by strong opposition and sometimes obstruction by the main opposition party, the PSD. The "no" camp was also supported by former president Mário Soares. This was a major blow for Prime Minister Antonio Guterres. In the end, the no camp comprised the leadership of the right-center parties, PSD and CDS-PP, and many other movements that emerged before and during the campaign. The main argumentation was of a financial nature and about territorial integrity. The first argument centered around the belief that regionalization would create another tier of administration that would lead to more costs. The second argument involved the danger that regionalization would lead to regionalism and the fragmentation of Portugal into eight little Portugals. This strange argumentation, the lack of interest of the population, and the ingrained political culture of national unitarianism prevented an important step towards decentralization by the Portuguese administration.[23]

There was some optimism during the negotiations of the CSFIII that Portugal could move towards a regionalized structure. However, in the end, alternatives based on the principle of deconcentration had to be devised to achieve a higher level of deconcentrated and decentralized decision-making. The submission of the economic and social development plan under the heading, *A Strategic Vision to Win the Twentieth-First Century 2000-2006*, and the Regional Development Plan to the European Commission in view of negotiating the Common Support Framework for the next six years, makes it crucial to further decentralize, coordinate, and improve the administrative structures in view of maximizing the impact of the structural funds in Portugal.[24]

One of the major problems that Portuguese public administration is facing at the present time is overcoming the deficiencies inherited from forty-eight years of authoritarian, patrimonial approaches to public policy. This inability to overcome its authoritarian past led Portuguese policymakers, in the first decade of membership in the European Union, to a very passive, receptive attitude in the process of negotiations with the European Commission. Changes to the original CSF had to be agreed upon after consultation of the monitoring committee on the implementation of the structural funds by the responsible Commissioner himself. It took a long time before adjustments could be made. Also the ideology of partnership between the public and the private sectors took a long time to materialize, or not to materialize at all, because of a lack of tradition of cooperation between state and civil society as well as lack of cooperation between firms.[25] The first decade could be viewed also as a means to educate the management of small- and medium-sized enterprises to modernize their enterprise culture in view of the forthcoming SEM and EMU. Naturally, the ideology did not match the reality. Despite the drawbacks, after 1995 all these efforts to create and recreate the Portuguese economic strategy began to pay off. The transnationalization of cooperation of Portuguese businesses created a dynamic, daring, and self-confident economy. A process of internalization and administrative learning led to the establishment of a more citizen-friendly and transparent political system.

At the same time, the experience of the CSF has led to a simplification of procedures of approval, implementation, and adjustment of projects. All in all, although Portugal had to internalize within a decade a reflective mode of policymaking and overcome the legacy of authoritarian governance, the verdict is positive. There are still many problems to overcome, but the transition to democratic governance, reinforced by being part of a community of democratic countries and monitored by a supranational institutional framework, has transformed public administrative practices of the country.

The Common Support Framework Programs: The Strategic Impact on Portuguese Public Policy

The two main aims of the three CSFs since the reform of the structural funds are to reduce the disparities of development between the European countries and also within the country. One has to acknowledge that the CSFs have helped to reduce the disparity between countries, but not within the country. The Portuguese case clearly shows that the GDP/capita in relation to the EU average is highest between Lisbon and Porto, while lowest in the peripheral regions of inner and southern Portugal. A particular problem continues to be Alentejo, which is stagnating in terms of economic and social development. This shows that Common Support Framework programs have certainly helped to boost the macroeconomic performance of the country and improve the linkages to other countries of the European Union, but still has difficulties in improving conditions in the less-advantaged regions of Portugal. Although the CSFs were and are a major strategic device to an integrated approach to development, mobilizing civil society and economic actors to play their parts still remains a major problem. The European Union finances most of the CSFIII in Portugal, but it is counting on the governmental counterpart and, naturally, the private sector to help. It is the latter that has been weak and only partially contributing to the CSF, which leads to a larger intervention of the public sector in financing projects that are designed to attract private investment. This problem has been highlighted in a study by Isabel Mota where she makes note of

> the excessive use of non-reimbursable subsidies to the private sector, to the detriment of other financial engineering schemes, creating excessive dependence on the part of investors on this type of support and removing the incentive from some innovative measures.[26]

This situation may pose a problem for the period after 2006, which, in turn, will lead to a substantial reduction of structural funds and their diversion to the new member-states in central and eastern Europe. In some ways, the Portuguese leadership is well aware of the future problems, although it is clearly in support of further enlargement. Indeed, it was during the Portuguese presidency that negotiations with the first-wave candidates were initiated.[27]

Although the CSFs are strategic devices to strengthen the Portuguese economy in long-term perspective, the level of need was so widespread that the whole country had to be declared as belonging to Objective 1, related to lagging behind regions. This, of course, helped to develop integrated CSFs with specific operational programs for individual policy areas such as health, education, industry, fisheries, agriculture, and so on. In sum, eighteen Operational Programs are part of the overall CSFIII, almost the same number of programs as in CSFII: The overall CSFIII will comprise over 42 billion euros over the period 2000 to 2006.

Most of the funding will go to a transformation of the economic profile of the country, particularly in the industry and services fields and naturally in regional cohesion. While upgrading the qualifications of the Portuguese population is still important, infrastructures have become less important in this CSFIII, which results in a priority shift towards the challenges of the information and knowledge society.

It will require a huge effort by the Portuguese private sector to come up with a more innovative approach towards upgrading their economic basis. A major report, by a team led by Jorge A. Vasconcellos, on the possibilities of the Portuguese economy making a seismic cultural change in relation to innovation, research and development, and competitiveness is rather critical. Indeed, the well-researched report predicts that Portugal may diverge instead of converging into the European Union. One of the main causes is the very low productivity of the Portuguese economy. There is a social psychological explanation for this related to the lack of transformation of the values of Portuguese society, which tend to go counter with a competitive ethos and emphasize a lack of ambition in pushing through major objectives. [28] Quite clearly, the authors make the point that the present education system is inadequate, because instead of teaching, it tends to deform the students towards the status quo. This well-researched report shows that cultural factors may account for the inability to transform the private sector. The entrepreneurial

Figure 8.1
The Five Administrative Deconcentrated Regions and the Two Autonomous Governments of the Islands Azores and Madeira

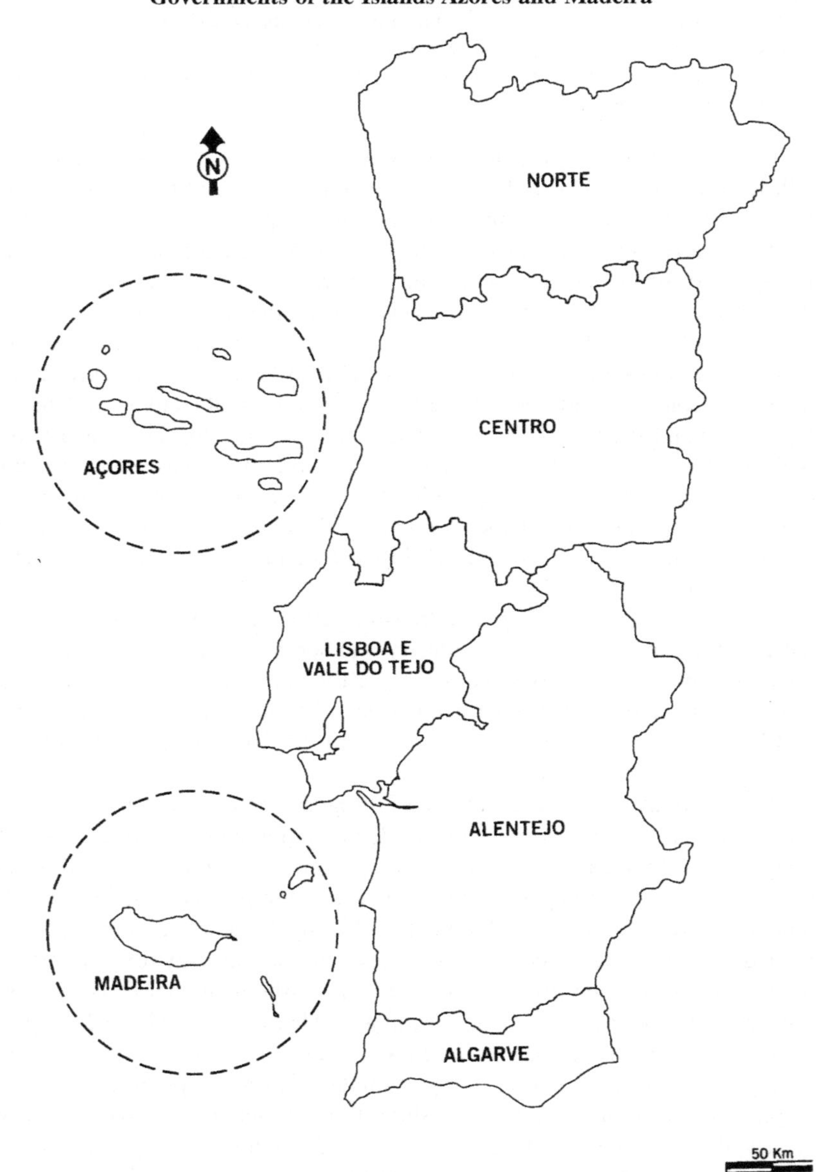

Source: Ministério do Planeamento, Comissão Europeia, *Portugal 2000-2006. Plano de Desenvolvimento Regional* (Lisbon: DGDR, 2000), 138.

Table 8.1
The Portuguese CSFIII (2000-2006) According to Axis and Source of Financing in ε Million

Axis	EU	Government	Private	Total
AXIS ONE: Upgrading the Level of Qualifications of Portuguese Employment and social cohesion	4,266,826	2,461,597	366,322	7,094,745 (16.8%)
AXIS TWO: Changing the Productive Profile towards activities of the future	4,131,581	1,962,504	7,015,475	13,109,560 (31.1%)
AXIS THREE: Affirm the value of the national territory and the geoeconomic position of the country	1,721,041	1,794,415	309,038	3,824,494 (9.1%)
AXIS FOUR: Promotion of s ustainable development in the regions and national cohesion	8,977,782	5,209,224	1,087,970	15,274,976 (36.3%)
RESERVE	1,356,460	810,176	620,906	2,787,542 (6.6%)
TOTAL	20,453,690 (48.6%)	12,237,916 (29.1%)	9,399,711 (22.3%)	42,091,317

Source: Author's own calculations based on data provided by the Financing Framework in Ministério do Planeamento, Comissão Europeia, *Quadro Comunitário de Apoio QCAIII* (Lisbon: Direcção Geral de Desenvolvimento Regional, 2000).

spirit is still underdeveloped in Portugal. At the center of all reforms, however, remains the lack of improvement of the education sector. Although the structural funds are financing an operational program on education, it is targeted towards infrastructures and the training of teachers, and is less designed to find a solution to the problem of Portugal having the highest dropout rates in the European Union and the lowest number of people with a secondary education. A large gap exists between people with a primary education and people with higher education, leading to a disparity of salaries (see chapter 4).

The coalition government under Manuel Durão Barroso is anxious to push towards a more competitive Portugal. He clearly wants to overcome the subsidy culture inherent in Portuguese society. However, in spite of these intentions, it is extremely difficult to transform a country that has mostly capital-poor, small- and medium-sized enterprises. The hand of the state is essential in raising the Portuguese economy to a certain level.

Naturally, the low level of investment in Research and Development does not lead to major successes. Less than 1 percent of GDP is invested in R&D and firms clearly do not show much ambition to change the structure of R&D financing, which leads to a technologically, highly dependent economy. Indeed, in the CSFII, the target of 42 percent financing of R&D by enterprises had to be abandoned as well as the Communications and Technology subprogram, which did not create a continuity of networks.[29] This becomes evident

Figure 8.2
The Sources of Research and Development Financing

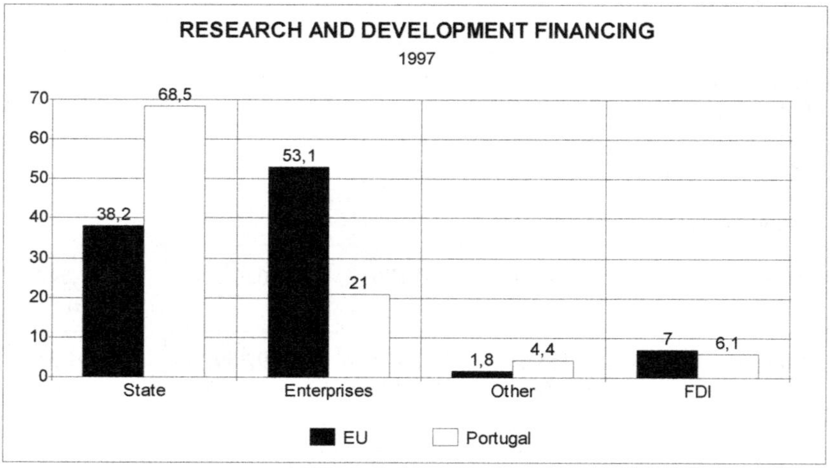

Source: Ministério do Planeamento, Comissão Europeia, *Portugal 2000-2006. Plano de Desenvolvimento Regional* (Lisbon: DGDR, 2000), I-14.

in terms of Internet and email use. Portugal is within the cluster of countries such as Greece, Italy, Spain, and France that are at the bottom of the European Union in this respect. Only 10 percent of Portuguese tend to use the Internet, in comparison to Sweden were almost two-thirds of the population have become acquainted with the new technologies (Figure 8.3). It should be mentioned that Sweden is the country that is investing the most in R&D of the EU. One of the basic problems of the Portuguese industry, apart from its low productivity and low investment, is its low performance in terms of marketing and distribution. Together, all of these deficiencies tend to keep Portuguese products uncompetitive. The branding of textiles or other clothing products as has been done by the Spaniards and Italians, is still underdeveloped in Portugal. In the future, this will create problems for Portugal in relation to similar products coming from Southeast Asia.[30]

If we look closely at the aspect of economic and social cohesion across the Portuguese territory including the islands, we have to reach the conclusion that not much national cohesion and reduction of regional disparities has been achieved. The most problematic areas seem to be Alentejo and the islands of Azores and Madeira, which are clearly still markedly distant from the Portuguese average and clearly even more so from the EU average. Alentejo, along with Madeira and Azores, are among the poorest regions of the European Union. Portuguese planners find the stagnation of Alentejo's economy,

Figure 8.3
Internet Users in the European Union (per 100 inhabitants)

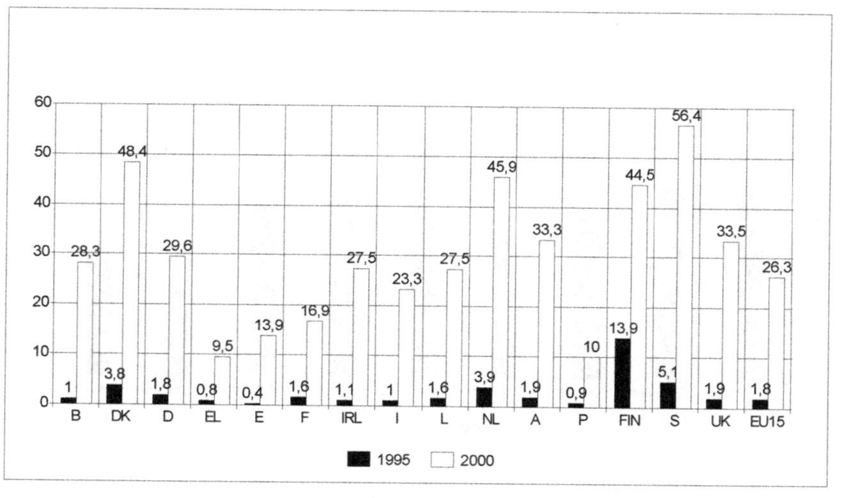

Source: Graph created based on data provided by Eurostat, *Eurostat Yearbook 2002. The Statistical Guide to Europe. Data 1990-2000* (Luxembourg: Office of the Official Publications of the European Communities, 2002), 296.

which is extremely dependent on agriculture, a major problem. The construction of the Alqueva dam may help to restore the economy of Alentejo, but an equally critical issue is the need to retain the young population that is migrating to the larger towns of Algarve or directly to Lisbon. Many of the young cross the border to work in Extremadura or even Andalusia in the agricultural sector.[31] Apart from the Algarve and the Lisbon Vale do Tejo region, all other Portuguese regions are still struggling to achieve the Portuguese average. The changes towards cohesion have been thus far minimal, which prevents a more cohesive economic and social development of the country. One cannot deny that many efforts have been made to overcome this situation with the approval of several projects in order to raise education and quality of life standards of the peripheral populations, but there is yet a long way to go in the direction of more equality of access to public goods and the market. In terms of country specific social and economic cohesion towards other European Union members one has to say that much improvement has been achieved in this area. The main worry is whether this dynamic will be sustainable when the flow of structural funds begins to dry up and the Portuguese have to find strategic funding from within their economy.

Figure 8.4
GDP per Capita (EU15)

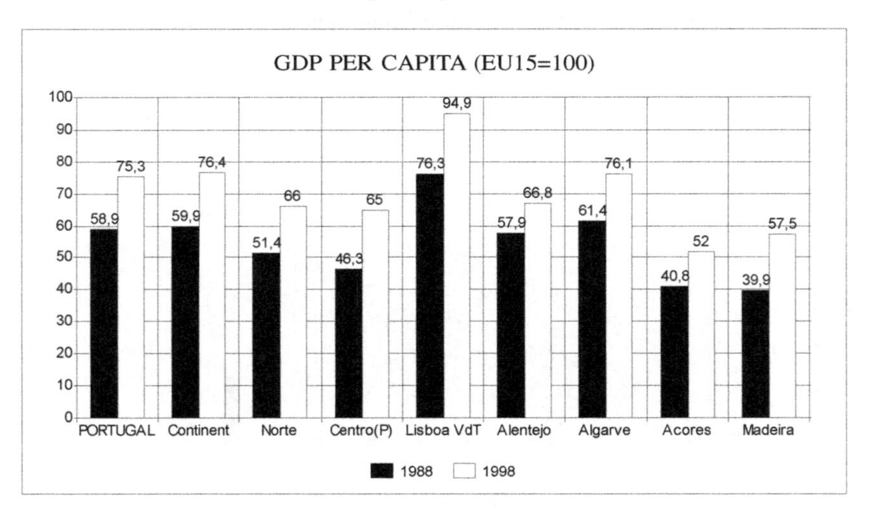

Source: Author's own graph based on data provided by European Commission, *Unity, Solidarity, Diversity for Europe, Its People and Its Territory. Second Report on Economic and Social Cohesion. Vol.2* (Luxembourg: Office of the Official Publications of the European Communities, 2001), 70-71.

Figure 8.5
Regional Disparities in Portugal

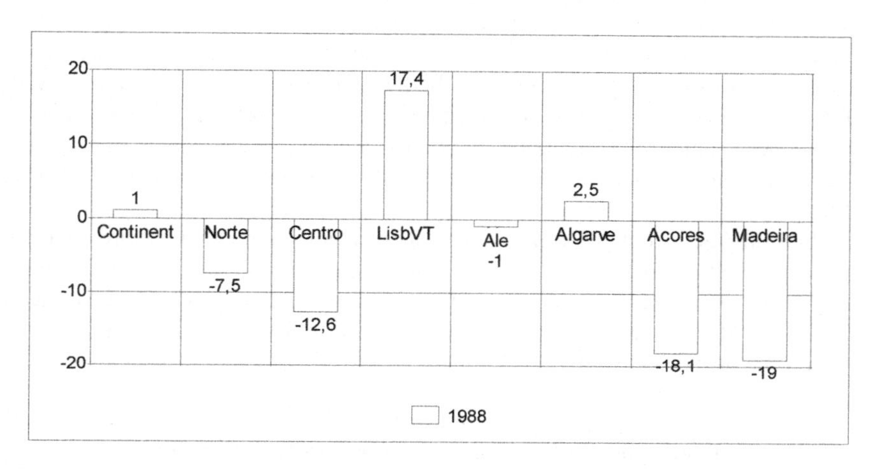

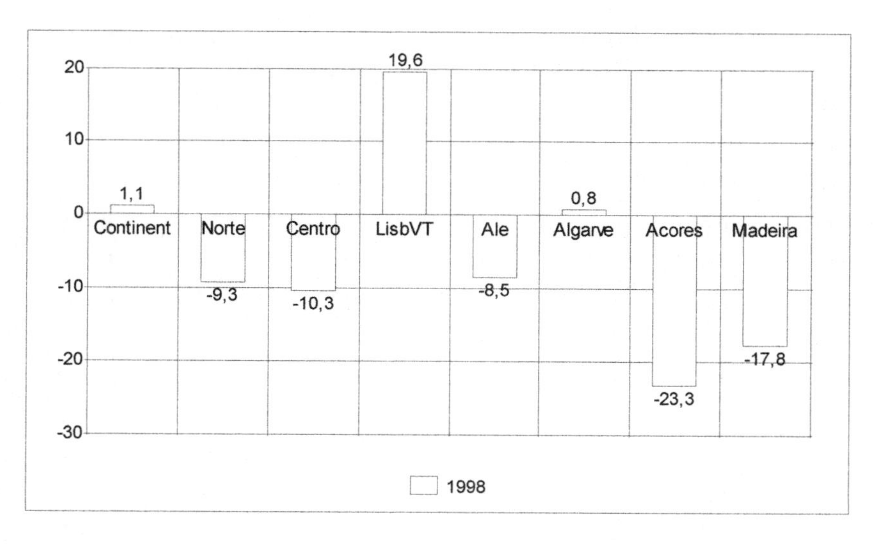

Source: Author's own graph based on data provided by European Commission, *Unity, Solidarity, Diversity for Europe, Its People and Its Territory. Second Report on Economic and Social Cohesion. Vol.2* (Luxembourg: Office of the Official Publications of the European Communities, 2001), 70-71. Ale=Alentejo; LisbVT=Lisbon and Vale do Tejo.

The regional asymmetries also have their expression in the comfort fields in terms of sanitation, electricity access, education/literacy, and life expectancy. In sum, the CSFs have contributed to the economic and social situation in absolute terms, but in relative terms the asymmetrical nature of Portuguese society and its economy continues to be a major obstacle to social mobility. Education, as already mentioned in chapter 4, is the single major problem of Portuguese society. It is not only about having more graduates, but, mainly, a better educated workforce that has successfully completed a secondary education.

In sum, the structural funds have only partially helped to improve the main problem of Portuguese society, which is related to the lack of innovating forces that would develop new products able to compete in the Single European Market. In spite of the enormous amount of work done thus far to overcome decades of underdevelopment there still remains much to be done.

Table 8.2
Distribution of Structural Funds among EU Members

	Objective 1	Transitional Objective 1	Objective 2	Transitional Objective 2	Objective 3	Total
B	0	625	368	65	737	1,795
DK	0	0	156	27	365	548
D	19,229	729	2,984	526	4,581	28,049
EL	20,961	0	0	0	0	20,961
E	37,744	352	2,553	98	2,140	42,887
F	3,254	551	5,437	613	4,540	14,395
IRL	1,315	1,773	0	0	0	3,088
I	21,935	187	2,145	377	3,744	28 388
L	0	0	34	6	38	78
NL	0	123	676	119	1,686	2,604
A	261	0	578	102	528	1,469
P	16,124	2,905	0	0	0	19 029
FIN	913	0	459	30	403	1,805
S	722	0	354	52	720	1,848
UK	5,085	1,166	3,989	706	4,568	15 514
TOTAL	127,543	8,411	19,733	2,721	24,050	182 458

Source: European Commission, *Working for the Regions* (Luxembourg: Office of the Official Publications of the European Communities, 2001), 11.

The main goal that needs to be met is a major review of all policy objectives and the introduction of new ways of adequately pursuing those objectives, to ensure that they are adjusted and compatible with the problems of Portuguese society and its economy. For the moment, the European structural funds have pushed the Portuguese government to come up with projects so that the funding can be absorbed, but there is still a lack of integration of all policy areas towards the common goal, which is necessary to building a strong society that will be able to sustain an innovative and competitive economic structure. A look at the overall problems concerning the management of the programs may highlight why it is still difficult to assess the impact of the structural funds as a completely positive experience. In a sense, a parallel can be drawn to the time when Portugal received gold and other precious minerals from Brazil, but was unable to transform this into real economic power. Eventually, it led to the semiperipheral position that Portugal is still trying to overcome. It appears that the major efforts of Portuguese governments since the mid-1980s have not been thought out completely.

An Assessment of the Management of the Structural Funds

Despite all the criticisms, one has to acknowledge that structural funds are generally well managed in Portugal, and particularly well managed in relation to the European Regional Development Fund (ERDF). It is obvious that the European Union changed the quality of life across the country through the upgrading of infrastructures. One impressive architectural masterpiece is the multimodal station of Oriente, which clearly helped to transform an area of Lisbon and give it new life. Indeed, the station of Oriente was built for Expo'98 and became an important part of life in the Portuguese capital; the linkage Lisbon-Oporto has to pass through the station of Oriente.[32] The same can be said about the new metro stations in Lisbon, which are really examples of the self-confidence the Portuguese have gained by being part of the European Union. These illustrations can be multiplied across the country, with examples such as the renovation of the old town of Guimarães, which is considered to be the birthplace of Portugal,[33] and the cultural infrastructures in Alentejo.[34]

The main problem lies more with the European Social Fund (ESF) and the European Agricultural Guarantee and Guidance Fund (EAGGF). Neither was able to contribute significantly to transforming the profile of both the qualifications structures and the agricultural sector. As previously stated, Portugal has the lowest number of people taking part in vocational training courses. Portugal fits into a southern European pattern in comparison to the northern European pattern where lifelong learning is a crucial part of employability strategies. Not only is it the low demand, it is also the quality of supply that may affect the low rate of people participating in vocational courses. Nor does Portugal's past history of vocational training give credibility to it. Even the trade union confederation General Workers Union (*União Geral dos Trabalhadores*-UGT) was involved in fraudulent activities in terms of vocational training courses, using the money for their own meetings.[35] Moreover, pre-1988 funds were characterized by fraudulent activities, all of which indicates that the running of the European Social Fund was not without problems.[36] In the intercalating report of CSFII, which took place in 1996, it was determined that the European Social Fund in Portugal lacked a reliable system of information for data on all courses and participants. Measures were taken to overcome this deficit. Also a lack of integration exists with the systems of information of the other funds. This disorganization of internal data collection became a major worry for policymakers, who clearly want to avoid duplication of this or other negative aspects of project approval and management. Because of this, information organization became a major issue after the second half of the 1990s, with a major shift to looking for quality of project management rather than quantity. It meant that after difficulties in CSFI, CSFII was able to attract more projects and ideas.[37]

The transformation of the agricultural sector towards a more dynamic competitive pattern has been progressing slowly. Nevertheless, there is a new group of well-qualified, young farmers who used the structural funds to replace the older generations. This embryonic development will only show results when the structural funds run out in the case of Portugal.[38]

One major problem that was partly solved in CSFIII is the high level of concentration/centralization in the management structures. There was somewhat of an improvement to adjust it to the necessities of the regional and local levels. This meant that the existing teams of technical assistance had to be decentralized and adjusted to the regional and local levels to achieve a better submission of projects. In some cases, the regulations of the competitions were nonexistent, creating delays in the approval of programs. This was further complicated by the fact that the bureaucratic structures would take a long time to approve projects or would delay the payment of structural funds. Moreover, the monitoring mechanisms of projects were, in some cases, inadequate because they lacked consistency in terms of criteria. There was some overlapping of projects, too, which clearly led or could lead to duplication. All of this relates to what was initially identified as the lack of a functioning integrated information system covering all structural funds.[39]

Thus, this, created problems for potential clients taking part in these projects. Indeed, the lack of information, the lack of consistency in the use of instruments, the overlapping of projects, the lack of knowledge as to how to run new innovating initiatives coming from the European Commission within a particular fund, especially in the European Social Fund, and the lack of an adequate bureaucratic structure to cope with the increased demand led many potential clients, particularly in the industry sector, to desist from application.[40]

One has to acknowledge that most of the demand was created by the structural funds and it takes some time to create a decentralized social capital system. Indeed, the main source for pushing through the operational programs at the regional level is the already mentioned CCRs. Since 1979 the CCRs have decentralized technical support services in each of the regions. These so-called Technical Assistance Offices (*Gabinetes de Assistencia Técnica*-GATs) normally have a small staff of about 10 to 20 people. These teams consist of engineers, architects, and other specialized staff, who are able to advise and support the projects initiated at the local level. This is quite important because local authorities are underfunded in Portugal and unable to get the necessary expertise for any projects they might want to implement. Over the past three decades of democratic local government, it should be noted, however, that some policy learning has improved this situation. Some local authorities have contracted environmental engineers due to the growing demand to implement environmental standards in all projects.

The GATs are located in the cities of the region. While in the CCR Norte there will be a continuation of the thirteen GATs,[41] in the CCR Lisboa Vale do Tejo there is a process going on to reduce the existing six GATs to three. The main reason is that there is a need to move towards a more integrated approach. There is discussion going on related to Associations of Municipalities, which would, in some sense, be a substitute for full-fledged regionalization. The main problem so far is that local authorities tend to rival each other, instead of cooperating with each other towards supramunicipality structures.[42] According to Rui Jacinto, vice president of the CCR Centro, the sixteen GATs in his region lack financial and human resources to perform a good job. He also sees as the only alternative a growing cooperation between the different local authorities so that projects become more viable and the structures of technical assistance can be rationalized.[43]

Naturally, all this relates back to the lack of preliminary research in order to make a proper allocation of funding tailored to the needs of a sector or region. Had previous studies been done, finding synergies and complementarities would not have been so difficult, and would have led to savings and probably debureaucratization of many programs.[44]

Another aspect that has been highlighted is the still incipient participation of civil society in the whole process of policy formulation, decision-making, and implementation of the structural funds. There is a growing effort within the Portuguese governments to overcome this democratic deficit. In the approval of the most recent CSFIII, the regional development plan was opened to public discussion in 1998 and 1999. According to official figures, more than 3,000 persons took part in these consultation meetings. Participants were invited to submit proposals and ideas for both the National Plan for Economic and Social Development (*Plano Nacional de Desenvolvimento Economico e Social*-PNDES) as well as the Regional Development Plan (*Plano de Desenvolvimento Regional*-PDR).[45] The main problem was and is to make this participation sustainable throughout the decision-making and implementation phases. The so-called units of management must, in some way, integrate the main social and economic agents so that the process of decision-making and monitoring becomes more democratic. In spite of this, regional civil societies are still relatively weak and unable to influence policy. The best organized is normally the business sector. Indeed, the so-called associations of enterprises (*associações empresariais*) are regarded as important economic agents in the different administrative regions.[46]

In the CCR Lisboa e Vale do Tejo, they were strongly involved in the ad hoc Strategic Council of the *Region* (*Conselho Estratégico da Região*), which was created to formulate a Strategic Plan of the Region Lisboa e Vale do Tejo (*Plano Estratégico para a Região Lisboa e Vale do Tejo*). This distinctive document demonstrates that there is a will to modify forms of policymaking by including social and economic actors and overcome the self-referential practices of state agencies of the past. The document is full of detailed analysis and long-term planning. It clearly is a response to the main bottleneck of the previous CSFI, the lack of framework studies for the proper allocation of the structural funds. This well-documented strategic plan was also the basis for negotiations with the European Commission to concede transitional Objective 1 status to the whole region of Lisboa e Vale do Tejo. In terms of the continuing participation of civil society, there was the plan to create regional Economic and Social Councils (*Conselhos Economico e Sociais Regionais*-CESRs) that would complement the already existing national Economic and Social Committee. However, in the end, they were never implemented. Alternatives are the Regional Councils (*Conselho da Região*), consisting of Local Council Presidents (70 percent), trade union confederations, and associations of enterprises.[47]

It appears that the main actors of civil society are the so-called environmental associations that have been noticeably active in calling attention to the lack of environmental assessments for many projects. Recently, there were protests by environmental associations against the intention to situate a new airport in Lisbon on the northern rim of the estuary. These disruptions naturally affect planning and create delays in the implementation of major projects. Indeed, Portuguese authorities perceive that the European Commission is highly sensitive to any environmental concerns from the population.[48]

Overall, the European Commission views Portuguese management and implementation of the funds as quite efficient. According to the official responsible for monitoring the Portuguese programs, the Portuguese administrative system is quite adequate for the management and implementation of the structural funds, because it is a simple system in which the decision-making process is sufficiently centralized. The Portuguese administrative system does not go through different levels of decision-making, as does, for example, Spain. The annual meetings of the European Commission with the government agencies in Brussels can be regarded as an important instrument to control and monitor the progress made by Portuguese authorities. The European Commission can make critical remarks and even send an official letter asking for adequate response. If such queries by the Commission are not properly answered, a blocking of payments may occur, which is normally a last resort only in cases where there is a clear dissonance between the European institution and the corresponding government. There is also a feeling that after a boom of demand in the 1990s, the whole dynamics and pace of presenting new innovative projects slowed down. Indeed, environmental concerns contributed to a more moderate rate of project submission.[49]

In sum, structural funds in Portugal continue to fulfill the strategic function of bringing the country up to the social and economic standards of the EU average or beyond. This has been a most difficult task to fulfill, because of decades of stasis in the 1930s to the 1950s that targeted the education sector in particular. Only in the 1960s did the authoritarian regime recognize the importance of modernizing the country. Nevertheless, it was only after accession to the European Union that a more long-term perspective was developed. The strategic use of the structural funds affected all sectors of politics, the economy, and society. In spite of now over fifteen years of accelerated qualitative development, meaning the taking into account of social and environmental costs, many areas, particularly education and health, have still to be reformed accordingly to allow better use of the recent transformations. As long as the drop-out rate of students in the secondary sector is the highest in the European Union, it will be difficult to raise the standard of qualifications in the Portuguese labor market, a fact that will adversely affect all sectors of the economy. Cheap labor is not the most positive strategy for creating real improvement and sustainability of the Portuguese economy. Instead, the riches of a poor country such as Portugal lie in its investment in its own human resources.

Conclusions

Despite the strong innovative potential in Portuguese society, the present situation is worrisome. The failing education and health systems are causing problems in upgrading the Portuguese labor market and, consequently, the Portuguese economy. A lack of investment in research and development in Portuguese enterprises makes them vulnerable to the highly competitive world economy and particularly to the emerging single European market. Although the structural funds helped finally to build an internal market with new roads and an expanded, modernized railway system, and other important infrastructures, the Portuguese industrial and services sectors have yet to be successfully turned around. Developments in these areas are slow. Portugal was able to increase its number of scientists in the past fifteen years; however, that number is far below the EU average.

All of these aspects indicate the high dependency of social and economic actors on state paternalism in terms of subsidies. Pivotal to this crucial turning around are the Portuguese primary and secondary sectors, which need more attention and need a better strategy to be integrated into the social and labor market policies. One of the main reasons for the drop-out rate in the secondary sector seems to be the fact that underprivileged families are not able to sustain the education of their children and as a result students are under pressure to search for work at an early age. For a large underprivileged part of the population that still lives on the verge of poverty, children at school are perceived as loss of income.[50] This means that the social dimension of education needs to be reassessed in a long-term perspective, and will need to be a priority until there is a more balanced number of people leaving school with a full education and, thus, better prepared for the labor market.

At the moment, there is a segment of the Portuguese population that is highly educated, well-off, and able to obtain high paying jobs, sometimes with salaries beyond the EU average, but the vast majority of the population has low paying jobs under the EU average. Indeed, as mentioned in chapter 4, Portugal's income disparity is the highest, along with the United Kingdom, which means that the highest income, on the average, is 7.2 times higher than the lowest income in Portugal.[51] This fact, naturally, is neither sensible nor adequate for establishing a proper consumer market and equality of opportunities. Although the structural funds have helped to improve Portugal's access to the market, they have not been able to change the cultural patterns of behavior in Portuguese society.

Notes

1. Liesbet Hooghe, Michael Keating, "The Politics of European Union Regional Policy," *Journal of European Public Policy*, 1, 3, 1996: 367-393.
2. José Magone, "The Third Level of European Integration: New and Old Insights," in José Magone (ed.), *Regional Institutions and Governance in the European Union* (Westport, CT: Praeger, 2003), 1-28.
3. Robert Putnam, "Diplomacy and Domestic Politics," *International Organization* 42, 1988: 427-461.
4. Ingeborg Tömmel, "Transformation of Governance: The European Commission´s Strategy for Creating a 'Europe of the Regions'" *Regional and Federal Studies* 8, 2, summer 1998: 52-80.
5. European Commission/Netherlands Economic Institute, *New Location Factors for Mobile Investment in Europe* (Luxembourg: Office of the Official Publications of the European Communities, 1993).

6. Richard Balme, "Las Condiciones de la Acción Colectiva Regional," in F. Letamendia (Coord.), *Nacionalidades Y Regiones En La Unión Europea* (Madrid: Fundamentos, 1999), 69-91.
7. John Loughlin, "Representing the Regions in Europe: The Committee of the Regions," *Regional and Federal Studies* .6, 1996: 147-165; Federiga Bindi Calussi, "The Committee of the Regions: An Atypical Influential Committee?" in M.P.C.M. Van Schendelen (ed.), *EU Committees as Influential Policy-makers* (Aldershot: Ashgate, 1999), 225-249.; José Maria Munoa, "El Comité de las Regiones y la democracia regional y local en Europa," in Francisco Letamendia, (ed.), *Nacionalidades y Regiones en la Unión Europea* (Madrid: Fundamentos, 1998), 51-68.
8. European Commission, "Agenda 2000. For a Stronger and Wider Union," *Bulletin of the European Union*, Supplement 5/97.
9. Interview with Dr. Alzira Cabrita, 24 November 1998.
10. Interview with Eng. Antonio Fonseca Ferreira, president of Regional Coordinating Commission of Lisbon and Vale do Tejo, Lisbon, 8 July 2002.
11. According to the OECD, Portugal invests only 0.76 percent of GDP in research and development compared to Sweden and Finland, which invest more than 3.5 percent. Portugal fits into the cluster of laggards, along with Spain, Greece, and Italy (see *La Repubblica*, 8 November 2002, p.27).
12. Here is not the place to bring in a detailed history of the CCRs; nevertheless, a note may suffice. Such Commissions have existed since the late phase of the authoritarian regime. Indeed, so-called Commissions for Regional Planning (*Comissões de Planeamento Regional*-CPR) were created in November 1969. Nevertheless, before 1979, not much had been done in terms of institution-building, particularly in terms of regional planning agencies. The CPRs were linked to the ambitious plans of development (*planos de fomento*) of the previous authoritarian regime. For a more detailed account, see Comissão de Coordenação Região Norte, *Autonomia Administrativa e Financeira do Estado. O Caso das Comissões de Coordenação Regional* (Porto: CCRN, 1999), 61-73.
13. After the new Barroso government came to power a new name was given to the ministry—Ministry of Cities, Territory Organization and Environment (*Ministério das Cidades, Ordenamento do Territorio e Ambiente*). Ministries had to merge, due to the fact that the Portuguese government had to reduce the budget deficit in order to continue within the guidelines of the stability pact and avoid penalization by the EU.
14. Luis Madureira Pires, *Politica Regional Europeia e Portugal* (Lisbon: Fundação Gulbenkian, 1998), 42-44.
15. In the Eurostat annual statistical yearbook on the regions, figures for Portugal existed only in 1987 for the whole of Portugal and in 1988 for the individual regions. See also Carlos Oliveira, Romeu Costa Reis, Carlos Nunes da Silva, Maria Lucinda Fonseca, "A construção do poder local democrático 1976-1993," in Carlos Oliveira (ed.), *História dos Municipios e Poder Local* (Lisbon: Temas e Debates, 1996), 361-493, 393.
16. Pires, *Politica*, 45-46.
17. European Commission, *Common Support Framework II. Portugal 1994-1999* (Luxembourg: Office of the Official Publications of the European Communities, 1994).
18. Comissão Europeia, Ministério do Planeamento, *Quadro Comunitário de Apoio III. Portugal 2000-2006* (Lisbon: Direcção Geral de Desenvolvimento Regional, 2000).

19. The Community allocation for the Portuguese CSFI was 6, 958 billion ECUs (Pires, *Politica*, 96). Portugal was entitled to receive, between 1986 and 1988, 1,119 billion ECUs. It was only able to absorb 1,083 billion, losing out on 116 million ECU. Most of the funds were only absorbed by 1995 (Pires, *Politica*, 58: Antonio José Cabral, "Community Regional Policy towards Portugal, " in José da Silva Lopes (ed.), *Portugal and EC Membership Evaluated* (London: Pinter, 1994), 133-145. A delay in absorption happened also in CSFI. In CSFII, after the approval of the Delors II Package, the amount was raised to 13,980 billion ECUs plus 2,601 billion coming from the new cohesion fund (Pires, *Politica*, 244).
20. Pires, *Politica*, 160-166.
21. Conselho Economico e Social, "Parecer to Conselho Economico e Social sobre o Plano de Desenvolvimento Regional-PDR Aprovado no Plenário de 30 de Julho de 1993," in Conselho Economico e Social, *Pareceres e Reuniões do Conselho Economico e Social (Setembro 1992 a Fevereiro 1996)* (Lisbon: CES, 1996), 177-187.
22. Assembleia da Republica, *Programa do XIII Governo. Apresentação e Debate* (Lisbon: AR, 1996), 20-29.
23. On the argumentation of the anti-regionalization movement, which is sometimes appealing to a dormant nationalism, see Ernani Rodrigues Lopes (eds.), *Uma Experiencia Unica 1998; MPU. Um Movimento Civico Contra a Regionalização* (Porto: Porto Editora, 2001).
24. Ministério do Equipamento, Planeamento e Administração do Territorio (MEPAT), *Portugal 2000-2006: Plano de Desenvolvimento Regional* (Lisbon: MEPAT, 1999) In Agenda 2000, Portugal received a total of 19,029 billion Euros over the six-year period under the heading of Objective 1 and ex-objective 1 region in transition regime (mainly for the regions of Lisbon and Vale do Tejo). The number of objectives was reduced from 6 to 3 to achieve a higher more integrated and concentrated use of the structural funds.
25. Stephen Syrett, "Local Power and Economic Policy: Local Authority Economic Initiatives in Portugal," *Regional Studies* 28/1, 1993: 53-67; Stephen Syrett, *Local Development: Restructuring, Locality and Economic Initiative in Portugal* (Aldershot: Avebury, 1994); Stephen Syrett, "The Politics of Partnership: The Role of Social Partners in Local Economic Development in Portugal," *European Urban and Regional Studies* 4, 2, 1997; 99-114; particularly 104-111; Michael Eaton, "Regional Development Funding in Portugal," *Journal of the Association for Contemporary Iberian Studies* 7/2, 1994: 36-46; Maria do Rosário de Matos da Silva Almeida Rozek, *Die Entwicklung der Strukturpolitik der Europäischen Gemeinschaften. Ziele und Auswirkungen des EFRE auf die regionale Infra- und Industriestruktur am Beispiel der Region Norden in Portugal* (Frankfurt a. M.: Peter Lang, 1995); Bernhard Iking, *Die Auswirkungen des EG-Beitritts auf die Industriepolitik Portugals. Die Entwicklung der technologischen Wettbewerbsfähigkeit der Portugiesischen Industrie* (Frankfurt a. M.: Peter Lang, 1997).
26. Isabel Mota, "Application of the Structural Funds," in Alvaro de Vasconcelos, Maria João Seabra (eds.), *Portugal. A European Story* (Lisbon: Principia, 2000), 131-163; particularly 149.
27. João Pedro de Silveira de Carvalho, "Prioridades e resultados da Presidencia do Conselho da UE," *Europa. Novas Fronteiras* 7, June 2000: 14-23; particularly 16.
28. Jorge A. Vasconcellos, Miguel Frasquilho, Watson Wyatt Limited, Margarida Palla Garcia, Clara Goncalves, *Portugal Europeu?* (Lisbon: Vida Economica, 2001), 454-455.

29. Direcção Geral de Desenvolvimento Regional (DGDR), *Quadro Comunitário de Apoio 1994-1999. Balanço Final* (Lisbon: DGDR, 1999), 66.
30. M. Emerson, D. Gros, "Impact of Enlargement, Agenda 2000 and EMU on Poorer Regions—The Case of Portugal," Working Document 125 (Brussels: Center for European Policy Studies, 1998), 23-29.
31. José M. Magone, *Iberian Trade Unionism. Democratization Under the Impact of the European Union* (New Brunswick, NJ: Transaction Publishers, 2001), 274-275.
32. Comissão Europeia, *Projectos para o futuro. Politica regional da UE em Portugal* (Bruxelas: Servico de Publicações Oficiais das Comunidades Europeias, 2001), 17.
33. Ibid., 14.
34. Comissão de Gestão dos Fundos Comunitários, *Um Olhar sobre o QCAII. Encerramento do Periodo de Programação 1994-1999* (Lisbon: DGDR, 2000), 139-140.
35. José Magone, *Iberian Trade Unionism,* 163, 173, 178.
36. Rainer Eisfeld, "Portugal in the European Community 1986-88.The Transition of the First Half of the Transition Period," *Iberian Studies* 18/2, 1989: 156-65.
37. DGDR, *Quadro*, 132, 134.
38. Ibid., 54.
39. Ibid., 130-132.
40. Ibid., 132-133.
41. Interview with Cristina de Azevedo, vice president of Regional Coordinating Commission North (CCRN), Porto, 4 July 2002.
42. Interview with Antonio Fonseca Ferreira, president of the Regional Coordinating Commission Lisboa e Vale do Tejo (CCRLVT), Lisbon, 8 July 2002.
43. Interview with Rui Jacinto, vice president of the Regional Coordinating Commission Centro (CCRC), Coimbra, 12 July 2002.
44. Ibid., 134.
45. DGDR, *Portugal 2000-2006. Plano de Desenvolvimento Regional* (Lisbon: DGDR, 1999), VII, 1-9.
46. Interview with Cristina de Azevedo, vice president of CCRN, Porto, 4 July 2002; Rui Jacinto, vice president of CCRC, Coimbra, 8 July 2002.
47. Interview with Antonio Fonseca Ferreira, president of the CCRLVT, Lisbon, 8 July 2002. See also the CCRLVT, *Plano Estratégico da Regiao de Lisboa Oeste Vale do Tejo. 2000-2010 O Horizonte de Excelencia* (Lisbon: CCRLVT, 1999), 11.
48. Interview with Antonio Fonseca Ferreira, president of the CCRLVT, Lisboa, 8 July 2002.
49. Interview with Marco Orani, responsible for Portuguese programs, European Commission, DG XVI, Brussels, 12 september 2002.
50. Pedro Hespanha, Alcina Monteiro, A. Cardoso Ferreira, Fernanda Rodrigues, M. Helena Nunes, M. José Hespanha, Rosa Madeira, Rudy van den Hoven, Silvia, *Portugal, Entre o Estado e o Mercado. As fragilidades das instituições de protecção social em Portugal* (Coimbra: Quarteto, 2000), 61-64.
51. European Commission, *The Social Situation in the European Union 2002* (Luxembourg: Office of the Official Publications of the European Communities, 2002), 89.

9

The Return of Portuguese Foreign Policy: Bridging the European Union and the Lusophone World

Introduction

In spite of Portugal's small size, Portuguese foreign policy cannot be underestimated. Portugal is a country full of pride in its past achievements, particularly in the Age of Discoveries. This knowledge of a strong dynamic past, based on high levels of maritime technology, is a major factor that pushes Portuguese diplomacy to continue to play an active role in international relations. The collapse of the authoritarian regime led to the end of the Portuguese colonial empire, which was an early part of the collective identity of the Portuguese. It was difficult for Portugal to separate itself from its former colonies, but the process of democratization was so turbulent and came so fast that by the time Portugal became a democracy with a new constitution of 1976 all colonies had become independent countries, more or less with the blessing of the new Portuguese establishment, which was represented by leaders such as Mário Soares, Melo Antunes, and José Medeiros Ferreira. The only open wound of the whole process was the annexation of East Timor by Indonesian troops, which was regarded as one aspect of the decolonization that did not go Portugal's way. East Timor would remain the single issue that would determine Portuguese foreign policy up until its recent independence. Portuguese diplomacy was crucial in making the voice of East Timorenses heard in the European Union and in the United Nations. The end of Indonesian occupation and the declaration of independence by East Timor can be regarded as the highest achievement of foreign policy for democratic Portugal.

One particular element of Portuguese foreign policy that changed forever once Portugal became a member of the European Union is the fact that the country is slowly becoming part of European common foreign and security policy. The current discussion of a network of EU embassies across the world, which is even supported by the United Kingdom, shows that there is a growing need to develop a single voice in European foreign policy. To that end, the Europeanization of Portuguese foreign policy is the most important transformation in the last fifteen years. There was some reluctance to become part of a larger whole, but in the end the idea of a European security community is beginning to become part of Portuguese foreign policy. Parallel to the Europeanization of Portuguese foreign policy, there was also a growing Mediterraneanization of Portuguese foreign policy, which clearly led to military contributions to Eurofor and Euromarfor rapid intervention forces that were designed to play a role in the Mediterranean in cases related to the Petersberg tasks. In this new European security architecture, one has to take into account the importance of NATO, of which Portugal has been a loyal member since 1949. Being a poor country with meager military, human, and material resources, Portugal clearly sees this security community as an important element in any national strategy.

The restructuring of Portuguese foreign policy first showed results in the 1990s when, under the Socialist government of Prime Minister Antonio Guterres, the Community of Portuguese Speaking Countries (*Comunidade de Paises de Lingua Portuguesa*-CPLP) was founded. This important project of Portuguese foreign policy is naturally a bilateral organization and tries to emulate the *British Commonwealth* and the *Communauté Francaise*. It clearly wants to restore its relationships to the former African colonies, Brazil, and East Timor, but now on the basis of partnership and respect of their national sovereignties. The importance of this reconstruction of Portuguese foreign policy cannot be underestimated because it enhances the role of the country in the southern hemisphere.

In sum, this chapter will concentrate on an analysis of the transformation of Portuguese foreign policy in the past thirty years and the implications for the country. In the first section, I will present the main developments since the collapse of the authoritarian regime, which could be called a reequilibration of Portuguese foreign policy after the difficult transition years of 1974-75. Afterward I will deal with the Europeanization and Mediterraneanization of Portuguese foreign policy since the 1990s. In the third section, I will discuss the CPLP project more thoroughly as well as relations with Brazil and Latin America, and briefly analyze the role of Portuguese diplomacy in relation to the independence of East Timor. The chapter will end with some conclusions.

The Restructuring of the Administrative Structures and Priorities of Portuguese Foreign Policy

One can roughly divide the past thirty years of Portuguese foreign policy into two main periods. The first period can be called the period of reequilibration of Portuguese foreign policy after the collapse of the authoritarian regime. It was a period of confusion and identity crisis that began with the Revolution of 25 April 1974, continued through the transition process, and finished at the end of 1985, the last day before Portugal's accession to the European Union. The second period was one of integration into and adaptation to the EC/EU structures. It also led to the reorganization and reformulation of Portuguese foreign policy priorities. This process can be called the Europeanization of Portuguese foreign policy.

The structure of foreign policy inherited from the authoritarian regime was extremely inadequate for the agenda of the provisional governments between 1974 and 1975. Indeed, the main priority of the agenda was unconditional de-colonization, in spite of resistance coming from the establishment, particularly General Antonio de Spinola. In this first two years, any restructuring of the Ministry of Foreign Affairs was almost impossible because of the short time span between the six provisional governments. After the decolonization process and the transition process, political and economic instability prevented any reform of the structures of the Ministry of Foreign Affairs. Foreign Policy lacked direction and a guiding document. The main preoccupation of the government was to achieve a civilianization of the political system as soon as possible, which meant mainly a retreat of the military from the political decision-making process. The revolutionary process had led to a constitution that allowed for a political and a military realm. While the political realm was controlled by the politicians, more or less, the military realm embodied in the Council of the Revolution was still dominated by the Movement of Armed Forces (MFA). This was the reason why Francisco Sá Carneiro and later Francisco Balsemão as leaders of the right-center coalition government, Aliança Democratica, had as their priority between 1979 and 1982 the revision of the constitution, so that the Council of the Revolution could be abolished and replaced by a civilian Constitutional Court. The coalition government wanted also to reduce the powers of the president, who, at that time, was General Antonio Ramalho Eanes, who clearly supported the MFA. Parallel to the revision, a new law of defense was approved by Parliament that established civilian tutelage over the military establishment. This action was quite important because it established the military as an instrument of a civilianized Portuguese foreign policy. The whole process of civilianization ended with the election of Mário Soares as president of the Republic, replacing General Ramalho Eanes.[1]

According to José Medeiros Ferreira, the entire conceptualization of Portuguese foreign policy was extremely linked to defense policy. It meant that Portuguese foreign policy was still highly dominated by the protection of national sovereignty. The documents on Portuguese foreign policy still did not reflect the growing interdependence of Portuguese foreign policy with the other European countries. Medeiros Ferreira quoted, in particular, the *White Book on National Defence,* published in early 1986, which clearly emphasized the protection of national sovereignty.[2] In this, one can recognize a disjunction between Portuguese defense policy, which was still fully enshrined in the parameters of national sovereignty, and a foreign policy that clearly was moving towards regimes of shared sovereignty. The high level of governmental instability did not allow for a major reform of the administrative structure of Portuguese foreign policy. Indeed, it was only in 1985, under the leadership of foreign minister Jaime Gama, that a major adaptation of the structures to the European Union took place. It was more or less a measure taken five minutes before midnight, meaning that it was undertaken to adjust to the forthcoming accession of Portugal to the European Union on 1 January 1986.[3]

It was only during the second period of Europeanization of Portuguese foreign policy that a proper, gradual, long-term reform of administrative structures was undertaken. First of all, the Ministry of Foreign Affairs became the main and only interface between the EU and the national institutions, facilitating communication between the supranational and national levels. This was done after careful study of all the existing models available in the European Union. The General Directorate of Community Affairs (*Direcção Geral de Assuntos Comunitários*-DGAC) became the interface between national and European institutions (see chapter 5). In terms of European foreign policy, Portugal became an integral part of the European Political Cooperation (EPC), which existed since the 1970s. Up until 1992, the administrative structures of Portuguese foreign policy had to integrate themselves into the structures of the EPC. The main task was to adopt the COREU telegraphic system and allocate appropriate staff to it. Moreover, the socialization and training of civil servants into the structures of EU foreign policy became a priority.[4] This investment would become a major asset in the running of the presidency of 1992, which was assessed as well organized. After the Maastricht Treaty, adopted in 1993, the new foreign minister Manuel Durão Barroso undertook a second major reform of the structures of the Ministry of Foreign Affairs in 1994. This action was important, because now Portugal was part of the Common Foreign and Security Policy (CFSP).[5] After this reform of the departments, Portuguese administrative structures remained quite stable throughout the Socialist government period.

In sum, the administrative structures of Portuguese foreign policy were able to become part of the process towards Europeanization. Indeed, it could be said that Portuguese diplomacy gained in self-confidence after a difficult period of transition from authoritarianism to democracy. The Ministry of Foreign Affairs is certainly an efficient and strong machinery that is able to support Portuguese diplomacy in its quest for European and international influence.

The Europeanization and Mediterraneanization of Portuguese Foreign Policy: Integration into Common Foreign and Security Policy

Portugal joined the EC/EU during a period of major transformations, after almost twenty years of Eurosclerosis. The importance of this fact cannot be underestimated, because most of the initiatives that would lead to the Europeanization of national foreign policy were related to this factor. Indeed, it was an acknowledged fact that both EPC, as well as the West European Union (WEU), were not adequate instruments to project the formation of a European foreign policy. The declarations of EPC were without teeth. There was a general feeling among the pro-integrationists that the European Union had to speak with a single voice to the outside world. The adoption of the second pillar Common Foreign and Security Policy (CFSP) in the Maastricht Treaty helped to change the situation. Indeed, the fratricide wars in former Yugoslavia made it imperative that the European Union would lead any peacekeeping forces to ensure the end of conflict and violence on the Continent. After years of trial and error and the experiences of Bosnia-Herzegovina and Kosovo, the Amsterdam Treaty finally allowed the establishment of structures and corresponding instruments for the working of the CFSP, which included also the long-term creation of a defense industry in the European Union. Moreover, after the Helsinki Council of December 1999, a working structure was agreed upon so that the Common European Security and Defense Policy (CESDP) could be established. The newly created Mr./Mrs. CFSP attached to the Council had the important task of coordinating all efforts and establishing the necessary structures for a functioning CESDP. The main objective was to achieve by 2003 a European army of 60,000 to 80,000 that could be deployed mainly for so-called Petersberg tasks (including peacekeeping operations, natural catastrophy management, and other similar tasks). Portugal was fully integrated into this process towards a more efficient CEDSP.[6] This meant that it was taking part in the new-standing Political and Security Committee (PSC) and the transitional military committee (MC), set up after March 2000, both of which were designed to create a permanent, flexible, and fast-reacting response to crisis situations.

The West European Union (WEU), the then European defense organization, lost complete credibility when it was unable to play a major role in the Kosovo conflict of 1999. Indeed, it was the Kosovo conflict that would lead to full integration of theWEU into the European Union structures, particularly in view of a dynamization of Common Foreign and Security Policy in the person of Javier Solana as the high representative of CFSP and secretary general of the Council.[7] Most likely, the WEU will become the European arm of NATO, meaning also that for the next twenty years NATO will continue to be the major military organization on the European continent and highly involved in shaping Common Foreign and Security Policy. This process of redefinition is still in flux and Portugal has to keep its defense and foreign policy structures flexible enough to cope with the change. The basic problem is that European Union foreign policy is still shared by the Council in the person of Javier Solana, and the European Commission in the person of commissioner Chris Patten. This means that presently the European Union is in a transitional phase that will most likely lead to a unification of the two positions, probably after 2004.

In the meantime, one can observe a growing synergy among the foreign policies of the member-states in many areas, so that the European Union is able to speak with one voice to the outside world. In a sense, discussion about European foreign policy has become domestic policy within the European Union. This certainly will gain more momentum in the future, because it is also about the transposition of a community of values (democracy, human rights, social market economy, security community) into a workable European foreign policy. It takes time to create such taken-for-granted reality.

Indeed, Portuguese foreign policy became strongly involved in the whole process towards CFSP and now CEDSP. Portuguese José Cutileiro became secretary general of the West European Union, of which Portugal had been member since 1988. The reconstruction of Portuguese foreign policy meant also a rethinking of its role in the North Atlantic Treaty Organization. It was no longer the only military organization to which Portugal belonged. Indeed, when Spain became a member in 1982, and further confirmed in a referendum in 1986, the Portuguese became clearly nervous about the possibility that Portugal would remain under Spanish command. The problem was solved by integrating Portugal and Spain into different geographical commands of NATO. While Spain was part of the European command, SACEUR, with seat in Naples, Portugal remained under the Atlantic command, SACLANT, which was headed by the Americans and had its seat in Norfolk, Virginia. Fears of the past were slowly replaced by trust between these two military structures.[8] Indeed, General Pedro Cardoso, who was commander-in-chief of the army in the 1980s, recalls that the relationship of Spaniards and Portuguese was very friendly and cooperative during and after the process of Spanish accession to NATO. He even makes note of the fact that such a relationship between Portugal and Spain had existed already after 1954, with regular annual meetings between the two institutions.[9]

Integration into the European Union considerably changed the perception of Spain among the political and military elites. One has to realize that until 1988, NATO was the only military organization to which Portugal belonged. After this period in time, Portugal became more and more integrated into the European structures, which contributed to a change of mentality. NATO remains an important institution for Portuguese defense and foreign policy, but now both are part of the new European security architecture that was established at the end of the Cold War. The recent expansion of NATO to the East means that Portugal will be more strongly involved in the CESDP, which is still highly shaped by NATO.[10]

Traditionally, Portugal had an Atlanticist strategic vocation close to the United States and directed towards the lusophone world, but integration into the European Union meant a complete shift of the parameters and priorities of Portuguese foreign and defense policy. The so-called Europeanization of Portuguese foreign and defense policy began in 1991 shortly before Portugal's first presidency of the European Union in the first half of 1992. The main reason was the ongoing breakdown of former Yugoslavia. The Portuguese government, as incumbent of the presidency, had to get involved in the diplomatic and military efforts to solve the Yugoslavia crisis. Clearly, it was particularly important in mediating between the representatives of the three ethnic groups of Bosnia-Herzegovina: Serbs, Croats, and Moslems. This was the first time since the First World War that Portugal had become so explicitly involved in European affairs, both diplomatically and militarily.[11]It meant naturally a complete change in the overall priorities of Portuguese foreign policy, which now was becoming fully integrated into the European structures. This clearly meant that the Atlanticist position had been more or less replaced by a primarily European one. In this sense, the European Union helped Portugal to overcome its nationalist position, which was very much related to the defense of the country, not the defense of the external borders of the European Union.[12] Such a transition of defense mentality is still going on, particularly in relation to the air bases in Lajes, Azores, which in the past were of central importance to the United States, but since 1989 have lost their importance. During Salazar's time, these were still a leverage to achieve foreign and defense policy concessions from the United States, for example, during the late phase of the Kennedy administration.[13] However, since the early 1990s, the United States, due to technological advancement of their aircraft, has found alternative air bases and become less dependent on the Azores. Although the airbases in the Azores are still used, they have less strategic significance. Naturally, in this transition of mentality from Atlanticism to Europeanization there remain a number of representatives of the political class that hold on to the myth of a "special relationship" between Portugal and the United States, similar to what is happening in the UK. In reality, any so-called "special relationship" with the United States is only of an instrumental nature, and doomed to be abandoned when the interest of the superpower wanes.[14]

Although Portugal is one of the most loyal members of NATO, in which American supremacy is unquestionable, it clearly is now engaged in building up the already mentioned CEDSP. In this sense, after the presidency of the European Union in 1992, the Portuguese government was extremely active in the peacekeeping missions of NATO under the United Nations authority in former Yugoslavia. This extended to Bosnia-Herzegovina with participation in the implementation force (IFOR) and the stability force (SFOR) as well as in the peacekeeping force in Kosovo (KFOR) and now Macedonia. In IFOR (1995-96), there were 924 Portuguese soldiers involved.[15] Afterwards, the number of Portuguese troops has declined. While in December 2001 there were 369 troops, particularly in SFOR and KFOR, in October 2002 there were only 338 troops. This corresponds to 0.7 percent of 47,690 troops present in the Balkans. Apart from seven military, all of them are stationed in Bosnia-Herzegovina. One is attached to the Kosovo headquarters and six are involved in the new peacekeeping mission in Macedonia.[16]

This so-called Europeanization of Portuguese foreign policy became firmly established during the Socialist government of former Prime Minister Antonio Guterres, and a level of continuity has been sustained by the present government under Manuel Durão Barroso. After September 11, 2001, Portugal has become an integral part of the fight against terrorism, which has meant also that the overall strategic concept has had to be reviewed and adapted to that of NATO and the European Union. Several actors of civil society were consulted in the establishment of the new strategic guidelines. According to

Figure 9.1
Portugese Contribution to Balkan Troops

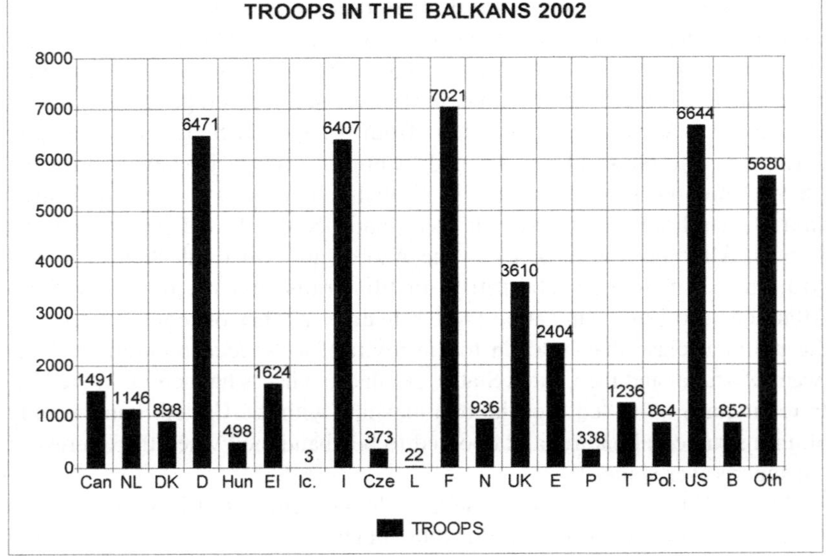

Source: Ministério da Defesa Nacional, *Participação de Militares e unidades Portuguesas em operações de paz fora do território nacional e em acções de cooperação bilateral na area de defesa nacional*, 31 October 2002 (Lisbon: MDN, 2002), 4.

the document, The *Major Options of the Strategic Concept of National Defense Policy*, apart from national territory, the European space is the main priority, followed by the relationship with neighboring countries, the relationship with the United States and the Mediterranean.[17] This again confirms the orientation towards Europeanization. Parallel to the changing nature of the European security architecture, the Portuguese military is adjusting to the new arrangements of a broader security concept, which will look at non-military threats as well, such as global criminality, cyberspace criminality, terrorism, and immigration. The "*White Book on National Defense*" adopts the concept of *cooperative security* within the international community. The United Nations, the EU, NATO, and the OSCE are the four institutions that serve as reference for Portuguese defense and security policies. In this sense, the synergy between foreign and defense policies has become a matter of fact in dealing with global threats.[18]

One of the main problems for a Portuguese defense policy will be recruitment of a sufficient number of troops. Indeed, since 1999, Portugal has moved from a compulsory military service to a voluntary, and/or based on contract, military service. The transition to the new system, which is regarded as the best one in periods of peace, will take four years to be in full operation. In-between there are transition measures. This is part of a major transformation of the Portuguese armed forces in terms of the numbers of active personnel. While in 1990, the military consisted of 72,000 troops, most of them in the territorial army, its number declined in 1995 to 57,325 and to 47,235 in 1999. Further reductions are expected, but stability of the numbers is predicted after 2003.[19] In December 2001, 39,295 troops were active in the armed forces (see figure 9.2), while 21,155 were either in the reserves or on pension (the vast majority of 90 percent was to be found in the latter category). The different branches of the military are already complaining about difficulties in recruiting enough people, mainly due to the fact that the salaries are not competitive enough. The reduction of personnel is to be accompanied by more investment in military equipment and technology. Nevertheless, this has been quite difficult to achieve and Portuguese military personnel perceives itself as disadvantaged in relation to its counterparts in NATO or in other operations. This recruitment and technological gap will be difficult to bridge in a period of budget austerity.[20] In sum, major changes are taking place in light of creating a professionalized armed forces in Portugal. It is also the best time for undertaking such restructuring, because the overall European security architecture is itself changing.

In the future, one can expect a stronger integration of Portuguese troops in cooperative security arrangements. For this effect, the Portuguese military will request a stronger investment in the technological capabilities of the Portuguese armed forces. In terms of foreign policy, Portugal is anchored in the European integration process, which means that in the past thirty years

Portuguese foreign policy has moved from a rigid foreign policy directed to the protection of the collapsing colonial empire to one of a small country in a community of democracies.

This major achievement of redirection of Portuguese foreign policy is firmly enshrined in article seven of the Portuguese constitution, which clearly emphasizes anti-colonialism, the right of self-determination, the importance of international law and, most recently, the role of the International Criminal Court after the revision of 2001.[21]

Europeanization means also Mediterraneanization of Portuguese foreign policy by paying more attention to the unstable situation in the southern rim of the Mediterranean. Portugal is, along with Spain, Italy, and France actively involved in the European Rapid Reaction Force (Eurofor) and the European Maritime Force (Euromarfor) units with headquarters in Florence, Italy. The purpose of these troops is to fulfill the Petersberg tasks in the Mediterranean. They are rapid reaction forces for army and sea troops. Their availability will become strategically important within the new, changing European security architecture.[22] Indeed, the Euro-Mediterranean partnership established during the Spanish presidency of the European Union in 1995, is an important issue for Portuguese foreign policy. In this sense, Portugal has become a major supporter of the Spanish project, although the results have been quite poor. The process of structuration and institutionalization is still going on. After seven years, the problems of the Euro-Mediterranean partnership have begun to be more salient. After the euphoric stage, one has to recognise that

Figure 9.2
Active Portuguese Armed Forces (December 2001)

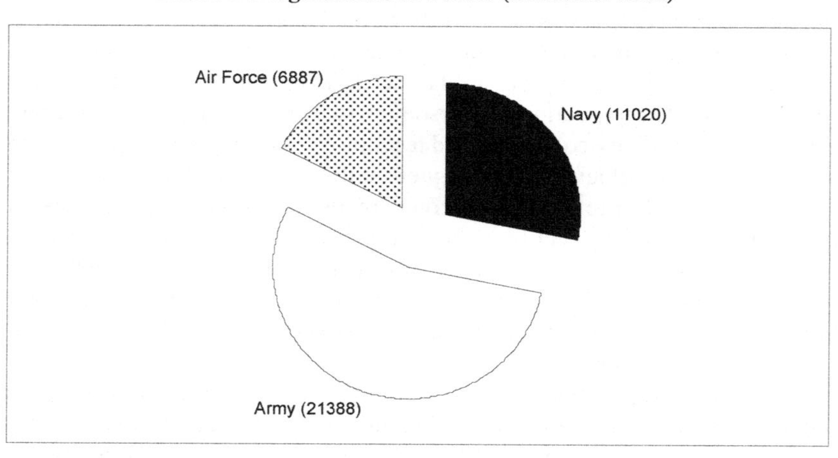

Source: Ministério da Defesa Nacional, *Anuário Estatistico 2001* (Lisbon: MDN, 2002), 66.

the involvement of patrimonial democracies such as the ones in the Maghreb, Mashreq, and the Middle East prevent complete transparency and accountability of the process when it goes wrong. The main objective is to create a Mediterranean Free Trade Area by 2010. This certainly seems a very difficult goal, when one thinks of the fact that many of these Mediterranean countries have relatively weak or non-integrated markets. The intra-regional trade among the southern rim countries is decidedly weak. Although Portugal has not been affected as badly by emigration flows from the Mediterranean, it regards it as a high priority area in view of creating new markets for Portuguese economy. One of the most important projects, of course, is the export of gas from Algeria into Spain and Portugal. This is a highly risky business, when one considers that Algeria has been in civil war since the early 1990s.[23]

Inspite of all these concerns, Portugal is committed to the Euro-Mediterranean partnership in order to improve the living conditions of the southern rim populations, and to create a security community around the Mediterranean, which would become more efficient to tackle Islamic fundamentalism and terrorism, illegal emigration and criminal gangs related to it, and overcome potential misunderstanding between the northern and southern rims. In sum, this Mediterraneanization is a consequence of stronger involvement and integration into the European Union structures and it was not sought out independently, apart from Morocco, by the Portuguese government.[24]

Portugal and the Community of Portuguese Speaking Countries (CPLP)

Although there was a change in parameters towards the European continent and the Mediterranean, it has been the ambition of successive Portuguese governments to reconstruct the relationship to the former colonies, which today are sovereign nations. This has been one of the most continuous elements of Portuguese foreign policy since the transition to democracy in 1974-75. It was felt that Portugal had to promote some kind of community spirit between the Portuguese-speaking countries. Such efforts were doomed to fail until 1989, due to the fact that the African nations had a extremely negative image of Portuguese foreign policy in terms of its capacities.

Everything began to change after 1989, when Portugal was able to present a more coordinated and organized foreign policy, in which cooperation with the Portuguese-speaking countries became more important. It took five years of meetings and negotiations to set up the Community of Portuguese Speaking Countries (*Comunidade de Paises de Lingua Portuguesa*-CPLP). It was finally founded on 17 July 1996 and has to be regarded as a major achievement of Portuguese diplomacy and the perseverance of politicians from the two main parties. Although the Guterres government was able to announce the new organization to the world, it was the hard work of the Cavaco Silva administration that really prepared the ground. The CPLP consisted originally of seven countries, of which Brazil and Portugal were the richest, while the others, Angola, Mozambique, Guinea-Bissau, Cape Verde Islands, and São Tomé and Principe, were markedly poor. East Timor was already a country with an observer status and only became a full-member after the declaration of independence. This project was quite interesting, because clearly is bringing to the fore the old myth of "Portuguese-speaking countries." The political elites of the African member-states, although they spoke Portuguese, they were also characterized by a lack of homogeneity.[25] This meant that Portuguese influence in the inner parts of these countries was always quite weak.

There was always a weak penetration of Portuguese administration in the hinterland of the countries, as the Portuguese colonial elite tended to settle on the coast of these countries and not venture into the vast inner territory. Portuguese administration was also unable to stand up against the major powers, particularly the British, in the late phase of the empire. The ultimatum of the British government against Portugal's intention to create a corridor link between its colonies in Mozambique and Angola in southern Africa in 1891 is a most explicit example of how weak the Portuguese empire was. Weak penetration is also a major problem for these countries that are still in the process in building up their public administration and structuring the territory.

Despite the lack of homogeneity, this project is quite interesting, because it really focuses on solidarity with these countries. Moreover, it includes Brazil, one of the superpowers of the Southern Hemisphere, which was always an advocate of south-south cooperation. A look at economic and social data clearly shows that the CPLP is a development community.

The main objective of the lusophone community is to achieve a high degree of multilateral cooperation that will lead, in the end, to the creation of a lobby in international organizations such as the United Nations and the European Union (through the Lomé Agreements). The CPLP has been quite active since its foundation on 17-18 July 1996. One of its major projects is, naturally, the promotion of Portuguese among the African countries. The creation of a channel for Africa by Portuguese national public television RTP Africa, which preceded the CPLP, is regarded as an important form of influence. Most of the projects have been of a cultural nature. It should be mentioned that the CPLP is still very much in its beginnings, but the fact that Brazil is actively engaged strengthens the resolve of Portuguese diplomacy. For decades, strengthening the relationship with Brazil has been a major objective of Portuguese diplomacy. Such a relationship enhances the position of Portugal in the world. Democratic Portugal has had to acknowledge, more or less, that the center of the Portuguese-speaking world moved a long time ago to Brazil, mainly because the Brazilian markets is much larger than the Portuguese ones. This naturally means also changes to the orthography of

Table 9.1
Some Data on the Member-States of the CPLP

	Territory 1,000 Sq Kilometers	Population Millions	GDP/per capita1998 Index1998	Human Development	Government form
Portugal	92,345	9,968	14,569	0.858	Democratic Republic
Brazil	8547,4	165,874	6,460	0.736	Democratic Republic
Angola	1246,7	12	380	0.405	Democratic Republic
Mozambique	779,38	16,947	210	0.326	Democratic Republic
São Tomé and Principe Islands	1,001	0,142	1 289	0.547	Democratic Republic
Cape Verde Islands	4,033	0,416	1 200	0.675	Democratic Republic
Guinea-Bissau	36,125	1,161	160	0.298	Democratic Republic
East Timor	14,609	0.748	-	-	Democratic Republic

Figure 9.3
The CPLP in Terms of Geographical Position

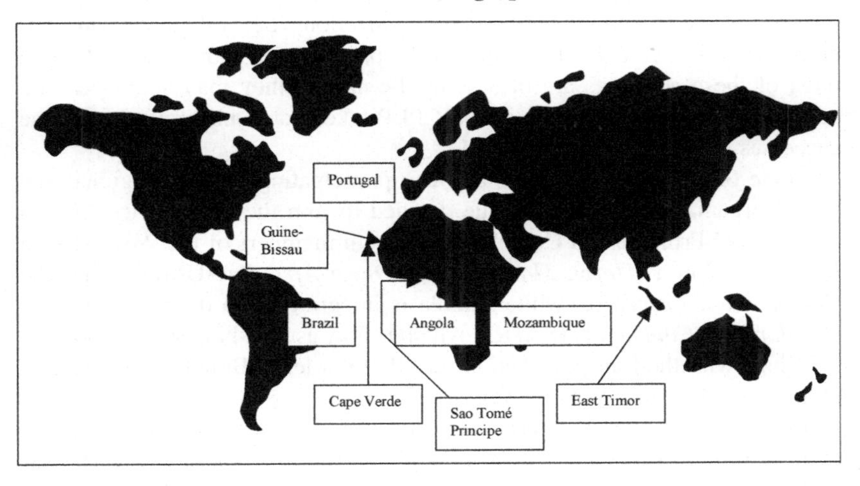

Portuguese. Such battles between the two countries have been fought in the past. Brazil has become quite important for the CPLP, because of its unconventional way of tackling the problem of HIV/AIDS. The ability to achieve concessions in terms of patent rights in relation to medication is becoming a model for most African countries, including the Portuguese-speaking, which are extremely affected by this disease. Cooperation in this field has become a priority in this millennium. This issue was a prominent part of the agenda in the third conference of the Heads of State and Chiefs of Government in Maputo, Mozambique, on 17-18 July 2000 and most recently in the fourth conference in Brasilia, Brazil, on 31 August-1 September 2002.[26]

Meanwhile, the activities of the CPLP have increased considerably. There are yearly meetings of the ministers of the CPLP in view of achieving coordination in major areas, which include police cooperation and coordination of HIV/AIDS strategy. Quite important also is the participation of the CPLP in other international organizations, namely the Organization for American States (OAS), the Latin Union, and the Ibero-American summits. CPLP is also represented in the different international conferences of the United Nations. Quite interesting has been the attempt to achieve cooperative arrangements with the *Communauté Francaise* and the Spanish-led Ibero-American summits. There are also some relationships with the Commonwealth, but the CPLP finds a stronger affinity to the Latin-speaking corresponding communities. The African member-states are pushing Portugal and Brazil to establish a lusophone citizenship across the community, which is regarded as problematic by Portugal, because of the constraints related to being member of the European Union.

Quite comforting is the fact that several initiatives were started by civil society around the CPLP. This covers both the business community, which is interested in developing cooperative links in the pursuit of building new markets, as well as nongovernmental organizations. Several cultural and scientific events have been developed in the past three to four years. Although most of these activities are of a symbolic nature, they may spill-over into something concrete. In a sense, the CPLP takes some inspiration from the successes of the European Union.

Some of the CPLP members are also participating in other regional and global organizations. Mozambique decided to join the *Commonwealth* and S.Tomé and Principe and Cape Verde are both members of the West African Monetary Union (*Union Monetaire de Ouest Africaine*-UMOA) and the *Communauté Francaise*, while Angola is integrated into the *South African Development Community* (SADC), which is now establishing strong cooperative links with the European Union. Last but not least, Brazil is nurturing its own regional project of Mercosur.

In this respect, one has to acknowledge the fact that Portugal is making major efforts to support the democratization process in these countries, par-

Figure 9.4
Quantitative Dimensions of CPLP Activities

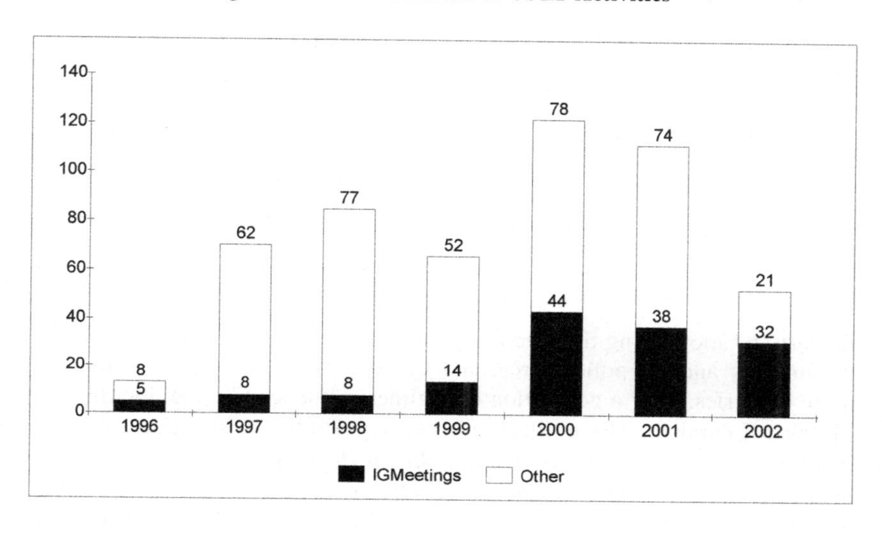

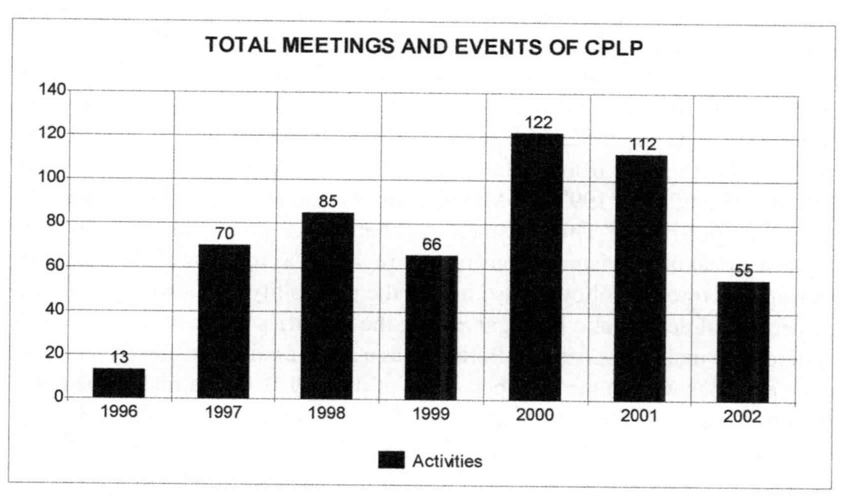

Source: Author's own graph based on data provided by web-page of CPLP, http//:www.cplp.org.

Table 9.2
The Meetings of the Chiefs of State and Government of CPLP (1996-2002)

Meetings	Place	Date
1st meeting	Lisbon, Portugal	17-18 July 1996
2nd meeting	Praia, Cape Verde	13-17 July 1998
3rd meeting	Maputo, Mozambique	17-18 July 2000
4th meeting	Brasilia, Brazil	31 August-1 September 2002

Source: web-page of CPLP, http://www.cplp.org.

ticularly by monitoring the election processes, improving the capabilities of the military and the police force. and by supporting institution-building in these countries, after a generation of regimes influenced by the doctrines of Marxism-Leninism. The military bilateral cooperation with these so-called PALOPs (*Paises Africanos de Lingua Oficial Portuguesa-African Countries with Official Portuguese Language*-PALOPs) tends to be less extensive than the engagement in the Balkan forces.[27] By 31 October 2002, there were only 94 military personnel involved in technical military cooperation in the PALOPs.[28] Nevertheless, throughout the 1990s, Portuguese military presence was noticeably important in pacifying some of the societies, such as Angola.

Moreover, Portugal is training several military units in Portuguese military institutions. In 2002, 164 trainees were taking courses in Portugal.[29] In Angola, Portuguese troops played an important role in the UN missions UNAVEM until June 1997 and MONUA until 30 June 1998, with 214 and 215 troops, respectively.[30] This regained trust between Portugal and the new Portuguese-speaking African nations can be regarded as a major achievement of Portuguese foreign policy. It also means the possibility of a stronger external projection of democratic Portugal among the countries of the Southern Hemisphere. The main reason is that Portugal, as a small country, is clearly less able to impose her will on the member-states of the CPLP, which makes the community quite egalitarian in its approach. Economically, Portugal´s trade with the CPLP countries is still very low. In the 1990s, it did not reach more than 2 percent of imports and less than 3 percent of exports. This, naturally, may change in the future, if integration processes occur in view of building the CPLP.[31]

The Highest Achievement of Democratic Foreign Policy: The Independence of East Timor (1975-2002)

It was in the 1996 award ceremony of the Nobel peace prize to Archbishop Ximenes Belo and the exiled politician Francisco Ramos Horta that Portugal achieved a major breakthrough in relation to the abuse of human rights in occupied East Timor. East Timor was a colony of Portugal up until it was occupied by force by Indonesian troops. Indeed, during the turbulent democratic transition in Portugal, negotiations were going on between the Portuguese government and the political factions in East Timor to pave the way for independence. (The situation in East Timor was one of instability and civil war in 1975.) In the end, the Timorese Front for National Liberation (*Frente Timorense de Libertação Nacional*-FRETILIN) was able to gain the hegemonic position in the country. The difficult transition in Portugal and the civil war in East Timor were major factors allowing Indonesian troops to occupy the country on 7 December 1975 and stay there for the next twenty-five years.[32] East Timor may be regarded as the most important foreign policy issue of post-authoritarian Portugal. Throughout the ensuing decades Portugal persevered in pushing forward the cause of East Timor. Although in the early days of the Indonesian occupation the United Nations was instrumental in condemning the act, East Timor slowly was sidelined from the agenda of the International Community. Between 1982 and 1998, East Timor was not a major issue for the United Nations.[33] During this period Portugal tried with the limited means at its disposal to draw attention to the East Timorese case.

Until 1985 Portugal was quite isolated in its effort to bring world attention to the abuse of human rights in East Timor. Only when she became a member of the European Union was its voice heard. Portugal used the EPC instruments to bring about an awareness of the situation in East Timor and was able to gain support from the European Parliament in relation to a condemnation of the Indonesian occupation. Portugal's position was that the East Timorese had the right to self-determination, which has been denied by Indonesia up to that point. Portugal achieved a first EPC declaration in relation to East Timor in the second half of 1988 during the Greek presidency, which can be regarded as the first major breakthrough of Portuguese diplomacy within the EU. It led to the inclusion of East Timor in the speech of the Greek presidency, given in name of the European Community, at the United Nations.[34]

Such pressure upon the Indonesian government continued throughout the 1990s. In 1991, the massacre in Dili was condemned and human rights abuses in East Timor were included in speeches presented during the Luxembourg and Dutch presidencies in the Commission of Human Rights in Geneva and in the UN General Assembly.[35] This persistent pressure began to show some results after the so-called killing of thousand of Timorese in Santa Cruz in 1991. The media reported extensively how the Indonesian army had brutally dispersed thousands of Timorese who were demonstrating peacefully for self-determination. A major charismatic figure of this movement was Xanana Gusmão, who led a small guerrilla group in the fight against the Indonesian occupation. His imprisonment led to major publicity for the Timorese cause in Portugal and around the world. Gusmão would remain a major reference point for the transition towards independence in East Timor. After 1996, awareness of the situation in East Timor was growing. In a sense, it led again to a stronger engagement of the UN in solving the East Timor problem.

After 1998, under the new president of Indonesia, Habibie, there was some hope that the problem in East Timor could be solved peacefully. Negotiations in the UN in New York led to the agreement that a referendum should be undertaken in East Timor, which would lead to independence. The referendum on 30 August 1999, which was announced on 4 September, led to an overwhelming vote of 78.5 percent for independence of the 450,000 eligible voters. Violence had preceded the referendum, but it became organized murder of East Timorese civilians by Indonesian paramilitary groups after the results were announced. The United Nations Assistance Mission for East Timor (UNAMET), which was in charge of preparing the referendum in East Timor, had to flee from the capital Dili when it came under continuous attack by the paramilitary groups, which had some support from the Indonesian army. The international community put pressure on President Habibie, which led to the deployment of an International Force East Timor (INTERFET) to fight against the paramilitary groups and pacify the country. It led also to the return of the UN civil administration. INTERFET, which remained in East Timor until January 2001, was replaced by United Nations Transitional Authority for East Timor (UNTAET), under the leadership of Brazilian Sergio Vieira de Mello. Meanwhile, on 20 May 2002, East Timor became independent and the first president became José Xanana Gusmão. The UN is still in East Timor supporting the East Timorese government in institution-building,[36] which has proven to be quite a difficult process because of the lack of financial resources. Portugal contributed troops and other staff (police) to the contingent of UNTAET. Indeed, two-thirds of all Portuguese soldiers engaged in peacekeeping operations are stationed in East Timor. By October 2002, there were 654 troops in East Timor, which indicates how important East Timor still is for Portuguese foreign policy. Apart from the military troops, there were 125 members of the National Republican Guard (*Guarda Nacional Republicana*-GNR) and 105 members of the Portuguese Security Police (*Policia de Segurança Portuguesa*-PSP) fulfilling policing tasks in this newly independent country.[37]

Spain, Portugal, and Latin America

In recent times, one can observe a closer engagement of Portuguese diplomacy in the Spanish project of the Ibero-American summits. Before 1998, Portuguese governments hesitated to take part in Spanish projects due to the past history between the two countries. This changed considerably after Expo´98 in Lisbon. The Ibero-American summit 1998 was celebrated in Lisbon and contributed to a better integration of Portugal into the Spanish Ibero-American project.[38]

Clearly, the developments related to integration of the national markets of Latin America in Mercosur, the Economic Association of Latin America (*Asociacion Economica de America Latina*-AELA), the Andean Community, and the Central American Economic Community are important new projects that may strengthen the role of the two Iberian countries in the world. Indeed, the Spaniards feel that they are the bridge between the EU and Latin America, while the Portuguese have always wanted to strengthen the links to Brazil.[39] The Ibero-American summits, undertaken since 1991, were initiated by former Spanish prime minister Felipe Gonzalez. In the twelfth Ibero-American summit (2001) in Playa Bavaro in the Dominican Republic, it was agreed to reform the institution towards a more European-like format, which would be able to make a difference in terms of improving living conditions in Latin America.[40] Although Portugal is not a major player in these gatherings, its participation shows a growing cooperation with Brazil and Spain in the integration of the Latin American continent.[41]

In sum, Portugal has become markedly integrated in several projects that may lead to stronger links with Latin America and Africa. Until the mid-1990s, what was once wishful thinking on the part of Portuguese diplomacy has, in the beginning of the new milennium, become, so to speak, a reconstructed Portuguese foreign policy, one that is based on the principles of the UN Charter and guided by the extradionary events of Portuguese democratic transition.

Conclusions: The Reconstruction of Portuguese Foreign Policy

The full integration of Portugal into the regimes of cooperative security of NATO, the EU, OSCE, and the UN adds leverage to the small country that, until the mid-1980s, was suffering under a major identity crisis after loss of an empire. The new democratic Portugal, which has an anti-colonialist agenda enshrined in its constitution, has learned a great deal from the European integration process in the past fifteen years. Indeed, integration into EPC, CFSP, and CESDP made it possible to gain credibility in bringing attention to the occupation of East Timor by Indonesian troops. Moreover, it became a platform for launching an embryonal community of Portuguese-speaking countries integrating new African nations and East Timor, which had emerged from the decolonization process in 1974-75. It also gained the strong support of Brazil in pushing through a lusophone agenda. The return of Macau to China at the end of 1999 was clearly a further landmark in this anti-colonialist agenda. In this sense, we are witnessing a reconstruction of Portuguese foreign policy that was and still is guided by past images of an experienced diplomacy that was able to leave its vestiges across five continents. In this sense, it is not a constructed foreign policy, but a reconstructed one. This means that learning from the past and preserving a strong memory about the past has been the main strength of a changing Portuguese foreign policy.

Notes

1. For a thorough discussion of the making of the law of defense and the relationship to democratic consolidation, see Vasco Rato, "A Aliança Atlantica e a consolidação democratica," in José Medeiros Ferreira (ed.), *Politica Externa e Politica de Defesa em Portugal* (Lisbon: Colibri, 2002), 126-136. Vasco Rato clearly shows that NATO membership was an important factor in pushing towards civilianization of the political system and professionalization of the armed forces after the revolutionary process of 1974-75. On civilianization and democratization, see the excellent study by Felipe Agüero, "Democratic Consolidation and the Military in Southern Europe and South America," in Richard Gunther, Nikiforos P. Diamandouros, Hans-Jurgen Puhle (eds.), *The Politics of Democratic Consolidation. Southern Europe in Comparative Perspective* (Baltimore: John Hopkins University Press, 1995), 124-165; particularly 131, 144.
2. José Medeiros Ferreira, "Politica Externa e Politica de Defesa no Portugal Democrático," in Medeiros Ferreira (ed.) *Politica Externa,* 11-27; particularly 20.
3. Actually the decree-law allowing for the restructuring of the Ministry of Foreign Affairs was only issued on 31 December 1985. It clearly was intended to adjust the structures to the European institutions. Centralization and reorganization were the major issues of the reform as well as the establishment of the General Directorate for Community Affairs (Decree Law no. 529/1985 and Decree Law no. 526/1985, both issued on 31 December; see Ministério dos Negocios Estrangeiros, *A reestruturação do ministério dos negocios estrangeiros* (Lisbon: MNE, 1995), 11-13.
4. P. S. da Costa Pereira, "Portugal, Public Administration and EPC/CFSP—A Fruitful Adaptation Process," in Elfriede Regelsberger and Franco Algieri (eds.), *Synergy at Work: Spain and Portugal in European Foreign Policy* (Bonn: Europa Union Verlag, 1996), 207-229; particularly 378 and 386.
5. Ministério dos Negócios Estrangeiros, *A Restruturação*, 16-23. The main reasons were related to the need to articulate better the different policy areas of Portuguese foreign policy, rationalization of structures and improvement of coordination.
6. For a summary of latest developments, see Anthony Forster and William Wallace, "Common Foreign and Security Policy. From Shadow to Substance," in Helen and William Wallace (eds.) *Policy-Making in the European Union* (Oxford: Oxford University Press, 2000), 461-491; Helene Sjursen, "The Common Foreign and Security Policy: Limits of Intergovernmentalism and the Search for a Global Role," in Svein S. Andersen, Kjell A. Eliassen (eds.), *Making Policy in Europe* (London: SAGE, 2001), 187-205.
7. Peter Van Ham, "Europe's Precarious Centre: Franco-German Co-operation and the CFSP," *European Security* 8, 4, 1999: 1-26; particularly 16.
8. Alvaro Vasconcelos, "Portuguese Defence Policy: Internal Politics and Defence Commitments," in John Chipman (ed.), *NATO's Southern Allies: Internal and External Challenges* (London, New York: Routledge, 1988), 86-139; 117-118.
9. General Pedro Cardoso, "Antecedentes e Repercussões da Entrada de Portugal na OTAN," in José Medeiros Ferreira (ed.), *Politica Externa*, 137-161; 155-157.
10. *El Pais*, 17 November 2002, p.6. President George W. Bush obviously wants the Europeans to carry a heavier burden in defense spending within the NATO struc-

tures. For too long the Europeans have been highly dependent on the military strength of the United States. Portugal is the example par excellence.

11. For a review of Portuguese foreign and defense policies in Europe, see José Medeiros Ferreira, *A Nova Era Europeia* (Lisbon: Editorial Noticias, 1999), 15-52; 75-91.
12. João Mira Gomes, "O Envolvimento Diplomatico de Portugal na Bósnia-Herzegovina," 61-69; José Cutileiro, "Bósnia-Herzegovina. Contribuição Portuguesa para uma Solução Politica," *Nação e Defesa* 92, Inverno 2000: 51-60, 2 Série. The Europeanization of foreign policy was ancillary to the Europeanization of Portuguese defense policy; see the article by Alvaro de Vasconcelos, "A Europeização da Politica de Defesa," *Estratégia* 14, 2° Semestre, 1999: 7-19; particularly; 10-13.
13. See the excellent study by Luis Nuno Rodrigues, *Salazar-Kennedy: a crise de uma aliança. As relações luso-americanas entre 1961 e 1963* (Lisbon: Editorial Noticias, 2001).
14. Miguel Mojardino, "A base indispensável? As Lajes e a 'Pax Americana,'" *Politica Internacional* 3, 22 (October-November 2000): 185-215. See also José Medeiros Ferreira, "Os Açores na encruzilhada da politica europeia e de segurança comum, 175-183.
15. Octávio de Cerqueira Rocha, "Portugal e as Operações de Paz na Bósnia: A Preparação das Forças," *Nação e Defesa* 92, Inverno 2000: 71-92, 81, 2 serie.
16. Ministério da Defesa Nacional, *Participação de Militares e unidades Portuguesas em operações de paz fora do território nacional e em acções de cooperação bilateral na area de defesa nacional, 31 de Dezembro 2001* (Lisbon: MDN, 2001); Ministério da Defesa Nacional, *Participação de Militares e unidades Portuguesas em operações de paz fora do território nacional e em acções de cooperação bilateral na area de defesa nacional, 31 de Outubro 2002* (Lisbon: MDN, 2002). On the transformation of the understanding of the Portuguese armed forces in the 1990s, see the excellent contribution by Maria Carrilho, "Os Conflitos nos Balcãs e a Redefinição das Missões Internacionais," *Estratégia* 14, 2 Semestre, 1999: 45-64.
17. Ministério da Defesa Nacional, Grandes Opções do Conceito Estratégico de Defesa Nacional, 2002, http: //www.mdn.gov.pt. Accessed Novenber 2002.
18. Ministério da Defesa Nacional, *Livro Branco sobre a Defesa Nacional* (Lisbon: MDN, 2002), 4-25.
19. Ministério da Defesa Nacional, 50-51.
20. For a review about the problems in Portugal, see Rui Lobato de Faria Ravara, "O Reequipamento e a Indústria de Defesa. Subsidios para uma Politica de Armamento," *Nação e Defesa* 98, Verao 2001: 115-145. One of the main problems is related to the low level of research and development of Portuguese enterprises. They are far too small for economies of scale and the Portuguese market is too small. The only alternative is to join forces with other EU member-states in creating a European Armament Agency and shift nationally spent defense armament investments to the European internal market. This is slowly happening through the West European Armament Group (WEAG) and the Joint Cooperation Organization in the field of Armament (OCCAR), which is leading to cooperation among the main European armament producers France, the UK, Germany, and Italy. Sweden and Spain are associated with it (ibid., 128-129).
21. See Assembleia da Republica, *Constituição Portuguesa. Quinta Revisão 2001* (Lisbon: AR, 2002), art. 7; on the historical background of the transformation of the rationale, see Nuno Severiano Teixeira, "Between Africa and Europe: Portu-

guese Foreign Policy, 1890-1986," in A. C. Pinto (ed.), *Modern Portugal* (Palo Alto: SPOSS, 1998), 60-87.

22. Maritheresa Frain, "A Peninsula Ibérica e a Europa: Uma convergencia nas politicas da defesa espanhola e portuguesa no pós-Guerra Fria?" *Politica Internacional* 1, 15/16 (October-November 1997): 249-282; particularly 260, 266-267.
23. This is not the place to make a full accounting of the Euro-Mediterranean Partnership. For the development and assessment of the Euro-Mediterranean Partnership, see Richard Gillespie (ed.) *The Euro-Mediterranean Partnership* (London: Frank Cass, 1997); Alvaro Vasconcelos, George Joffé (eds.), *The Barcelona Process. Building a Euro-Mediterranean Regional Community* (London: Frank Cass, 2001); a critical assessment can be found in Richard Youngs, *The European Union and the Promotion of Democracy. Europe's Mediterranean and Asian Policies* (Oxford: Oxford University Press, 2001), 47-93.
24. Fernanda Faria, "The Mediterranean: A New Priority in Portuguese Foreign Policy," *Mediterranean Politics*, 1996: 212-230.
25. It is estimated that only 60 percent of Angolans speak Portuguese, 80 percent of Cape Verdians, 11.1 percent of Guineans, 25 percent of Mozambicans, and 80 percent of the population of S. Tomé and Principe. See Américo Madeira Bárbara, "Dinamicas e tendencias da lusofonia," *Janus 99-2000* (Lisbon: Publico-Universidade Aberta de Lisboa, 1999), 138-139. See also Manfred Wöhlke, "Die Gemeinschaft Portugiesisch-sprachiger Staaten und die EU," *Aus Politik und Zeitgeschichte* B29-30, 2000: 14-21; 17-18.
26. *Publico*, 19 July 2000, 4-5; http: //www.cplp.org.
27. Ministério de Defesa Nacional, *Anuario Estatistico de Defesa Nacional 2001* (Lisbon: MDN, 2001), 52-58.
28. Ministério da Defesa Nacional, *Participação de Militares*, op.cit., 1.
29. Ibid.
30. See João Marco Domingues, "Participação Portuguesa em exercicios e operações conjuntas," in *As Forças Armadas no novo contexto internacional, Janus 98, suplemento especial* (Lisbon: *Publico*, UAL, 1998), 80-81; particularly 80, and Marisa Abreu Safaneta, "A Cooperação Técnico Militar de Portugal com as PALOP," 82-83.
31. Américo Madeira Bárbara, "Dinamicas e tendencias da lusofonia," in Janus 99-2000 (Lisbon: Publico-Universidade Aberta de Lisboa, 1999), 138-139.
32. Patricia Galvão Teles, "O Estatuto juridico de Timor-Leste: Um case study sobre as relações entre os conceitos de autodeterminação e soberania," *Politica Internacional* 15/16, 1997: 195-202.
33. Paula Escarameia, "Um mundo em mudança: Timor, a ONU e o Direito Internacional," *Politica Internacional* 3, 23, Primavera-Verão 2001: 99-119; particularly 102-103.
34. Ministério dos Negócios Estrangeiros, *Portugal nas Comunidades Europeias. Terceiro Ano 1988* (Lisbon: MNE, 1989), 342. Already in the first year, Portugal was reluctant to participate in a meeting of the ministers of foreign affairs between EC and ASEAN, because it took place in Djakarta, but it did not create problems in preserving European solidarity. See Ministério de Negócios Estrangeiros, *Portugal nas Comunidades Europeias.Primeiro Ano 1986* (Lisbon: MNE, 1987), 200.
35. Ministério de Negocios Estrangeiros, *Portugal na União Europeia. Sexto Ano 1991* (Lisbon: MNE, 1992), 342-343. Similarly, in 1992, Ministério dos Negocios Estrangeiros, *Setimo Ano 1992* (Lisbon: MNE, 1992), 391.
36. *The Economist*, 18 May 2002: 72-73; trials of Indonesians who committed atrocities in East Timor in 1999 did not lead to convictions. The Indonesian courts were

lenient with some of the protagonists of the violence and murder. See *The Economist*, 24 August 2002: 51.

37. Ministério da Defesa Nacional, *Participação de Militares*, 2002, op. cit., 1.
38. Nancy Gomes, "As relações externas da América Latina," *Janus 98* (Lisbon: Publico-Universidade Aberta de Lisboa, 1997), 130-131.
39. One has to acknowledge that overall Portuguese trade with Latin America has been low; nevertheless private investment increased considerably in the 1990s; see Henrique Morais, Anabela Sousa, "As relações económicas de Portugal com a América Latina," *Janus 98* (Lisbon: Publico-Universidade Aberta de Lisboa, 1997), 132-133.
40. *El Pais*, 17 November 2002, pp.2-4.
41. Nancy Gomes, "Cenários no espaco ibero-americano," *Janus 99-2000* (Lisbon: Publico, Universidade Aberta de Lisboa, 2000), 142-143.

10

Conclusions: Challenges to Portuguese Democracy within the European Union

One of the main problems of Portuguese democracy is its weak economic infrastructures. Portugal was one of the first countries to be hit by asymmetrical shocks related to the Economic and Monetary Union (EMU) and the slow growth of the world economy since the beginning of 2000. Although unemployment is still low, according to the official figures, the need for major reforms in the public administrative sector and the deteriorating economy will no doubt lead to a different picture. Portugal is a country on the semiperiphery of the European economy, and as such it is highly vulnerable to the policies of the European Central Bank and the European Commission. According to figures of the Ministry of the Economy, Portuguese industry is losing its competitiveness. The loss of market share in the Portuguese economy by Portuguese firms has led to an increase in imports. Because of this, the Durão Barroso government is trying to reverse the trend by presenting a package of enterprise-oriented policies. At the same time, a reduction in the role of the state in the economy will occur. Although these enterprise-friendly measures are crucial for a revival of Portuguese industry, there are other crucial issues in Portugal, which, after thirty years of democracy, require major reform. Success in the industrial sector will need an integrated set of policy reforms, which will lead to a change in the pattern of the Portuguese economy in the next two decades. A strong economy is the basis for the improvement of living conditions of the population.

After 2007, Portugal will be faced with less funds from the European Union, which, in turn, will then be transferred to the Central and Eastern European countries. Any set of reforms will have to revise the whole way of doing politics and economics in Portugal. Reform is about continuing a process of cultural change that will make democracy more egalitarian in terms of opportunities and sustainability. Any set of reforms will need to include the following areas, which are interlinked:

1. Reduction of the gap between the political class and the population
2. Reform of the education sector
3. Reform of the health sector
4. Change of the business culture
5. Reform of public administration and decentralization

Reduction of the Gap between the Political Class and the Population

In spite of thirty years of democracy, the Portuguese political class consists in the vast majority of academics, lawyers, or members of the liberal professions. They simply inherited the social, cultural, and political capital of their parents. This situation has led to a continuing autonomization of the highly educated political class from the vast majority of the population, which is still plagued by a low level of qualifications. In this sense, the political class monopolizes access to power by controlling the gateway to political participation, namely the political parties. The structure of public party funding in Portugal further strengthens the link between parties and the state against the vast majority of the population. Indeed, Portuguese parties have become highly dependent on state funding, which makes them office-seeking cartel parties.

The lack of cross-party cooperation in the past five years has had a negative effect on the country. The best example is the referendum on regionalization, which led to a trivial discussion with poor arguments, some of them devised to distort reality. Now, there is no alternative to regionalization, only the idea of association of municipalities, for which there is also no tradition. There is no constructive engagement in discussions; most of the debate is highly superficial. This naturally creates a negative climate among the political class and a negative perception of the autonomized political class among the population.

The political class tends to look at the constitution or the electoral system as the reason for the growing gap with the population, but, in reality, it has more to do with their own behavior in the parliamentary forum and outside. Indeed, parliamentary culture is still well behind other European Union countries in terms of proper scrutiny of the government, which means that the quality of parliamentary reports and other parliamentary acts are still far from being challenging documents in relation to the work of the government. Although due partly to the lack of human and financial resources, it is also due to the lack of commitment of a vast majority of MPs. There are naturally exceptions to the rule, such as José Barros Moura, Francisco Torres, and José Medeiros Ferreira, who clearly have worked hard as responsible parliamentarians.[1]

Reform of the Education Sector: Tackling the Drop-Out Rate in Secondary Education

Although there have been major achievements in the past thirty years, the Portuguese secondary sector is still in crisis. One of the main factors was the late development of the secondary sector under the previous authoritarian system. The secondary sector had to be built up during the first decades of Portuguese democracy; nevertheless, many problems remain that have led to Portugal having the highest drop-out rate of the European Union. First of all, the secondary education sector is not properly linked to the needs of the Portuguese labor market, a fact that creates disjunctions between the education and labor market sector. More studies on making the transition from school to the labor market are necessary.

One of the main reasons for the collapse of the secondary sector is the fact that the vast majority of school children are struggling to stay in school because they originate from poorer backgrounds. While primary education is still tolerated in most poor families, secondary education is regarded as a luxury and it prevents children from earning an income for the household. This reality makes it exceptionally important for Portugal to strengthen its support services in relation to school attendance and completion for at least a decade to reequilibrate this situation. More attention needs to be given to the fact that the poorer segments of the population still struggle to keep the household afloat. Thus, it is important, in order to strengthen the position of children from poorer backgrounds, to change completely the present education culture that tends to create a two-tier society of highly educated people earning sometimes above the EU average and poorly educated people living on the verge of poverty. This is essential for democratization of society and enrichment of the Portuguese economy. A better qualified workforce will certainly raise the standards in different fields of the Portuguese economy, while, at the same time, it will also contribute to higher salaries and an improvement of living conditions for the next generations.

The challenge of reform of secondary education is extremely linked to a strengthening of civil society and to the transition from a subject to a participant, or at least, civic culture. A better understanding of the dynamics of the drop-out rates (*insucesso escolar*) and the measures needed to tackle the problem would certainly be a crucial element in renewed efforts to enhance participation and democratization. The approach has to be integrated into lifelong strategies and other vocational training strategies, so that within a decade the level of qualifications of the Portuguese population can be raised to the EU average and the gap between rich and poor in Portugal reduced. For the moment, on average, in Portugal the highest income is 7.2 times that of the lowest income, which is the largest income gap in the European Union, along with the United Kingdom. Such a long-term strategy would certainly be welcome by the European Commission and the Council of the European Union, both of which have so far made this a priority of the Portuguese labor market policy.

Reform of the Health Sector

Many efforts have been made to reform the health sector in Portugal. However, the reforms of this sector have been a disorganized and inconsequent. Although living conditions of the population have improved considerably, there is still much to be done to strengthen the health of the Portuguese population. There is a lack of a long-term strategy connected with other policy areas, particularly the labor market. The Portuguese decision makers have to recognize that any proper long-term strategy must take into account the fact that a vast majority of the population is affected by poverty and has a tendency to withdraw from public institutions, which includes going to the hospital for treatment. The health sector has to become better organized in order to fulfill the needs of the population. For the moment, health policy is characterized by inconsequence, non-decision-making, and inertia. A transformation of the Portuguese National Health Service can only be achieved by a consensus strategy between the two main parties; otherwise the pattern of non-decision making will prevail.

Change of the Business Culture

A well-educated and healthy workforce is essential for any improvement in the Portuguese economy. The other part of the equation requires a major change of the business culture. Portugal is characterized by small- and medium-sized enterprises with low levels of capital investment. If Portuguese firms are to compete in the future, they will need to create corresponding economies of scale, which means that enterprises will have to become more bold and join forces with other Portuguese or foreign enterprises to compete in the market place. At the same time, the business culture needs to begin looking for highly qualified staff to generate new ideas for production, distribution, and marketing. Such a transformation is already going on, but it needs to accelerate and it should be linked to the transformation of the secondary and health sectors. Portuguese enterprises have to be more engaged in search of market niches. Latin America, Africa, and Central and Eastern Europe are future markets for Portuguese enterprises. Dynamization of the business sector has to be supported by the state with tax incentives and other mechanisms. One major issue is the growing need to overcome Portuguese individualism and create partnerships at local, regional, national, and transnational levels. Also a better linkage should occur between the financial and banking sector and the small- and medium-sized enterprises so that they can undertake new risks in the global economy.

Perhaps the most crucial issue is the need for a growing cooperation between universities and enterprises so that research and development can be increased and shared between the public and the private sectors. For the moment, Portugal is at the bottom of the European Union in terms of research and development expenditure. Most of the expenditure is provided by the state. There is a need to reverse this trend within the decade.

Reform of Public Administration and Decentralisation: From Government to Governance

A crucial aspect of any transformation of Portuguese democracy is the reform of public administration. Public administration, as the main motor of the state, needs to be dynamic, flexible, and able to cope with new challenges of democracy. Reform of public administration is already taking place in Portugal. The Durão Barroso government is eager to modernize public administration. Thus, the OECDization of Portuguese public administration is important, because it pushes the country to achieve a better relation between public administration and the citizens. The consulting of citizens in relation to policymaking processes will become a major element of democratic governance.

Indeed, Portugal is moving slowly towards a governance system, that has been induced by the relationship with other national public administrations in the European Union, all of them integrated into the OECD. Governance means that governments must pay more attention to the demands of civil society. For Portugal, civil society is still weak, but emerging. Reforms in the education sector would certainly raise the quality of civil society. In continuing on a path of reform, the need to decentralize public administration cannot be overlooked. After the rejection of regionalization in a referendum, which is not binding due to the fact that less than 50 percent of eligible voters took part in it, the Portuguese elite is disoriented. However, a proposal has been made to establish associations municipalities as an alternative to the failed regionalization plan.

In my view, regionalization continues to be on the agenda. It is the most sensible way of decentralizing public administration, which is concentrated mainly in Lisbon and Oporto. I believe that the regionalization discussion showed that the Portuguese political elite is more interested in achieving party political gain than moving forward towards a more democratic, citizen-friendly structure. Even if there is no regionalization, Portugal should aim for a high degree of decentralization so that citizens are better served. This would also allow more flexible locally and regionally adjusted policies to be firmly embedded in nationally formulated general policy strategies.

In thirty years, Portuguese democracy has already achieved multiple successes, but it is still characterized by high levels of inequality which are based on educational achievements. The next decade has to target poverty by raising the educational standards of the population. From there, benefits for democratic civil society, the business culture and the labor market will emerge. This factor is firmly embedded in policymaking proposed by the European Union, so that it will fit into the overall EU strategy of achieving a better workforce able to compete in the global economy by 2010.

Note

1. See José M. Magone, "Portugal: The Patrimonial Heritage and the Emergence of a Democratic Political Class," in Jens Borchert, Jürgen Zeiss (eds.), The Political Class in the Western World (Oxford: Oxford University Press, forthcoming).

Selected Bibliography

A Classe Politica Portuguesa. Lisbon: Edição, 1989.

Agh, Attila. "The Europeanization of ECE Polities and the Emergence of the New ECE Democratic Parliaments. In Attila Agh (ed.), *The Emergence of East Central Parliaments: The First Steps,* Budapest: Hungarian Centre of Democracy Studies, 1994.

_____. *The Politics of Central Europe.* London: SAGE, 1998.

Agüero, Felipe. "Democratic Consolidation and the Military in Southern Europe and South America." In Richard Gunther, P. Nikiforos Diamandouros, Hans-Jürgen Puhle eds.), *The Politics of Democratic Consolidation. Southern Europe in Comparative Perspective,* 124-165. Baltimore: Johns Hopkins University Press 1995.

Aguiar, Joaquim. "Partidos, estruturas patrimonialistas e poder funcional: A crise de legitimidade." In *Análise Social* 21 (1985): 759-783.

_____. "Portugal: The Hidden Fluidity in a Ultra-Stable Party System." In Walter C. Opello and Eduardo de Sousa Ferreira (eds.), *Conflict and Change in Modern Portugal 1974-1984,* 101-126. Lisbon: Teorema, 1985.

_____. *O Pós-Salazarismo. 1974-1984.* Lisbon: Dom Quixote, 1986.

_____. "Partidos, eleições, dinamica politica (1975-1991)." *Análise Social* XXIX, 125-126 (1994): 171-236.

_____. "Eleições, configurações e clivagens: Os resultados eleitorais de 1995." In *Análise Social* XXXV, 154-155 (2000): 55-84.

Albuquerque, José Luis, Teresa Bomba, Isabel Matias, Carlos Farinha Rodrigues e Gisela Santos. "Distribuição de Rendimentos e Condições de Vida." In DEPP/MTS (ed.), *Portugal 1995-2000. Perspectivas de Evolução Social,* 67-86. Lisbon: Celta, 2002).

Almeida, Ana Nunes de Maria das Dores Guerreiro, Cristina Lobo, Amália Torres, Karin Wall. "Relações Familiares: Mudanças e Diversidade." In José Manuel Leite Viegas, António Firmino da Costa (eds.), *Portugal, Que Modernidade?,* 45-78. Lisbon: Celta, 1998.

Almeida, João Ferreira de Luis Capucha, Antonio Firmino da Costa, Fernando Luis Machado, Isabel Nicolau, and Elisabeth Reis. *Exclusão Social. Factores e Tipos de Pobreza em Portugal.* Oeiras: Celta, 1992.

Almond, Gabriel A., Sidney Verba. *The Civic Culture. Political Attitudes and Democracy in Five Nations.* London: SAGE, 1989.

Andersen, Mikael Skou, Lise Nordvig Rasmussen. "The Making of Environmental Policy in the European Council." *Journal of Common Market Studies* 36, 4 (1998): 585-97.

André, Isabel, Jorge Gaspar. "Geografia eleitoral 1974 e 1987." In Mário Baptista Coelho (ed.), *Portugal. O Sistema Politico e Constitucional.1974-1987,* 257-277. Lisbon: ICS, 1989.

Antunes José Freire. *Os Americanos e Portugal. Vol I: Os Anos de Richard Nixon 1969-1974*. Lisbon: Publicacoes Dom Quixote, 1986.

Aragão, Rui, *Portugal: O Desafio Nacionalista.Psicologia e Identidade Nacionais*. Lisbon: Editorial Teorema, 1985.

Araújo, António de. *O Tribunal Constitucional (1989-1996). Um estudo de comportamento judicial*. Coimbra: Coimbra Editora, 1997.

Araújo, Antonio de, Pedro Coutinho Magalhães, "A justica constitucional: Uma instituição contra as maiorias." *Análise Social* XXXV, 154-155 (2000): 207-246.

Assemblée Parlementaire Européenne. "Aspects politiques et institutionels de l´adhesion ou de l´association à la Communauté-Discussion d´un rapport de M. Birkelbach, fait au nom de la Commission politique." Séance du Mardi 23 Janvier 1962.

Assembleia da Republica. *Biografias dos Deputados. VI Legislatura*. Lisbon: AR, 1993.

_____. *Biografias dos Deputados. VII Legislatura.* Lisbon: AR, 1997.

_____. *Biografias dos Deputados. VIII Legislatura*. Lisbon: AR, 2000.

_____. *Constituição Portuguesa. Quinta Revisão 2001*. Lisbon: AR, 2002.

_____. *Programa do XIII Governo. Apresentação e Debate*. Lisbon: AR, 1996.

_____. *Programa do XIV Governo. Apresentação e Debate*. Lisbon: AR, 1999.

_____. Programa do XV Governo. Texto do Programa." *Diário da Assembleia da Republica* 18.4.2003, II-Série-A, No. 2, Suplemento.

Attinà, Fulvio, "Integrazione e Democrazia: Un´analisi evoluzionista dell´Unione Europea." *Rivista Italiana di Scienza Politica* a.XXX, 2 (2000): 227-256.

Bach, Maurizio. *Die Bürokratisierung Europas. Verwaltungseliten, Experten und politische Legitimation in Europa*. New York: Campus, 1999.

Baganha, Maria Ioannis João Ferrão, Jorge Macaista Malheiros. Os imigrantes e o mercado de trabalho: O caso português." *Análise Social* XXXIV, 150 (1999): 147-173.

Balme, Richard, "Las Condiciones De La Acción Colectiva Regional."In F. Letamendia (coord.), *Nacionalidades Y Regiones En La Unión Europea*, 69-91. Madrid: Fundamentos, 1999.

Bárbara, Américo. "Madeira Dinâmicas e tendencias da lusofonia." *Janus 99-2000*: 138-139. Lisbon: Publico-Universidade Aberta de Lisboa, 1999.

Barbier, Cécile. "La répartition des pouvoirs dans l'Union européenne aprés Nice." *Notabene* 119 (Février 2001): 11-17.

Barreto, António (ed.). *Regionalização Sim ou Não*. Lisbon: Dom Quixote, 1998.

_____ (ed.). *A Situação Social em Portugal 1960-1999. Vol. II. Indicadores sociais em Portugal e na União Europeia*, 197-199. Lisbon: Instituto de Ciencias Sociais, 2001.

Barros Moura, José António Nazaré Pereira, *Relatório sobre a proposta de resolução n°59/VIII que aprova para ratificação, o Tratado de Nice que altera o Tratado da Uniao Europeia, os Tratados que instituem as Comunidades Europeias e alguns actos relativos a esses tratados assinado em Nice, em 26 de Fevereiro de 2001*. Lisbon: Comissão de Assuntos Europeus, 24 Outubro 2001; http://www.parlamento.pt, seen in December 2001.

Bartolini, Stefano, Peter Mair. *Identity, Competition and Electoral Availability: The Stabilization of European Electorates 1885-1985*. Cambridge: Cambridge University Press, 1990.

Baum, Michael A., André Freire. "Political Parties, Cleavage Structures and Referendum Voting: Electoral Behaviour in the Portuguese Regionalization Referendum 1998." *South European Society and Politics* 6, 1 (Summer 2001): 1-26.

_____. "Clivagens, economia e voto em Portugal 1999: Uma análise das eleições parlamentares com dados agregados." *Sociologia-Problemas e Práticas* 37 (November 2001): 115-140.

Bergman, Torbjörn. "National Parliaments and EU Affairs Committees: Notes on Empirical Variation and Competing Explanations." *Journal of European Public Policy* 3 (1997): 373-87.

Bermeo, Nancy. *A Teoria da Democracia e as Realidades da Europa do Sul*, 154-167. Lisbon: Difel, 2000.

Beyers, Jan, Guido Dierickx. "The Working Groups of the Council of the European Union: Supranational or Intergovernmental Negotiations?" *Journal of Common Market Studies* 36, 3 (1998): 289-317; 305-306.

Beyme, Klaus von. "Party Leadership and Change in Party Systems: Towards a Postmodern Party State?" *Government and Opposition* 31, 2 (1996): 135-159.

Biezen, Ingrid van. "Sobre o equilibrio interno do poder: as organizações partidárias nas novas democracias." *Análise Social* 33 (1998): 685-708.

Börzel, Tanja. "Why There is No Southern Problem: On Environmental Leaders and Laggards in the EU." *Journal of European Public Policy* 7 (1): 141-162.

_____. "Non-compliance in the European Union. Pathology or Statistical Artefact?" *Journal of European Public Policy* 8, 5 (2001): 803-824.

Braga da Cruz, Manuel. *O Partido e o Estado no Salazarismo*. Lisbon: Editorial Presenca, 1988.

_____. "A revisão falhada do sistema eleitoral" *Analise Social* XXXV, 154-155 (Summer 2000): 45-53.

Bruneau, Thomas. *Politics and Nationhood. Postrevolutionary Portugal*. New York: Praeger, 1984.

Bruto da Costa, Alfredo, Manuela Silva, J. Pereirinha, Madalena Matos. *A Pobreza em Portugal*. Lisbon: Fundação Calouste Gulbenkian, 1985.

Burnham, June, Moshe Maor. "Converging Administrative Systems: Recruitment and Training in EU Member States." *Journal of European Public Policy* 2:2 (June 1995): 185-204.

Cabral, Antonio José. "Community Regional Policy towards Portugal." In José da Silva Lopes (ed.), *Portugal and EC Membership Evaluated*, 133-145. London: Pinter, 1994.

Cabral, Manuel Villaverde. "O exercicio da cidadania em Portugal." In Manuel Villaverde Cabral, Jorge Vala, João Freire (eds.), *Trabalho e Cidadania*. Lisbon: Imprensa de Ciencias Sociais, 2000, 123-171.

Calussi, Federiga Bindi. "The Committee of the Regions: An Atypical Influential Committee?" In M.P.C.M. Van Schendelen (ed.), *EU Committees as Influential Policy-makers*, 225-249. Aldershot: Ashgate, 1999.

_____. "O processo de tomada de decisões em politica comunitária." *Analise Social* 154-155 (2000): 383-404.

Campinos, Jorge. *O Ministro dos Negocios Estrangeiros. Estudo de Direito Internacional Publico e de Direito Constitucional Comparado*. Lisbon: Moraes Editores, 1977.

Capucha, Luis. "Pobreza, Exclusão Social e Marginalidades." In José Manuel Leite Viegas, Antonio Firmino da Costa (eds.), *Portugal, Que Modernidade?*, 209-12. Lisbon: Celta, 1998.

Capucha, Luis, Ana Sofia Marques, José Luis Castro. "Carlos Pereira e Paula Monteiro, Vulnerabilidade e Exclusão Social." In DEPP/MTS (ed.), *Portugal 1995-2000. Perpectivas da Evolucao Social*, 215-251. Lisbon: Celta, 2002.

Carrilho, Maria. "Os Conflitos nos Balcãs e a Redefinição das Missões Internacionais." *Estratégia* 14, (2 Semester1999): 45-64.

Castells, Manuel. *The Power of Identity. Volume II of the Information Age, Economy, Society and Culture*. London: Blackwell, 1997.

Castilho, Manuel Tavares. *A Ideia de Europa no Marcelismo (1968-1974)*. Lisbon: Colecção Parlamento, 2000.

Caupers, João, João Raposo. *A nova justiça administrativa*. Lisbon: Ancors editoras, 2002.

Christiansen, Thomas. "Tensions of European Governance: Politicized Bureaucracy and the Multiple Accountability in the European Commission." *Journal of European Public Policy* 4, 1 (March 1997): 73-90.

Christiansen, Thomas, Knud-Erik Jorgensen. "Transnational Governance 'Above' and 'Below' the State: The Changing Nature of Borders in the New Europe." *Regional Studies* 10, 2 (Summer 2000): 62-77.

Cole, Alastair. "National and Partisan Contexts of Europeanization: The Case of French Socialists." *Journal of Common Market Studies* 39, 1 (March 2001): 15-36.

Collins, Neill, Mary O´Shea. "The Republic of Ireland." In J. A.Chandler (ed.), *Comparative Public Administration*, 98-125. London: Routledge, 2000.

Comissão de Assuntos Europeus. *Acompanhamento parlamentar da Revisão do Tratado da União Europeia na Conferencia Intergovernmental de 1996*. 2 vols. Lisbon: Assembleia da Republica, 1995.

_____. *Portugal na União Europeia em 1995 e 1996. Apreciação Parlamentar*. Lisbon: Assembleia da Republica, 1997.

_____. *Portugal Na União Europeia em 1996 e 1997. Apreciação Parlamentar.* Lisbon: Assembleia da Republica, 1998.

_____. *Relatório sobre a Proposta n°59/VIII que aprova para ratificação, o tratado de Nice que altera o Tratado da União Europeia, Os Tratados que instituem as Comunidades Europeias e alguns actos relativos a esses Tratados, assinado em Nice, em 26 de Fevereiro de 2001.* Lisbon: Assembleia da Republica, 2001.

_____. *Opções Europeias de Portugal. União Económica e Monetária.* Lisbon: Assembleia da Republica, 1998.

_____. *Mesa Redonda sobre o Tratado de Nice e o Futuro da Europa.* Lisbon: Assembleia da Republica, 2001.

Comissão de Coordenação Lisboa e Vale do Tejo (CCRLVT). *Plano Estratégico da Região de Lisboa Oeste Vale do Tejo. 2000-2010 O Horizonte de Excelencia.* Lisbon: CCRLVT, 1999.

Comissão de Coordenação Região Norte (CCR-N). *Autonomia Administrativa e Financeira do Estado. O Caso das Comissões de Coordenação Regional,* 61-73. Porto: CCRN, 1999.

Comissão de Gestão dos Fundos Comunitários. *Um Olhar sobre o QCAII.Encerramento do Periodo de Programação 1994-1999.* Lisbon: DGDR, 2000.

Comissão Europeia. *Ministério do Planeamento, Quadro Comunitário de Apoio III. Portugal 2000-2006.* Lisbon: Direcção Geral de Desenvolvimento Regional, 2000.

_____. *Projectos para o futuro. Politica regional da UE em Portugal.* Bruxelas: Servico de Publicações Oficiais das Comunidades Europeias, 2001.

Comissão para a Qualidade e Racionalização da Administração Pública. *Renovar Administração.* Lisbon: Secretaria do Estado da Modernização Administrativa, 1998.

Commission of the European Communities. *Council Recommendation on the Implementation of Member States´ Employment Policies.* Brussels, 12.9.2001, COM (2001): 512 final; 17.

Conselho Economico e Social. *Pareceres e Reuniões do Conselho Economico e Social (Setembro 1992 a Fevereiro 1996).* Lisbon: CES, 1996.

Corkill, David. "Portugal's 1998 Referendums." *West European Politics* 22, 2 (1999): 186-92.

_____. *The Portuguese Economy. A Case of Europeanization.* London: Routledge, 1999.

Covas, António. *Integração Europeia, Regionalização Administrativa e Reforma do Estado-Nacional.* Oeiras: INA, 1997.

Cram, Laura. *Policy Making in the European Union. Conceptual Lenses and the Integration Process.* London: Routledge, 1997.

_____. "Whither the Commission? Reform, Renewal and Issue-Attention." *Journal of European Public Policy* 8, 5 (October 2001): 770-786.

Cunha, Carlos. "The Portuguese Communist Party." In Thomas C. Bruneau (ed.), *Political Parties and Democracy in Portugal,* 23-54. Boulder, CO: Westview Press, 1997).

Cunha, Isabel Ferin, Verónica Policarpo, Teresa Líbano Monteiro, Rita Figueiras. "Media e discriminacao: Um estudo exploratório do caso portugues." *Observatório* 5 (May 2002): 27-38.

Cutileiro, José. "Bósnia-Herzegovina. Contribuição Portuguesa para uma Solução Politica." *Nação e Defesa* 92, 2 Série (Winter 2000): 51-60.

den Boer, Monica, William Wallace. "Justice and Home Affairs: Integration through Incrementalism." In Helen and William Wallace (eds.), *Policy-Making in the European Union*, 494-525. Oxford: Oxford University Press, 2000.

Direcção Geral de Desenvolvimento Regional (DGDR). *Quadro Comunitário de Apoio 1994-1999. Balanço Final.* Lisbon: DGDR, 1999.

Domingues, João Marco. "Participação Portuguesa em exercicios e operações conjuntas." In *As Forças Armadas no novo contexto internacional, Janus 98, suplemento especial.* Lisbon: O Publico, UAL, 1998.

Dyson, Kenneth. "EMU as 'Europeanization': Convergence, Diversity and Contingency." *Journal of Common Market Studies* 38, 4 (2000): 645-66; particularly 657.

Dyson, Kenneth, Kevin Featherstone. "Italy and EMU as a 'Vincolo Esterno': Empowering the Technocrats, Transforming the State." *South European Society and Politics* 1, 2 (Autumn 1996): 272-299.

Eaton, M. "Regional Development Funding in Portugal." *Journal of the Association for Contemporary Iberian Studies* 7, 2 (Autumn 1994): 36-46.

Eisfeld, Rainer. *Sozialistischer Pluralismus in Europa. Ansätze und Scheitern am Beispiel Portugal.* Köln: Verlag Wissenschaft und Politik, 1984.

_____. "Portugal in the European Community 1986-88.The Transition of the First Half of the Transition Period." *Iberian Studies* 18, 2 (1989): 156-65.

Ekengreen, Magnus, Bengt Sundelius. "Sweden: The State Joins the European Union." In Ben Soetendorp, Kenneth Hanf (eds.), *Adapting to European Integration.Small States and the European Union*, 131-148. London: Longman, 1998.

Emerson, M., D.Gros. *Impact of Enlargement, Agenda 2000 and EMU on Poorer Regions—The Case of Portugal. Working Document 125.* Brussels: Centre for European Policy Studies, 1998.

Escarameia, Paula. "Um mundo em mudança: Timor, a ONU e o Direito Internacional." *Politica Internacional* 3, 3 (Primavera-Verao 2001): 99-119.

Eurobarometro. *As fontes de informação sobre a União Europeia, O Alargamento e as Relações entre as Instituições, os Estados Membros e os Cidadãos. Estudo realizado para a Representação da Comissão Europeia em Portugal.* 2002.

European Commission/Netherlands Economic Institute. *New Location Factors for Mobile Investment in Europe*. Luxembourg: Office of the Official Publications of the European Communities, 1993.

European Commission. *Common Support Framework II. Portugal 1994-1999.* Luxembourg: Office of the Official Publications of the European Communities, 1994.

_____. "Agenda 2000. For a Stronger and Wider Union." *Bulletin of the European Union.* Supplement 5/97.

_____. *Reforming the Commission. A White Paper.* Brussels, 1.3.2000, COM (2000), 200 final, 2 vols.

_____. *The Social Situation in the European Union 2002.* Luxembourg: Office of the Official Publications of the European Union, 2002.

European Companion 1990. London: Dod's Publishing and Research Limited. 1990.

European Companion 1995. London: Dod's Publishing and Research Limited, 1995.

European Institute for Public Administration. *Annual Report 2000.* Maastricht: EIPA, 2001.

Eurostat. *Como somos los europeos? Todos los Datos.* Madrid: El Pais, 1999.

Everson, Michelle. "Administering Europe?" *Journal of Common Market Studies* 36, 2 (June 1998): 195-215.

Faria, Fernanda. "The Mediterranean: A New Priority in Portuguese Foreign Policy." *Mediterranean Politics* 1 (1996): 212-230.

Ferrão, João. "Terciarização e território: Emergência de novas configurações espaciais?" *Análise Social* XXVI, 5 (1991): 829-845.

Ferreira, José Medeiros. *A Nova Era Europeia. De Genebra a Amsterdão.* Lisbon: Noticias Editorial, 1999.

_____. "Os Açores na encruzilhada da politica europeia e de segurança comum." *Politica Internacional* 22, 3 (2000): 175-183.

_____ (ed.). *Politica Externa e Politica de Defesa em Portugal.* Lisbon: Colibri, 2002.

Filipe, António. *As Oposições Parlamentares em Portugal. Práticas e Intervenções (1976-2000).* Lisbon: Vega, 2002.

Follesdal, Andreas, Peter Koslowski (eds.). *Democracy and the European Union.* New York: Springer, 1998.

Forster, Anthony, William Wallace. "Common Foreign and Security Policy. From Shadow to Substance." In Helen and William Wallace (eds.) *Policy-Making in the European Union*, 461-491. Oxford: Oxford University Press, 2000.

Fraga, Ana. "The Parliament in Portugal: Loyal Scrutiny and Informal Influence." In Andreas Maurer, Wolfgang Wessels (eds.), *National Parliaments on their Ways to Europe: Losers or Latecomers?*, 359-376. Baden-Baden: Nomos Verlagsgesellschaft, 2001.

_____. *O Papel dos Parlamentos Nacionais e a Legitimidade da Construção Europeia.* Lisbon: Cosmos, 2002.

Frain, Maritheresa. "Relações entre o Presidente e o primeiro-ministro em Portugal: 1985-1995." *Análise Social* XXX, 133, 4 (1995): 653-578.

_____. "A Peninsula Ibérica e a Europa: Uma convergência nas politicas da defesa espanhola e portuguesa no pós-Guerra Fria?" *Politica Internacional* 1, 5/16 (Winter 1997): 249-282.

_____. *PPD/PSD e a consolidação do regime democrático.* Lisbon: Editorial Noticias, 1998.

Freire, André. "Participação e abstenção nas eleições legislativas portuguesas, 1975-1995." *Analise Social* 154-155 (2000) 115-145.

Freire, André, Pedro Magalhães. *A abstenção eleitoral em Portugal*. Lisbon: ICS, 2002.

Freitas do Amaral, Diogo. "A crise da justiça." *Analise Social* XXXV, 154-155 (2000): 247-257.

Gallagher, Tom. "Unconvinced by Europe of the Regions: The 1998 Regionalization Referendum in Portugal." In *South European Society and Politics* 4, 1 (1999): 132-148.

Gaspar, Carlos. "Portugal e o alargamento da União Europeia." *Analise Social* 154-155 (2000): 327-372.

Giacometti, Pierre. "Les Européens face au cas Haider. La question Haider divise les opinions européennes." In Bruno Cautrés, Dominique Reyniè (eds.), *L'Opinion Européenne 2000*, 193-195. Paris: Presses Sciences Po, 2000.

Giddens, Anthony. *Modernity and Self-Identity. Self and Society in the Late Modern Age*. Cambridge: Polity Press, 1993.

Gillespie, Richard (ed.). *The Euro-Mediterranean Partnership*. London: Frank Cass, 1997.

Goetz, Klaus H., Simon Hix. "Introduction: European Integration and National Political Systems." In Klaus H. Goetz, Simon Hix (eds.), "Europeanised Politics? European Integration and National Political Systems." *West European Politics* 23, 4 (October 2000): 1-26.

Gonçalves, Júlio da Mesquita. *Desburocratização. Uma administração para o século XXI*. Lisbon: SMA, 1997.

González Hernandez, Juan Carlos. *Desarollo Político y Consolidación Democrática en Portugal (1974-1998)*. Madrid: Centro de Investigaciones Sociologicas, 1999.

Gomes, João Mira. "O Envolvimento Diplomatico de Portugal na Bósnia-Herzegovina." *Nação e Defesa* 92, 2a serie (Winter 2000): 61-69.

Gomes, João Salis. "Perspectivas da Moderna Gestão Pública." In Juan Mozzicafreddo, João Salis Gomes (eds.), *Administração e Política. Perspectivas de Reforma da Administração Pública na Europa e nos Estados Unidos*, 77-102. Oeiras: Celta, 2001.

Gomes, Nancy. "As relações externas da América Latina." *Janus 98*, 130-131. Lisbon: Publico-Universidade Aberta de Lisboa, 1997.

_____. "Cenários no espaco ibero-americano." *Janus 99-2000*: 142-143. Lisbon: Publico-Universidade Aberta de Lisboa, 2000.

Graham, Lawrence S. *Portugal. The Decline and Collapse of an Authoritarian Order*. London, Beverly Hills: SAGE, 1975.

_____. "Bureaucratic Politics and the Problem of Reform in the State Apparatus." In Lawrence S. Graham and Douglas L. Wheeler (eds.), *In Search of Modern Portugal: The Revolution and Its Consequences*. Madison: The University of Wisconsin Press, 1982.

_____. "Administração publica central and local: Mudança e continuidade." *Analise Social* XXI, 87-88-89 (1985): 903-924.

_____. *The Portuguese Military and the State. Rethinking Transitions in Europe and Latin America*. Boulder, CO: Westview Press, 1993.

Gray, Oliver. "The Structure of Interest Group Representation in the EU: Observations from a Practitioner. Paul-H. Claeys, Corinne Gobin, Isabelle Smets, and Pascaline Winand (eds.), *Lobbying, Pluralism and European Integration*, 281-302. Brussels: European Inter-University Press, 1998.

Grupo Parlamentar do Partido Socialista. *Regionalizar. Cumprir a Constituição e Concretizar uma Reforma*. Lisbon: PS, 1998.

Guibentif, Pierre. "Rechtskultur und Rechtsproduktion: Das Beispiel Portugal." *Zeitschrift für Rechtssoziologie*, issue 2 (1989): 148-169.

Guterres, António. *Regionalização Faz a Força. Discurso de António Guterres na Comissão Nacional do PS*. Lisbon: PS, 1998.

Hayes-Renshaw, Fiona, Helen Wallace. *The Council of Ministers*. Basingstroke: Macmillan, 1997.

Henderson, Douglas. "The UK Presidency: An Insider´s View." *Journal of Common Market Studies* 36, 4 (1998): 563-72.

Hespanha, A. M. "As transformações revolucionárias e o discurso dos juristas." *Revista Critica de Ciencias Sociais* 18/19/20 (February 1986): 311-341.

Hespanha, Pedro, Alcina Monteiro, A. Cardoso Ferreira, Fernanda Rodrigues, M. Helena Nunes, M. José Hespanha, Rosa Madeira, Rudy van den Hoven, Silvia Portugal. *Entre o Estado e o Mercado.As fragilidades das instituições da protecção social em Portugal*. Coimbra: Quarteto, 2000.

Hooghe, Liesbet. "The Dynamics of Constitution Building in Belgium." In Patrick Dunleavy, Jeffrey Stanyer (eds.), *Contemporary Political Studies 1994, Vo. 1. Proceedings of the Annual Conference Held at the University of Wales, Swansea, March 29-31, 1994*, 314-324. Belfast: PSA, 1994.

Hooghe, Liesbet, Michael Keating. "The Politics of European Union Regional Policy." *Journal of European Public Policy* 1, 3 (1996): 367-393.

Hooghe, Liesbet, Gary Marks. *Multilevel Governance and European Integration*. Lanham, MA: Rowman and Littlefield, 2001.

Hrbek, Rudolf. "Nationalstaat und Europäische Integration. Die Bedeutung der Nationalen Komponente für den Integrationsprozess." In P. Haungs (ed.), *Europäisierung Europas?*, 81-108. Baden-Baden: Nomos, 1989.

Iking, Bernhard. *Die Auswirkungen des EG-Beitritts auf die Industriepolitik Portugals.Die Entwicklung der technologischen Wettbewerbsfähigkeit der Portugiesischen Industrie*. Frankfurt a. M.: Peter Lang, 1997.

Imig, Doug, Sidney Tarrow. "Political Contention in a Europeanising Polity." In Klaus H. Goetz, Simon Hix (eds.), "Europeanised Politics? European Integration and National Political Systems."*West European Politics* 23, 4 (October 2000): 73-93.

Instituto para a Inovação da Administração do Estado. *Missão e Linhas Estratégicas. Iniciativas a desenvolver em 2002*. Lisbon: IIAE, 2001.

Iturra, Raul. *A Construção Social do Insucesso Escolar. Memória e Aprendizagem em Vila Ruiva*. Lisbon: Escher, 1990.

Jachtenfuchs, M. "The Governance Approach to European Integration." *Journal of Common Market Studies* 39, 2 (2001): 245-64.

Jones, Robert A. "The European Union." In J. A. Chandler (ed.), *Comparative Public Administration*, 173-219. London, New York: Routledge 2000.

Katz, Richard, Peter Mair. "Changing Models of Party Organisation and Party Democracy: The Emergence of the Cartel Party." Party Politics *(1995): 5-28.*

Katz, Richard, Bernhard Wessels (eds.). *The European Parliament, National Parliaments and European Integration.* Oxford: Oxford University Press, 1999.

Kitschelt, Herbert. *The Transformation of European Social Democracy.* Cambridge: Cambridge University Press, 1994.

_____. "European Party Systems: Continuity and Change." In Martin Rhodes, Paul Heywood, Vincent Wright (eds.), *Developments in West European Politics*, 136-147. Basingstroke: Macmillan, 1997.

_____. "A Silent Revolution in Europe?" In Jack Hayward, Ed Page (eds.), *Governing the New Europe*, 123-165. Oxford: Oxford University Press, 1995.

Knigge, Pia. "The Ecological Correlates of Right-Wing Extremism in Western Europe." *European Journal of Political Research* 34, 2 (October 1998): 249-279.

Knill, Christoph. *The Europeanisation of National Administrations.* Cambridge: Cambridge University Press, 2001.

Kohler-Koch, Beate. "Regieren in der Europäischen Union. Auf der Suche nach demokratischer Legitimität." *Aus Politik und Zeitgeschichte* B (6/2000): 30-38.

Kommission der Europaeischen Gemeinschaften. "Stellungnahme zum Beitrittsantrag Portugals (von der Kommission am 19. Mai 1978 dem Rat vorgelegt)." *Bulletin der Europaeischen Gemeinschaften*, Beilag 5/78.

König, Thomas, Elmar Rieger, Hermann Schmitt (Hg.). *Das europäische Mehrebenensystem.* Frankfurt a. M.: Campus, 1996.

Ladrech, Robert. "Europeanization of Domestic Politics and Institutions: The Case of France" *Journal of Common Market Studies* 32, 1 (March 1994): 69-88.

Laffan, Brigid, Etain Tannam. "Ireland: The Rewards of Pragmatism." In Kenneth Hanf, Ben Soetendorp (eds.), *Adapting to European Integration. Small States and the European Union*, 69-83. London: Longman, 1998.

Lampreia, Laura. *Contributos para uma nova Cultura da Gestão Pública.* Lisbon: SMA, 1997.

Lepsius, M. Rainer. "Nationalstaat oder Nationalitätenstaat als Modell für die Weiterentwicklung der Europäischen Gemeinschaft." In Rudolf Wildenmann (ed.), *Staatswerdung Europas? Optionen für eine Europäische Union*, 19-40. Baden-Baden: Nomos Verlagsgesellschaft, 1991.

_____. "Die Europäische Union. Ökonomische-Politische Integration und kulturelle Identität." In Reinhold Viehoff, Rien T. Segers (eds.), *Kultur,Identität, Europa.Über Schwierigkeiten und Möglichkeiten einer Konstruktion*, 201-222. Frankfurt a. M.: Suhrkamp, 1999.

Lerch, Wolfgang. "Neu in Europa: Der interregionale Wirtschafts-und Sozialauschuß in the Großregion Saar-Lor-Lux." *WSI Mitteilungen* (6/ 1999): 396-406.

Leston-Bandeira, Cristina. *Da Legislação à Legitimação: O Papel do Parlamento Portugues*. Lisbon: ICS, 2002.

Lewis, Jeffrey. "Is the 'Hard Bargaining' Image of the Council Misleading? The Committee of Permanent Representatives and the Local Elections Directive." *Journal of Common Market Studies* 36, 4 (1998): 479-504.

Lipset, Martin Seymour. *Political Man. The Social Conditions of the Political Order.* London: Heinemann Group of Publishers, 1964.

Lobo, Marina Costa. "A evolução do sistema partidário portugues á luz de mudanças económicas e politicas" *Analise Social* XXXI, 139 (1996): 1085-1116.

Lobo, Marina Costa, Pedro C. Magalhaes. "From 'Third Wave' to 'Third Way': Europe and the Portuguese Socialists." *Journal of Southern Europe and the Balkans* 3, 1 (2001): 25-35.

Lopes, Ernani Rodrigues (ed.). *Uma Experiencia Unica 1998; MPU. Um Movimento Civico Contra a Regionalização*. Porto: Porto Editora, 2001.

Lopes, José da Silva (ed.). *Portugal and EC Membership Evaluated*. London: Pinter, 1994.

Lopez Mira, Alvaro Xosé. "Portugal: The Resistance to Change in the State Model." *Regional and Federal Studies* 9, 2 (1999): 98-115.

Loughlin, John. "Representing the Regions in Europe: The Committee of the Regions." *Regional and Federal Studies* 6 (1996): 147-165.

_____. "La autonomia en Europa ocidental: Un estudio comparado." In Francisco Letamendia (coord.), *Nacionalidades y Regiones en la Unión Europea*, 109-159. Madrid: Editorial Fundamentos, 1998.

Ludlow, Peter. "The UK Presidency: A View from Brussels." *Journal of Common Market Studies* 36, 4 (1998): 573-83.

Machado, Fernando Luis, Antonio Firmino da Costa. "Processos de Uma Modernidade Inacabada. Mudanças Estruturais e Mobilidade Social." José Manuel Leite Viegas, António Firmino da Costa (eds.), *Portugal, Que Modernidade?*, 17-58; particularly 33-43. Lisbon: Celta, 1998.

Macmullen, Andrew. "Fraud, Mismanagement and Nepotism: The Committee of Independent Experts and the Fall of the European Commission 1999." *Crime, Law and Social Change* 31 (1999): 173-192.

Magalhães, Pedro. "Desigualdade, desinteresse e desconfiança: A abstenção nas eleições legislativas de 1999." *Análise Social* XXXV, 157 (2001): 1079-1093.

Magone, José. *The Iberian Members of the European Parliament and European Integration. Their Background, Their Attitudes and the Prospects for Transforming Elite Cultures*. Occasional Paper No. 7, June 1993. Bristol: Centre for Mediterranean Studies (University of Bristol).

_____. "The Portuguese Assembleia da República: Discovering Europe." In Philip Norton (ed.), *National Parliaments and the European Union*, 151-165. London: Frank Cass, 1996.

_____. *The Changing Architecture of Iberian Politics (1974-1992). An Investigation on the Structuring of Democratic Political Systemic Culture in Semiperipheral Southern European Countries*. Lewiston, NY: Edwin Mellen Press, 1996.

_____. "Portugal." In Juliet Lodge (ed.), *The 1994 European Parliament Elections*, 147-156. London: Pinter, 1996.

_____. *European Portugal. The Difficult Road to Sustainable Democracy*. Basingstroke: Macmillan, 1997.

_____. "A integração e a construção da democracia portuguesa." *Penelope* 18 (1998): 123-63.

_____. "Portugal: Party System Installation and Consolidation." In David Broughton, Mark Donovan (eds.), *Changing Party Systems in Western Europe*, 232-253. London: Pinter, 1999.

_____. "Portugal: Das patrimoniale Erbe und die Entstehung einer demokratischen politischen Klasse." In Jens Borchert, Mitarbeit von Jürgen Zeiß (eds.), *Politik als Beruf. Die politische Klasse in westlichen Demokratien*, 396-414. Opladen: Leske+Budrich, 1999.

_____. "The Portuguese Socialist Party." In Robert Ladrech, Philippe Marliére (eds.), *Socialdemocratic Parties in the European Union.History, Organization, Policies*, 166-175. Basingstoke: Macmillan, 1999.

_____. *"La construzione di una societá civile europea: Legami a più livelli tra comitati economici e sociali." In Antonio Varsori (ed.),* Il Comitato Economico e Sociale nella construzione europea*, 222-242. Venice: Marsilio, 2000.*

_____. "Political Recruitment and Elite Transformation in Modern Portugal 1870-1999: The Late Arrival of Mass Representation." In Heinrich Best, Maurizio Cotta (eds.), *Parliamentary Representatives in Europe 1848-2000. Legislative Recruitment and Careers in Eleven European Countries*, 341-370. Oxford: Oxford University Press, 2000.

_____. "Portugal: The Rationale of Democratic Regime Building." In Wolfgang C. Müller, Kaare Strom (eds.), *Coalition Governments in Western Europe*, 529-558. Oxford: Oxford University Press, 2000.

_____. "The Transformation of the Portuguese Political System: European Regional Policy and Democratization in a Small EU Member State." *South European Society and Politics* 5, 2 (Autumn 2000): 119-140.

_____. "EU Territorial Governance and National Politics: Reshaping Marginality in Spain and Portugal." In Noel Parker, Bill Armstrong (eds.), *Margins in European Integration*, 155-177. Basingstroke: Macmillan, 2000.

_____. "Portugal." In Ruud Koole, Richard S. Katz (eds.), Political Data Yearbook 2000. Special Issue of *European Journal of Political Research* 38, 3-4 (December 2000): 499-510.

_____. "Portugal." In Special Issue Political Data Yearbook 2001. *European Journal of Political Research* 40, 3-4 (December 2001): 396-401; particularly 399-400.

_____. "Portugal." In Juliet Lodge (ed.), *The 1999 Elections to the EuropeanParliament*, 171-184. Basingstroke: Palgrave, 2001.

_____. *Iberian Trade Unionism. Democratization under the Impact of the European Union*. New Brunswick, NJ: Transactions Publishers, 2001.

_____. "The Third Level of European Integration: New and Old Insights." In José Magone (ed.), *Regional Institutions and Governance in the European Union*, 1-28. Westport, CT: Praeger, 2003.

_____. *The Politics of Southern Europe. Integration into the European Union*. Westport, CT: Praeger, 2003).

Mair, Peter. "The Limited Impact of Europe on National Party Systems." In Klaus H. Goetz, Simon Hix (eds.), "Europeanised Politics? European Integration and National Political Systems." Special Issue of *West European Politics* 23, 4 (October 2000): 27-50.

Makler, Harry M. "The Portuguese Industrial Elite and Its Corporative Relations: A Study of Compartmentalization in an Authoritarian Regime." In Lawrence S. Graham and Harry M. Makler (eds.), *Contemporary Portugal. The Revolution and Its Antecedents*, 123-145. Austin: University of Texas. 1974.

Marks, Gary. "Structural Policy and Multilevel Governance in the European Community." In A. W. Cafruny, G. C. Rosenthal (eds.), *The State of the Community, vol. 2: The Maastricht Debates and Beyond*, 391-410. Boulder, CO: Lynne Rienner, 1993.

Marks, Gary, Fritz Scharpf, Philippe Schmitter, Wolfgang Streck. *Governance in the European Union*. London: SAGE, 1996.

Martin, Andrew, George Ross. "European Integration and the Europeanisation of Labour." In Emilio Gabaglio and Reiner Hoffmann (eds.), *The ETUC in the Mirror of Industrial Relations Research*, 247-293. Brussels: European Trade Union Institute, 1998.

Martins, Vitor. "Introdução." In Ministerio dos Negocios Estrangeiros, *Portugal nas Comunidades Europeias 1992, setimo ano*, I-XI. Lisbon: MNE 1993.

Mateus, Rui. *Contos Proibidos. Memórias para um PS Desconhecido*. Lisbon: Dom Quixote, 1996.

Maurer, Andreas. "National Parliament after Amsterdam: Adaptation, Recalibration and Europeanisation by Process." Paper for working group meeting, XXIVth COSAC, 8-9 April 2001.

_____. *National Parliaments in the European Architecture: Elements for Establishing a Best Practice Mechanism*. Working the European Convention, The Secretariat, Group IV-Role of National Parliaments, Brussels, 9 July 2002.

Maurer, Andreas, Jürgen Mittag, Wolfgang Wessels. "Theoretical Perspectives on Administrative Interaction in the European Union." In Thomas Christiansen, Emil Kirchner (eds.), *Committee Governance in the European Union*. 21-44. Manchester: Manchester University Press, 2000.

Menon, Anand. "France." In Hussein Kassim, Anand Menon, Guy Peters (eds.), *The National Co-ordination of EU Policy. The Brussels Level*. Oxford: Oxford University Press, 2001.

Merlingen, Michael. "Identity, Politics and Germany's Post-TEU Policy on EMU." *Journal of Common Market Studies* 39, 3 (September 2001): 463-483.

Merlingen, Michael, Cas Mudde, Ulrich Sedelmeier. "The Right and the Righteous? European Norms, Domestic Politics and the Sanctions Against Austria." *Journal of Common Market Studies* 38, 1 (March 2001): 59-77.

Metcalfe, Les. "Reforming the Commission: Will Organizational Efficiency Produce Effective Governance?" *Journal of Common Market Studies* 38, 5 (1998): 817-41.

Ministério de Defesa Nacional (MDN). *Participação de Militares e unidades Portuguesas em operações de paz fora do território nacional e em acções de cooperação bilateral na area de defesa nacional, 31 de Dezembro 2001*. Lisbon: MDN, 2001.

_____. *Anuario Estatistico de Defesa Nacional 2001*. Lisbon: MDN, 2001.

_____. *Livro Branco sobre a Defesa Nacional*. Lisbon: MDN, 2002.

_____. *Participação de Militares e unidades Portuguesas em operações de paz fora do território nacional e em acções de cooperação bilateral na area de defesa nacional*. 31 October 2002. Lisbon: MDN, 2002.

Ministério do Equipamento e da Administração do Território (MEPAT). *Descentralização, Regionalização e Reforma do Estado*. Lisbon: MEPAT, 1998.

Ministério do Equipamento, Planeamento e Administração do Territorio (MEPAT). *Portugal 2000-2006:Plano de Desenvolvimento Regional*. Lisbon: MEPAT, 1999.

Ministério dos Negocios Estrangeiros (MNE). *Portugal nas Comunidades Europeias. Annual Volumes 1986-2000*. Lisbon: MNE, 1986-2001.

_____. *A reestruturação do ministério dos negocios estrangeiros*. Lisbon: MNE, 1995.

_____. *Portugal e a Conferencia Intergovernmental para a Revisão do Tratado da Uniao Europeia*. Lisbon: MNE Marco, 1996.

_____. *Rumo á União Europeia*. Lisbon: MNE, 1991.

_____. *Presidencia Portuguesa no Conselho de Ministros das Comunidades Portuguesas*. Lisbon: Casa da Moeda, 1992.

_____. *Anuário Diplomático e Consular Portugues*. 2 vols. Lisbon: MNE, 2000.

Ministério da Reforma do Estado e da Administração Publica (MREAP). *CAF: Common Assessment Framework*. Lisbon: MREAP, 2000.

_____. *Intervenção do Senhor Ministro da Reforma do Estado e da Administração Publica, Sessão de apresentação do 2°Recenseamento Geral da Administração Publica*. Centro Cultural de Belém, 19 September 2001(http://www.mreap.gov.pt/docs/resenc.html), seen in November 2001.

Miranda, Berta Alvarez. "On the Edge of Europe: Southern European Political Debates on Membership." *South European Society and Politics* 1, 2 (1996): 206-118.

_____. "*El Sur de Europa y la adhesion a la Comunidad. Los debates politicos*. Madrid: CIS, 1996.

Mojardino, Miguel. "A base indispensável? As Lajes e a 'Pax Americana.'" *Politica Internacional* 3, 22 (October-November 2000): 185-215.

Morais, Henrique Anabela Sousa. "As relações económicas de Portugal com a América Latina." *Janus 98*: 132-133. Lisbon:Publico-Universidade Aberta de Lisboa, 1997.

Moreira, Adriano. "O Regime: O presidencialismo do primeiro ministro." In Mário Baptista Coelho (org.), *Portugal. O Sistema Politico e Constitucional 1974-1987*, 31-37. Lisbon: ICS, 1989.

Morlino, Leonardo Mario Tarchi. "The Dissatisfied Society: The Roots of Political Change in Italy." *European Journal for Political Research* 30 (July 1996): 41-63.

Mota, Isabel. "Application of Structural Funds." In Alvaro de Vasconcelos, Maria João Seabra (eds.), *Portugal. A European Story*, 131-152. Cascais: Principia, 2000.

Mozzicafreddo, Juan. *Estado Providencia e Cidadania em Portugal*. Oeiras: Celta, 1997.

_____. "Modernização da Administração Pública e Poder Politico." In Juan Mozzicafreddo, Joao Salis Gomes, *Administração e Politica. Perspectivas de Reforma da Administração Pública na Europa e nos Estados Unidos*, 1-33. Oeiras: Celta, 2001.

Munoa, José Maria. "El Comité de las Regiones y la democracia regional y local en Europa." In Francisco Letamendia (ed.), *Nacionalidades y Regiones en la Unión Europea*, 51-68. Madrid: Fundamentos, 1998.

Nielsen, Hans Joergen. "Denmark." In Juliet Lodge (ed.), *The 1994 Election to the European Parliament*, 54-65. London: Pinter, 1996.

_____. "Denmark." In Juliet Lodge (ed.), *The 1999 Elections to the European Parliament*, 60-71. Basingstroke: Macmillan, 2001.

Oliveira, César. "A questao da regionalização." In César Oliveira (ed.), *História dos Municipios e Poder Local*, 495-509. Lisbon: Temas e Debates, 1996.

O'Nuallain, Colm (ed.). *The Presidency of the European Council of Ministers. Impacts and Implications for National Governments*. London: Croom Helm, 1985.

Pagh, Peter. "Denmark's Compliance with European Community Environmental Law." *Journal of Environmental Law* 11, 2 (1999): 301-319.

Partido Socialista, Fundação Mário Soares. *Fontes Para a História do PS, Fontes para a História do PS 1, 25 Anos em Documentos e Imagens-Fontes Para a História do Partido Socialista*. Lisbon, 1998, CD Rom.

Pennings, Paul, Jan-Erik Lane (eds.), *Comparing Party System Change*. London: Routledge, 1998.

Pereira, Pedro Sanchez da Costa. "Portugal: Public Administration and EPC/CFSP—A Fruitful Adaptation Process." In Franco Algieri, Elfriede Regelsberger (eds.), *Synergy at Work: Spain and Portugal in European Foreign Policy*, 207-229. Bonn: Europa Union Verlag, 1996.

Pernthaler, Peter, Peter Hilpold. "Sanktionen als Instrument der Politikkontrolle-der Fall Österreich." *Integration* 23Jg, 2 (2000): 105-110.

Peters, B. Guy, Vincent Wright. "The National Co-ordination of European Policy-making. Negotiating the Quagmire." In Jeremy Richardson (ed.),

European Union. Power and Policy-Making, 155-178. London: Routledge, 2001.

Pinto, António Costa. "Dealing with the Legacy of Authoritarianism: Political Purges and Radical Right Movements in Portugal's Transition to Democracy 1974-1980." In Stein Ugelvik Larsen (ed.), *Modern Europe After Fascism.1943-1980s*, 1679-1717. New York: Columbia, 1998.

Pinto, Carlos. "Gouveia, Saúde e Cuidados de Saúde." In *Portugal Hoje*, 162-178. Oeiras: INA, 1995.

Pires, Luis Madureira. *A Politica Regional Europeia e Portugal.* Lisbon: Fundação Calouste Gulbenkian, 1998,

Pollack, Mark. "Creeping Competence: The Expanding Agenda of the European Community." *Journal of Public Policy* 14, 2 (1994): 95-140.

_____. "The End of Creeping Competence? EU Policy-making Since Maastricht." *Journal of Common Market Studies* 38, 3 (September 2000): 519-538.

Poulantzas, Nicos. *Die Krise der Diktaturen.Portugal, Griechenland und Spanien.* Frankfurt a. M.: Suhrkamp, 1977.

Pridham, Geoffrey. "The politics of the European Community, Transnational Networks and Democratic Transition in Southern Europe." In Geoffrey Pridham (ed.), *Encouraging Democracy: The International Context of Regime Transition in Southern Europe*, 211-245. London: Leicester University Press, 1991.

Putnam, Robert. "Diplomacy and Domestic Politics." *International Organization* 42 (1988): 427-461.

Quirke, Brendan. "Fraud against European Public Funds." *Crime, Law and Social Change* 31 (1999): 193-208.

Raunio, Tapio. "Always One Step Behind? National Legislatures and the European Union." *Government and Opposition* 34, 2 (1999): 180-202.

Ravara, Rui Lobato de Faria. "O Reequipamento e a Indústria de Defesa. Subsidios para uma Politica de Armamento." *Nação e Defesa* 98 (2001): 115-145.

Rebelo de Sousa, Marcelo. *A Revolução e o Nascimento do PPD.* 2 vols. Lisbon: Bertrand Editora, 2000.

Republique Francaise, Ministére de la fonction publique de la reforme d´Etat et de la decentralization. *Rapport annuel de relations internationales et de la cooperation administrative.1998-99.* Paris: MFPRED, 1999.

Rocha, Octávio de Cerqueira. "Portugal e as Operações de Paz na Bósnia: A Preparação das Forças." *Nação e Defesa* 92, 2-serie (2000): 71-92.

Rodrigues, Luis Nuno. *Salazar e Kennedy: a crise de uma aliança.* Lisbon: Editorial Noticias, 2002.

Rodrigues, Maria João. "A Estratégia de Lisbon: Das Politicas Europeias às Politicas Nacionais." *Europa. Novas Fronteiras* 7 (June 2000): 42-45.

Rollo, Maria Fernanda. "Salazar e a construção europeia." In António Costa Pinto, Nuno Severiano Teixeira (eds.), Portugal e a Unificação Europeia. Special Issue of *Penélope* 18 (1998): 51-76.

Ross, George. *Jacques Delors and European Integration*. Cambridge: Polity, 1995.

Rozek, Maria do Rosário de Matos da Silva Almeida. *Die Entwicklung der Strukturpolitik der Europäischen Gemeinschaften. Ziele und Auswirkungen des EFRE auf die regionale Infra-und Industriestruktur am Beispiel der Region Norden in Portugal*. Frankfurt a. M.: Peter Lang, 1995.

Sablovsky, Juliet Antunes. *PS e a transição para a democracia*. Lisbon: Editorial Noticias, 2000.

Safaneta, Marisa Abreu. "A Cooperação Técnico Militar de Portugal com as PALOP." In *As Forcas Armadas no novo contexto internacional, Janus 98, suplemento especial*, 82-83. Lisbon: *O Publico*, UAL, 1998.

Santos, Boaventura de Sousa. "Crise e Reconstituição do Estado em Portugal (1974-1984)." *Revista Critica de Ciencias Sociais* 14 (November 1984): 7-29.

_____. "Social Crisis and the State." In Kenneth Maxwell (ed.), *Portugal in the 1980s. Dilemmas of Democratic Consolidation*, 168-195. New York: Greenwood, 1986.

_____. *O Estado e a Sociedade em Portugal (1974-1988)*. Porto: Afrontamento, 1990.

_____, (org.). *Portugal: Um Retrato Singular*. Porto: Edições Afrontamento, 1993.

Santos, Boaventura Sousa, Maria Manuel Leitão Marques, João Pedroso, Pedro Lopes Ferreira. *Os Tribunais nas Sociedades Contemporaneas.O Caso Portugues*. Porto: Afrontamentos, 1995.

Santos, Norberto Pinto dos. *A Sociedade de Consumo E Os Espacos Vividos pelas Familias.A Dualidade dos espaços, a turbulencia dos percursos e a identidade social*. Lisbon: Edições Colibri, 2001.

Santos, Rogério, Isabel Ventura e Vanda Calado. "Congressos e convenções partidárias-como se relacionam os políticos e os jornalistas de televisão." *Observatório* 5 (May 2002): 9-25.

Schmitt, Hermann Jacques Thomassen (eds.), *Political Representation and Legitimacy in the European Union*. Oxford: Oxford University Press, 1999.

Schmitter, Philippe. "Examining the Present Euro-Polity with Past Theories." In Marks, Scharpf, Schmitter, Streeck, *Governance in the European Union*, 1-14. London: SAGE, 1996.

_____. "Some Alternative Futures for the European Polity and Their Implications for European Public Policy." In Yves Meny, Pierre Muller, Jean-Louis Quermonne (eds.), *Adjusting to Europe. The Impact of the European Union on National Institutions and Policies*, 25-40. London: Routledge, 1996.

_____. "The 'Regime d'Exception' That Became the Rule: Forty-Eight Years of Authoritarian Domination in Portugal." In Lawrence S. Graham, Harry M. Makler (eds.), *Contemporary Portugal. The Revolution and Its Antecedents*, 3-46. Austin: University of Texas, 1974.

_____. *How to Democratize the European Union and Why Bother?* Lanham, MA: Rowman and Littlefield, 2000.

Schoutheete, Philippe. *Una Europa para todos. Diez ensayos sobre la construccíon europea*. Madrid: Alianza Editorial, 1998.

Sebastião, João. "Os Dilemas da Escolaridade. Universalização, diversidade e inovação." In José Manuel Leite Viegas, António Firmino da Costa (eds.), *Portugal, que Modernidade?*, 311-327. Lisbon: Celta, 1998.

Secretaria do Estado da Integração Europeia (SEIE). *Guia para o Exercicio da Presidencia*. Lisbon: SIE, 1992.

Secretariado para a Modernização Administrativa (SMA). *Gestão da Qualidade.Conceitos, Sistemas de gestão, Instrumentos*. Lisbon: SMA, 1995.

_____. *Os direitos do cidadão face à Administração Pública*. Lisbon: SMA, 1996.

_____. *Comissão de Empresas-Administração. Plano de Actividades 1997/99, Regulamento de Funcionamento*. Lisbon: SMA, 1998.

_____. *Forum Cidadãos-Administração. Regulamento e Funcionamento*. Lisbon: SMA, 1998.

_____. *Qualidade em Serviços Publicos*. Lisbon: SMA, 1998.

_____. *Carta de Qualidade.Um Compromisso com o Cidadão*. Lisbon: SMA, 1998.

_____. *Serviços Publicos, Da Burocracia à Qualidade*. Lisbon: SMA, 1999.

_____. *Auto-Avaliação da Qualidade em Serviços Publicos*. Lisbon: SMA, 1999.

_____. *First Quality Conference for Public Administrations in the European Union*. Lisbon, 10-12 May 2000.

Seixas da Costa, Francisco. "Tratado de Amsterdão: História de uma negociação." *Politica Internacional* 1, 15-16 (Winter 1997): 23-47.

_____. "Portugal e o Desafio Europeu." *Nação e Defesa* 85, 2 Serie Primavera 98: 17-28.

_____. "Uma Reforma Indispensável." *Europa, Novas Fronteiras* (June 1999): 4-10.

_____. "Portugal e o Tratado de Nice. Notas sobre a estratégia negocial portuguesa." *Negócios Estrangeiros* 1 (March 2001): 40-70.

Sejersted, Fredrik. "The Norwegian Parliament and European Integration—Reflections from Medium-Speed Europe." In Eivind Smith (ed.), *National Parliaments as Cornerstones of European Integration*, 124-156. London: Kluwer, 1996.

Sieber, Wolfgang. *Agrarentwicklung und ländlicher sozialer Wandel in Portugal*. Saarbrücken: Breitenbach, 1990.

Siedentopf, Heinrich, Jacques Ziller (eds.). *Making European Policies Work? The Implementation of Community Legislation in the Member-States*, 2 vols. London: SAGE, 1988.

Silva, Anibal Cavaco. *As Reformas da Decada (1986-1995)*. Lisbon: Bertrand Editora, 1995.

Silveira de Carvalho, João Pedro. "Prioridades e resultados da Presidencia do Conselho da UE." *Europa. Novas Fronteiras* 7 (June 2000): 14-23.

Sjursen, Helene. "The Common Foreign and Security Policy: Limits of Intergovernmentalism and the Search for a Global Role." Svein S. Andersen,

Kjell A. Eliassen (eds.), *Making Policy in Europe*, 187-205. London: SAGE, 2001.

Soares, Francisco, Teresa Evaristo. "Recenseamento eleitoral: Disfuncionamentos e novas perspectivas." *Análise Social* XXXV, 154-155 (2000): 25-43; particularly 35-42.

Soares, Mario. "Democratic Transition in Portugal and the Enlargement of the European Union." In Alvaro de Vasconcelos, Maria João Seabra (eds.), *Portugal. A European Story*, 39-54. Lisbon: Instituto de Estudos Estratégiçõs e Internacionais, 2000.

Sousa, Luis de. "Political Parties and Corruption in Portugal." *West European Politics* 24, 1 (January 2001): 157-180.

Spence, David. "Plus ca change, plus c´est la meme chose? Attempting to Reform the Commission." *Journal of European Public Policy* 7, 1 (March 2000): 1-25.

Stock, Maria José. *Os Partidos do Poder. Dez Anos depois do 25 de Abril.* Évora: Universidade de Évora, 1986.

_____. *Elites, Facções e Conflito Interpartidário: O PPD/PSD e o processo político portugues de 1974 a 1985*. Ph.d. diss., University of Évora, 1989.

Stoehr, Stephen. *Educação e Mudança Social em Portugal 1970-1980.Uma decada de transição*. Porto: Edições Afrontamento, 1986.

Syrett, Stephen. "Local Power and Economic Policy: Local Authority Economic Initiatives in Portugal." *Regional Studies* 28/1 (1993): 53-67.

_____. *Local Development: Restructuring, Locality and Economic Initiative in Portugal*. Aldershot: Avebury, 1994.

_____. "The Politics of Partnership: The Role of Social Partners in Local Economic Development in Portugal." *European Urban and Regional Studies* 4, 2 (1997): 99-114; particularly 104-111.

Teixeira, Nuno Severiano. "Between Africa and Europe: Portuguese Foreign Policy, 1890-1986." In A. C. Pinto (eds.), *Modern Portugal*, 60-87. Palo Alto: SPOSS, 1998.

Teles, Patricia. "Galvão O Estatuto juridico de Timor-Leste: Um case study sobre as relações entre os conceitos de autodeterminação e soberania." *Politica Internacional* 15/16 (1997):195-202.

The Economist. "A Survey of Portugal.Half-Way There."2 December 2000.

Tömmel, Ingeborg. "Transformation of Governance: The European Commission's Strategy for Creating a 'Europe of the Regions'." In *Regional and Federal Studies* 8, 2 (Summer 1998): 52-80.

Torres Campos, J. M. "Empresas Públicas." In Manuela Silva (ed.), *Portugal Contemporaneo. Problemas e Perspectivas*, 437-459. Lisbon: INA, 1986.

Torres, Francisco. "The Case for Economic and Monetary Union: Europe and Portugal" *Nação e Defesa* 85, 2 Série (Spring 1998): 29-69.

_____. "Portugal Towards Economic and Monetary Union: A Political Economy Perspective." In Jeffry Frieden, Francisco Torres (eds.), *Joining Europe´s Monetary Club: The Challenges for Smaller Member States*, 171-202. New York: St. Martin's Press, 1998.

_____. "A dinamica das novas adesões à UE e as opções europeias." *Europa. Novas Fronteiras* (December 1999): 85-87.

_____. "Lessons from Portugal's Long Transition to Economic and Monetary Union." In Alvaro de Vasconcelos, Maria João Seabra (eds.), *Portugal. A European Story*, 99-130. Lisbon: Instituto de Estudos Estratégicos e Internacionais-Principia, 2000.

Vala, Jorge, Rodrigo Brito, Diniz Lopes. *Expressões dos racismos em Portugal. Estudos e Investigações 11*. Lisbon: Imprensa de Ciencias Sociais, 1997.

Van der Eijk, Cees, Mark N. Franklin (eds.). *Choosing Europe?The European Electorate and National Politics in the Face of the Union*. Ann Arbor: University of Michigan Press, 1996.

Van Ham, Peter. "Europe's Precarious Centre: Franco-German Co-operation and the CFSP." *European Security* 8, 4 (1999): 1-26.

Vasconcelos, Alvaro. "Portuguese Defence Policy: Internal Politics and Defence Commitments." In John Chipman (ed.), *NATO's Southern Allies: Internal and External Challenges*, 86-139. London, New York: Routledge, 1988.

_____. "A Europeização da Politica de Defesa" *Estratégia* 14, 2 Semestre (1999): 7-19.

Vasconcelos, Alvaro, Maria João Seabra (eds.). *Portugal. A European Story*. Lisbon: Instituto de Estudos Estratégicos e Internacionais-Principia, 2000.

Vasconcelos, Alvaro, George Joffé (eds.). *The Barcelona Process. Building a Euro-Mediterranean Regional Community*. London: Frank Cass, 2001.

Vasconcellos, Jorge A., Miguel Frasquilho, Watson Wyatt Limited, Margarida Palla Garcia, Clara Goncalves. *Portugal Europeu?* Lisbon: Vida Economica, 2001.

Vitorino, Antonio. "A Democracia Representativa." In *Portugal Hoje*, 329-350. Oeiras: INA, 1995.

Youngs, Richard. *The European Union and the Promotion of Democracy. Europe´s Mediterranean and Asian Policies*. Oxford: Oxford University Press, 2001.

Wall, Karin, Cristina Lobo. "Familias monoparentais em Portugal." *Analise Social* XXXIV (October 1999): 123-145.

Wallace, Helen. *National Governments and the European Communities*. London: Chatham House: PEP, 1973.

Weiler, J.H.H. "European Neo-constitutionalism: In Search of Foundations for the European Constitutional Order." *Political Studies* 44, 3 (1996): 517-533.

_____. "Epilogue: 'Comitology' as Revolution-Infranationalism, Constitutionalism and Democracy." In Christian Joerges, Ellen Vos (eds.), *EU Committees: Social Regulation, Law and Politics*, 339-350. Oxford: Hart Publishing, 1999.

Wessels, and Dietrich Rometsch. "German Administrative Interaction and European Union. The Fusion of Public Policies." In Yves Meny, Pierre Muller, Jean-Louis Quermonne (eds.), *Adjusting to Europe. The Impact of the European Union on National Institutions and Policies*, 73-109. London: Routledge, 1997.

Westlake, Martin. *Britain´s Emerging Euro-elite?The British in the Directly-Elected European Parliament, 1979-1992*. Aldershot: Dartsmouth, 1994.

_____. "The View from Brussels." In Philip Norton (eds.), *National Parliaments and the European Union*, 166-176; particularly 171-173. London: Frank Cass, 1995.

Wheeler, Douglas. *Republican Portugal. A Political History 1910-1926*. Madison: University of Wisconsin Press, 1978.

Wöhlke, Manfred. "Die Gemeinschaft Portugiesisch-sprachiger Staaten und die EU." *Aus Politik und Zeitgeschichte* B29-30 (2000): 14-21.

Wright, Vincent. "La coordination nationale de la politique européenne: Le bourbier de la négociation." *Revue Francaise d´Administration Publique* 93 (2000): 103-124.

Zwaan, Jaap W. de. *The Permanent Representatives Committee. Its Role in European Union Decision-Making*. Amsterdam: Elsevier, 1995.

List of Interviews

Luis Inez Fernandes, director of the juridical issues department of General-Directorate for Community Affairs, Ministry of Foreign Affairs (DGAC-MNE), 22 September 1998.

Josefina Carvalho, Interministerial Committee for Community Affairs (CIAC), DGAC-MNE, Lisbon, 22 september 1998.

Rui Marques, Department of Information, Training and Documentation, DGAC-MNE, Lisbon, 23 September 1998.

Alzira Cabrita, DGAC-MNE, 24 November 1998.

Manuel Carvalho, Portuguese Permanent Representation to the European Union in Brussels, 8 February 1999.

Cristina de Azevedo, vice president of Regional Coordinating Commission North (CCRN), Porto, 4 July 2002.

Antonio Fonseca Ferreira, president of Regional Coordinating Commission of Lisbon and Vale do Tejo (CCLVT), Lisbon, 8 July 2002.

Heloisa Cid, Department for European and International Affairs, Ministry of Cities, Planning and Environment, 10 July 2002.

Rui Jacinto, vice president of Regional Coordinating Commission Centre (CCRC), Coimbra, 12 July 2002.

Ana Fraga, Committee of Foreign and European Affairs, Assembly of the Republic, Lisbon, 13 July 2002.

Marco Orani, responsible for Portuguese programmes, European Commission, DG XVI, Brussels, 12 September 2002.

Pedro Lourdie, Portuguese Permanent Representation of Portugal in Brussels, 13 September 2002.

Index

Alentejo, *see* Regions
Algarve, *see* Regions
Algeria, 251
Alqueva dam, 228
Angola, 92, 252
Armed Forces, 249
  Common European Defence and Security Policy (CEDSP), *see* foreign policy or European Union
  Common Foreign and Security Policy (CFSP), *see* foreign policy or European Union
  Eurofor 242, 250
  Euromarfor, 242, 250
  Lajes, Azores, 247
  Movement of Armed Forces (MFA), *see* Portugal
  North Atlantic Treaty Organization (NATO), 30, 242, 245-249, 259
  Peacekeeping forces, 256
  Petersberg tasks, 242
  SACEUR, 246
  SACLANT, 246
  West European Union (WEU), 30
Attitudes
  EU, 96-97
  National Democracy, 94
  political participation, 95
  power distance, 93-94
Austria, 13, 18
Aznar, José Maria, 57, 173
Azores, 219, 227

Balsemao, Francisco, 243
Barroso, Manuel Durão, 30, 35, 40, 63, 65, 73, 74, 147, 244, 248, 265
Belgium, 34, 41, 170, 216
Berlin Wall, 5
Blair, Tony, 14, 34, 57
Bosnia-Herzegovina, 32, 247
Braga da Cruz, Manuel, 67
Brazil, 2, 92, 242, 252, 254, 259

Caetano, Marcelo, 26
Cape Verde Islands, 92, 252
Carneiro, Francisco Sá, 243
Carvalhas, Carlos, 69
Castelo da Paiva, 35
Cavaquismo, 64, 65
Centro, *see* Regions
Charities, 91
China, 259
CIAC, *see* Portugal
Civil society, 18, 19, 20, 44, 94
Consumerism, 86, 91
Constancio, Vitor, 66
Constitution, 1, 28, 35-38
  Revision, 36, 37
Constitutional Court, 17, 29, 36, 47, 58, 243
Constitutional Court, Germany, 47
Community of Portuguese Speaking Countries (CPLP), 2, 242, 251-256
Council of the Revolution, 28-29, 36, 243
Criminality, 249
  cyberspace criminality, 249
  global criminality, 249

Cuba, 16

Decolonization, 241
Delors, Jacques, 11
Denmark, 13, 18, 27, 131, 170, 173, 216
Douro river, 35

Eanes, Antonio Ramalho, 36, 38, 39, 243
East Timor, 2, 241, 242, 257, 258
  Timorese Front for National Liberation (Fretilin), 257
  United Nations, 258
Economic and Social Committees, 14, 169, 172

Economy
Portuguese business culture, 223, 226, 268-269
Portuguese economy, 16, 223
research and development, 226-227
semiperipheral, 20, 23, 59
Education, 1, 19, 230, 267-268
education divide, 85, 86
illiteracy, 87
School leavers, 88
secondary education, 85, 86, 268
Elections
abstention, 59, 60
Americanization, 57, 59, 75
concentration of vote, 56
D'Hondt electoral system, 56
electoral cleavages, 76
electoral geography, 76
electoral results, 72-73
European, 17, 73-74
legislative, 71-73
local, 73
marketization of elections, 57, 71, 76
mediatization 71
regional 75
voters 59
Electorate
value-oriented, 75, 76
Euro-elites 1, 16, 166-192
Euro-Mediterranean partnership, 250
European Union
Agenda 2000, 217
Amsterdam Treaty, 25, 44
Birkelbach report, 26, 133
Charter of Fundamental Workers' Rights, 41
Committee of Regional and Local Authorities, 172, 216
Common Agricultural Policy 215
Common European Defence and Security Policy (CEDSP), 41, 245, 247
Common Foreign and Security Policy (CFSP), 14, 41, 244, 245-251
Comitology, 105, 168
COREPER, 150, 176, 177, 196
Delors Package I, 31
Delors Package II, 33
Economic and Monetary Union (EMU), 5, 11, 31, 34, 68, 203, 222, 265
employment policy, 12, 14
Euro, 5, 33, 47
European Central Bank, 265
European Commission, 168-169, 172, 232, 265
European Economic Community (EEC), 27, 28
European Free Trade Area (EFTA), 28
European law, 6
European Parliament, 26, 105
European Political Cooperation (EPC), 244, 245
European Regional Development Fund (ERDF), 219, 231
European Social Fund (ESF), 231, 232
European System of Central Banks, 114
Europol, 14
Eurosclerosis, 5
Extradionary Council of Lisbon, 14, 200, 202-204
Infra-nationalism, 6
intergovernmental conferences, 14, 40, 141-142
Intergovernmental Conference 1996, 41, 42, 141
Intergovernmental Conference 2000, 41, 42, 142, 201
Interreg, 106
Justice and Home Affairs, 14, 41
lobbyists, 169-170
Lomé Agreements, 252
Maastricht Treaty, 10
Multi-Level Governance System (MLG), 6-9, 10, 5, 106
Nice Treaty, 44
Open Method of Coordination (OMC), 204
Permanent Representation Brussels (REPER), *see* Portugal
Presidency of European Union 2000, *see* Presidency of European Union 2000
Political system, 5-6, 7
Reflection Group of Intergovernmental Conference 2000, 204-206
Rio Environment summit, 1992 32, 140
Rome Treaties, 133
Single European Market (SEM), 11, 31, 36, 203, 222, 280

Stabilization state, 20
Transnational European Space, 8
Transnational policy communities, 6
Europeanization, 6, 19
definition, 9-12
European public space, 11
National public space, 11
Bottom-Up, 12, 14
Horizontal, 12, 14-15
Top-down, 12-14
European Institute for Public Administration (EIPA), 103
Euroskepticism, 75
Eusebio, 2
Exchange Rate Mechanism, 31
Expo'98, 2, 92, 231, 258

Ferreira, José Medeiros, 44, 142, 241, 266
Finland, 41
Fischer, Joschka, 142, 205
Foreign policy, 241-263
Anti-colonialism, 250
Common European Defence and Security Policy (CEDSP), 41, 245, 247
Common Foreign and Security Policy (CFSP,) 14, 41, 244, 245-251
EU, 243, 249, 259
Latin America, 258-259
Mediterranean 250-251
Mediterraneanization, 272
Ministry of Foreign Affairs (MFA), 29-30
period of reequilibration, 243
Peacekeeping forces, *see* Armed Forces
right of self-determination, 250
France, 11, 12, 13, 17, 40, 131, 173, 205, 256, 227
Fundamentalism, Islamic, 251

Gama, Jaime, 30, 198, 205
Germany, 12, 17, 40-42, 131, 173, 216
Gipsy Communities, 92
Goncalves, Vasco, 27
Gonzalez, Felipe, 173
Government, 19
Greece, 11, 26, 40, 41, 79, 131, 170, 173, 205, 217
Guinea-Bissau, 92, 252, 254
Gusmao, Xanana, 257
Guterres, Antonio, 34, 40, 66, 71, 74, 114, 177, 194, 221, 251
Guterrismo, 67

Haider, Jörg, 14
Health, 19
National Health Service, 268

Ibero-American summits, 258-259
Identity
National, 2
Immigration, 91-92
Indochina, 26
International Criminal Court, 38, 250
International Monetary Fund (IMF), 29
Internet access, 227
Ireland, 18, 24
Italy, 11, 12, 13, 26, 34, 40, 79, 131, 173, 205, 217

Japan, 5
Jardim, Alberto Joao, 75
Jospin, Lionel, 14, 34
Judiciary, 47-48

Kinnock, Neil, 173

Lajes, Azores, 247
Latin American summits, 258-259
Lisboa e Vale do Tejo, *see* Regions
Louca, Antonio, 63
Louca, Francisco, 63, 70
Luxembourg, 41, 131

Madeira, 219, 227
Maghreb, 251
Martins, Vitor, 141
Mashreq, 251
Mozambique, 252, 254
Macau, 259
Marxism-Leninism, 256
Mediterranean Free Trade Area, 251
Mercosur, 254
Middle classes
New middle classes, 86, 89
traditional, 89
Monteiro, Manuel, 32, 68
Moura, José Barros, 200, 266

National Employment Plans (NEP), 88
NATO, *see* Armed Forces
Netherlands, 41, 131

New public management, 173
Nogueira, Fernando, 63,
Nogueira, Franco, 133
Norte, *see* Regions
North America, 92
Norway, 26

Organization for Economic Cooperation and Development (OECD), 102, 106
Oecdisation, 102
Open Method of Coordination (OMC), *see* European Union
Organization for Security and Cooperation in Europe, 249, 259

PALOPs, 256
Palace of Sao Bento, 1
Parliament, 1, 17, 37, 42-47,
  Comité des organs specialisés en affaires communautaires (COSAC)
  Committees, 14, 45-46, 169, 178, 202
  Committee of European Affairs, 42-45, 178
Parties
  Block of the Left (BE), 17, 56, 64, 79
  Cartel parties, 59, 61,
  Communist parties, 26
  Democratic Alliance (AD,) 243
  Democratic People's Union (UDP), 63, 79
  Euroskeptic parties, 13
  French Socialist Party, 12
  National parties, 12
  People's Democratic Party, 27
  People's Party (PP), 17, 31, 35, 38, 55, 68, 69, 77
  Portuguese Communist Party (PCP), 17, 33, 35, 36, 38, 61, 63, 69-70, 77, 135
  Portuguese party system, 55-61
  Socialdemocratic Party (PSD), 17, 33, 34, 63, 64-66, 76-77
  Socialist Party (PS), 17, 33, 36, 38, 62, 63, 66-68, 71, 77
  Socialist Revolutionary Party (PSR), 63, 79
  Partyocracy, 64
  party membership, 62-63
  trust in, 64
Party system
  bipolarization, 78
Patten, Chris, 246
Pereira, Antonio Nazaré, 266
Pereira, José Pacheco, 75
Permanent Representation in Brussels (REPER), *see* Portugal,
Political culture, 85-100
Portas, Paulo, 35, 63, 68, 69, 75
Portugal
  Administrative law, 174
  authoritarian dictatorship, 18, 86
  budget deficit, 35
  Central block government, 218
  Commission for European Integration, 135
  Constitutional change, 35-38
  Common support framework, 18, 113, 122, 217, 219, 220, 221, 222, 230, 232, 233, 234
  Development towards EU membership, 25-35
  11 September 2001, 27
  EU membership, 17
  EU Presidency, 1992, 138-140
  Europeanization of political system, 25-53, 101
  Movement of Armed Forces (MFA), 27, 38, 135
  Free trade agreement with European Union, 28
  General-Directorate for Community Affairs (DGAC), 137, 144, 145, 146, 244
  Government, 40-42
  Judiciary, 47-48
  Interministerial Committe for Community Affairs (CIAC), 142, 147-149, 177
  National Assembly, 110
  National EU policy coordination, 131-163
  National Institute of Public Administration (INA), 194
  Negotiations with European Community, 29
  Parliament, 42-47
  People's democracy, 27
  People's power democracy, 27
  Permanent Representation in Brussels (REPER), 149-158
  Presidency, 38-40
  Presidentialization of the Prime Minister, 57
  Public administration, 101-129

Quantum (National Framework of Adjustment to the Transition towards Economic and Monetary Union), 31-32
regional coordinating commissions, 110, 113, 217, 218, 219, 220
Revolution of Carnations, 26, 87
Secretariat for European Integration, 136, 144
Social democracy, 27
structural funds, 18, 215-239
Poverty, 90, 267
Presidency of EU, 174-176
Portuguese presidency of EU, 165-213
Working Groups, 196
Prison system, 48
Privatization, 3, 6, 110
Public administration, 18, 19
Civil service, 34
Europe of Administrations/European Administrative Space, 101, 102-108, 173
European Commission, 102
New public management, 173
Oecdisation, 102
Reform of public administration, 103

Racism, 92
Rebelo de Sousa, Marcelo, 58, 63, 65, 68, 69
Regions
Alentejo, 35, 222, 227
Algarve, 228
Centro, 233
four-motor, 216
Europe of the regions, 33
Lisboa e Vale do Tejo, 217, 227, 233, 234
Regional offices at European Union level, 216
Regionalization referendum, 33, 113, 114, 221
Rodrigues, Eduardo Ferro, 67-68, 73
Rodrigues, Maria João, 34, 203
Russia, 193

Salazar, Antonio Oliveira, 26, 86, 88
Sampaio, Jorge, 39-40, 66, 67
Santos, Manuel dos, 44, 198
Sao Tomé e Principe, 252, 254
Seixas da Costa, Francisco, 41, 141, 142, 198, 204-205
Silva, Anibal Cavaco, 32, 34, 36, 39, 47, 56, 65,
71, 73, 75, 113, 136, 194, 251, 66, 74, 135, 221, 241, 243
Soames, Christopher, 27, 28
Soares, João, 75
Soares, Mário, 27, 28, 29, 36, 39, 40, 58, 64, 66
Social benefits, 91
Social change, 85-100
Social expenditure, 91
Society
debt, 90
income distribution, 90
individualization, 90
marketization of society, 90
tertiarization, 90
Solana, Javier, 245
South African Development Community (SADC), 254
Spain, 11, 26, 40, 79, 96, 170, 173, 216, 217, 227, 259
Sweden, 11, 13, 17, 26, 131, 173, 227

Television
RTP1, 71
RTP2, 71
SIC, 71
TVI, 71
Terrorism, 249
Thatcher, Margaret, 31
Thomaz, Américo, 133
Torres, Francisco, 266

United Nations, 247, 257, 259
United States, 5
United Kingdom, 12, 13, 17, 18, 26, 79, 96, 131, 170, 133, 174, 216, 268

Védrine, Hubert, 142, 205
Vieira de Mello, Sergio, 258
Vitorino, Antonio, 66

West African Monetary Union (UMOA), 254
West European Union, 245

Yugoslavia
breakdown, 247

For Product Safety Concerns and Information please contact our EU representative GPSR@taylorandfrancis.com Taylor & Francis Verlag GmbH, Kaufingerstraße 24, 80331 München, Germany

Batch number: 08153793

Printed by Printforce, the Netherlands